# 15th SIGMORPHON Workshop on Computational Research in Phonetics, Phonology, and Morphology (SIGMORPHON 2018)

Brussels, Belgium
31 October 2018

ISBN: 978-1-5108-7426-8

SIGMORPHON 2018

# The 15th SIGMORPHON Workshop on Computational Research in Phonetics, Phonology, and Morphology

## Proceedings of the Workshop

October 31, 2018
Brussels, Belgium

Order copies of this and other ACL proceedings from:

Association for Computational Linguistics (ACL)
209 N. Eighth Street
Stroudsburg, PA 18360
USA
Tel: +1-570-476-8006
Fax: +1-570-476-0860
acl@aclweb.org

# Preface

Welcome to the 15th SIGMORPHON Workshop on Computational Research in Phonetics, Phonology, and Morphology, to be held on October 31, 2018 in Brussels, Belgium. The workshop aims to bring together researchers interested in applying computational techniques to problems in morphology, phonology, and phonetics. Our program this year highlights the ongoing and important interaction between work in computational linguistics and work in theoretical linguistics. This year, however, a new focus on low resource approaches to morphology is emerging as a consequence of the SIGMORPHON 2016 and CoNLL shared tasks on morphological reinflection across a wide range of languages.

We received 36 submissions, and after a competitive reviewing process, we accepted 19. Due to time limitations, 6 papers were chosen for oral presentations, the remaining papers are presented as posters. The workshop also includes a joint poster session with CoNLL, on the CoNLL–SIGMORPHON 2018 Shared Task: Universal Morphological Reinflection.

We are grateful to the program committee for their careful and thoughtful reviews of the papers submitted this year. We are looking forward to a workshop covering a wide range of topics, and we hope for lively discussions.

Sandra Kübler
Garrett Nicolai

**Organizers:**

Sandra Kübler, University of Indiana
Garrett Nicolai, Johns Hopkins University

**Program Committee:**

Noor Abo Mokh, Indiana University
Adam Albright, MIT
Jane Chandlee, Haverford College
Çağrı Çöltekin, University of Tübingen
Ryan Cotterell, Johns Hopkins University
Daniel Dakota, Indiana University
Thierry Declerck, DFKI
Ewan Dunbar, Laboratoire de Sciences Cognitives et Psycholinguistique, Paris
Jason Eisner, Johns Hopkins University
Micha Elsner, The Ohio State University
Sharon Goldwater, University of Edinburgh
Kyle Gorman, Google
Nizar Habash, NYU Abu Dhabi
Mike Hammond, University of Arizona
Mans Hulden, University of Colorado
Adam Jardine, Rutgers University
Gaja Jarosz, University of Massachusetts Amherst
Christo Kirov, Johns Hopkins University
Greg Kobele, University of Chicago
Grzegorz Kondrak, University of Alberta
Kimmo Koskenniemi, University of Helsinki
Andrew Lamont, University of Massachusetts Amherst
Karen Livescu, TTI Chicago
Arya McCarthy, Johns Hopkins University
Kevin McMullin, University of Ottawa
Kemal Oflazer, CMU Qatar
Jeff Parker, Brigham Young University
Gerald Penn, University of Toronto
Jelena Prokic, Ludwig-Maximilians-University Munich
Mohamad Salameh, CMU-Qatar
Miikka Silfverberg, University of Colorado
Andrea Sims, The Ohio State University
Kairit Sirts, Macquarie University
Richard Sproat, Google
Kenneth Steimel, Indiana University
Reut Tsarfaty, The Open University of Israel
Francis Tyers, Higher School of Economics
Richard Wicentowski, Swarthmore University
Anssi Yli-Jyrä, University of Helsinki
Kristine Yu, University of Massachusetts Amherst

# Table of Contents


*Efficient Computation of Implicational Universals in Constraint-Based Phonology Through the Hyperplane Separation Theorem*
Giorgio Magri . . . . . . . . . . . . . . . . . . . . . . . . . . . . . . . . . . . . . . . . . . . . . . . . . . . . . . . . . . . . . . . . . . . . . . . 1

*Lexical Networks in !Xung*
Syed-Amad Hussain, Micha Elsner and Amanda Miller . . . . . . . . . . . . . . . . . . . . . . . . . . . . . . . . . . 11

*Acoustic Word Disambiguation with Phonogical Features in Danish ASR*
Andreas Søeborg Kirkedal . . . . . . . . . . . . . . . . . . . . . . . . . . . . . . . . . . . . . . . . . . . . . . . . . . . . . . . . . . . . 21

*Adaptor Grammars for the Linguist: Word Segmentation Experiments for Very Low-Resource Languages*
Pierre Godard, Laurent Besacier, François Yvon, Martine Adda-Decker, Gilles Adda, Hélène Maynard and Annie Rialland . . . . . . . . . . . . . . . . . . . . . . . . . . . . . . . . . . . . . . . . . . . . . . . . . . . . . . . . . . . . 32

*String Transduction with Target Language Models and Insertion Handling*
Garrett Nicolai, Saeed Najafi and Grzegorz Kondrak . . . . . . . . . . . . . . . . . . . . . . . . . . . . . . . . . . . 43

*Complementary Strategies for Low Resourced Morphological Modeling*
Alexander Erdmann and Nizar Habash . . . . . . . . . . . . . . . . . . . . . . . . . . . . . . . . . . . . . . . . . . . . . . . . 54

*Modeling Reduplication with 2-way Finite-State Transducers*
Hossep Dolatian and Jeffrey Heinz . . . . . . . . . . . . . . . . . . . . . . . . . . . . . . . . . . . . . . . . . . . . . . . . . . . 66

*Automatically Tailoring Unsupervised Morphological Segmentation to the Language*
Ramy Eskander, Owen Rambow and Smaranda Muresan . . . . . . . . . . . . . . . . . . . . . . . . . . . . . . . 78

*A Comparison of Entity Matching Methods between English and Japanese Katakana*
Michiharu Yamashita, Hideki Awashima and Hidekazu Oiwa . . . . . . . . . . . . . . . . . . . . . . . . . . . . 84

*Seq2Seq Models with Dropout can Learn Generalizable Reduplication*
Brandon Prickett, Aaron Traylor and Joe Pater . . . . . . . . . . . . . . . . . . . . . . . . . . . . . . . . . . . . . . . . 93

*A Characterwise Windowed Approach to Hebrew Morphological Segmentation*
Amir Zeldes . . . . . . . . . . . . . . . . . . . . . . . . . . . . . . . . . . . . . . . . . . . . . . . . . . . . . . . . . . . . . . . . . . . . . . . 101

*Phonetic Vector Representations for Sound Sequence Alignment*
Pavel Sofroniev and Çağrı Çöltekin . . . . . . . . . . . . . . . . . . . . . . . . . . . . . . . . . . . . . . . . . . . . . . . . . . 111

*Sounds Wilde. Phonetically Extended Embeddings for Author-Stylized Poetry Generation*
Aleksey Tikhonov and Ivan Yamshchikov . . . . . . . . . . . . . . . . . . . . . . . . . . . . . . . . . . . . . . . . . . . . . 117

*On Hapax Legomena and Morphological Productivity*
Janet Pierrehumbert and Ramon Granell . . . . . . . . . . . . . . . . . . . . . . . . . . . . . . . . . . . . . . . . . . . . . 125

*A Morphological Analyzer for Shipibo-Konibo*
Ronald Cardenas and Daniel Zeman . . . . . . . . . . . . . . . . . . . . . . . . . . . . . . . . . . . . . . . . . . . . . . . . . 131

*An Arabic Morphological Analyzer and Generator with Copious Features*
Dima Taji, Salam Khalifa, Ossama Obeid, Fadhl Eryani and Nizar Habash . . . . . . . . . . . . . . . 140

*Sanskrit n-Retroflexion is Input-Output Tier-Based Strictly Local*
Thomas Graf and Connor Mayer . . . . . . . . . . . . . . . . . . . . . . . . . . . . . . . . . . . . . . . . . . . . . . . . . . . . 151

*Phonological Features for Morphological Inflection*
Adam Wiemerslage, Miikka Silfverberg and Mans Hulden . . . . . . . . . . . . . . . . . . . . . . . . . . . . . . . . . . . 161

*Extracting Morphophonology from Small Corpora*
Marina Ermolaeva . . . . . . . . . . . . . . . . . . . . . . . . . . . . . . . . . . . . . . . . . . . . . . . . . . . . . . . . . . . . . . . . . . . . 167

# Conference Program

**Wednesday, October 31**

**08:50–09:00**      **Session Opening: Opening Session**

**09:00–10:30**      **Session 1: Phonology**

09:00–09:30      *Efficient Computation of Implicational Universals in Constraint-Based Phonology Through the Hyperplane Separation Theorem*
Giorgio Magri

09:30–10:00      *Lexical Networks in !Xung*
Syed-Amad Hussain, Micha Elsner and Amanda Miller

10:00–10:30      *Acoustic Word Disambiguation with Phonogical Features in Danish ASR*
Andreas Søeborg Kirkedal

**10:30–11:00**      *Tea Break 1*

**11:00–12:30**      **Session ST: CoNLL – SIGMORPHON 2018 Shared Task: Universal Morphological Reinflection**

**12:30–14:00**      *Lunch*

**Wednesday, October 31**

**14:00–15:30**    **Session 2: Low-Resource Morphology**

14:00–14:30    *Adaptor Grammars for the Linguist: Word Segmentation Experiments for Very Low-Resource Languages*
Pierre Godard, Laurent Besacier, François Yvon, Martine Adda-Decker, Gilles Adda, Hélène Maynard and Annie Rialland

14:30–15:00    *String Transduction with Target Language Models and Insertion Handling*
Garrett Nicolai, Saeed Najafi and Grzegorz Kondrak

15:00–15:30    *Complementary Strategies for Low Resourced Morphological Modeling*
Alexander Erdmann and Nizar Habash

**15:30–16:00**    *Tea Break 2*

**16:00–17:30**    **Session P: Poster Session**

*Modeling Reduplication with 2-way Finite-State Transducers*
Hossep Dolatian and Jeffrey Heinz

*Automatically Tailoring Unsupervised Morphological Segmentation to the Language*
Ramy Eskander, Owen Rambow and Smaranda Muresan

*A Comparison of Entity Matching Methods between English and Japanese Katakana*
Michiharu Yamashita, Hideki Awashima and Hidekazu Oiwa

*Seq2Seq Models with Dropout can Learn Generalizable Reduplication*
Brandon Prickett, Aaron Traylor and Joe Pater

*A Characterwise Windowed Approach to Hebrew Morphological Segmentation*
Amir Zeldes

*Phonetic Vector Representations for Sound Sequence Alignment*
Pavel Sofroniev and Çağrı Çöltekin

*Sounds Wilde. Phonetically Extended Embeddings for Author-Stylized Poetry Generation*
Aleksey Tikhonov and Ivan Yamshchikov

*On Hapax Legomena and Morphological Productivity*
Janet Pierrehumbert and Ramon Granell

*A Morphological Analyzer for Shipibo-Konibo*
Ronald Cardenas and Daniel Zeman

*An Arabic Morphological Analyzer and Generator with Copious Features*
Dima Taji, Salam Khalifa, Ossama Obeid, Fadhl Eryani and Nizar Habash

*Sanskrit n-Retroflexion is Input-Output Tier-Based Strictly Local*
Thomas Graf and Connor Mayer

*Phonological Features for Morphological Inflection*
Adam Wiemerslage, Miikka Silfverberg and Mans Hulden

*Extracting Morphophonology from Small Corpora*
Marina Ermolaeva

**17:30–17:40    Session Closing: Closing Session**

# Efficient Computation of Implicational Universals in Constraint-Based Phonology Through the Hyperplane Separation Theorem

**Giorgio Magri**
CNRS, SFL, UPL
`magrigrg@gmail.com`

## Abstract

This paper focuses on the most basic *implicational universals* in phonological theory, called *T-orders* after Anttila and Andrus (2006). It develops necessary and sufficient constraint characterizations of T-orders within *Harmonic Grammar* and *Optimality Theory*. These conditions rest on the rich convex geometry underlying these frameworks. They are phonologically intuitive and have significant algorithmic implications.

## 1 Introduction

A *typology* $\mathfrak{T}$ is a collection of grammars $G_1, G_2, \ldots$ For instance, $\mathfrak{T}$ could be the set of syntactic grammars corresponding to all possible combinations of values of a set of parameters (Chomsky, 1981). Or the set of phonological grammars corresponding to all possible orderings of an underlying set of phonological rules (Chomsky and Halle 1968). Or the set of grammars corresponding to all rankings of an underlying constraint set (Prince and Smolensky, 2004).

The structure induced by a typology $\mathfrak{T}$ can be investigated though its *implicational universals* of the form (1). This implication holds provided every grammar in the typology $\mathfrak{T}$ that satisfies the *antecedent* property $P$ also satisfies the *consequent* property $\widehat{P}$ (Greenberg 1963).

$$P \xrightarrow{\mathfrak{T}} \widehat{P} \qquad (1)$$

To illustrate, suppose that $\mathfrak{T}$ is the typology of syntactic grammars. Consider the antecedent property $P$ of having VSO as the basic word order. And the consequent property $\widehat{P}$ of having prepositions (as opposed to postpositions). In this case, (1) is Greenberg's implicational universal #3.

In this paper, we are interested in typologies of *phonological grammars*. We assume a rep-resentational framework which distinguishes between two representational levels: *underlying representations* (URs), denoted as $x, \widehat{x}, \ldots$; and *surface representations* (SRs), denoted as $y, \widehat{y}, \ldots$ or $z, \widehat{z}, \ldots$. A *phonological grammar* $G$ is a function which takes a UR $x$ and returns a SR $y$. For instance, the phonology of German maps the UR $x = $ /bɛːd/ to the SR $y = $ [bɛːt] ('bath'). A *phonological typology* $\mathfrak{T}$ is a collection of phonological grammars $G_1, G_2, \ldots$ that we assume are all defined over the same set of URs (*Richness of the Base* assumption; Prince and Smolensky 2004).

Since phonological grammars are functions from URs to SRs, the most basic or atomic antecedent property $P$ of an implicational universal (1) is the property of mapping a certain UR $x$ to a certain SR $y$. Analogously, the most basic consequent property $\widehat{P}$ is the property of mapping a certain UR $\widehat{x}$ to a certain SR $\widehat{y}$. We thus focus on implicational universals of the form (2). This implication holds provided every grammar in the typology $\mathfrak{T}$ that succeeds on the antecedent mapping (i.e., it maps the antecedent UR $x$ to the antecedent SR $y$), also succeeds on the consequent mapping (i.e., it also maps the consequent UR $\widehat{x}$ to the consequent SR $\widehat{y}$). This definition makes sense because every grammar in the typology $\mathfrak{T}$ is defined on every UR, so that every grammar can be applied to the two URs $x$ and $\widehat{x}$.

$$(x, y) \xrightarrow{\mathfrak{T}} (\widehat{x}, \widehat{y}) \qquad (2)$$

The relation $\xrightarrow{\mathfrak{T}}$ thus defined over mappings turns out to be a partial order (under mild additional assumptions). It is called the *T-order* induced by the typology $\mathfrak{T}$ (Anttila and Andrus, 2006).

A familiar example concerns coda cluster simplification in English. Suppose that a coda t/d deletes before vowels in a certain dialect, so that the UR /cost us/ is realized as the SR [cos' us].



*Proceedings of the 15th SIGMORPHON Workshop on Computational Research in Phonetics, Phonology, and Morphology*, pages 1–10
Brussels, Belgium, October 31, 2018. ©2018 The Special Interest Group on Computational Morphology and Phonology
https://doi.org/10.18653/v1/P17

Then the coda also deletes before consonants in that same dialect, so that the UR /cost me/ is realized as the SR [cos' me] (Guy, 1991; Kiparsky, 1993; Coetzee, 2004). In other words, the implication $(/tV/, [V]) \xrightarrow{\mathfrak{T}} (/tC/, [C])$ holds relative to the typology $\mathfrak{T}$ of English dialects.

Two important phonological frameworks explored in the literature are *Harmonic Grammar* (HG; Legendre et al., 1990; Smolensky and Legendre, 2006; Potts et al., 2010) and *Optimality Theory* (OT; Prince and Smolensky, 2004). The crucial idea shared by HG and OT is that the relevant properties of phonological mappings are extracted by a set of $n$ phonological *constraints* that effectively represent discrete phonological mappings as points of $\mathbb{R}^n$. The goal of this paper is to express an implication $(x, y) \to (\widehat{x}, \widehat{y})$ in HG and OT in terms of the constraint violations of the two mappings $(x, y)$ and $(\widehat{x}, \widehat{y})$ and their competitors.

Section 2 presents the constraint condition for HG T-orders. It rests on the rich geometry underlying HG, as it follows from a classical result of convex geometry (the *Hyperplane Separation Theorem*), as detailed in section 3. Section 4 presents the constraint condition for OT T-orders. It rests on an equivalence between OT and HG T-orders established in section 5.

These constraint conditions admit a straightforward interpretation and thus help us better understand the phonological import of T-orders. Furthermore, they allow us to compute T-orders efficiently, circumventing the laborious computation of the entire HG or OT typology (as it is currently done in the literature; see for instance the OT *T-order Generator* by Anttila and Andrus, 2006).

## 2 Constraint Conditions for HG T-orders

HG assumes a relation *Gen* which pairs each UR x with a set $Gen(x)$ of *candidate* SRs. It also assumes a set of $n$ phonological constraints $C_1, \ldots, C_n$. Each *constraint* $C_k$ takes a phonological mapping $(x, y)$ of a UR x and a candidate SR y in $Gen(x)$ and returns the corresponding *number of violations* $C_k(x, y) \in \mathbb{N}$, a nonnegative integer which quantifies the "badness" of that mapping $(x, y)$ from the phonological perspective encoded by that constraint $C_k$. A *weight vector* $\mathbf{w} = (w_1, \ldots, w_n) \in \mathbb{R}_+^n$ assigns a nonnegative weight $w_k \geq 0$ to each constraint $C_k$.

The $\mathbf{w}$-*harmony* of a mapping $(x, y)$ is the weighted sum of the constraint violations multi-plied by $-1$, namely $-\sum_{k=1}^{n} w_k C_k(x, y)$. Because of the minus sign, mappings with a large harmony have few constraint violations. The *HG grammar* corresponding to a weight vector $\mathbf{w}$ maps a UR x to the candidate SR y in $Gen(x)$ such that the mapping $(x, y)$ has a larger $\mathbf{w}$-harmony than the mapping $(x, z)$ corresponding to any other candidate z in $Gen(x)$ (Legendre et al., 1990; Smolensky and Legendre, 2006; Potts et al., 2010). The *HG typology* (relative to a candidate relation and a constraint set) consists of the HG grammars corresponding to all weight vectors.

We denote by $(x, y) \xrightarrow{\text{HG}} (\widehat{x}, \widehat{y})$ the implication between an antecedent mapping $(x, y)$ and a consequent mapping $(\widehat{x}, \widehat{y})$ relative to the HG typology. We assume that the antecedent UR x comes with only a finite number $m$ of *antecedent loser* candidates $z_1, \ldots, z_m$ besides the *antecedent winner* candidate y. Analogously, we assume that the consequent UR $\widehat{x}$ comes with only a finite number $\widehat{m}$ of *consequent loser* candidates $\widehat{z}_1, \ldots, \widehat{z}_{\widehat{m}}$ besides the *consequent winner* candidate $\widehat{y}$. This assumption is nonrestrictive. In fact, a UR admits only a finite number of HG optimal candidates (Magri, 2018). Candidate sets can thus be assumed to be finite without loss of generality.

For each antecedent loser $z_i$, we define the *antecedent difference vector* $\mathbf{C}(x, y, z_i)$ as in (3). It has a component for each constraint $C_k$ defined as the *violation difference* $C_k(x, y, z_i)$ between the number $C_k(x, z_i)$ of violations assigned by $C_k$ to the loser mapping $(x, z_i)$ minus the number $C_k(x, y)$ of violations assigned to the antecedent winner mapping $(x, y)$.

$$\mathbf{C}(x, y, z_i) = \begin{bmatrix} C_1(x, z_i) - C_1(x, y) \\ \vdots \\ C_k(x, z_i) - C_k(x, y) \\ \vdots \\ C_n(x, z_i) - C_n(x, y) \end{bmatrix} \quad (3)$$

The *consequent difference vector* $\mathbf{C}(\widehat{x}, \widehat{y}, \widehat{z}_j)$ is defined analogously, as pitting the consequent winner mapping $(\widehat{x}, \widehat{y})$ against one of its losers $(\widehat{x}, \widehat{z}_j)$.

The definition of the HG implication $(x, y) \xrightarrow{\text{HG}} (\widehat{x}, \widehat{y})$ requires every HG grammar which succeeds on the antecedent mapping to also succeed on the consequent mapping. This condition is trivially satisfied if no HG grammar succeeds on the antecedent mapping, namely the mapping $(x, y)$ is HG unfeasible. Thus, let's suppose that is not the case. The following proposition then provides a

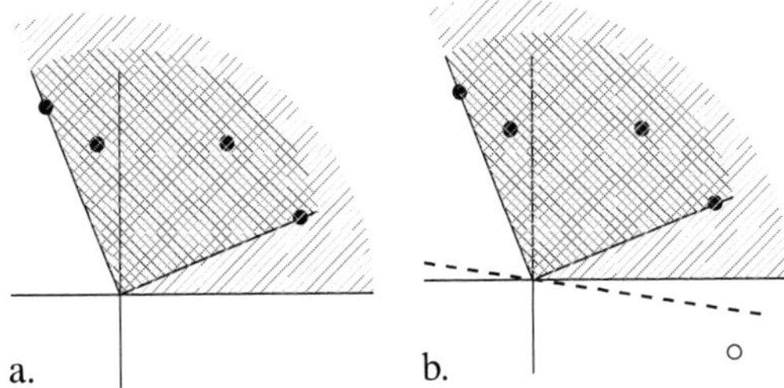

a.     b.

Figure 1: Geometric representation of condition (4).

| | | ONSET | NOCODA | MAX | DEPV | DEPC |
|---|---|---|---|---|---|---|
| /CC/ | [null] | 0 | 0 | 2 | 0 | 0 |
| | [CV.CV] | 0 | 0 | 0 | 2 | 0 |
| | [CVC] | 0 | 1 | 0 | 1 | 0 |
| /CCC/ | [null] | 0 | 0 | 3 | 0 | 0 |
| | [CV.CV.CV] | 0 | 0 | 0 | 3 | 0 |
| | [CV.CVC] | 0 | 1 | 0 | 2 | 0 |
| | [CVC] | 0 | 1 | 1 | 1 | 0 |

Table 1: Violation profiles for the mappings of the URs /CC/ and /CCC/ to their non-harmonically bounded candidates.

complete (both necessary and sufficient) characterization of the HG implication $(x, y) \overset{HG}{\mapsto} (\widehat{x}, \widehat{y})$ in terms of condition (4) stated entirely in terms of antecedent and consequent difference vectors.

**Proposition 1** *If the antecedent mapping $(x, y)$ is HG feasible, the HG implication $(x, y) \overset{HG}{\mapsto} (\widehat{x}, \widehat{y})$ holds if and only if for every consequent loser candidate $\widehat{z}_j$ with $j = 1, \ldots, \widehat{m}$, there exist $m$ nonnegative coefficients $\lambda_1, \ldots, \lambda_m \geq 0$ (one for each antecedent loser candidate $z_1, \ldots, z_m$) such that*

$$\mathbf{C}(\widehat{x}, \widehat{y}, \widehat{z}_j) \geq \sum_{i=1}^{m} \lambda_i \, \mathbf{C}(x, y, z_i) \qquad (4)$$

*and furthermore at least one of these coefficients $\lambda_1, \ldots, \lambda_m$ is different from zero.* □

Proposition 1 admits the following phonological interpretation. Condition (4) says that each consequent loser $\widehat{z}_j$ violates the constraints at least as much as (some conic combination of) the antecedent losers $z_1, \ldots, z_m$. In other words, the consequent losers are "worse" than the antecedent losers. The consequent winner $\widehat{y}$ thus has an "easier" time beating its losers than the antecedent winner $y$, as required by the definition of T-order.

Proposition 1 has important algorithmic implications. In fact, checking the definition of T-order (in general, of any implicational universal) directly is costly, because it requires computing the entire typology, which can be large. But proposition 1 says that, in the case of HG, T-orders can be determined locally, by only looking at the antecedent and consequent mappings together with their losers. Indeed, this proposition effectively reduces the problem of computing HG T-orders to the problem of finding coefficients $\lambda_i$ which satisfy the inequality (4). The latter is a polyhedral feasibility problem that can be solved efficiently with standard linear programming technology. A Python package to compute HG T-orders using condition (4) will be released shortly.

Proposition 1 admits the following geometric interpretation. Suppose there are only $n = 2$ constraints and $m = 4$ antecedent difference vectors $\mathbf{C}(x, y, z_i)$, represented as the black dots in figure 1a. The region $\{\sum_{i=1}^{m} \lambda_i \mathbf{C}(x, y, z_i) \mid \lambda_i \geq 0\}$ is the *convex cone* generated by these antecedent difference vectors, depicted in dark gray in figure 1a. The region in light gray singles out the points which are at least as large (component by component) as some point in this cone. Condition (4) thus says that each consequent difference vector $\mathbf{C}(\widehat{x}, \widehat{y}, \widehat{z}_j)$ must belong to this light gray region.

Indeed, suppose that some consequent difference vector does not belong to this light gray region, as represented by the white dot in figure 1b. The dashed line leaves the antecedent difference vectors (black dots) and the consequent difference vector (white dot) on two different sides. This means that the HG grammar corresponding to a nonnegative weight vector orthogonal to this line succeeds on the antecedent mapping $(x, y)$ but it fails on the consequent mapping $(\widehat{x}, \widehat{y})$, defying the implication $(x, y) \overset{HG}{\mapsto} (\widehat{x}, \widehat{y})$.

The existence of (a weight vector corresponding to) a dashed line such as the one depicted in figure 1b is geometrically obvious in the case with only $n = 2$ constraints. For an arbitrary number $n$ of constraints, a fundamental result of convex geometry, the *Hyperplane Separation Theorem* (HST; Rockafellar, 1970, §11; Boyd and Vandenberghe, 2004, §2.5), indeed guarantees the existence of a weight vector which separates the cone generated by the antecedent difference vectors from the outlier consequent difference vector. This is the core of the proof of proposition 1 provided in section 3.

Let's finally look at a couple of examples (based on Bane and Riggle 2009). We assume $n = 5$ con-

$$
\begin{array}{r}
\text{ONSET} \\ \text{NOCODA} \\ \text{MAX} \\ \text{DEPV} \\ \text{DEPC}
\end{array}
\begin{bmatrix} 0 \\ 0 \\ 3 \\ -3 \\ 0 \end{bmatrix} \geq 1.5
\begin{bmatrix} 0 \\ 0 \\ 2 \\ -2 \\ 0 \end{bmatrix} + 0
\begin{bmatrix} 0 \\ 1 \\ 0 \\ -1 \\ 0 \end{bmatrix} , \quad
\begin{bmatrix} 0 \\ 1 \\ 0 \\ -1 \\ 0 \end{bmatrix} \geq 0
\begin{bmatrix} 0 \\ 0 \\ 2 \\ -2 \\ 0 \end{bmatrix} + 1
\begin{bmatrix} 0 \\ 1 \\ 0 \\ -1 \\ 0 \end{bmatrix} , \quad
\begin{bmatrix} 0 \\ 1 \\ 1 \\ -2 \\ 0 \end{bmatrix} \geq 0.5
\begin{bmatrix} 0 \\ 0 \\ 2 \\ -2 \\ 0 \end{bmatrix} + 1
\begin{bmatrix} 0 \\ 1 \\ 0 \\ -1 \\ 0 \end{bmatrix}
$$

Table 2: Verifying that condition (4) holds for the HG implication (CC, CV.CV) → (CCC, CV.CV.CV).

straints: ONSET, which penalizes surface syllables starting with a vowel (V); NOCODA, which penalizes surface syllables ending with a consonant (C); MAX, which penalizes deletion of underlying segments; and DEPV and DEPC, which penalize epenthetic vowels and consonants, respectively. We focus on the two URs /CC/ and /CCC/. We only consider their non-harmonically bounded candidates, listed in table 1 with their constraint violations (the candidate [CVC.CV] is omitted because indistinguishable by the constraints from [CV.CVC]).

We focus on the implication (CC, CV.CV) → (CCC, CV.CV.CV). The antecedent UR $x$ = /CC/ comes with the winner candidate $y$ = [CV.CV] and the $m = 2$ loser candidates $z_1$ = [null] and $z_2$ = [CVC]. There are therefore two antecedent difference vectors $C(x, y, z_i)$, repeated on the right hand side of each of the three inequalities in table 2. The consequent UR $\widehat{x}$ = /CCC/ comes with the winner candidate $\widehat{y}$ = [CV.CV.CV] and the $\widehat{m} = 3$ loser candidates $\widehat{z}_1$ = [null], $\widehat{z}_2$ = [CV.CVC], and $\widehat{z}_3$ = [CVC]. There are therefore three consequent difference vectors $C(\widehat{x}, \widehat{y}, \widehat{z}_j)$, which appear on the left hand side of the three inequalities in table 2. Condition (4) holds: each consequent difference vector is at least as large as a conic combination of the antecedent difference vectors, as shown in table 2. Proposition 1 thus establishes the HG implication (CC, CV.CV) $\overset{\text{HG}}{\to}$ (CCC, CV.CV.CV).

Proposition 1 can also be used to show that an implication fails in HG. To illustrate, we focus on the implication (CC, CVC) → (CCC, CV.CVC). We consider the consequent difference vector $C(/CCC/, [CV.CVC], [null])$, which appears on the left hand side of (5). There are two antecedent difference vectors $C(/CC/, [CVC], [null])$ and $C(/CC/, [CVC], [CV.CV])$, which appear on the right hand side of (5).

$$
\begin{array}{r}
\text{ONSET} \\ \text{NOCODA} \\ \text{MAX} \\ \text{DEPV} \\ \text{DEPC}
\end{array}
\begin{bmatrix} 0 \\ -1 \\ 3 \\ -2 \\ 0 \end{bmatrix} \not\geq \lambda_1
\begin{bmatrix} 0 \\ -1 \\ 2 \\ -1 \\ 0 \end{bmatrix} + \lambda_2
\begin{bmatrix} 0 \\ -1 \\ 0 \\ 1 \\ 0 \end{bmatrix}
\tag{5}
$$

Condition (4) fails: the consequent difference vector is not larger than any conic combination of the two antecedent difference vectors, no matter the choice of the coefficients $\lambda_1, \lambda_2 \geq 0$. In fact, the inequality (5) for DEPV requires $\lambda_1 \geq 2$, whereby the inequality fails for MAX. Proposition 1 thus establishes that the implication (CC, CVC) $\overset{\text{HG}}{\not\to}$ (CCC, CV.CVC) fails in HG.

## 3 Proof of Proposition 1

The HST has a number of algebraic consequences known as *theorems of the alternatives*.[1] One of these theorems is the *Motzkin Transposition Theorem* (MTT; Bertsekas, 2009, proposition 5.6.2), which is particularly suited to our needs. It states that conditions (C1) and (C2) below are mutually exclusive (one and only one of them holds) for any two matrices $A \in \mathbb{R}^{p \times n}$ and $B \in \mathbb{R}^{q \times n}$.

(C1) There exists a vector $w \in \mathbb{R}^n$ such that $Aw < 0$ and $Bw \leq 0$.

(C2) There exist two nonnegative vectors $\xi \in \mathbb{R}^q_+$ and $\mu \in \mathbb{R}^p_+$ with $\mu \neq 0$ such that $A^\top \mu + B^\top \xi = 0$.

It is useful to specialize the MTT as follows. Consider some vectors $a_1, \ldots, a_m, b \in \mathbb{R}^n$. Let $A$ be the matrix whose $p = m$ rows are $-a_1^\top, \ldots, -a_m^\top$. Let $B$ be the matrix whose $q = n + 1$ rows are $-e_1^\top, \ldots, -e_n^\top, b^\top$ (where $e_i \in \mathbb{R}^n$ has all components equal to 0 but for the $i$th component which is equal to 1). The two conditions (C1) and (C2) thus become (C1′) and (C2′).

(C1′) There exists a nonnegative vector $w \in \mathbb{R}^n_+$ such that $a_1^\top w > 0, \ldots, a_m^\top w > 0$ but $b^\top w \leq 0$.

(C2′) There exist some nonnegative coefficients $\mu_1, \ldots, \mu_m, \xi \geq 0$ with at least one of the coefficients $\mu_1, \ldots, \mu_m$ different from 0 such that $\xi b \geq \sum_{i=1}^m \mu_i a_i$.

---

[1] Throughout this section, all vectors are column vectors; T stands for matrix transposition. Vector inequalities must hold component-wise.

With these preliminaries in place, we now consider the HG implication $(x, y) \overset{\text{HG}}{\Rightarrow} (\widehat{x}, \widehat{y})$. Suppose that the HG grammar corresponding to some nonnegative weight vector $\mathbf{w} \in \mathbb{R}^n_+$ succeeds on the antecedent mapping $(x, y)$. This means that the $\mathbf{w}$-harmony of this mapping $(x, y)$ is larger than that of every antecedent loser mapping $(x, z_i)$. This condition can be stated in terms of the antecedent difference vectors as in (6), taking advantage of the linearity of the HG harmony.

$$\mathbf{C}(x, y, z_i)^{\mathsf{T}} \mathbf{w} > 0, \qquad i = 1, \ldots, m \quad (6)$$

The implication $(x, y) \overset{\text{HG}}{\Rightarrow} (\widehat{x}, \widehat{y})$ then requires the HG grammar corresponding to that weight vector $\mathbf{w}$ to also succeed on the consequent mapping $(\widehat{x}, \widehat{y})$. This means that the $\mathbf{w}$-harmony of this mapping $(\widehat{x}, \widehat{y})$ is larger than that of every consequent loser mapping $(\widehat{x}, \widehat{z}_j)$. This condition can be stated in terms of the consequent difference vectors as in (7).

$$\mathbf{C}(\widehat{x}, \widehat{y}, \widehat{z}_j)^{\mathsf{T}} \mathbf{w} > 0, \qquad j = 1, \ldots, \widehat{m} \quad (7)$$

In other words, the HG implication $(x, y) \overset{\text{HG}}{\Rightarrow} (\widehat{x}, \widehat{y})$ holds if and only if every nonnegative weight vector $\mathbf{w}$ which satisfies (6) also satisfies (7). Equivalently, the HG T-order holds if and only if for every $j = 1, \ldots, \widehat{m}$, it is false that there exists a nonnegative weight vector $\mathbf{w} \in \mathbb{R}^n_+$ such that $\mathbf{C}(x, y, z_i)^{\mathsf{T}} \mathbf{w} > 0$ for every $i = 1, \ldots, m$ but $\mathbf{C}(\widehat{x}, \widehat{y}, \widehat{z}_j)^{\mathsf{T}} \mathbf{w} \leq 0$. In other words, for every $j = 1, \ldots, \widehat{m}$, condition (C1$'$) is false, with the positions $\mathbf{a}_i = \mathbf{C}(x, y, z_i)$ and $\mathbf{b} = \mathbf{C}(\widehat{x}, \widehat{y}, \widehat{z}_j)$. By the MTT, condition (C2$'$) must therefore be true for every $j = 1, \ldots, \widehat{m}$. This means that there exist some non-negative coefficients $\mu_1, \ldots, \mu_m, \xi \geq 0$ such that at least one of the coefficients $\mu_1, \ldots, \mu_m$ is strictly positive and furthermore the inequality (8) holds.

$$\xi \, \mathbf{C}(\widehat{x}, \widehat{y}, \widehat{z}_j) \geq \sum_{i=1}^{m} \mu_i \, \mathbf{C}(x, y, z_i) \quad (8)$$

The coefficient $\xi$ in (8) must be strictly positive. In fact, suppose by contradiction that $\xi = 0$, whereby inequality (8) becomes (9).

$$\mathbf{0} \geq \sum_{i=1}^{m} \mu_i \, \mathbf{C}(x, y, z_i) \quad (9)$$

Consider a weight vector $\mathbf{w}$ whose corresponding HG grammar maps the antecedent UR x to

the antecedent winner y, which exists by hypothesis. This weight vector $\mathbf{w}$ thus satisfies condition (6). Since $\mathbf{w}$ is non-negative, the scalar product of both sides of (9) with $\mathbf{w}$ preserves the inequality, yielding (10). But the latter inequality requires $\mu_1 = \cdots = \mu_m = 0$, contradicting the assumption that at least one of the nonnegative coefficients $\mu_1, \ldots, \mu_m \geq 0$ is strictly positive.

$$0 \geq \sum_{i=1}^{m} \mu_i \underbrace{\mathbf{C}(x, y, z_i)^{\mathsf{T}} \mathbf{w}}_{>0} \quad (10)$$

Since the coefficient $\xi$ is strictly positive, both sides of (8) can be divided by $\xi$, yielding the inequality (4) with the position $\lambda_i = \mu_i / \xi$.

## 4 Constraint Conditions for OT T-orders

This section extends the convex geometric analysis of T-orders developed in the preceding sections from HG to OT. We start by recalling that in OT a constraint $C_k$ is said to *prefer* a mapping $(x, y)$ to another mapping $(x, z)$ provided $C_k$ assigns less violations to the former than to the latter, namely $C_k(x, y) < C_k(x, z)$. A *constraint ranking* is an arbitrary linear order $\gg$ over the constraint set. A constraint ranking $\gg$ *prefers* a mapping $(x, y)$ to another mapping $(x, z)$ provided the highest $\gg$-ranked constraint which distinguishes between the two mappings $(x, y)$ and $(x, z)$ prefers $(x, y)$. The fact that the highest $\gg$-ranked relevant constraint defines the preference of the entire ranking, irrespectively of the preferences of lower $\gg$-ranked constraints, is captured by saying that the former constraint *strictly dominates* the latter constraints. The *OT grammar* corresponding to a ranking $\gg$ maps a UR x to that SR y such that $\gg$ prefers the mapping $(x, y)$ to the mapping $(x, z)$ corresponding to any other candidate z in $Gen(x)$ (Prince and Smolensky, 2004). The OT typology (for a given candidate relation and constraint set) consists of the OT grammars corresponding to all rankings.

We denote by $(x, y) \overset{\text{OT}}{\Rightarrow} (\widehat{x}, \widehat{y})$ the implication between an antecedent mapping $(x, y)$ and a consequent mapping $(\widehat{x}, \widehat{y})$ relative to the OT typology. By definition, this implication holds provided every constraint ranking that succeeds on the antecedent mapping also succeeds on the consequent mapping. Thus, a natural strategy to check the OT implication $(x, y) \overset{\text{OT}}{\Rightarrow} (\widehat{x}, \widehat{y})$ would be to use Recursive Constraint Demotion (RCD; Tesar and Smolensky, 1998) to check that for every $j =$

$1, \ldots, \widehat{m}$, no ranking is consistent simultaneously with the two mappings $(x, y)$ and $(\widehat{x}, \widehat{z}_j)$. In this section, we develop instead an alternative strategy which uses the HG-to-OT-portability result of Magri (2013) to extend to OT the convex geometric characterization of HG T-orders developed in sections 2-3.

To start, we recall that an OT grammar can be construed as an HG grammar (as long as the constraint violations are bounded, which is the case when the set of URs and the candidate sets are finite). In fact, OT's strict domination can be mimicked through HG weights which decrease exponentially. Indeed, if a weight is much larger than every smaller weight, the preferences of the constraint with the larger weight cannot be overcome by the preferences of the constraints with smaller weights (Prince and Smolensky, 2004; Keller, 2006). Since the OT typology is a subset of the HG typology, whenever an implication $(x, y) \overset{\text{HG}}{\to} (\widehat{x}, \widehat{y})$ holds in HG, the implication $(x, y) \overset{\text{OT}}{\to} (\widehat{x}, \widehat{y})$ holds in OT.

Lemma 1 slightly strengthens this conclusion. In fact, OT only cares about constraints' preferences. Equivalently, about the sign of the violation differences. Thus, the HG implication $(x, y) \overset{\text{HG}}{\to} (\widehat{x}, \widehat{y})$ entails not only the corresponding OT implication $(x, y) \overset{\text{OT}}{\to} (\widehat{x}, \widehat{y})$ but also any other OT implication $(x^*, y^*) \overset{\text{OT}}{\to} (\widehat{x}^*, \widehat{y}^*)$ whose antecedent and consequent mappings $(x^*, y^*)$ and $(\widehat{x}^*, \widehat{y}^*)$ yield violation differences with the same sign as the original antecedent and consequent mappings $(x, y)$ and $(\widehat{x}, \widehat{y})$. The proof of this lemma simply uses the observation that exponentially decaying HG weights mimic OT strict domination and it is therefore omitted.

**Lemma 1** *Given an antecedent mapping $(x, y)$ with its $m$ antecedent loser candidates $z_1, \ldots, z_m$, consider another mapping $(x^*, y^*)$ with the same number $m$ of loser candidates $z_1^*, \ldots, z_m^*$ such that the $m$ corresponding violation differences have the same sign, in the sense that condition (11) holds for $k = 1, \ldots, n$ and $i = 1, \ldots, m$.*

$$C_k(x, y, z_i) \gtreqless 0 \iff C_k(x^*, y^*, z_i^*) \gtreqless 0 \quad (11)$$

*Analogously, given the consequent mapping $(\widehat{x}, \widehat{y})$ with its $\widehat{m}$ consequent loser candidates $\widehat{z}_1, \ldots, \widehat{z}_{\widehat{m}}$, consider another mapping $(\widehat{x}^*, \widehat{y}^*)$ with the same number $\widehat{m}$ of loser candidates $\widehat{z}_1^*, \ldots, \widehat{z}_{\widehat{m}}^*$ such that the $\widehat{m}$ corresponding violation differences have the same sign, in the sense*
that condition (12) holds for $k = 1, \ldots, n$ and $j = 1, \ldots, \widehat{m}$.

$$C_k(\widehat{x}, \widehat{y}, \widehat{z}_j) \gtreqless 0 \iff C_k(\widehat{x}^*, \widehat{y}^*, \widehat{z}_j^*) \gtreqless 0 \quad (12)$$

*The HG implication $(x, y) \overset{\text{HG}}{\to} (\widehat{x}, \widehat{y})$ then entails the OT implication $(x^*, y^*) \overset{\text{OT}}{\to} (\widehat{x}^*, \widehat{y}^*)$.*

The preceding lemma establishes an entailment from HG to OT implications. We now want to investigate the reverse entailment from OT to HG implications. Thus, we suppose that an implication $(x, y) \overset{\text{OT}}{\to} (\widehat{x}, \widehat{y})$ holds in OT. Of course, that does not entail that the implication $(x, y) \overset{\text{HG}}{\to} (\widehat{x}, \widehat{y})$ between the same two mappings also holds in HG. That is because the HG typology is usually a *proper* superset of the OT typology. And a larger typology yields sparser T-orders. Thus, it makes no sense to try to establish that the OT implication $(x, y) \overset{\text{OT}}{\to} (\widehat{x}, \widehat{y})$ entails the HG implication $(x, y) \overset{\text{HG}}{\to} (\widehat{x}, \widehat{y})$ between the same two mappings.

We will try to establish something weaker instead: the OT implication $(x, y) \overset{\text{OT}}{\to} (\widehat{x}, \widehat{y})$ entails an HG implication $(x^{\text{dif}}, y^{\text{dif}}) \overset{\text{HG}}{\to} (\widehat{x}^{\text{easy}}, \widehat{y}^{\text{easy}})$ between an antecedent mapping $(x^{\text{dif}}, y^{\text{dif}})$ different from $(x, y)$ and a consequent mapping $(\widehat{x}^{\text{easy}}, \widehat{y}^{\text{easy}})$ different from $(\widehat{x}, \widehat{y})$. And we will choose this new antecedent mapping $(x^{\text{dif}}, y^{\text{dif}})$ and this new consequent mapping $(\widehat{x}^{\text{easy}}, \widehat{y}^{\text{easy}})$ in such a way that the new HG implication $(x^{\text{dif}}, y^{\text{dif}}) \overset{\text{HG}}{\to} (\widehat{x}^{\text{easy}}, \widehat{y}^{\text{easy}})$ is "more likely to hold" than the original implication $(x, y) \overset{\text{HG}}{\to} (\widehat{x}, \widehat{y})$ and thus validates the entailment from OT to HG implications.

What does it mean that an implication is "more likely to hold"? Intuitively, an implication from an antecedent to a consequent mapping is "likely to hold" when the antecedent mapping is "difficult" to obtain, namely it is consistent with very few grammars. In the limit, the implication holds trivially when the antecedent mapping is consistent with no grammars at all. Thus, we want to define the new antecedent mapping $(x^{\text{dif}}, y^{\text{dif}})$ in such a way that it is "more difficult" to obtain in HG than the original antecedent mapping $(x, y)$, whereby the superscript "diff". Analogously, an implication from an antecedent to a consequent mapping is intuitively "likely to hold" when the consequent mapping is "easy" to obtain, namely it is consistent with very many grammars. In the limit, the implication holds trivially when the consequent mapping is consistent with every grammar. Thus, we want to define the new consequent mapping $(\widehat{x}^{\text{easy}}, \widehat{y}^{\text{easy}})$ in such a way that it is "easier" to obtain in HG than the original consequent mapping $(\widehat{x}, \widehat{y})$, whereby the superscript "easy".

Let us now turn to the details. As discussed above around (6), it suffices to define the difference vectors corresponding to the new difficult mapping antecedent $(x^{\text{dif}}, y^{\text{dif}})$. Given the original antecedent mapping $(x, y)$ with its $m$ loser candidates $z_1, \ldots, z_m$, we assume that the new antecedent mapping $(x^{\text{dif}}, y^{\text{dif}})$ comes with the same number $m$ of loser candidates $z_1^{\text{dif}}, \ldots, z_m^{\text{dif}}$ whose violation differences are defined as in (13). Here, $\Omega_i$ is the total number of constraints $C_k$ such that $C_k$ prefers the original antecedent winner mapping $(x, y)$ to the original antecedent loser mapping $(x, z_i)$, in the sense that $C_k(x, y, z_i) > 0$.

$$C_k(x^{\text{dif}}, y^{\text{dif}}, z_i^{\text{dif}}) =$$
$$= \begin{cases} 1 & \text{if } C_k(x, y, z_i) > 0 \\ 0 & \text{if } C_k(x, y, z_i) = 0 \\ -\Omega_i - 1 & \text{if } C_k(x, y, z_i) < 0 \end{cases} \quad (13)$$

The intuition behind this definition (13) is as follows. OT only cares about the sign of the violation differences. Thus, the new violation difference $C_k(x^{\text{dif}}, y^{\text{dif}}, z_i^{\text{dif}})$ is defined in such a way that it has the same sign as the original violation difference $C_k(x, y, z_i)$: one is positive or negative if and only if the other is as well. HG also cares about the size of the violation differences, not only about their sign. In order for the mapping $(x^{\text{dif}}, y^{\text{dif}})$ to be "difficult" in HG, we want its positive violation differences to be as small as possible. For this reason, the positive violation differences in (13) have been set equal to 1, which is the smallest positive integer. Analogously, in order for the mapping $(x^{\text{dif}}, y^{\text{dif}})$ to be "difficult" in HG, we want its negative violation differences to be large (in absolute value) relative to the strength of the positive violation differences they have to "fight off". Since the positive entries are all equal to 1 in (13), the "strength" of the positive entries only depends on their number $\Omega_i$. For this reason, the absolute value of the negative violation differences in (13) has been set equal to $\Omega_i + 1$. In conclusion, this definition (13) ensures that the mapping $(x^{\text{dif}}, y^{\text{dif}})$ is "difficult" in HG, because the positive violation differences are small and the negative ones are large (in absolute value).

We now turn to the consequents. Given the original consequent mapping $(\widehat{x}, \widehat{y})$ with its $\widehat{m}$ loser candidates $\widehat{z}_1, \ldots, \widehat{z}_{\widehat{m}}$, we assume that the new consequent mapping $(\widehat{x}^{\text{easy}}, \widehat{y}^{\text{easy}})$ comes with the same number $\widehat{m}$ of loser candidates $\widehat{z}_1^{\text{easy}}, \ldots, \widehat{z}_{\widehat{m}}^{\text{easy}}$ whose violation differences are defined as in (14). Here $\widehat{\Lambda}_j$ is the total number of constraints $C_k$ such that $C_k$ prefers the original consequent loser mapping $(\widehat{x}, \widehat{z}_j)$ to the original consequent winner mapping $(\widehat{x}, \widehat{y})$, in the sense that $C_k(\widehat{x}, \widehat{y}, \widehat{z}_j) < 0$.

$$C_k(\widehat{x}^{\text{easy}}, \widehat{y}^{\text{easy}}, \widehat{z}_j^{\text{easy}}) =$$
$$= \begin{cases} \widehat{\Lambda}_j + 1 & \text{if } C_k(\widehat{x}, \widehat{y}, \widehat{z}_j) > 0 \\ 0 & \text{if } C_k(\widehat{x}, \widehat{y}, \widehat{z}_j) = 0 \\ -1 & \text{if } C_k(\widehat{x}, \widehat{y}, \widehat{z}_j) < 0 \end{cases} \quad (14)$$

The intuition behind this definition (14) is as follows. Whenever the original violation difference $C_k(\widehat{x}, \widehat{y}, \widehat{z}_j)$ is positive or negative, the new violation difference $C_k(\widehat{x}^{\text{easy}}, \widehat{y}^{\text{easy}}, \widehat{z}_j^{\text{easy}})$ is positive or negative as well, so that the original and the new violation differences have the same sign. The size of the new violation differences has been chosen as follows. In order for the mapping $(\widehat{x}^{\text{easy}}, \widehat{y}^{\text{easy}})$ to be "easy" in HG, we want its negative violation differences to be as small as possible (in absolute value). For this reason, the negative violation differences in (14) have been set equal to $-1$, which is the negative integer smallest in absolute value. Analogously, in order for the mapping $(\widehat{x}^{\text{easy}}, \widehat{y}^{\text{easy}})$ to be "easy" in HG, we want its positive violation differences to be large relative to the strength of the negative violation differences they have to "fight off". Since the negative entries are all equal to $-1$ in (14), the "strength" of the negative entries only depends on their number $\widehat{\Lambda}_j$. For this reason, the positive violation differences in (14) have been set equal to $\widehat{\Lambda}_j + 1$. In conclusion, this definition (14) ensures that the mapping $(\widehat{x}^{\text{easy}}, \widehat{y}^{\text{easy}})$ is "easy" in HG, because the positive violation differences are large and the negative violation differences are small (in absolute value).

We are now ready to put the pieces together. As anticipated, the OT implication $(x, y) \overset{\text{OT}}{\to} (\widehat{x}, \widehat{y})$ might not entail the HG implication $(x, y) \overset{\text{HG}}{\to} (\widehat{x}, \widehat{y})$ with the same antecedent and consequent mappings. Nonetheless, the following lemma 2 ensures that the OT implication $(x, y) \overset{\text{OT}}{\to} (\widehat{x}, \widehat{y})$ does entail the HG implication $(x^{\text{dif}}, y^{\text{dif}}) \overset{\text{HG}}{\to} (\widehat{x}^{\text{easy}}, \widehat{y}^{\text{easy}})$. The intuition is that the latter is less demanding than the HG implication $(x, y) \overset{\text{HG}}{\to} (\widehat{x}, \widehat{y})$, because its antecedent is "difficult" (namely, consistent with few HG grammars) and its consequent is "easy" (namely, consistent with many HG grammars). The proof of this lemma is provided in section 5, mimicking a reasoning in Magri (2013).

**Lemma 2** *The OT implication $(\mathsf{x}, \mathsf{y}) \overset{OT}{\to} (\widehat{\mathsf{x}}, \widehat{\mathsf{y}})$ entails the HG implication $(\mathsf{x}^{dif}, \mathsf{y}^{dif}) \overset{HG}{\to} (\widehat{\mathsf{x}}^{easy}, \widehat{\mathsf{y}}^{easy})$ between the antecedent mapping $(\mathsf{x}^{dif}, \mathsf{y}^{dif})$ and the consequent mapping $(\widehat{\mathsf{x}}^{easy}, \widehat{\mathsf{y}}^{easy})$ whose violation differences are defined in (13) and (14).* $\square$

As remarked explicitly above, (13) ensures that the original antecedent violation differences $C_k(\mathsf{x}, \mathsf{y}, \mathsf{z}_i)$ and the new antecedent violation differences $C_k(\mathsf{x}^{\mathrm{dif}}, \mathsf{y}^{\mathrm{dif}}, \mathsf{z}_i^{\mathrm{dif}})$ have the same sign. In other words, condition (11) holds with the positions $\mathsf{x}^* = \mathsf{x}^{\mathrm{dif}}$, $\mathsf{y}^* = \mathsf{y}^{\mathrm{dif}}$, and $\mathsf{z}_i^* = \mathsf{z}_i^{\mathrm{dif}}$. Analogously, (14) ensures that the original consequent violation differences $C_k(\widehat{\mathsf{x}}, \widehat{\mathsf{y}}, \widehat{\mathsf{z}}_j)$ and the new consequent violation differences $C_k(\widehat{\mathsf{x}}^{\mathrm{easy}}, \widehat{\mathsf{y}}^{\mathrm{easy}}, \widehat{\mathsf{z}}_i^{\mathrm{easy}})$ have the same sign. In other words, condition (12) holds with the positions $\widehat{\mathsf{x}}^* = \widehat{\mathsf{x}}^{\mathrm{easy}}$, $\widehat{\mathsf{y}}^* = \widehat{\mathsf{y}}^{\mathrm{easy}}$, and $\widehat{\mathsf{z}}_i^* = \widehat{\mathsf{z}}_i^{\mathrm{easy}}$. The two lemmas 1 and 2 can therefore be combined into the following conclusion: the OT implication $(\mathsf{x}, \mathsf{y}) \overset{OT}{\to} (\widehat{\mathsf{x}}, \widehat{\mathsf{y}})$ holds if and only the HG implication $(\mathsf{x}^{\mathrm{dif}}, \mathsf{y}^{\mathrm{dif}}) \overset{HG}{\to} (\widehat{\mathsf{x}}^{\mathrm{easy}}, \widehat{\mathsf{y}}^{\mathrm{easy}})$ holds. We can thus extend to OT the characterization of HG T-orders provided by the HG proposition 1 above, obtaining the following:

**Proposition 2** *If the antecedent mapping $(\mathsf{x}, \mathsf{y})$ is OT feasible, the OT implication $(\mathsf{x}, \mathsf{y}) \overset{OT}{\to} (\widehat{\mathsf{x}}, \widehat{\mathsf{y}})$ holds iff for every $j = 1, \ldots, \widehat{m}$, there exist $m$ nonnegative coefficients $\lambda_1, \ldots, \lambda_m \geq 0$ such that*

$$\mathbf{C}(\widehat{\mathsf{x}}^{easy}, \widehat{\mathsf{y}}^{easy}, \widehat{\mathsf{z}}_j^{easy}) \geq \sum_{i=1}^{m} \lambda_i \, \mathbf{C}(\mathsf{x}^{dif}, \mathsf{y}^{dif}, \mathsf{z}_i^{dif}) \tag{15}$$

*and furthermore at least one of these coefficients $\lambda_1, \ldots, \lambda_m$ is different from zero.* $\square$

To illustrate, we have seen at the end of section 2 that the HG implication $(\mathrm{cc}, \mathrm{cvc}) \overset{HG}{\to} (\mathrm{ccc}, \mathrm{cv.cvc})$ fails in HG because condition (4) fails, as shown in (5). But this entailment $(\mathrm{cc}, \mathrm{cvc}) \overset{OT}{\to} (\mathrm{ccc}, \mathrm{cv.cvc})$ does hold in OT. In fact, the three "easy" consequent difference vectors $\mathbf{C}(\widehat{\mathsf{x}}^{\mathrm{easy}}, \widehat{\mathsf{y}}^{\mathrm{easy}}, \widehat{\mathsf{z}}_j^{\mathrm{easy}})$ in this case are listed on the left hand side of the three inequalities in table 3. The two "difficult" antecedent difference vectors $\mathbf{C}(\mathsf{x}^{\mathrm{dif}}, \mathsf{y}^{\mathrm{dif}}, \mathsf{z}_i^{\mathrm{dif}})$ are repeated on the right hand side of the three inequalities. The table thus shows that condition (15) holds.

## 5  Proof of Lemma 2

We assume that the OT implication $(\mathsf{x}, \mathsf{y}) \overset{OT}{\to} (\widehat{\mathsf{x}}, \widehat{\mathsf{y}})$ holds. We consider an arbitrary nonnegative weight vector $\mathbf{w} = (w_1, \ldots, w_n)$ which succeeds on the "difficult" antecedent mapping $(\mathsf{x}^{\mathrm{dif}}, \mathsf{y}^{\mathrm{dif}})$ and we prove that it is also succeeds on the "easy" consequent mapping $(\widehat{\mathsf{x}}^{\mathrm{easy}}, \widehat{\mathsf{y}}^{\mathrm{easy}})$, thus securing the HG implication $(\mathsf{x}^{\mathrm{dif}}, \mathsf{y}^{\mathrm{dif}}) \overset{HG}{\longrightarrow} (\widehat{\mathsf{x}}^{\mathrm{easy}}, \widehat{\mathsf{y}}^{\mathrm{easy}})$.

The assumption that the weight vector $\mathbf{w}$ succeeds on the "difficult" antecedent mapping $(\mathsf{x}^{\mathrm{dif}}, \mathsf{y}^{\mathrm{dif}})$ means that $\sum_{k=1}^{n} w_k C_k(\mathsf{x}^{\mathrm{dif}}, \mathsf{y}^{\mathrm{dif}}, \mathsf{z}_i^{\mathrm{dif}}) > 0$ for every $i = 1, \ldots, m$. The latter inequality can be unpacked as in (16). In step (16a), we have used the definition (13). Here $W(\mathsf{x}, \mathsf{y}, \mathsf{z}_i)$ and $L(\mathsf{x}, \mathsf{y}, \mathsf{z}_i)$ are the sets of winner-preferring and loser-preferring constraints relative to the winner $(\mathsf{x}, \mathsf{y})$ and the loser $(\mathsf{x}, \mathsf{z}_i)$. In step (16b), we have upper bounded the sum $\sum_{h \in W(\mathsf{x}, \mathsf{y}, \mathsf{z}_i)} w_h$ with its largest term $\max_{h \in W(\mathsf{x}, \mathsf{y}, \mathsf{z}_i)} w_h$ times the number $\Omega_i$ of its addenda. In step (16c), we have lower bounded the sum $\sum_{k \in L(\mathsf{x}, \mathsf{y}, \mathsf{z}_i)} w_k$ with one of its terms, as the addenda are all non-negative.

$$
\begin{aligned}
\sum_{k=1}^{n} & w_k C_k(\mathsf{x}^{\mathrm{dif}}, \mathsf{y}^{\mathrm{dif}}, \mathsf{z}_i^{\mathrm{dif}}) > 0 \\
&\overset{(a)}{\Longleftrightarrow} \sum_{h \in W(\mathsf{x}, \mathsf{y}, \mathsf{z}_i)} w_h > (\Omega_i + 1) \sum_{k \in L(\mathsf{x}, \mathsf{y}, \mathsf{z}_i)} w_k \\
&\overset{(b)}{\Longrightarrow} \Omega_i \max_{h \in W(\mathsf{x}, \mathsf{y}, \mathsf{z}_i)} w_h > (\Omega_i + 1) \sum_{k \in L(\mathsf{x}, \mathsf{y}, \mathsf{z}_i)} w_k \\
&\overset{(c)}{\Longrightarrow} \Omega_i \max_{h \in W(\mathsf{x}, \mathsf{y}, \mathsf{z}_i)} w_h > (\Omega_i + 1) w_k \\
&\qquad\qquad \text{for every } k \in L(\mathsf{x}, \mathsf{y}, \mathsf{z}_i) \\
&\Longrightarrow \max_{h \in W(\mathsf{x}, \mathsf{y}, \mathsf{z}_i)} w_h > w_k
\end{aligned}
\tag{16}
$$

We now show that the conclusion reached in the last line of (16) entails that the strict inequality (17) holds for every $j = 1, \ldots, \widehat{m}$.

$$\max_{h \in W(\widehat{\mathsf{x}}, \widehat{\mathsf{y}}, \widehat{\mathsf{z}}_j)} w_h > \max_{k \in L(\widehat{\mathsf{x}}, \widehat{\mathsf{y}}, \widehat{\mathsf{z}}_j)} w_k \tag{17}$$

In fact, suppose by contradiction that (17) fails for some $j = 1, \ldots, \widehat{m}$. Consider a ranking $\gg$ which respects the relative size of the weights, in the sense that conditions [A] and [B] hold for any two constraints $C_s, C_t$ with weights $w_s, w_t$.

**[A]** If $w_s > w_t$, then $C_s$ is $\gg$-ranked above $C_k$.

**[B]** If $w_s = w_t$ and $C_s \in L(\widehat{\mathsf{x}}, \widehat{\mathsf{y}}, \widehat{\mathsf{z}}_j)$ and $C_t \in W(\widehat{\mathsf{x}}, \widehat{\mathsf{y}}, \widehat{\mathsf{z}}_j)$, then $C_s$ is $\gg$-ranked above $C_k$.

$$\begin{array}{c}\text{\small ONSET}\\\text{\small NOCODA}\\\text{\small MAX}\\\text{\small DEPV}\\\text{\small DEPC}\end{array}\begin{bmatrix}0\\-1\\3\\-1\\0\end{bmatrix}\geq 0.5\begin{bmatrix}0\\-2\\1\\-2\\0\end{bmatrix}+0\begin{bmatrix}0\\-2\\0\\1\\0\end{bmatrix}\qquad \begin{bmatrix}0\\-1\\0\\2\\0\end{bmatrix}\geq 0\begin{bmatrix}0\\-2\\1\\-2\\0\end{bmatrix}+0.5\begin{bmatrix}0\\-2\\0\\1\\0\end{bmatrix}\qquad \begin{bmatrix}0\\0\\2\\-1\\0\end{bmatrix}\geq 0.5\begin{bmatrix}0\\-2\\1\\-2\\0\end{bmatrix}+0\begin{bmatrix}0\\-2\\0\\1\\0\end{bmatrix}$$

Table 3: Verifying that condition (15) holds for the OT implication (CC, CVC) → (CCC, CV.CVC).

The ranking $\gg$ succeeds on the antecedent mapping $(x, y)$. In fact, the condition obtained in the last line of (16) says that there exists a constraint which prefers the winner $(x, y)$ to the loser $(x, z_i)$ whose weight is strictly larger than the weight of every constraint which instead prefers the loser $(x, z_i)$ to the winner $(x, y)$. By [A], this means that a constraint which prefers the winner $(x, y)$ is $\gg$-ranked above every constraint that instead prefers the loser $(x, z_i)$. The ranking $\gg$ therefore prefers the winner $(x, y)$ to the loser $(x, z_i)$. Since this conclusion holds for every $i = 1, \ldots, m$, the ranking $\gg$ succeeds on the antecedent mapping $(x, y)$.

On the other hand, the ranking $\gg$ fails on the consequent mapping $(\widehat{x}, \widehat{y})$. In fact, the contradictory assumption that (17) fails means that $\max_{h \in W(\widehat{x}, \widehat{y}, \widehat{z}_j)} w_h \leq \max_{k \in L(\widehat{x}, \widehat{y}, \widehat{z}_j)} w_k$. In other words, there exists a constraint which prefers the loser $(\widehat{x}, \widehat{z}_j)$ to the winner $(\widehat{x}, \widehat{y})$ whose weight is strictly larger than or equal to the weights of the constraints which instead prefer the winner $(\widehat{x}, \widehat{y})$ to the loser $(\widehat{x}, \widehat{z}_j)$. By [A] and [B], the ranking $\gg$ cannot prefer $(\widehat{x}, \widehat{y})$ to $(\widehat{x}, \widehat{z}_j)$.

The conclusion that $\gg$ succeeds on the antecedent $(x, y)$ but fails on the consequent $(\widehat{x}, \widehat{y})$ contradicts the assumption that the implication $(x, y) \overset{\text{OT}}{\to} (\widehat{x}, \widehat{y})$ holds in OT, thus establishing the inequality (17). This inequality can in turn be unpacked as in (18). In step (18a), we have lower bounded $\widehat{\Lambda}_j \max_{k \in L(\widehat{x}, \widehat{y}, \widehat{z}_j)} w_k$ with the sum $\sum_{k \in L(\widehat{x}, \widehat{y}, \widehat{z}_j)} w_k$, because $\widehat{\Lambda}_j$ is the number of addenda in the sum. In step (18b), we have upper bounded the maximum $\max_{h \in W(\widehat{x}, \widehat{y}, \widehat{z}_j)} w_h$ with the sum $\sum_{h \in W(\widehat{x}, \widehat{y}, \widehat{z}_j)} w_h$, because the weights being summed over are all non-negative. In step (18c), we have used the definition (14) of the con-

straint differences $C_k(\widehat{x}^{\text{easy}}, \widehat{y}^{\text{easy}}, \widehat{z}_j^{\text{easy}})$.

$$\begin{aligned}
&\max_{h \in W(\widehat{x}, \widehat{y}, \widehat{z}_j)} w_h > \max_{k \in L(\widehat{x}, \widehat{y}, \widehat{z}_j)} w_k \Longrightarrow\\
&\Longrightarrow (\widehat{\Lambda}_j + 1) \max_{h \in W(\widehat{x}, \widehat{y}, \widehat{z}_j)} w_h > \widehat{\Lambda}_j \max_{k \in L(\widehat{x}, \widehat{y}, \widehat{z}_j)} w_k\\
&\overset{(a)}{\Longrightarrow} (\widehat{\Lambda}_j + 1) \max_{h \in W(\widehat{x}, \widehat{y}, \widehat{z}_j)} w_h > \sum_{k \in L(\widehat{x}, \widehat{y}, \widehat{z}_j)} w_k\\
&\overset{(b)}{\Longrightarrow} (\widehat{\Lambda}_j + 1) \sum_{h \in W(\widehat{x}, \widehat{y}, \widehat{z}_j)} w_h > \sum_{k \in L(\widehat{x}, \widehat{y}, \widehat{z}_j)} w_k\\
&\overset{(c)}{\Longrightarrow} \sum_{k=1}^{n} w_k C_k(\widehat{x}^{\text{easy}}, \widehat{y}^{\text{easy}}, \widehat{z}_j^{\text{easy}}) > 0
\end{aligned}$$
$$(18)$$

The inequality in the last line of (18) holds for every $j = 1, \ldots, \widehat{m}$, ensuring that the weights $\mathbf{w}$ succeed on the consequent mapping $(\widehat{x}^{\text{easy}}, \widehat{y}^{\text{easy}})$.

## 6 Conclusions

A central task of linguistic theory is to characterize the typological structure predicted by a grammatical formalism in order to match it to linguistic data. A classical strategy to characterize typological structure is to chart the implicational universals predicted by the formalism. In this paper, we have focused on the two constraint-based phonological formalisms of HG and OT. And we have considered the simplest type of implicational universals, namely *T-orders*. The main result of this paper has been a complete constraint characterization of T-orders in HG and OT. These constraint conditions rely on an elegant underlying convex geometry. These conditions are phonologically intuitive and have important algorithmic implications.

### Acknowledgments

The research reported in this paper has been funded by the *Agence National de la Recherche* (project title: 'The mathematics of segmental phonotactics'). This paper is part of a larger project on T-orders, developed in collaboration with Arto Anttila. His comments on this paper are gratefully acknowledged.

9

## References

Arto Anttila and Curtis Andrus. 2006. T-orders. Manuscript and software (Stanford).

Maximilian Bane and Jason Riggle. 2009. Evaluating Strict Domination: The typological consequences of weighted constraints. In *Proceedings of the 45th annual meeting of the Chicago Linguistics Society*, pages 13–27.

Dimitri P. Bertsekas. 2009. *Convex Optimization Theory*. Athena Scientific, Belmont, MA, USA.

Stephen Boyd and Lieven Vandenberghe. 2004. *Convex Optimization*. Cambridge University Press.

Noam Chomsky. 1981. *Lectures on Government and Binding*. Mouton de Gruyter.

Noam Chomsky and Morris Halle. 1968. *The Sound Pattern of English*. Harper and Row, New York.

Andries W. Coetzee. 2004. *What it Means to be a Loser: Non-Optimal Candidates in Optimality Theory*. Ph.D. thesis, University of Massachusetts, Amherst.

Joseph H. Greenberg. 1963. Some universals of grammar with particular reference to the order of meaningful elements. In Joseph H. Greenberg, editor, *Universals of Language*, pages 73–113. MIT Press, Cambridge, MA.

G. Guy. 1991. Explanation in variable phonology. *Language Variation and Change*, 3:1–22.

Frank Keller. 2006. Linear Optimality Theory as a model of gradience in grammar. In Gisbert Fanselow, Caroline Féry, Ralph Vogel, and Matthias Schlesewsky, editors, *Gradience in Grammar: Generative Perspectives*, pages 270–287. Oxford University Press, Oxford.

Paul Kiparsky. 1993. An OT perspective on phonological variation. Handout (Stanford).

Géraldine Legendre, Yoshiro Miyata, and Paul Smolensky. 1990. Harmonic Grammar: A formal multi-level connectionist theory of linguistic well-formedness: Theoretical foundations. In *Annual conference of the Cognitive Science Society 12*, pages 388–395, Mahwah, NJ. Lawrence Erlbaum.

Giorgio Magri. 2013. HG has no computational advantages over OT: towards a new toolkit for computational OT. *Linguistic Inquiry*, 44.4:569–609.

Giorgio Magri. 2018. Finiteness of optima in constraint-based phonology. Manuscript, CNRS.

Christopher Potts, Joe Pater, Karen Jesney, Rajesh Bhatt, and Michael Becker. 2010. Harmonic Grammar with Linear Programming: From linear systems to linguistic typology. *Phonology*, 27(1):1–41.

Alan Prince and Paul Smolensky. 2004. *Optimality Theory: Constraint Interaction in generative grammar*. Blackwell, Oxford. Original version, Technical Report CU-CS-696-93, Department of Computer Science, University of Colorado at Boulder, and Technical Report TR-2, Rutgers Center for Cognitive Science, Rutgers University, April 1993. Available from the Rutgers Optimality Archive as ROA 537.

R. Tyrrell Rockafellar. 1970. *Convex Analysis*. Princeton Landmarks in Mathematics; Princeton University Press.

Paul Smolensky and Géraldine Legendre. 2006. *The Harmonic Mind*. MIT Press, Cambridge, MA.

Bruce Tesar and Paul Smolensky. 1998. Learnability in Optimality Theory. *Linguistic Inquiry*, 29:229–268.

# Lexical Networks in !Xung


**Syed-Amad Hussain**
Department of Computer Science
The Ohio State University
amadh881@gmail.com

**Micha Elsner**
Department of Linguistics
The Ohio State University
melsner0@gmail.com

**Amanda Miller**
[24]7.ai
San Jose, California
amanda.miller@247.ai



## Abstract

We investigate the lexical network properties of the large phoneme inventory Southern African language Mangetti Dune !Xung as it compares to English and other commonly-studied languages. Lexical networks are graphs in which nodes (words) are linked to their minimal pairs; global properties of these networks are believed to mediate lexical access in the minds of speakers. We show that the network properties of !Xung are within the range found in previously-studied languages. By simulating data ("pseudolexicons") with varying levels of phonotactic structure, we find that the lexical network properties of !Xung diverge from previously-studied languages when fewer phonotactic constraints are retained. We conclude that lexical network properties are representative of an underlying cognitive structure which is necessary for efficient word retrieval and that the phonotactics of !Xung may be shaped by a selective pressure which preserves network properties within this cognitively useful range.


## 1 Introduction

We investigate the lexical network properties (LNPs) of the Southern African language Mangetti Dune !Xung (hereafter !Xung) as they compare to previously-studied languages. !Xung has 87 consonant phonemes, substantially larger than most of the world's languages (Miller, 2016; Miller-Ockhuizen, 2003; Dickens, 1994; Maddieson, 2013). Many of these sounds are clicks, typologically rare sounds found mostly in Southern Africa. In !Xung, close to 90% of content words begin with an initial click. While these properties place !Xung distinctly apart from most commonly-studied languages at the phonemic level, we analyze its lexical network (LN) to determine whether its mental lexicon is structurally different from those of languages with

smaller inventories.

In a LN, as shown in Figure 1, nodes represent words and edges between nodes represent minimal pairs (Vitevitch, 2008). Vitevitch (2008) argues that the high connectivity and tendency toward clustering found in the English language lexicon are important aids to word learning and retrieval; later work finds similar properties in other lexicons (Arbesman et al., 2010; Shoemark et al., 2016). Some claims about the linguistic relevance of LNPs have been qualified by experiments showing that certain property values are inherent to the construction process of the network and can be replicated even when words are sampled from simple generative processes (Stella and Brede, 2015; Gruenenfelder and Pisoni, 2009; Turnbull and Peperkamp, 2016; Brown et al., 2018), though all these studies except Brown et al. point out that the LNs of natural languages maintain some distinctive properties.

Because !Xung has a very large phoneme inventory, it might in principle have very different network properties from previously studied languages. Any given word might have far more minimally different neighbors; alternately, the words might be spread out more thinly across a wider phonemic space. Our main questions in this study are (1) whether the network properties of !Xung differ from those of previously-studied languages, and, (2) if not, what phonological properties of the language lead to this network structure despite the large phoneme inventory?

Our initial analysis shows that most of the LNPs of !Xung lie within the range of values found for other languages in previous work. We next look at how these properties might vary over a range of lexicon sizes. Because large lexicons for !Xung are not available, we conduct these analyses on simulated data ("pseudolexicons") sampled from trigram models, following Gruenen-

11


*Proceedings of the 15th SIGMORPHON Workshop on Computational Research in Phonetics, Phonology, and Morphology*, pages 11–20
Brussels, Belgium, October 31, 2018. ©2018 The Special Interest Group on Computational Morphology and Phonology
https://doi.org/10.18653/v1/P17

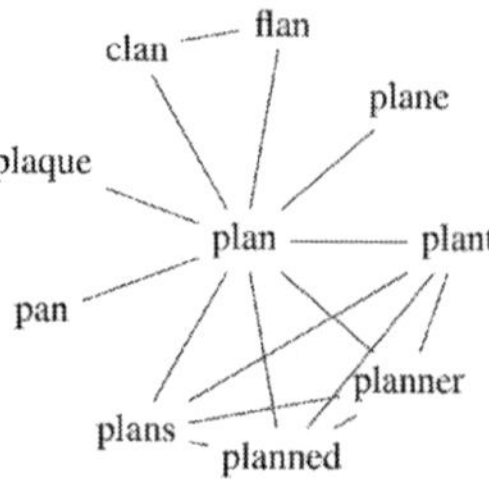



Figure 1: Example lexical network centered around the word "plan": (Turnbull and Peperkamp, 2016, Fig. 1).

felder and Pisoni (2009). Though this analysis must be considered preliminary due to the weakness of the trigram model, a comparison against the reported values from Shoemark et al. (2016) again finds no substantial difference. Having answered our first question, we turn to the second: we construct pseudolexicons with varying degrees of phonological structure, following Turnbull and Peperkamp (2016), and compare them to one another. We show that !Xung is more susceptible to the loss of phonotactic structure than English; simplistic sampling procedures create extremely unnatural lexicons due to the inventory size. To determine what phonotactic properties give the actual lexicon its shape, we create additional pseudolexicons that focus on specific phonological properties of !Xung. We find that pseudolexicons based on syllabic structure, including the syllable type inventory and co-occurrence restrictions on onset and rhyme within the syllable, move closer to the properties of the actual language, although a disparity still remains present. Overall, we find that !Xung has similar LNPs to previously studied languages. However, experiments with sampled lexicons show that when its syllable structure is disrupted, disparities between !Xung and English arise, hinting at a greater reliance on phonotactics to maintain the shape of the network.

## 2 Background

We conduct our analysis on LNs to derive cognitive and phonotactic conclusions. Vitevitch (2008) first presents this network model which assigns words as nodes and minimal pairs between these words as edges. He finds that lexical retrieval and language acquisition is aided by higher network density – largely defined by the network properties of assortative mixing and average clustering coefficient. Vitevitch (2008) and subsequent work

on networks (Shoemark et al., 2016; Turnbull and Peperkamp, 2016) describe network structure in terms of four properties: **Fraction in Largest Island** is defined as the percent of the lexicon that is connected to the largest component, or island, in the network and characterizes the global connectivity of the network. The remaining three properties are calculated within this largest island: **Degree Assortativity Coefficient** shows the tendency of nodes to be connected to other nodes with similar degrees, where with higher values the central "hubs" of the network are connected to one another (Newman and Girvan, 2003); **Average Shortest Path Length (ASPL)** averages the minimum number of hops it takes to get between any two nodes in the largest island, similar to the game "Six Degrees to Kevin Bacon"; **average Clustering Coefficient (CC)** is defined as the number of edges that exist between neighbors divided by the number of possible edges between neighbors and can be thought of as "are my neighbors also neighbors with each other" or "do all my friends know each other?".

Later work on this model points out that network statistics are affected by lexicon size, phoneme inventory size, word length distribution, and the inclusion of morphological variants (Shoemark et al., 2016). Since these cannot all be controlled in cross-linguistic comparisons, indirect comparisons are often made. The phonological properties of the language can be used to generate pseudolexicons sampled from character language models, which are examined over several lexicon sizes. The trends for each language are then compared qualitatively against each other language.

Further work expands the use of pseudolexicons to determine the source of the network property statistics (Turnbull and Peperkamp, 2016). Instead of attempting to replicate the real phonotactic regularities of the language, pseudolexicons can vary in how many, and which, phonotactic properties of the original language they retain. By comparing several such pseudolexicons, Turnbull and Peperkamp (2016) conclude that the typical range of values of average CC are intrinsic to all LNs, typical values of largest island size and ASPL are determined by phonological rules, and degree assortativity may reflect some higher-level organization principle within the lexicon.

While this kind of previous research has established that some lexical network properties depend on phonology, their experiments tell us relatively little about what specific phonological constraints have the greatest effect. In order to do so, we must move beyond comparing real languages to samples from generic statistical processes like ngram models and create distributions which enforce individual phonotactic constraints.

We employ a series of pseudolexicons which preserve various aspects of !Xung phonology to determine which phonological rules within these languages are responsible for preserving the typical values of largest island size and ASPL. We find that constraints on click placement and syllable structure can explain most, but not all the difference between randomly generated pseudolexicons and the real data.

## 3 Phonological Properties of !Xung

Mangetti Dune !Xung belongs to the Kxa language family (formerly known as the Northern Khoisan branch of the Khoisan family), and is a member of the Northern branch of the Juu subgroup, according to the classification of Sands (2003). The complete sound inventory of Mangetti Dune !Xung is provided in Miller (2016). Mangetti Dune !Xung contains 87 consonants, 45 of which are click consonants; its vowel inventory is also extremely large. There are only five contrastive vowel qualities, but there are many contrastive vocalic phonation types (modal, breathy, epiglottalized and glottalized), and the language also contrasts oral vs. nasal vowels. Nasality can combine with all the different phonation types, though there are some restrictions on which vowel qualities can combine with epiglottalization and nasalization. In addition, !Xung is a tone language; each mora may bear one of 4 distinct tone levels with some restrictions on their co-occurrence (Miller-Ockhuizen, 2003), leading to 7 possible contrastive tone patterns that occur on content words. (In our analysis, for purposes of determining minimal pairs, the tones are considered as contrastive features of the vowels.) Over 90% of content words in !Xung commence with a click consonant, while function words largely begin with a pulmonic (non-click) consonant.

Miller-Ockhuizen (2003) describes the phonology of a related Juu lect, Ju'hoansi. All native roots within Ju'hoansi (and !Xung) are either monosyllabic or bisyllabic with loan words constituting any trisyllabic roots. A syllable consists of an onset consonant followed by a 1 or 2-vowel nucleus with 2-vowel nuclei only occurring within the first syllable. The only coda consonants are nasals which end some monosyllabic roots. Within a word, 89 consonant types can occur in the initial position while only 4 types occur in medial position. Initial consonants are 91% pulmonic and velaric plosives, which includes all click types, with fricatives and nasal or liquid sonorants constituting the rest of the occurrences. Medial consonants are effectively limited to the sonorants β and ɾ (98% of medial consonants) and the nasals m and n. Guttural consonants and vowels only occur within the initial syllable and both never co-occur within the same syllable. The extensive co-occurrence restrictions in !Xung continue between tone and guttural vowels and consonants where, for instance, roots with partially epiglotalized vowels are always bitonal while roots with fully epiglottalized vowels are level toned. There are also several co-occurrence restrictions based on place of articulation with cross-height cross-place dipthongs only occurring in roots with back clicks and dipthongs with epiglottalized vowels and pharyngeal consonants causing the dipthongization of following front vowels. See Miller (2016) and Heikkinen (1986) for differences between Ju'hoansi and !Xung.

## 4 Basic properties

We begin by establishing the actual LNPs of the !Xung lexicon and comparing them to previous work.

### 4.1 Methodology

Our !Xung corpus contains 974 words, collected and transcribed into IPA as part of field work (Miller et al., 2008). For comparison, we use an English lexicon containing the 974 highest frequency words from the Fisher corpus (Cieri et al., 2004), converted to IPA using the CMU dictionary— though we do not believe that the !Xung lexicon contains strictly the most frequent words of the language, we do believe that the field workers chose to record words which they encountered frequently in storytelling and conversation.

We build each LN by assigning words as nodes and minimal pairs as edges. We build and analyze our networks using the python NetworkX package. From these networks, we derive the Fraction in Largest Island, Degree Assortativity, ASPL, and

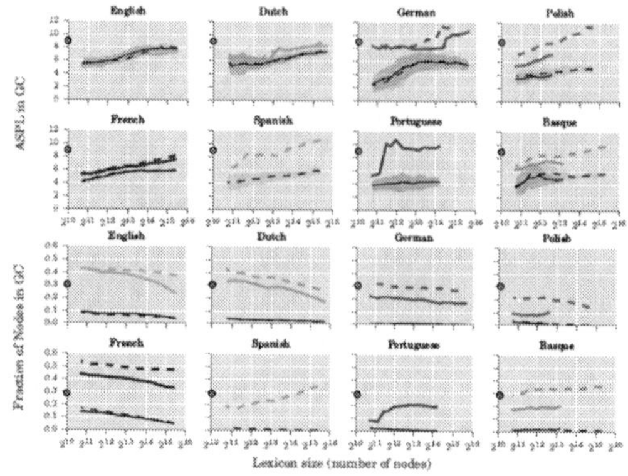

Figure 2: Two panels of Figure 4 from Shoemark et al., with superimposed dots for !Xung; colored lines show real language, dotted lines show pseudolexicons.

| Property | !Xung | Closest value |
|---|---|---|
| % Lgst. Island | 36.5 | 32 (Dutch) |
| ASPL | 8.74 | 8 (German) |
| Deg. Assrt. | 52.8 | 52 (German) |
| CC | 52.4 | 35 (Polish) |

Table 1: Lexical network properties of !Xung, along with closest comparison values from Shoemark et al. (2016).

| Median degree | 4 |
|---|---|
| Mean degree | 4.357 |
| Min degree | 1 |
| Max degree | 14 |
| Degree std. dev. | 2.749 |

Table 2: Degree (minimal pair) statistics of !Xung.

Average Clustering Coefficient. We then qualitatively compare these results to the values for the 8 reported languages[1] in Shoemark et al. (2016).

## 4.2 Results

The LN degree statistics are summarized in Table 2. Despite the potential for very large or small numbers of minimal pairs per word, we find that the actual maximum degree (number of pairs) is 14, the minimum is 1, and most words have about 4 neighbors. Lexical network properties are shown in Table 1. (Comparison values for the LNPs are derived from Shoemark's Figure 4 by reading the graph at the smallest lexicon size available; two panels of this graph are reproduced as Figure 2.) !Xung's value for Fraction in Largest Island falls within the observed range of variation; for Average Shortest Path and Degree Assortativity, !Xung represents an extreme of the observed values, but falls quite close to the measurements for German. Only for Clustering Coefficient is the !Xung value an outlier; !Xung is more tightly clustered than the other languages in the sample.

## 5 Analysis 1

The analysis above did not show definitive differences between !Xung and previously studied languages, but, as argued by Shoemark et al. (2016), LN measurements are best viewed as trends over several lexicon sizes rather than point measurements. With the limited data available for !Xung,

we cannot obtain more than 974 actual words; instead, we follow previous work in using sampled data as a proxy. Though sampled data cannot be considered fully reliable, it can help us to understand whether !Xung phonology would probably create extreme LNP values if more data were available, or whether the outcomes would likely remain in the typical range.

## 5.1 Methodology

To create pseudolexicons that most accurately capture the phonotactics of each language, we use a trigram model with Ney's absolute discounting(Ney et al., 1994)[2]. Using these probabilities, we can extend the lexicon size by simulating "words" similar to those in the actual language.

We train the trigram models using the SRI Language Modeling (SRILM) Toolkit (Stolcke, 2002; Stolcke et al., 2011). We generate pseudolexicons of size $2^{10}$, $2^{11}$, $2^{12}$, and $2^{13}$ for each language (we did not generate a $2^{13}$ length pseudolexicon for English) and average relevant network statistics over 50 trials.

## 5.2 Results

The trendlines appear in Figure 3. In an initial overview, we see that !Xung trend lines are similar to those for trigram-sampled English for most of the properties; Fraction in Largest Island trends upward (the network grows more connected), as does Degree Assortativity ("hubs" in the network

---

[1] Seven Indo-European languages of Europe: English, Dutch, German, Polish, French, Spanish and Portuguese—and one language isolate: Basque.

[2] Previous work used Kneser-Ney smoothing (Chen and Goodman, 1999); this is not as suitable for character-level modeling, since it uses a type-based backoff strategy designed for the sparsity of word rather than character statistics.

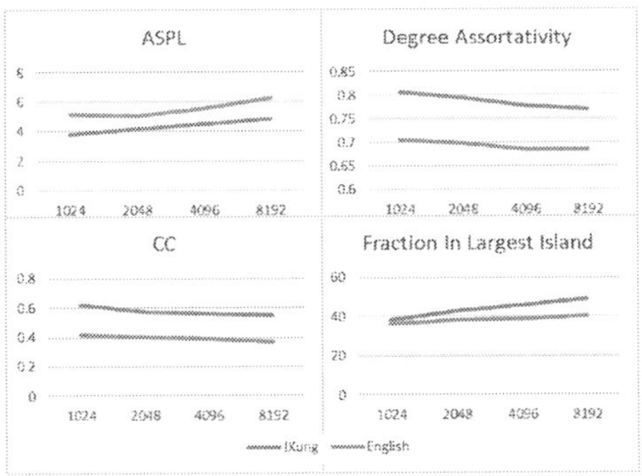

Figure 3: Trigram pseudolexicon network property values for trigram pseudolexicons of English and !Xung, and natural English data.

grow closer together), while clustering coefficient remains flat. The trend for ASPL differs (!Xung remains flat while English, like most languages in Shoemark's sample, increases). However, there are long flat intervals in Shoemark's trendlines for ASPL in German, Dutch and Portuguese.

For most of the LNPs, the slope of the natural English trendline is similar to that for trigram English, indicating that the language model is a reasonable proxy for additional data. However, for Fraction in Largest Island, the slope is reversed; real English grows less rather than more connected. This is probably due to the different lexical strata within English (less common words are often borrowings with different phonological patterns) (Shoemark et al., 2016). Without additional !Xung data, we cannot know how well the trigram LM corresponds to the real trendlines for !Xung, nor whether the real slope for Fraction in Largest Island would increase or decrease. However, increasing slopes are linguistically plausible; Spanish and Portuguese have increasing Largest Island sizes.

Overall, then, the trendlines for !Xung are plausibly within the range of variation shown by previously studied languages. The analysis below shows that trigrams are a poorer proxy for the !Xung lexicon than for English, generating a realistic size for the largest island but erroneous values for shortest path and assortativity, so these results must be taken with a substantial grain of salt. However, like the LNP statistics above, they represent converging evidence that !Xung's lexical network is not a linguistic outlier in the same way as its phonemic inventory.

# 6 Analysis 2

Analysis 1, like the preliminary examination, showed that the LNPs of !Xung broadly resemble those of previously studied languages. This raises the question: what phonological properties allow !Xung to have similar LNPs to these languages despite having a much larger phoneme inventory? In this analysis, we employ the methods used by Gruenenfelder and Pisoni (2009); Stella and Brede (2015); Turnbull and Peperkamp (2016) to create pseudolexicons with varying levels of phonological structure. A comparison of these pseudolexicons highlights the phonotactic disparities between !Xung and English.

## 6.1 Methodology

For each of our corpora, we generate the following pseudolexicons also used in Turnbull and Peperkamp (2016): Uniform – randomly selects from the phoneme inventory; Zipfian – randomly selects from the phoneme inventory given a Zipfian distribution; Scrambled – scrambles the phonemes of a word in place; Bigram – like the previously mentioned trigram LM; Trigram. We also create a Unigram pseudolexicon which randomly selects from the actual phoneme distribution. Pseudolexicons which sample single letters are given the same word length distribution as the original lexicon. Examples of words from these pseudolexicons are shown in Table 4 within the appendix. We compare the network properties of these pseudolexicons (averaged over 50 trials) within each language.

Since the pseudolexicons represent artificial distributions, which are known *a priori* to differ from the true distribution of words in the language, null hypothesis significance testing is inappropriate to assess the degree of difference— an arbitrarily small $p$-value could always be obtained by sampling more data. Instead, we use Cohen's $d$ as a measure of the effect size; $d$ measures the difference between means scaled by the standard deviation.

## 6.2 Results

Table 3 shows the results, also plotted in Figure 4. The lower right panel shows that only the bigram and trigram lexicons generate realistic sizes for the largest island. Other pseudolexicons are highly disconnected. This is especially the case for !Xung relative to English; for instance,

|  | Unif | Zipf | Scram | Unig | Bigr | Trigr | Natural |
|---|---|---|---|---|---|---|---|
| % Lgst. (mean) | 0.7 | 24.9 | 6.1 | 9.0 | 41.7 | 37.7 | 36.6 |
| % Lgst. ($d$) | -246.9 | -6.0 | -15.1 | -15.3 | 2.6 | 0.6 | |
| % Lgst. (mean) | 8.6 | 32.1 | 12.5 | 18.3 | 33.3 | 36.6 | 38.4 |
| % Lgst. ($d$) | -30.3 | -4.6 | -13.4 | -9.8 | -3.5 | -1.1 | |
| ASPL (mean) | 2.0 | 4.4 | 5.8 | 5.9 | 3.9 | 3.7 | 8.7 |
| ASPL ($d$) | -17.9 | -13.6 | -1.9 | -3.1 | -24.0 | -23.7 | |
| ASPL (mean) | 5.1 | 4.2 | 6.0 | 5.9 | 4.6 | 5.2 | 6.1 |
| ASPL ($d$) | -1.4 | -12.1 | -0.1 | -0.4 | -7.5 | -3.1 | |
| DA (mean) | -27.0 | 35.1 | 26.9 | 31.5 | 80.1 | 80.5 | 52.8 |
| DA ($d$) | -3.7 | -2.6 | -2.1 | -2.0 | 11.2 | 14.4 | |
| DA (mean) | 39.1 | 32.6 | 46.8 | 45.8 | 71.1 | 72.3 | 43.6 |
| DA ($d$) | -0.5 | -3.6 | 0.5 | 0.5 | 7.8 | 8.0 | |
| CC (mean) | 35.6 | 58.7 | 50.1 | 48.9 | 58.6 | 60.8 | 52.4 |
| CC ($d$) | -0.7 | 2.1 | -0.4 | -0.7 | 3.5 | 4.2 | |
| CC (mean) | 37.3 | 44.1 | 39.0 | 36.3 | 42.9 | 42.5 | 36.5 |
| CC ($d$) | 0.2 | 4.1 | 0.7 | -0.1 | 3.5 | 2.9 | |

Table 3: Pseudolexicon LNPs (!Xung in white, English in gray); mean and Cohen's $d$ versus the natural language.

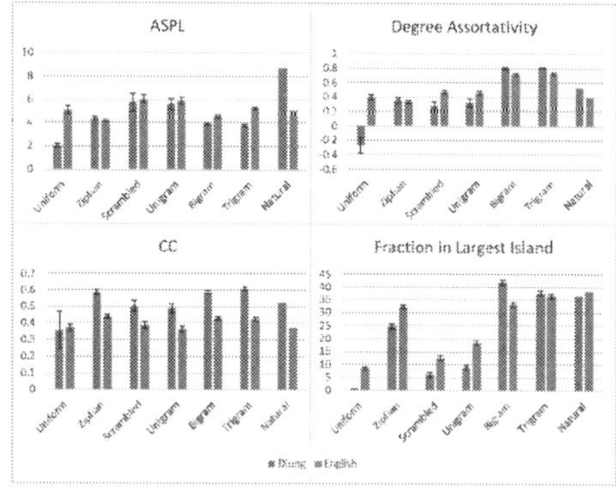

Figure 4: Network property values for pseudolexicon models of English and !Xung, ordered by phonotactic similarity to the natural language, with right-most being the natural language itself.

the English uniform pseudolexicon (far left) has nearly 10% of the nodes in the largest island, while !Xung has essentially none on average, with extremely high variance. This disparity between languages is caused by the large phonemic inventory, which creates fewer minimal pair matches when randomly sorted, as in the uniform, Zipfian, scrambled, and unigram pseudolexicons. !Xung thus serves as a counterexample to recent claims that simplistic random lexicons created with unigram sampling can mimic the properties of real LNs (Brown et al., 2018). The disparity begins to shrink as the pseudolexicons become more natural, suggesting that disparities due to the large

phonemic inventory are reduced by phonological structure and that phonotactic constraints on word forms in !Xung lead the lexicon to include more minimal pairs.

For the lexicons with reasonable island sizes, the values of clustering coefficient are relatively stable across all pseudolexicons, as in Turnbull and Peperkamp (2016), though again highly variable for the Uniform lexicon. The shortest path and associativity measures show that Bigram and Trigram lexicons are more compact and centralized than the actual lexicon for both !Xung and English (paths are shorter and associativity is higher). However, these differences are larger for !Xung than for English as measured by Cohen's $d$. The Unigram and Scrambled lexicons, meanwhile, are more realistically dispersed, but also disconnected ($< 10\%$ of nodes in the largest island).

Overall, the results show that the network structure of !Xung reflects properties which go beyond the frequencies of individual segments, including some characteristics which are poorly captured even by trigram models. The differences between simple pseudolexicons and the real properties of the language are generally greater (in terms of $d$) for !Xung than for English. Thus, we conclude that the !Xung network is less resilient to phonotactic disruption than the English network.

| | English | !Xung |
|---|---|---|
| Uniform | ŋsθ, iɛhh, iʒgmʊ | ü‡ʰë |
| Zipfian | oʊpə, ɔɔɛŋə, ŋɔæɔs | óm̀n\|n̊\|ʰ, g‖ǹ̊\|, g\|ho |
| Scrambled | ɛθlih, əwrdnəɪŋ, krljəɛaən | ə‖ŋ, eŋ̊!ʰe, äàʰ! |
| Semi-Scrambled | (N/A) | ‖ŋə̀, ŋ̊!ʰee, !àʰä |
| CV | ɛnfəzamɛs, vɪlɔkitdr, nnaəln | nő!'ùŋ\|, g‖áχúβ, ʃinòʒ |
| KCV | (N/A) | ŋ!dóm, ‡'zùs', g‖lʉ́s |
| Free O+R | (N/A) | !önä, dʒä, g‖öʔⁿ |
| Pos. O+R | (N/A) | g‡ɔ́, ŋ!ò?và, wì |
| Syllable | (N/A) | ŋ̊\|ʰúíⁿ, ‖àòⁿ, g!ə̈mɦè |
| Unigram | wjork, sɛgit, njŋe | úŋ́‖úlùb, téùχà?à, íl‖!iò |
| Bigram | rnɔsm, ɔjə, tekjks | !ʔm̀, má?ìi, \|'ùβäⁿ |
| Trigram | plæŋ, lɪŋ, hæv | ŋ̊\|ʰùì, ŋ̊\|ʰülà, täʰ |
| Natural Lexicon | hɛlθi, wəndərɪŋ, kɛrəlajnə | ‖ə̀ŋ, ŋ̊!ʰee, !äàʰ |

Table 4: Three random words from pseudolexicons.

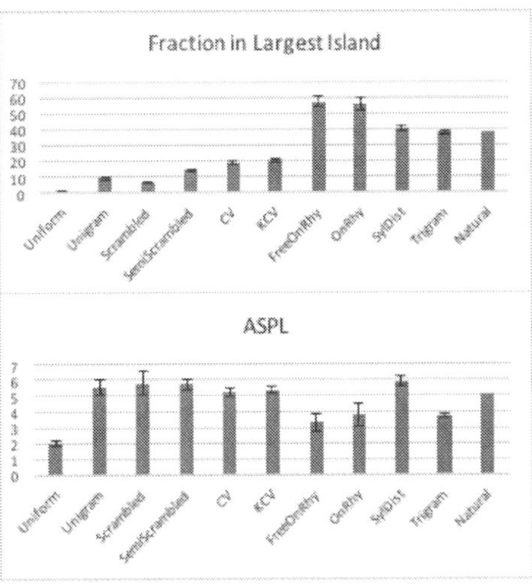



Figure 5: LNPs in Analysis 3.

## 7  Analysis 3

We continue our investigation by attempting to determine which phonotactic properties of !Xung might be most important in maintaining its structure. Several properties of !Xung phonology might be important in constraining its network structure. These include its relatively simple syllabic structure, the positional constraints on initial medial consonants, and the co-occurrence restrictions on consonants and vowels within the syllable. To highlight these properties, we compare our Scrambled pseudolexicon to pseudolexicons designed to respect some of these properties.

### 7.1  Methodology

In the CV lexicon, we extract a distribution over word templates by transforming each consonant into C and each vowel into V, then generate each word by sampling a template from this distribution and filling it with random consonants and vowels sampled from the unigram distribution. The CV pseudolexicon forces the generated words to contain reasonable proportions of vowels and consonants, but it does not enforce any positional constraints; words may contain unnatural features like illegal codas, sequences of vowels which do not form diphthongs, and medial clicks. We next test the effect of the constraint that !Xung content words tend to begin with a click, by generating a Semi-scrambled lexicon (scrambling each real word in place, but any present click stays at the initial position) and KCV (like CV, except that the initial syllable will begin with a click and subsequent ones will only contain vowels and pulmonic consonants). Examples of words from these pseudolexicons can be found in Table 4.

We next syllabify the !Xung corpus (treating each sequence of vowels as a syllable nucleus and maximizing onsets). We use this database of syllables to create a sequence of pseudolexicons which sample larger prosodic units rather than single segments. These pseudolexicons are length-matched to the original corpus in number of syllables (not segments). Free Onset+Rhyme forms syllables by sampling attested onsets and rhymes, but draws them from anywhere in the corpus, ignoring positional constraints. Positional Onset+Rhyme enforces placement constraints on consonants by sampling word-initial, medial and final onsets and rhymes from separate distributions. Finally, Syllable samples whole syllables from the correct positional distributions, enforcing the co-occurrence constraints between onsets and rhymes as well as the placement constraints.

### 7.2  Results

The results (averaged over 50 trials) are shown in Table 5. The CV lexicon, which forces words to contain realistic proportions of vowels and consonants, roughly triples the largest island size versus the Scrambled lexicon, but does not create a realistic LN. Forcing clicks to occur only at word beginnings does relatively little; neither the Semiscrambled nor KCV lexicons look very different from the CV lexicon. Lexicons formed using ac-

|  | Scram | Semi | CV | KCV | Free Ons+Rhy | Posit. Ons+Rhy | Syll | Trigr | Natural |
|---|---|---|---|---|---|---|---|---|---|
| % Lgst. (mean) | 6.1 | 13.6 | 18.6 | 20.3 | 57.4 | 55.7 | 40.6 | 37.7 | 36.6 |
| % Lgst. ($d$) | -15.1 | -17.2 | -9.2 | -8.4 | 3.5 | 2.6 | 1.2 | 0.6 | |
| ASPL (mean) | 5.8 | 5.7 | 5.2 | 5.4 | 3.3 | 3.8 | 5.9 | 3.7 | 8.7 |
| ASPL ($d$) | -1.9 | -5.0 | -5.5 | -7.6 | -5.1 | -3.6 | -4.1 | -23.7 | |
| DA (mean) | 26.9 | 38.8 | 43.8 | 43.0 | 47.0 | 43.6 | 59.6 | 80.5 | 52.8 |
| DA ($d$) | -2.1 | -3.7 | -1.1 | -1.3 | -1.1 | -1.1 | 2.5 | 14.4 | |
| CC (mean) | 50.1 | 55.2 | 47.4 | 46.1 | 63.1 | 62.9 | 51.2 | 60.8 | 52.4 |
| CC ($d$) | 0.0 | 0.0 | -0.1 | -0.1 | 0.1 | 0.1 | -0.1 | 0.1 | |

Table 5: Statistics of phonotactically targeted pseudolexicons (mean and Cohen's $d$ versus natural language).

tual onsets and rhymes attested from the corpus have much larger island sizes— in fact, larger than the real graph (56% vs 36%). The Positional Onset+Rhyme model is quite similar to the Onset+Rhyme model across all the LNPs. Finally, the Syllable lexicon has a realistic island size (41%), and is wider than the Onset+Rhyme or Trigram networks, with an average path length of 5.9 (vs 3.3-3.8, compared with the actual 8.7)[3].

Comparing the Onset+Rhyme models to the CV lexicon, we find that the syllabic structure of !Xung helps to ensure that the network is connected. Surprisingly, positional constraints on consonant placement (clicks at the beginning, restricted set of medials) have a limited impact on the shape of the network; KCV is similar to CV, and Positional Onset+Rhyme to Free Onset+Rhyme. However, the co-occurrence restrictions on onset and rhyme within the syllable, for instance, constraints on gutturals, are important in limiting connectedness and creating the long shortest-path distances of the real lexicon, since both these properties appear only in the pseudolexicon which samples whole syllables as units. Co-occurrence restrictions within the syllable widen the LN by preventing the formation of a minimal pair which would be phonologically unnatural, since its onset and rhyme would not match.

## 8 Conclusion

Overall, we find that the network properties of !Xung do not substantially differ from previously studied languages despite fundamental phonological disparities. This supports the argument of Vitevitch (2008) that the LNPs indicate an underlying cognitive structure. Vitevich proposed that the global shape of the network enables efficient word learning and retrieval from memory; it is also plausible that the network structure is necessary to avoid confusing large numbers of minimal pairs in auditory perception. In any case, the preservation of this global structure suggests a selective pressure shaping the phonotactics of these languages (and others with large inventories) — phonotactic rules may arise and change over time in ways that preserve the network properties within a cognitively useful range. For instance, the differences between randomly scrambled and syllabic pseudowords indicate that the restricted syllable inventories of !Xung and Ju may force words to cluster more tightly in the LN, compensating for the large number of contrastive phonemes. In other words, the underlying universal structure may be, not linguistic, but cognitive. This universal architecture may require certain patterns of connectivity within the lexicon, and these, in turn, may entail particular phonotactic patterns.

Looking forward, we plan to expand our current LN analysis to include data from relatives of !Xung such as Ju|'hoansi,[4] as well as languages with small phoneme inventories, such as certain Polynesian languages[5]. Through this, we hope to uncover how our hypothesis operates across a range of inventory sizes and types.

Additionally, we plan to investigate the func-

---

[3]Cohen's $d$ estimates a slightly *larger* effect separating the ASPL for Syllable from the natural language than Onset+Rhyme; this is because Syllable has a substantially lower variance.

[4]We conducted a preliminary analysis of a 3733-word lexicon of Ju|'hoansi collected by Biesele et al. (2006) and found similar results to those we obtained from !Xung. However, the IPA transcription of this data is not consistent, so we have chosen not to present it here.

[5]Hawai'ian was previously studied by Arbesman et al. (2010) who found a comparatively larger giant component and shorter average path lengths than several other languages; however, they did not control for lexicon size.

tional load and potential confusability of !Xung phonemic contrasts. A LN assumes real world speakers can distinguish perfectly between minimal pairs. However, with the large phoneme inventory of !Xung, these clicks may be confusable in real speech, cf. (Fulop et al., 2004). We hope to determine how the network properties change when potential confusions between sounds are taken into account.

## Acknowledgements

We thank Rory Turnbull, Philippa Shoemark, Eric Fosler-Lussier, the attendees of OSU's Workshop on the Emergence of Linguistic Universals and Phonies discussion group, and six anonymous reviewers for their many helpful comments and suggestions. This work was funded by NSF 1422987 to the second author.

## References

Samuel Arbesman, Steven H Strogatz, and Michael S Vitevitch. 2010. The structure of phonological networks across multiple languages. *International Journal of Bifurcation and Chaos*, 20(03):679–685.

M. Biesele, B. C. Boo, H. K. Gcao, G≠kao M. /K, Kaqece K N!., A. Miller, /A. F /Kunta, and C. N! Tsamkxao F. /U. /Ui. 2006. *Ju|'hoansi Dictionary, Revised version of Dickens, P. Ju|'hoan-English – English-Ju|'hoan Dictionary*. unpublished manuscript, The Kalahari People's Foundation and The Ju—hoan Transcription Group.

Kevin S. Brown, Paul D. Allopenna, William R. Hunt, Rachael Steiner, Elliot Saltzman, Ken McRae, and James S. Magnuson. 2018. Universal features in phonological neighbor networks. *Computing Research Repository*, arXiv:1804.05766. Version 1.

Stanley F Chen and Joshua Goodman. 1999. An empirical study of smoothing techniques for language modeling. *Computer Speech & Language*, 13(4):359–394.

Christopher Cieri, David Miller, and Kevin Walker. 2004. The Fisher corpus: a resource for the next generations of speech-to-text. In *Proceedings of LREC*, volume 4, pages 69–71.

P. Dickens. 1994. *Ju|'hoan-English English-Ju|'hoan Dictionary*. Koppe.

Sean A Fulop, Peter Ladefoged, Fang Liu, and Rainer Vossen. 2004. Yeyi clicks: Acoustic description and analysis. *Phonetica*, 60(4):231–260.

Thomas M Gruenenfelder and David B Pisoni. 2009. The lexical restructuring hypothesis and graph theoretic analyses of networks based on random lexicons. *Journal of Speech, Language, and Hearing Research*, 52(3):596–609.

Terttu Heikkinen. 1986. Outline of the phonology of the !Xũ dialect spoken in Ovamboland and western Kavango. *South African journal of African languages*, 6:18–28.

Ian Maddieson. 2013. Vowel quality inventories. In Matthew S. Dryer and Martin Haspelmath, editors, *The World Atlas of Language Structures Online*. Max Planck Institute for Evolutionary Anthropology.

A. Miller, L. Namaseb, S. Sands, S. Shah, M. Aromo, C. Augumes, R. Fransisko, T. Kaleyi, D. Prata, and S. Riem. 2008. *Mangetti Dune !Xung Dictionary*. unpublished manuscript, The Ju|'hoan Transcription Group, The Kalahari People's Foundation, The University of Namibia and Northern Arizona University.

Amanda L Miller. 2016. Posterior lingual gestures and tongue shape in Mangetti Dune !Xung clicks. *Journal of Phonetics*, 55:119–148.

Amanda Miller-Ockhuizen. 2003. *The Phonetics and Phonology of Gutturals: A Case Study from Ju|'hoansi*. Outstanding Dissertations in Linguistics Series. Routledge.

Mark EJ Newman and Michelle Girvan. 2003. Mixing patterns and community structure in networks. In *Statistical mechanics of complex networks*, pages 66–87. Springer.

Hermann Ney, Ute Essen, and Reinhard Kneser. 1994. On structuring probabilistic dependences in stochastic language modelling. *Computer Speech & Language*, 8(1):1–38.

Bonny Sands. 2003. Juu subgroups based on phonological patterns. In *Khoisan languages and linguistics: Proceedings of the 1st International Symposium*, pages 85–114.

Philippa Shoemark, Sharon Goldwater, James Kirby, and Rik Sarkar. 2016. Towards robust cross-linguistic comparisons of phonological networks. In *Proceedings of the 14th SIGMORPHON Workshop on Computational Research in Phonetics, Phonology, and Morphology*, pages 110–120.

Massimo Stella and Markus Brede. 2015. Patterns in the english language: phonological networks, percolation and assembly models. *Journal of Statistical Mechanics: Theory and Experiment*, 2015(5):P05006.

Andreas Stolcke. 2002. SRILM-an extensible language modeling toolkit. In *Seventh international conference on spoken language processing*.

Andreas Stolcke, Jing Zheng, Wen Wang, and Victor Abrash. 2011. SRILM at sixteen: Update and outlook. In *Proceedings of IEEE automatic speech recognition and understanding workshop*, volume 5.

Rory Turnbull and Sharon Peperkamp. 2016. What governs a language's lexicon? Determining the organizing principles of phonological neighbourhood networks. In *International Workshop on Complex Networks and their Applications*, pages 83–94. Springer.

Michael S Vitevitch. 2008. What can graph theory tell us about word learning and lexical retrieval? *Journal of Speech, Language, and Hearing Research*, 51(2):408–422.

# Acoustic word disambiguation with phonological features in Danish ASR

**Andreas Søeborg Kirkedal**
Interactions, LLC
Murray Hill, NJ, USA
akirkedal@interactions.com

## Abstract

Phonological features can indicate word class and we can use word class information to disambiguate both homophones and homographs in automatic speech recognition (ASR). We show Danish stød can be predicted from speech and used to improve ASR. We discover which acoustic features contain the signal of stød, how to use these features to predict stød and how we can make use of stød and stød-predictive acoustic features to improve overall ASR accuracy and decoding speed. In the process, we discover acoustic features that are novel to the phonetic characterisation of stød.

## 1 Introduction

Stød ([ˀ] in IPA notation) is usually described as (a kind of) creaky voice or as *laryngealisation* (Hansen, 2015; Grønnum et al., 2013). Stød can distinguish homophones and homographs and can identify word class by its presence. Danish *viˀser* is a noun that translates to *clock dial*, but pronounced without stød - *viser* - it can also be a verb that means *to show*. The presence of stød can change the meaning of an utterance, e.g. *de kendte folk* can mean *the famous people* if *kendte* is pronounced as [kɛnˀdə] and can also mean *they knew people* if *kendte* is pronounced as [kɛndə]. Stød is robust against some types of reduction and is an acoustic cue that can help distinguish *one* vs. *none* in colloquial Danish: [eˀn] and [eŋ].

Phonological features can often be determined from grammar and morphology (Grønnum, 2005) but stød may not occur in read-aloud or spontaneous speech when predicted by morphology and grammar, and stød can be difficult to perceive in both visualisations of spectrograms and in speech (Hansen, 2015).

Stød is not highly frequent in either read-aloud or spontaneous speech, but stød and similar phonological features like e.g. tones are interesting for two main reasons:

1. Relatively small languages like Nordic languages do not have large speech corpora available like English, Chinese etc. We should exploit all signals in the data to improve ASR performance for these languages.

2. The semantic disambiguation at both sentence and lexical level is appealing because ASR errors that disturb the meaning of an utterance are less acceptable for human consumers of ASR output (Mishra et al., 2011).

Our contributions are to:

- Show that stød annotation is reliable when annotated by trained phoneticians and can be the basis of statistical analyses.

- Discover novel audio features that are predictive of stød in speech.

- Demonstrate we can predict stød in speech as phone variant discrimination.

- Integrate stød in ASR and improve WER on read-aloud and spontaneous speech.

## 2 Related work

Henrichsen and Christiansen (2012) found a correlation between fundamental frequency (F0) and spectral tilt, and discrimination between *content* words and *function* words. We also investigate these features for their ability to predict stød.

Stød, stress and schwa-assimilation were studied in Kirkedal (2013) in an ASR context. The study found that WER improved when stød, stress, schwa and duration annotation were removed from the lexicon. However, the ASR system was trained on a single speaker corpus with read-aloud speech



*Proceedings of the 15th SIGMORPHON Workshop on Computational Research in Phonetics, Phonology, and Morphology*, pages 21–31
Brussels, Belgium, October 31, 2018. ©2018 The Special Interest Group on Computational Morphology and Phonology
https://doi.org/10.18653/v1/P17

| Dataset | Speech genre | Location | Speakers | Duration | Types | Tokens |
|---|---|---|---|---|---|---|
| Språkbanken-train | Read | Office | 560 | 316h | 65667 | 2366183 |
| Språkbanken-test | Read | Office | 56 | 77h | 72978 | 185049 |
| JHP | Spontaneous | High-school | 2 | 1 min | 178[†] | 995[†] |
| PAROLE48 | Read | Speech lab | 1 | 48 min | 181 | 4705 |
| DanPASS | Spontaneous | Speech lab | 18 | 2h 51 min | 1075 | 21170 |

Table 1: Summary table for the corpora used. [†] indicate that type/token counts are based on counts of phones instead of words.

and evaluated on a test set from the same corpus and we demonstrate that the findings do not generalise to a multi-speaker setting.

No single feature extracted from audio of spoken Danish can predict the presence of stød like F0 estimation can predict pitch (Fischer-Jørgensen, 1989). Because stød is related to irregular vibration of the vocal folds, previous research has focused on harmonics-to-noise (HNR) ratio, the difference between the first two harmonics in a spectrum (H1:H2) and diplophony (H1:H1$\frac{1}{2}$[1]) as well as F0 and intensity (Hansen, 2015), but this is the first large scale quantitative study of stød.

Stød can be audibly heard yet not be visible in a spectrogram to an experienced researcher (Hansen, 2015). Consequently, the annotation of stød is subject to annotator perception. Annotators need a considerable amount of training to be able to annotate stød and the high cost of annotation in terms of training and annotation time coupled with potential bias from annotator training or the specific annotator has been a barrier to quantitative studies of stød. We show that expert stød is reliable in Section 4.

Like stød in Danish, Tone 1 and Tone 2 in Norwegian and Swedish are the only difference between some homographs and homophones. Swedish and Norwegian are pitch accent languages that use tones to distinguish lexical items that would otherwise be homophones and homographs, e.g. *tanken*$_1$ vs. *tanken*$_2$ (*the tank* vs. *the thought* - subscript indicates Tone 1 and Tone 2) (Lahiri et al., 2005). Some theories suggest that stød originated from tones and the distribution of stød and Tone 1 & 2 also show similarities (Grønnum et al., 2013). Riad (2000) describe stød as a tonal pattern but this is refuted in a reply in Grønnum et al. (2013).

In tonal languages like Mandarin Chinese, tones or tonal contours disambiguate monosyllabic words as in the famous example of *ma* which has five different meanings depending on the tonal contour. ASR for tonal languages add suprasegmental information to ASR models either by extending the acoustic feature input (*embedded*) or rescoring word lattices (*explicit*) (wen Li et al., 2011). Embedded modelling requires that tones are modelled in the lexicon either as tonal variations of the same phoneme (Metze et al., 2013; Yoon et al., 2006) or as separate phonemes (Adams et al., 2018). Stød is related to irregular vibration of the vocal folds which occurs frequently in Danish with no connection to stød and we do not explore explicit modelling.

The duration of the stød-bearing (semi-)vowel or syllable has been considered important in previous literature. We do not consider duration in this paper for 2 reasons: 1) HMM-based ASR is the target application and implicitly model duration with self-loops in the HMM and 2) the investigations of duration where conducted in lab conditions with elicited speech in the Standard Copenhagen dialect. We use several corpora that cover most Danish dialects, also dialects that typically do not use stød.

The rest of the paper is structured as follows: Section 3 presents the data used and Section 4 presents the study of stød annotation. In Section 5 we discover novel acoustic features that are predictive of stød. We test and evaluate how well acoustic features predict stød in Section 6 and perform phone variant discrimination where we jointly predict phone and stød. In Section 7, we adapt an ASR recipe for Danish and train several ASR systems to determine the best way to use stød to improve ASR.

## 3 Data

Table 1 shows the corpus statistics for all corpora used in the rest of this paper.

---

[1]The ratio between the first harmonic H1 and the harmonic signal at F0 $* 1.5$. F0 is the frequency of H1.

We use an interview with a high school student in real-world conditions, denoted as JHP[2] to study the reliability of stød annotation. We use this short sample of speech because it is the only sample that is annotated by four Danish-speaking expert phoneticians trained in stød annotation. Another expert phonetician aligned and time-coded the four transcriptions.

We also use the monologues from Dan-PASS (Grønnum, 2006) and speech from PAROLE-DK[3] (Henrichsen, 2007). To compensate for the unequal corpus sizes, we sample only 48 minutes and refer to this subset as PAROLE48. We separate a random subset that contains speech from both DanPASS and PAROLE48 as a test set.

Nasjonalbiblioteket[4] hosts a language repository called Språkbanken. In the repository is a multilingual speech corpus also known as Språkbanken. The Danish 16 kHz part of Språkbanken contains recordings of phonetically-balanced utterances and covers 7 regions of Denmark and ages ranging from 18-70. The Swedish part was used in Vanhainen and Salvi (2014) to create an ASR recipe.

Språkbanken-test is 15 times larger than standard test sets from the Linguistic Data Consortium (LDC) such as HUB5 which is 5 hours long.[5] We decided to split Språkbanken-test into a development set SPDEV (ca. 9 hours) and test set SPTEST (ca. 17 hours). The remaining 51 hours are included in the training data (ca. 367 hours) while making sure that neither speakers nor utterances in SPDEV and SPTEST appear in the training set.

We create pronunciation lexicons with eSpeak (Duddington, 2010) from the training transcripts because the pronunciation lexicon distributed with Språkbanken has low coverage and eSpeak was found to produce transcriptions that are good enough for ASR (Kirkedal, 2014).

## 4   Stød annotation study

The data we use for training and testing needs to be reliable, i.e. if stød is annotated, we need to be sure that stød occurs. To test how reliable our data is, we calculate inter-annotator agreement measured

---

|            | IPA1 | IPA2 | IPA3 | IPA4 |
|------------|------|------|------|------|
| Phone avg. | 0.82 | 0.80 | 0.81 | 0.85 |
| Stød avg.  | 0.72 | 0.74 | 0.76 | 0.76 |

Table 2: Average $\kappa$ inter-annotator agreement on stød-bearing items.

by Cohen's $\kappa$ and an *annotator competence score* (ACS) with MACE (Hovy et al., 2013). ACS is based on an item-response model that assumes an annotator will produce the correct phone sequence if he tries to which is valid in this scenario. An *item* is a unit in the phone sequence and in this study each unit is labelled by 4 annotators. We use both $\kappa$ and ACS because $\kappa$ is a measure of the annotation whereas ACS is an estimate of annotator proficiency. For both $\kappa$ and ACS, higher scores are better. 7.8% of the items in JHP are annotated with phones with stød (stød-bearing) and the phones without stød (stød-less) will dominate $\kappa$ because the distribution of phones in JHP is Zipfian and all stød-bearing phones are in the long tail. To focus specifically on stød, we report $\kappa$ computed over stød-bearing items in two conditions:

1. Items that are labelled with stød by at least one annotator e.g. [ð$^?$], [ɑ$^?$], [n$^?$] etc.

2. The same items as in 1. but binarised such that e.g. [ð$^?$], [ɑ$^?$], [n$^?$] → 1 and [ð], [ɑ], [n] → 0.

We compute ACS over all phones and over the binarised stød annotation in 2.

We discovered 10 errors in the data, e.g. one label was [$^?$n], but should have been [n] and stød should have been annotated on the previous phone as [ð$^?$]. There were 7 alignment errors that was caused by the interpretation of a syllable nucleus as either two short vowels or a long vowel. This has an impact on the alignment because stød is annotated on a syllable rather than a phone and the data is aligned at the phone level.

We corrected the errors before calculating the $\kappa$ scores based on phones and binary stød in Table 2. Average $\kappa$ is a an average over all pairwise $\kappa$ scores where the specific annotator is involved. The annotators are referred to as IPA1, IPA2, IPA3 and IPA4.

The $\kappa$ scores in Table 2 and the ACS scores in Table 3 both indicate that stød annotation is reliable and we can base statistical models on stød

---

[2]The JHP sample was made available by Jan Heegård Petersen, Copenhagen University.

[3]This corpus was used in Kirkedal (2013).

[4]The Norwegian National Library service.

[5]See https://catalog.ldc.upenn.edu/ LDC2002S13.

| Annotator | # labels | Phone | # stød | Stød |
|---|---|---|---|---|
| IPA1 | 107 | 0.760 | 53 | 0.770 |
| IPA2 | 99 | 0.813 | 58 | 0.840 |
| IPA3 | 94 | 0.823 | 62 | 0.894 |
| IPA4 | 107 | 0.833 | 59 | 0.856 |

Table 3: Annotator competence scores for all items and stød-bearing items.

annotation. The high $\kappa$ scores show that the annotation in JHP is high quality and the ACS scores show that the annotators are able to annotate stød consistently and accurately.

## 5    Acoustic correlates of stød

Because we can rely on expert stød annotation, we can discover acoustic features that signal stød with statistical models. We use DanPASS and PAROLE48 as training and test data because they are also manually annotated and there is annotator overlap with JHP. We use the toolkits Kaldi (Povey et al., 2011), Covarep (Degottex et al., 2014) and Praat (Boersma, 2002) to extract features that may contain information that signals the occurrence of stød. The number of features extracted by the different toolkits can be seen in Table 4.

We sample the audio every 10 milliseconds and extract features over a context window the size which depends on the feature. Mel-feature cepstral coefficients (MFCC) and perceptual linear prediction (PLP) features use a 25 ms window while pitch estimation uses a 1.5 second window to extract robust features. Each 10 ms, we extract MFCC features, PLP features, Phase Distortion Mean (PDM) features, Phase Distortion Deviation (PDD) features, the Maxima Dispersion Quotient (MDQ), Peak slope (PS), Quasi-Open Quotient (QOQ), Normalised Amplitude Quotient (NAQ), Parabolic Spectral Parameter (PSP), the difference between first and second harmonic (H1-H2), Fant's basic shape parameter ($R_d$[6]), HNR and Intensity[7]. The first coefficient (C0) is replaced by an energy feature in both MFCC and PLP extraction and we choose to discard the energy feature from MFCC extraction and keep the log-energy feature with derivatives from PLP extraction. When referring to 1st and 2nd derivatives, we will suffix the feature name with -d and

---

[6]See (Fant, 1995) for a description.
[7]We use amplitude and intensity interchangeably, but we are aware that amplitude is the acoustic correlate of intensity.

| Toolkit | Dimension | Feature |
|---|---|---|
| Kaldi | 39 | PLP* |
| | 3 | PoV* |
| | 3 | log-pitch* |
| | 3 | $\Delta$-pitch* |
| Covarep | 24 | MFCC/MCEP |
| | 25 | PDM |
| | 13 | PDD |
| | 1 | MDQ |
| | 1 | PS |
| | 1 | QOQ |
| | 1 | NAQ |
| | 1 | PSP |
| | 1 | H1-H2 |
| | 1 | $R_d$ |
| Praat | 1 | HNR |
| | 1 | Intensity |
| | 1 | Pitch |

Table 4: Acoustic features. Features marked with * also include 1st order and 2nd order derivatives.

-dd, respectively. $\Delta$-pitch is a derivative on the raw unnormalised pitch estimate in log space computed over 5 frames and log-pitch is mean subtracted by an average pitch value over a 151 frame context window that is weighted by a probability of voicing feature (PoV). We also estimate pitch with Praat because Praat and Kaldi behave differently in unvoiced speech: Kaldi interpolates the pitch estimate across unvoiced regions and Praat sets it to 0.

We align each 120-dimensional feature vector to a single phone by first segmenting syllable and word level annotation to phone level and relying on the existing time-coding.

### 5.1    Ranking acoustic features

We want to rank the 120 features by how well they predict stød with Extremely-Randomised Trees (Geurts et al., 2006) which trains an ensemble of decision trees. Decision trees can use features without standardisation and the input is not assumed to be normally distributed, which is not the case for e.g. HNR which becomes undefined if the harmonic component of the speech signal becomes too noisy. The estimation of relative feature importance will also be less affected by differences between the toolkits.

The algorithm creates fully grown trees top-down by splitting nodes. To split a node, a random

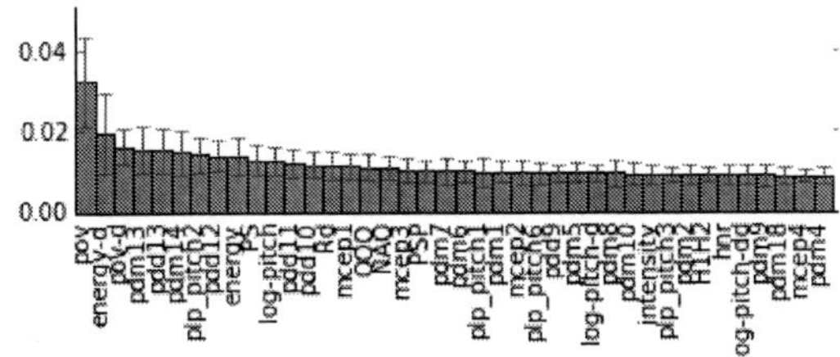

Figure 1: Feature salience for stød prediction (task 1). PLP are called *plp_pitch* and *energy* refers to C0 extracted with PLP features.

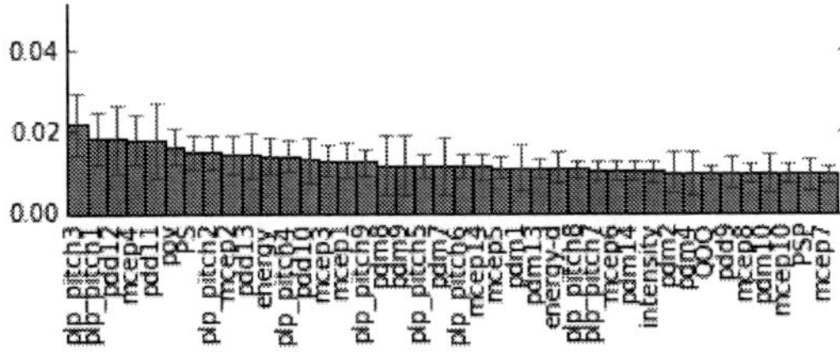

Figure 2: Feature salience for stød-bearing and stød-less phone variant discrimination (task 2).

subset $K = \sqrt{N}$ of all features $N$ in the current node is selected as candidates for splitting criterion. For each $k_j$ in $K$, a random cut-point $a_j$ is chosen. The feature $k_j$ with cut-point $a_j$ which most improves entropy after a split is used to split the data in the node. Each decision tree is estimated on a random subset of the training data and we use sub-sampling with replacement to mitigate the under-representation of samples labelled with stød-bearing phones.

Relative feature importance can be ranked by the depth at which a feature is used to split a node because features used as splitting criterion closer to the root node contribute to the prediction of a larger fraction of samples. Final prediction is achieved by majority voting across all trees (1024). The samples are not weighted and classes are represented by an equal number of samples. This balancing is necessary to prevent the tree growing algorithm to favour features that predict a majority class.

### 5.1.1 Rankings

We rank features according to *salience* measured as mean reduction in entropy across the ensemble in two tasks: 1) binary stød prediction and 2) multi-class discrimination between stød-less and stød-bearing phone variants (e.g. [a$^?$] vs. [a], [m$^?$] vs. [m]) at sample level. Figures 1 and 2 show the 40 most salient features for each task.

A common set of features that are salient for phone discrimination and stød prediction emerges from studying Figures 1 and 2. The top 17 features are PLP 1-4, MFCC 1-4, PDD 10-13, PDM 13-14, PS, POV and log-pitch. In the following sections, SELECT will refer to this feature set and ALL will denote a set with all 120 features.

PDM and PDD are novel features in stød characterisation. That phase information is salient for stød prediction is to our knowledge a novel insight and interesting because PDM and PDD rank higher than many ASR-related features such as PLP-d, PLP-dd and some MFCC features. If this finding can be corroborated in the analysis of other corpora, phase features might be useful information to add to acoustic models in ASR.

## 6 Predicting stød from acoustic input

With acoustic features that are predictive of stød and reliable annotation, we can train classifiers that predict stød directly from acoustics with supervised training. The features in SELECT were also chosen for their ability to discriminate between stød-bearing and stød-less phone variants and in an ASR context, discriminating these phone variants will be sufficient to identify word class. Yoon et al. (2006) conducted a similar experiment for American English with *creak* to improve WER and they achieve an overall phone classification accuracy of 69.23% on 25 minimal phone pairs.

Following the same methodology, we train an SVM classifier with an RBF kernel and do not perform any optimisation of parameter values. We compare classifiers trained on ALL and SELECT to a baseline trained on PLP features in a balanced[8] 1v1 evaluation where the phone variants are only distinguished by the presence or absence of stød. We evaluate on JHP and do 5-fold cross validation on the training set because we cannot meaningfully separate a test set when we reduce the training data to 1/10th the original size.

We can see from Table 5 that the classification accuracy is much better than chance. The variance increases for all feature sets on JHP because it is much harder data, but all feature sets contain information that can help discriminate between stød-bearing and stød-less variants of the same phone, including standard PLP features.

---

[8]Balanced in terms of training data.

| | **Train** | $\pm$ | **JHP** | $\pm$ |
|---|---|---|---|---|
| PLP | 0.769 | 0.144 | **0.713** | 0.266 |
| ALL | 0.781 | 0.168 | 0.685 | 0.220 |
| SELECT | **0.803** | 0.176 | 0.600 | 0.104 |

Table 5: 5-fold cross validation on the training data across 40 phone variant pairs and mean classification accuracy on JHP across 5 pairs.

| ID | Standard features | +stød | +pitch |
|---|---|---|---|
| 1 | PLP | × | × |
| 2 | PLP | ✓ | × |
| 3 | PLP | ✓ | ✓ |
| 4 | MFCC | × | × |
| 5 | MFCC | ✓ | × |
| 6 | MFCC | ✓ | ✓ |

Table 6: The 6 conditions we test in this set of experiments.

# 7 Stød in ASR

We have discovered that acoustic features normally used in ASR contain information that signal the occurrence of stød and can then annotate stød in the pronunciation lexicon used in lexicon-based ASR systems to create a baseline with standard ASR feature input. We can then add stød-related features to ASR features to improve stød modelling and performance further. We split this set of experiments because adding more features to the training data could also have an adverse effect: we could be improving stød prediction at the expense of other speech sounds and because stød is relatively infrequent this could increase WER.

We trained several ASR systems with features where we augment MFCCs with features from SE-LECT and also tried to train AMs with SELECT and ALL as input. Training on ALL worsened performance and was a very expensive experiment, SELECT did not consistently perform better or worse and we have chosen to report on experiments where we observed performance improvements over more than one training run. The features log-pitch and POV from SELECT are good predictors of stød and are standard features to include in ASR for tonal languages together with Δ-pitch. These *pitch features* and modelling stød in the lexicon will be investigated in Section 7.1. Results with other features from SELECT that are not standard ASR features will be reported in Section 7.2.

We will no longer train on manually annotated data because we need more data than is available in DanPASS, PAROLE48 and JHP. We will train AMs and an LM on data from Språkbanken which is much larger and designed for ASR tasks.

## 7.1 Modelling stød in the lexicon

To train AMs, we use a pronunciation lexicon to convert text sequences to phone sequences. Phones are further subdivided to triphones and to state-tied HMM states or senones. The lexicon is central to state-of-the-art ASR and to test if stød can actually improve WER, we will use both a lexicon with stød annotation and without stød annotation. eSpeak generates phonetic transcriptions with stød by default and we simply remove the annotation in the first case.

We want to see if adding pitch features improve WER in ASR systems where stød is in the lexicon, so we test the six conditions in Table 6.

We base our recipe on the Wall Street Journal and Librispeech recipes in the Kaldi repository which trains a series of GMM models and a DNN model from scratch. We use IRSTLM (Federico et al., 2008) to train a language model (LM) on the training transcripts. We also tried to train a LM on ngram frequency lists calculated over 290 million words from Danish newspapers, but the performance degraded when we used the newspaper LM both on it's own and interpolated with the transcript LM and we conclude that the text genre is too different from our data sets. We use Matched Pairs Sentence-Segment Word Error (MAPSSWE) from the SCTK toolkit (Fiscus, 2007) to calculate statistical significance.

We train a GMM-based ASR system where we stack features in an $\pm 5$ frame context and use LDA to project to 40 dimensions followed by a GMM with speaker-adaptive training using feature space MLLR (fMLLR) on top of LDA. The DNN is a 4-layer feed-forward network with 1024 nodes per layer and tanh-nonlinearities that we train on the same LDA+fMLLR transformed features. The learning rate starts at 0.01 and is decayed linearly to 0.001 over 15 epochs and trains for an additional 5 epochs at 0.001.

In Table 7, we see the impact on WER when we add stød annotation in the lexicon and add pitch features to the feature input (denoted +*pitch*) and evaluate on SPTEST. Adding stød consistently improves WER, but is not always statistically sig-

|        | PLP      |        |                  | MFCC     |                  |                  |
| ------ | -------- | ------ | ---------------- | -------- | ---------------- | ---------------- |
| AM     | Baseline | +stød  | +pitch           | Baseline | +stød            | +pitch           |
| GMM+LDA | 17.61 | 17.55 | $17.07^{\ddagger}$ | 17.72 | 17.54 | $\mathbf{16.88}^{\ddagger}$ |
| GMM+LDA+SAT | 16.85 | 16.64* | 16.49 | 17.14 | $16.81^{\dagger}$ | $\mathbf{16.17}^{\ddagger}$ |
| DNN | 13.50 | 13.33 | 13.17 | 13.28 | $\mathbf{13.08}^{\dagger}$ | 13.38 |

Table 7: %WER performance on SPTEST. The best performance for each AM is in bold. Statistical significance over the condition in the column to the left is denoted by * if $p < 0.05$, † if $p < 0.01$ and ‡ if $p < 0.001$.

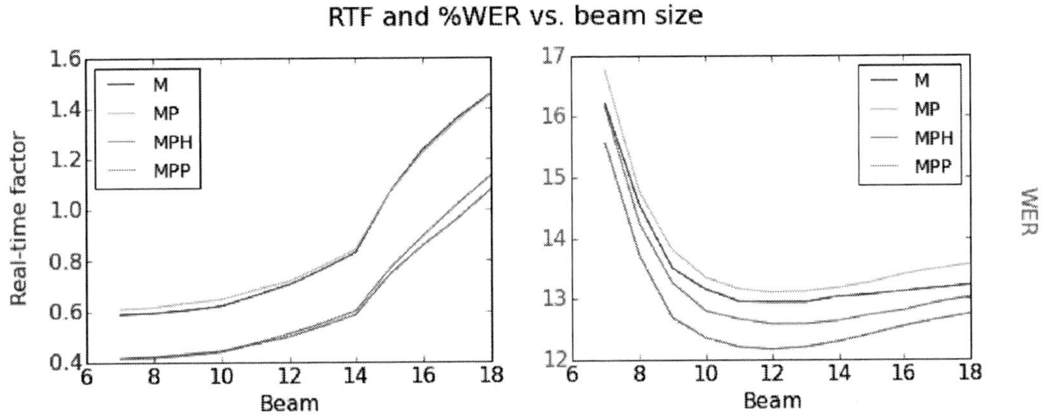

RTF and %WER vs. beam size



Figure 3: Beam parameters sweep on SPTEST. The optimal beam size is 12.

nificant. We found that adding stød annotation resolves many homophonic entries in the lexicon e.g. *hver, værd, vejr* and *vær* are transcribed as [vɛɐ] but stød resolves the ambiguity such that *værd, hver* and *vejr* transcribes as [vɛ$^{?}$ɐ] and *vær* as [vɛɐ$^{?}$]. Table 8 shows the impact of stød annotation on homophony in the pronunciation lexicon. The proportion of affected tokens in SPTEST, PAROLE48 and DanPASS are 27%, 26.7% and 7%, respectively and suggest that modelling stød can have a significant impact even though it appears infrequently.

| Polygraphy | -stød | +stød | difference |
| ---------- | ----- | ----- | ---------- |
| 4x | 5 | 0 | -5 |
| 3x | 54 | 27 | -27 |
| 2x | 930 | 662 | -268 |

Table 8: $2x$ denote the number of phonetic transcriptions that can be mapped to two words, $3x$ denotes the number of phonetic transcriptions that can be mapped to three words, etc.

Only when we evaluate the DNN AM trained in condition 6 do we not observe improved WER when we add pitch features. We also see that in general MFCC-based models outperform PLP-based models and that adding stød and pitch features gives a larger performance improvement in MFCC-based GMM AMs. The best performance is achieved with the DNN trained in condition 5.

We observe an interesting interaction between stød and pitch features in decoding speed. When we add stød and use the same decoder parameters, the real-time factor (RTF) becomes larger which means the ASR system takes more time to recognise a sentence. If we add pitch features to the acoustic input, decoding speed increases.

We encode stød-bearing phones as variants of stød-less phones when we estimate phonetic decision trees (PDT) and stød-bearing phones could become just an alias of the stød-less phone during state-tying because we do not increase the number of estimated probability density functions or leaves of the PDTs. We observe that state-tying tends to cluster together word position-dependent phones more often than stød variants such that clusters contain $[e_E^{?}, e_B^{?}]$, but not $[e_B]^9$. There are 43-45 clusters of stød-bearing phones and 15-19 clusters of mixed stød-bearing and stød-less variants which indicate that stød often is a more important feature than word position.

---

[9]Subscripts denote word position

We can conclude that modelling stød explicitly in the pronunciation lexicon improves WER for both GMM and DNN AMs. There is a statistically significant overall WER improvement and we can conclude that there was no adverse effect on performance despite of the infrequent occurrence of stød. In all cases but one we also observe improvement from adding pitch features.

We find expert annotation is not necessary to take advantage of stød in ASR. We used a g2p-system to generate the pronunciation lexicon and can observe consistent performance improvements when we add stød annotation to the lexicon.

### 7.2 Stød-related acoustic features in ASR

We further investigate several features from SE-LECT: PDD 10-13, PDM 13-14 and Peak slope. Early experiments with GMM AMs showed significantly worse empirical results with Peak Slope and we chose to discard that feature from the rest of the experiments. We bin together PDD 10-13 and PDM 13-14 and denote them as *phase features*.

| Abbr. | MFCC | Pitch | Extra |
|---|---|---|---|
| M | ✓ | ✗ | ✗ |
| MP | ✓ | ✓ | ✗ |
| MPH | ✓ | ✓ | HRF |
| MPP | ✓ | ✓ | PDD10-13 PDM13-14 |

Table 9: Feature combinations and their abbreviations.

Harmonic Richness Factor (HRF) is a measure of harmonicity in the speech signal that Fernandez et al. (2014) use to improve ASR for Zulu and Lao and we expect a relevant measure to include in our study. We discard PLP features because AMs trained on MFCC features generally perform better than the PLP counterparts both in WER and RTF. We also include pitch features because they tend to improve performance and decoding speed and we need to estimate F0 to estimate both phase features and HRF.

The feature combinations we use are in Table 9 and we use early feature integration before LDA because it gave better performance in Metze et al. (2013) and worked well in previous experiments.

We will depart from standard test methodology and optimise one set of decoder parameters on SPTEST, DanPASS, and PAROLE48 which we also use as test sets. We could not find a method to completely isolate the impact the new acoustic features have on WER, but this is our best effort to reduce the impact from other factors. We randomly choose to optimise decoder parameters with the MP model. We will do a second evaluation where we sweep the decoder beam size and visualise the impact on RTF.

Table 10[10] shows that we can get better performance by adding HRF and phase features to the feature input. The improvement is significant on the multispeaker test sets, but not PAROLE48, where the MFCC baseline shows the best performance. The RTF constraint does not affect WER on SPTEST and Figure 3 shows that increasing the beam will have no effect, but we could increase the beam to 17 when we decode with MPH and MPP, but only to 14 with M or MP.

On PAROLE48, we see that M takes a small performance hit to maintain real-time decoding capabilities, but on DanPASS we can further improve MPP and MPH performance because the faster decoding speed allows us to use a larger decoding beam. For MPP, the improvement is significant at $p < 0.01$. The speed up in Figures 3 and 4 is constant for MPP and MPH compared to M. The MP RTF varies considerably and we cannot draw conclusions on the relationship to MPP and MPH based on these experiments.

We can conclude that HRF, PDD10-13 and PDM 13-14 are beneficial acoustic features to use in Danish ASR. WER decreases and decoding speed increases when we add these features. While phase features seem to provide the best improvements, the phase feature extraction method is slower than real-time and our current recommendation is to use HRF. Notes in the Covarep source code suggest that real-time phase feature extraction is possible at the cost of precision, but implementing real-time phase feature extraction is beyond the scope of this research.

## 8 Conclusion

We discovered that stød annotation is reliable when it is annotated by expert phoneticians and used this insight to discover predictive acoustic features that are novel in the phonetic characterisation of stød.

We also discovered that we do not need expert annotation to use stød in ASR to improve

---

[10]See Table 1 for summaries of the corpora used as test sets.

| Features | SPTEST | PAROLE48 | | DanPASS | |
|---|---|---|---|---|---|
| M | 12.94 | **29.78** | **(29.89)** | 53.83 | |
| MP | 13.10 | 30.38 | | 54.73 | |
| MPH | 12.58‡ | 30.38 | | 51.06 | (50.46) |
| MPP | **12.16‡** | 30.05 | | **49.02*** | **(48.79*)** |

Table 10: WER performance using the same decoder parameters for each test set. WER under the $RTF < 1$ constraint are in parentheses if different. Statistical significance is compared to M. These numbers are not directly comparable to Table 7.

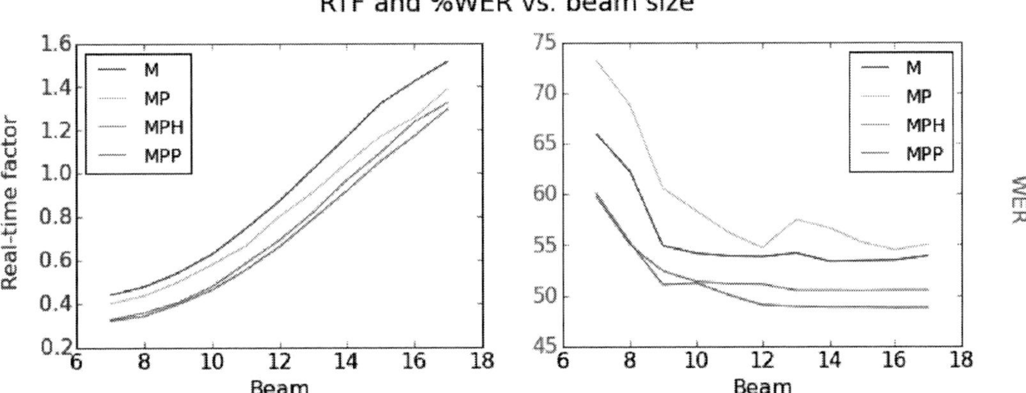


Figure 4: Beam parameter sweep on DanPASS.

performance. The harmonic richness factor and the phase features PDD10-13, PDM13-14 also improve ASR performance and this indicates we have successfully modelled stød explicitly in the lexicon and implicitly with predictive acoustic features without degrading overall performance. We believe that these features can improve performance in absence of stød annotation.

We tried to predict stød as a binary classification task, i.e. predict the presence or absence of stød regardless of the co-occurring phone, but this was not possible because creaky voice, laryngealisation and other acoustic signals that correlate with stød also occur when there is no stød-bearing phone. In future work, we want to experiment with pronunciation variants based on stød to accurately model the optional nature of stød and do an ablation study where we use more features from SELECT, and do not include pitch features in the feature input. We also need to investigate what impact these features have in the absence of stød annotation.

We used open source software and features from ASR and speech analytics so our experiments can be reproduced and reapplied to Swedish and Norwegian. Språkbanken also includes Swedish and Norwegian and eSpeak can generate pronunciations with tones for both languages.

There are no previously published results on Språkbanken or any of the test sets and this was state-of-the-art performance in early 2016. New state-of-the-art performance on Språkbanken-test[11] also model stød in the lexicon.[12]

## Acknowledgments


This work was supported by the Danish Agency for Science and Higher Education, Copenhagen Business School and Mirsk Digital ApS. We thank Klaus Akselsen, Peter Juul Henrichsen, Dirk Hovy and Srinivas Bangalore for support and mentoring through the long process.


---

[11]See https://github.com/kaldi-asr/kaldi/blob/master/egs/sprakbanken/s5/RESULTS

[12]See https://github.com/kaldi-asr/kaldi/blob/master/egs/sprakbanken/s5/local/dictsrc/complexphones.txt

## References

Oliver Adams, Trevor Cohn, Graham Neubig, Hilaria Cruz, Steven Bird, and Alexis Michaud. 2018. Evaluation phonemic transcription of low-resource tonal languages for language documentation. In *LREC*.

P. Boersma. 2002. Praat, a system for doing phonetics by computer. *Glot international*, 5(9/10):341–345.

Gilles Degottex, John Kane, Thomas Drugman, Tuomo Raitio, and Stefan Scherer. 2014. Covarep—a collaborative voice analysis repository for speech technologies. In *Acoustics, Speech and Signal Processing (ICASSP), 2014 IEEE International Conference on*, pages 960–964. IEEE.

Jonathan Duddington. 2010. *eSpeak Text to Speech*. Web publication: `http://espeak.sourceforge.net/`.

Gunnar Fant. 1995. The LF-model revisited. Transformations and frequency domain analysis. *Speech Trans. Lab. Q. Rep., Royal Inst. of Tech. Stockholm*, 2(3):40.

Marcello Federico, Nicola Bertoldi, and Mauro Cettolo. 2008. IRSTLM: an open source toolkit for handling large scale language models. In *Interspeech*, pages 1618–1621.

Raul Fernandez, Jia Cui, Andrew Rosenberg, Bhuvana Ramabhadran, and Xiaodong Cui. 2014. Exploiting Vocal-Source Features to Improve ASR Accuracy for Low-Resource Languages. In *Fifteenth Annual Conference of the International Speech Communication Association*.

Eli Fischer-Jørgensen. 1989. *A phonetic study of the stød in Standard Danish*. University of Turku, Phonetics.

J Fiscus. 2007. Speech recognition scoring toolkit ver. 2.3 (sctk).

Pierre Geurts, Damien Ernst, and Louis Wehenkel. 2006. Extremely randomized trees. *Machine learning*, 63(1):3–42.

Nina Grønnum. 2005. Fonetik og Fonologi, 3. udg. *Akademisk Forlag, København*.

Nina Grønnum. 2006. DanPASS-a Danish Phonetically Annotated Spontaneous Speech corpus. In *Proceedings of the 5th International Conference on Language Resources and Evaluation (LREC), Genova, Italy, May*.

Nina Grønnum, Miguel Vazquez-Larruscaín, and Hans Basbøll. 2013. Danish Stød: Laryngealization or Tone. *Phonetica*, 70(1-2):66–92.

Gert Foget Hansen. 2015. *Stød og stemmekvalitet: En akustisk-fonetisk undersøgelse af ændringer i stemmekvaliteten i forbindelse med stød*. Ph.D. thesis, Københavns Universitet, Faculty of Humanities, Department of Nordic Research. In Danish.

Peter Juel Henrichsen. 2007. The Danish PAROLE corpus-a merge of speech and writing. *Current Trends in Research on Spoken Language in the Nordic Countries*, 2:84–93.

Peter Juel Henrichsen and Thomas Ulrich Christiansen. 2012. Speech Transduction Based on Linguistic Content. In *Joint Baltic-Nordic Acoustics Meeting, Odense, Denmark*.

Dirk Hovy, Taylor Berg-Kirkpatrick, Ashish Vaswani, and Eduard H Hovy. 2013. Learning Whom to Trust with MACE. In *HLT-NAACL*, pages 1120–1130.

Andreas Søeborg Kirkedal. 2013. Analysis of phonetic transcriptions for Danish automatic speech recognition. *Proceedings of the 19th Nordic Conference of Computational Linguistics (NODALIDA 2013) May 22–24, 2013, Oslo University, Norway.*, NEALT Proceedings Series 16.

Andreas Søeborg Kirkedal. 2014. Automatic Phonetic Transcription for Danish Speech Recognition. *CRITT-WCRE Conference*.

Aditi Lahiri, Allison Wetterlin, and Elisabet Jönsson-Steiner. 2005. Lexical specification of tone in north germanic. *Nordic journal of linguistics*, 28(1):61–96.

Shang wen Li, Yow-Bang Wang, Liang-Che Sun, and Lin-Shan Lee. 2011. Improved tonal language speech recognition by integrating spectro-temporal evidence and pitch information with properly chosen tonal acoustic units. In *INTERSPEECH*.

Florian Metze, Zaid A. W. Sheikh, Alexander H. Waibel, Jonas Gehring, Kevin Kilgour, Quoc Bao Nguyen, and Van Huy Nguyen. 2013. Models of tone for tonal and non-tonal languages. *2013 IEEE Workshop on Automatic Speech Recognition and Understanding*, pages 261–266.

Taniya Mishra, Andrej Ljolje, and Mazin Gilbert. 2011. Predicting human perceived accuracy of ASR systems. In *Twelfth Annual Conference of the International Speech Communication Association*.

Daniel Povey, Arnab Ghoshal, Gilles Boulianne, Lukas Burget, Ondrej Glembek, Nagendra Goel, Mirko Hannemann, Petr Motlicek, Yanmin Qian, Petr Schwarz, Jan Silovsky, Georg Stemmer, and Karel Vesely. 2011. The Kaldi Speech Recognition Toolkit. In *IEEE 2011 Workshop on Automatic Speech Recognition and Understanding*. IEEE Signal Processing Society. IEEE Catalog No.: CFP11SRW-USB.

Tomas Riad. 2000. The origin of danish stød. *Analogy, Levelling and Markedness: Principles of Change in Phonology and Morphology*, pages 261–300.

Niklas Vanhainen and Giampiero Salvi. 2014. Free Acoustic and Language Models for Large Vocabulary Continuous Speech Recognition in Swedish. *training*, 965(307568):420–8.

Tae-Jin Yoon, Xiaodan Zhuang, Jennifer Cole, and
Mark Hasegawa-Johnson. 2006. Voice quality
dependent speech recognition. In *International
Symposium on Linguistic Patterns in Spontaneous
Speech*. Citeseer.

# Adaptor Grammars for the Linguist: Word Segmentation Experiments for Very Low-Resource Languages


**Pierre Godard*, Laurent Besacier[†], François Yvon*, Martine Adda-Decker*,**
**Gilles Adda*, Hélène Maynard*, Annie Rialland***

*LIMSI, CNRS, Université Paris-Saclay / Orsay, France
[†]LIG, UGA, G-INP, CNRS, INRIA / Grenoble, France
*LPP, CNRS / Paris, France

*{godard,yvon,gadda,hbm}@limsi.fr
[†]laurent.besacier@univ-grenoble-alpes.fr
*{martine.adda-decker,annie.rialland}@univ-paris3.fr


## Abstract


Computational Language Documentation attempts to make the most recent research in speech and language technologies available to linguists working on language preservation and documentation. In this paper, we pursue two main goals along these lines. The first is to improve upon a strong baseline for the unsupervised word discovery task on two very low-resource Bantu languages, taking advantage of the expertise of linguists on these particular languages. The second consists in exploring the Adaptor Grammar framework as a decision and prediction tool for linguists studying a new language. We experiment 162 grammar configurations for each language and show that using Adaptor Grammars for word segmentation enables us to test hypotheses about a language. Specializing a generic grammar with language specific knowledge leads to great improvements for the word discovery task, ultimately achieving a leap of about 30% token F-score from the results of a strong baseline.


## 1 Introduction

A large number of the world's languages are expected to go extinct during this century – as much as half of them according to Crystal (2002) and Janson (2003). Such predictions have subsequently fostered a growing interest for a new field, Computational Language Documentation (CLD), as it is now clear that traditional field linguistics alone will not meet the challenge of preserving and documenting all of these languages.

CLD attempts to make the most recent research in speech and language technologies available to linguists working on language preservation and documentation (e.g. (Anastasopoulos and Chiang, 2017; Adams et al., 2017)). A remarkable effort in this direction has improved the data collection

tools to be used on the field (Bird et al., 2014; Blachon et al., 2016), enabling to collect corpora for several endangered languages (Adda et al., 2016). In parallel, the language technology community is investing more efforts to design methodologies tailored for the new challenges posed by the analysis of such linguistic material: the extreme variability of the orthographic representation, the scarcity of annotated data (both written and oral), as well as the modeling of complex tonal systems.

This effort could greatly benefit from a tighter collaboration between the two main research communities involved in this endeavor, which often struggle to cooperate efficiently. Knowledge background differs between linguists and computer scientists; the definition of why a problem is interesting or not may not be the same for the two communities, theoretical and experimental platforms do not intersect much, etc. Consequently, for lack of investing enough energy working on the same problems with the same tools and towards the same goals, we might not achieve the efficiency that is needed, as time is running out for many languages. This view constitutes the underlying motivation of the work reported here.

We pursue two main goals in this spirit. The first one is to improve upon a strong baseline (Goldwater et al., 2009) for the unsupervised word discovery task[1] on two low-resource languages, by teaming up with linguist experts. A natural idea to achieve this goal is to engage them in formalizing their linguistic knowledge regarding the languages or language families under study, in the hope that it will compensate for the small amount of available data. In our case, this expertise corresponds to morphological and phonotactic constraints for

---

[1]We indifferently use the terms *word discovery* and *word segmentation* to denote the task defined in Section 2.2.




*Proceedings of the 15th SIGMORPHON Workshop on Computational Research in Phonetics, Phonology, and Morphology*, pages 32–42
Brussels, Belgium, October 31, 2018. ©2018 The Special Interest Group on Computational Morphology and Phonology
https://doi.org/10.18653/v1/P17

two Bantu languages displaying very similar structures (see Section 3). For one language, we were also able to elicit a list of prefixes and some additional knowledge regarding the consonantal system. Such expert knowledge can readily be integrated in grammar rules using the framework of Adaptor Grammars (see Section 6). Another interesting property of this framework is its compatibility with two strategies that are usually thought as being mutually exclusive: rule-based learning, still in wide use inside the linguistics community, and statistical learning, prevalent in natural language processing circles.

Our second goal is to study ways to help linguists explore language data when little expert knowledge is available. Our proposal is to complement the grammatical description activity with task-oriented search procedures, that will speed up the exploration of competing hypotheses. The intuition is that better grammars should not only truthfully match the empirical data, but also improve the quality of automatic analysis processes. The word discovery task considered below should thus be viewed as an extrinsic validation procedure, rather than a goal in and of itself. This process might also yield new linguistic insights regarding the language(s) under focus.

To sum up, the main contribution of this paper is a methodology for systematically exploring (a subpart of) the space of possible grammars, refining grammar rules (from the most generic to the most language specific) at four levels of description (see Section 4). This results in a comparison of 162 alternative accounts of the grammar for two languages. Our results (analyzed in Section 5) show that enriching grammar rules with language specific knowledge has a consistent positive impact in performance for the segmentation task. They validate our hypotheses that (a) improved grammatical descriptions actually correlate with better automatic analysis; (b) Adaptor Grammars provide a framework around which linguists and computer scientists can effectively collaborate, with tangible results for both communities.

## 2  Adaptor Grammars for Word Discovery

### 2.1  Adaptor Grammars

Formal grammars, and notably Context-Free Grammars (CFGs), are a cornerstone of linguistic description and provide a model for the structural description of linguistic objects. Our grammars capture simple aspects of the syntax and some less trivial aspects of the morphological and phonological structures. As discussed below, both levels of descriptions are useful for word discovery.

A CFG is a 4-tuple $G = (N, W, R, S)$ where $N$ and $W$ are respectively the non-terminal and terminal symbols, $R$ a finite set of rules of the form $A \rightarrow \beta$, with $A \in N$ and $\beta \in (N \cup W)^*$, and $S \in N$ the start symbol. Our grammars will be used to analyze the structure of complete utterances and the start symbol $S$ will always correspond to the sentence top-level. Assuming that $S$, Words, and Word belong to $N$, the top level rules will typically look like: $S \rightarrow$ Words; Words $\rightarrow$ Word Words; Words $\rightarrow$ Word, the last two rules abbreviated as Words $\rightarrow$ Word $+$.

Probabilistic CFGs (PCFGs) (Johnson, 1998) extend this model by associating each rule with a scalar value $\theta_{A \rightarrow \beta}$, such that for each $A \in N$, $\sum_\beta \theta_{A \rightarrow \beta} = 1$. Under some technical conditions (Chi, 1999), PCFGs define probability distributions over the set of parse trees, where the probability of a tree is a product of the probability of the rules it contains. PCFGs can be learned in a supervised way from treebanks or in a unsupervised manner using, for instance, the EM algorithm (Lari and Young, 1990).

PCFGs make unrealistic independence assumptions between the different subparts of a tree, an observation that has yielded many subsequent variations and extensions. Adaptor grammars (AGs) (Johnson et al., 2007) define a powerful mechanism to manipulate PCFG distributions to better match the occurrences of trees and subtrees observed in actual corpora. Informally, an AG is a CFG where non-terminals have the possibility to be *adapted*: when non-terminal $A$ is adapted, all subtrees rooted in $A$ are "reified", meaning that they are no-longer viewed only as decomposable objects, but can also be manipulated and stored as a whole. In our grammars below, adapted non-terminals are underlined, and optional non-terminals appear between brackets. Following (Johnson et al., 2007), we only adapt non-recursive non-terminals.[2]

AGs define a framework to implement Bayesian nonparametric learning of grammars, and are usually trained in an unsupervised manner using sampling techniques (Monte-Carlo Markov Chain,



---

[2]A non-terminal $A$ is recursive if $R$ contains a rule where $A$ appears both in the left and right-hand sides.

MCMC). A typical run will produce, for each sentence, a distribution of possible parses under the grammar, from which we can then retain the most frequent one as the "best" possible analysis.[3]

## 2.2 Word Segmentation using AGs

In this work, we are interested in the word segmentation task: from an unsegmented stream of symbols, the system must output delimited sequences corresponding to actual words in the language. For this, we assume a linguistic grammar $G$, which parses sequences of letters (or phones) as being organized into Words, which themselves recursively decompose into smaller units such as Morphs, Syllables, etc. To induce word segmentation from parse trees, we will consider that each span covered by the non-terminal symbol Word defines a linguistic word, even though in a fully unsupervised setting, this non-terminal might actually correspond to larger or smaller linguistic units. Figure 2 illustrates this on two example parses.

Likewise, when examining the output of the training process, we are in a position to collect sets of word types (or morph types, syllable types, etc.) and will do so based only on the identity of the root symbol, i.e. without any certainty regarding the linguistic status of the collected sequences.

## 3 Linguistic material

### 3.1 Mboshi and Myene

We experiment with two Northwestern Bantu Languages: Mboshi (Bantu C25), a language spoken in Congo-Brazzaville, and Myene (B10, Gabon), a cluster of six mutually intelligible varieties (Adyumba, Enenga, Galwa, Mpongwe, Nkomi and Orungu) spoken at the coastal areas and around the town of Lambarene in Gabon.[4] Unlike southern Bantu relatives such as Swahili, Sotho or Zulu, Mboshi and Myene are scarcely studied, protected, and resourced. We briefly describe the main aspects related to phonetics, phonology, morphology, and tonology of these languages.

**Phonetics and phonology.** Mboshi and Myene both have a seven vowel system (i, e, ɛ, a, ɔ, o, u). Mboshi has an opposition between long and short vowels, which does not exist in Myene. Mboshi consonantal system includes the following phonemes: p, t, k, b, d, β, l, r, m, n, ɲ, mb,

nd, ndz, ng, mbv, f, s, ɣ, pf, bv, ts, dz, w, j. It has a set of prenasalized consonants (mb, nd, ndz, ng, mbv) which is common in Bantu languages (Embanga Aborobongui, 2013; Kouarata, 2014). Myene includes the following phonemes: p, t, k, b, d, β, l, r, m, n, f, s, g, y, v, ŋ, w, z – many of them with variants of realization. Prenasalized consonants exist also in Myene (Ambouroue, 2007).

While both languages can be considered as rarely written, linguists have nonetheless defined a non-standard graphemic form for them, considered to be close to the language phonology. Affricates and prenasalized plosives are coded using multiple symbols (e.g. two symbols for dz, three for mbv). For Mboshi, long and short vowels are coded respectively as V and as VV. In Myene, the transcription of the corpus involves not only the phoneme set, but also the main variants (ɲ, tʃ, dz) and some marginal sounds found in loanwords.

Both languages display a complex set of phonological rules. The deletion of a vowel before another vowel in particular, common in Bantu languages, occurs at 40% of word junctions in Mboshi (Rialland et al., 2015). This tends to obscure word segmentation and introduces an additional challenge for automatic processing.

**Morphology.** Words are composed of roots and affixes, and almost always include at least one prefix, while the presence of several prefixes and one suffix is also very common. The suffix structure mostly consists of a single vowel V (e.g. -a or -i) whereas the prefix structure may be both CV or V (or CVV in Mboshi). The most common syllable structures are V and CV in both languages. CVC also occurs in Myene, and CVV in Mboshi.[5]

The noun class prefix system is another feature typical of Bantu languages. For both languages, the structure of the verbs, also common in Bantu languages, is as follows: Subject Marker — Tense/Mood Marker — Root-derivative Extensions — Final Vowel. A verb can be very short or quite long, depending on the markers involved.

**Tonology.** Prosodic systems for both Mboshi and Myene involve tones, but the transcribed data used for this work do not encode tone markers. Experiments to assess the usability of tonal information for word segmentation were conducted in (Godard et al., 2018b).

---

[3]In practice, we will retain the most frequent segmentation rather than the most frequent parse (see Section 2.2).

[4]Our Myene data correspond to the Orungu variant.

[5]CCV may also arise due to the presence of affricates and prenasalized plosives mentioned in this section.

| language | #sent | #tokens | #types | avg. token length |
|---|---|---|---|---|
| Mboshi | 5130 | 30,556 | 5,312 | 4.19 |
| Myene | 4,579 | 18,047 | 4,190 | 4.72 |

Table 1: Corpora Statistics

## 3.2 Corpora for Mboshi and Myene

Corpora for Mboshi and Myene were collected following a real language documentation scenario, using a mobile app dedicated to fieldwork language documentation (Blachon et al., 2016). These corpora contain manual transcriptions in the form of a non-standard graphemic form close to the languages' phonology. The correct word segmentations for these transcripts were also annotated by linguists. Basic statistics are in Table 1. The Mboshi corpus is more comprehensively described in (Godard et al., 2018a).[6]

## 4 Grammars

### 4.1 Structuring Grammar Sets

Our starting point is the set of grammars used in (Johnson and Goldwater, 2009) and (Eskander et al., 2016) which we progressively specialize through an iterative refinement process involving both field linguists and computer scientists. As we wish to evaluate specific linguistic hypotheses, the initial space of interesting grammars has been generalized in a modular, systematic, and hierarchical way as follows. We distinguish four sections in each grammar: sentence, word, syllable, character. For each section, we test multiple hypotheses, gradually incorporating more linguistic structure. Every hypothesis inside a given section can be combined with every hypothesis of any other section,[7] thereby allowing us to explore a large quantity of grammars and to analyze the contribution of each particular hypothesis.

### 4.2 The Full Grammar Landscape

All the grammar sections (sentence, word, syllable, character) experimented in this paper are detailed in Figure 1. We describe below the way each section was designed.

- sentence level: we model 3 different hierarchies of words. We introduce first the `flat` variety with two rules generating right-branching parse trees. `colloc` adds a single level of word collocation, aimed to capture recurrent local word associations (such as frequent bigrams); `colloc3` displays a deeper hierarchical structure with three levels of collocations. Exploring more realistic syntactic structures is left for future work.

- word level: here we propose 6 competing hypotheses. `flat` is similar to previous sentence variety but at the word level instead of the sentence level. `generic` corresponds to a more structured version of `flat`, as the specification of a sequence of 5 adapted morphemes allows, in principle, the Adaptor Grammar to learn some morphotactics. `bantu` defines a generic morphology for Bantu languages. `basaa` implements the morphology of a well-studied Bantu language, Basaa (A43 (Hamlaoui and Makasso, 2015)). `mboshi/myene` corresponds to a somewhat crude morphology of Mboshi, also applicable to Myene. Last `mboshi/myene_NV` refines `mboshi/myene` with a specification of the morphology of nouns and verbs. Additionally, for `basaa`, `mboshi/myene` and `mboshi/myene_NV` which introduce a notion of prefix, we also test a variant (called respectively `basaa+`, `mboshi/myene+` and `mboshi/myene_NV+`) containing an explicit list of prefixes in Mboshi.

- syllable level: we contrast 3 hypotheses : `flat` is similar to previous sentence and word varieties but at the syllable level, defining the syllable as a mere sequence of characters. `generic/basaa` is a generic set of rules modeling phonotactics applicable to a wide scope of languages (including Basaa mentioned in the preceding level). `bantu/mboshi/myene` displays a set of rules more specific to Mboshi and Myene.[8]

- character level: rules in the `chars` set simply rewrite the characters (terminals) ob-

---

[6]This dataset has already been used in several studies targeting endangered languages and is available at `http://www.islrn.org/resources/747-055-093-447-8/`.

[7]Note that if a non-terminal is absent from a hypothesis (e.g. Syllable in a word level hypothesis), the corresponding non-terminal in the subsequent hypotheses (e.g. at the syllable level) will be ignored.

[8]In theory, we should not include a coda in this last hypothesis, but loanwords and proper names in our data made the Adaptor Grammar fail to parse without a coda. To decrease the impact of this rule, we chose not to adapt the corresponding non-terminal, in contrast to `generic/basaa`.

**Sentence level (A)**

Words → Word+

flat(A1)

Collocs → Colloc+
Colloc → Words
Words → Word+

colloc(A2)

Colloc3s → Colloc3+
Colloc3 → Colloc2s
Colloc2s → Colloc2+
Colloc2 → Collocs
Collocs → Colloc+
Colloc → Words
Words → Word+

colloc3(A3)

**Word level (B)**

Word → Morphs
Morphs → Morph+
Morph → Chars

flat(B1)

Word → M1 (M2 (M3 (M4 (M5))))
M1 → Chars
M2 → Chars
M3 → Chars
M4 → Chars
M5 → Chars

generic(B2)

Word → (Prefixes) Stem (Suffixes)
Prefixes → Chars
Stem → Chars
Suffixes → Chars

bantu(B3)

Word → (Prefix) Stem (Suffix)
Prefix → Syllable
Suffix → Syllable
Stem → Syllable
Stem → Syllable Syllable

basaa(B4)

Word → (Prefix1 (Prefix2)) Stem (Suffix)
Prefix1 → Syllable
Prefix2 → Syllable
Suffix → Syllable
Stem → Syllable (Syllable)

mboshi/myene(B5)

Word → Noun
Word → Verb
Word → Chars
Noun → (PrefixNoun) Stem (Suffix)
Verb → (Prefix1 (Prefix2)) Stem
PrefixNoun → Syllable
Prefix1 → Syllable
Prefix2 → Syllable
Suffix → Syllable
Stem → Syllable (Syllable (Syllable))

mboshi/myene_NV(B6)

**Syllable level (C)**

Syllable → Chars
Chars → Char+

flat(C1)

Syllable → (Onset) Rhyme
Rhyme → Nucleus (Coda)
Onset → Consonants
Nucleus → Vowels
Coda → Consonants
Consonants → Consonant+
Vowels → Vowel+
Chars → Char+

generic/basaa(C2)

Syllable → (Onset) Rhyme
Rhyme → Nucleus (Coda)
Onset → Consonants
Nucleus → Vowel (Vowel)
Coda → Consonants
Consonants → Consonant+
Chars → Char+

bantu/mboshi/myene(C3)

**Character level (D)**

Char → Vowel
Char → Consonant
Vowel → u
Vowel → o
Vowel → i
Vowel → a
Vowel → e
...

chars(D1)

...
Consonant → m b
Consonant → n d
Consonant → n d z
...

chars+(D1+)

...
Prefix → o
Prefix → i
Prefix → e
Prefix → a
Prefix → l e
Prefix → l a
Prefix → l i i
...

{basaa,mboshi/myene,mboshi/myene_NV}+
(B{4,5,6}+)

Figure 1: Grammar rules for all the hypotheses presented in Section 4.

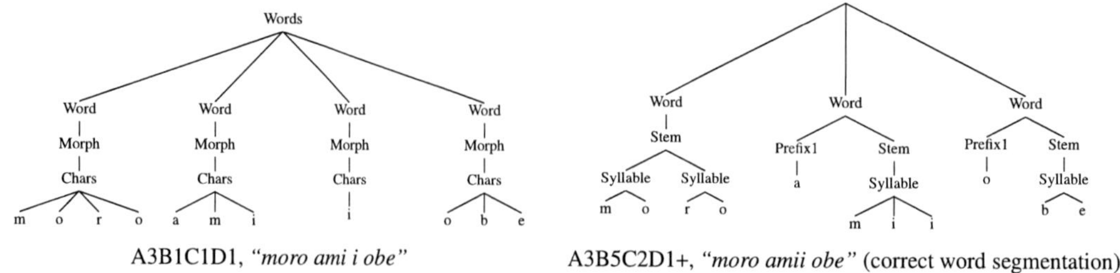

A3B1C1D1, *"moro ami i obe"*   A3B5C2D1+, *"moro amii obe"* (correct word segmentation)

Figure 2: Examples of parses – some non-terminals have been omitted for readability – obtained with two grammars, and the corresponding word segmentation for Mboshi sentence *"Moro a-mii o-be"*. (CL1.man 3SG-swallow.PST CL14-bad; since *Moro* is an irregular noun, the prefix and the stem are difficult to separate, which is signaled by a dot, following the Leipzig glossing rules.)

served in our data. `chars+` adds rules to capture the digraphs or trigraphs occurring in Mboshi (see details in Section 3).

## 5 Experiments and Discussion

We now experiment along the methodology presented in Section 4. We report word segmentation performance using precision, recall, and F-measure on tokens (WP, WR, WF), and types (LP, LR, LF). We also report the exact-match (X) metric which calculates the proportion of correctly segmented utterances.[9]

In all the figures, and in this section, we use the following compact names for grammatical hypotheses at each level:

- A1 (`flat`), A2 (`colloc`), A3 (`colloc3`),

- B1 (`flat`), B2 (`generic`), B3 (`bantu`), B4 (`basaa`), B5 (`mboshi/myene`), B6 (`mboshi/myene_NV`), with additional "+" variants for B4, B5, and B6 when a list of prefixes is provided, for instance B6+ (`mboshi/myene_NV+`),

- C1 (`flat`), C2 (`generic/basaa`), C3 (`bantu/mboshi/myene`),

- D1 (`chars`), D1+ (`chars+`).

For each language, we evaluate our 162 grammar configurations using Mark Johnson's code,[10] collecting parses after 2,000 sampling steps.[11] We adapt all non-recursive non-terminals and use a Dirichlet prior to estimate the rule probabilities. We place a uniform Beta prior on the discount parameter of the Pitman-Yor process, and a vague Gamma prior on the concentration parameter.

Figure 3 presents token metrics (WP, WR, WF) and type metrics (LP, LR, LF), as well as sentence exact-match (X) for both corpora on all grammars.

### 5.1 Word Segmentation Results

**Impact of sentence level variants** We can see in Figure 3 that A2 and A3 hypotheses globally yield better results than A1 in both languages. For Mboshi, the benefit of A3 vs. A2 appears especially on token metrics (WP, WR, WF), but this contrast is less clear on Myene. For both languages, however, our results confirm that modeling collocation-like word groups at the sentence level is important. These word dependencies seem indeed related to a universal linguistic property.

**Impact of word level variants** If we now focus solely on the A3 hypothesis for Myene in Figure 3, we observe a general trend upwards for all metrics. The benefit of gradually using more language-specific grammars, from B1 to B6+, is clear. While this trend is also observed for Mboshi, the less specific B3 hypothesis yields the strongest results on token metrics (WP, WR, WF). Precision on types (LP) with B3 is also the strongest, but B6+ achieves better performance on type recall and F-measure (LR and LF). The contrast between B1 and B2 for all metrics on both languages (keeping a focus on A3, but this can also be seen for A1 and A2) highlights the benefit of modeling some morphotactics inside the word-level hypotheses, which seems to correspond to another universal linguistic property (the dependency between morphemes inside a word).

**Impact of syllable level variants** It is difficult to see a clear trend for the impact of syllable-level variants in Figure 3. Importantly, the syllable level will only be effective when combined with word level variants B4, B5 and B6 (and their "+" versions) which model the concept of syllable: when combined with B1, B2 or B3, each C level hypothesis will default to its "Chars $\rightarrow$ Char +" rule. Figure 4 illustrates the impact of C1, C2, and C3 by averaging type and token F-measures (LF and WF) over all grammar sections with a syllable non-terminal (B4, B4+, B5, B5+, B6, and B6+). The benefit of C2/C3 vs. C1 appears more clearly, especially on type F-measures and on Myene.[12] Nevertheless, the impact of the syllable level, and the capacity to incorporate phonotactics in our models, seems of less significance for word segmentation than choices made at the word and sentence levels.

**Impact of character level variants** In Figure 3, it is also hard to see if there is any benefit in using D1+ over D1, i.e. adding digraphs or trigraphs

---



[9]The exact-match metric includes single-word utterances.

[10]`http://web.science.mq.edu.au/ ~mjohnson/Software.htm`

[11]The large number of experiments we are dealing with did not allow us to average over several runs. Stable results were obtained on a subset of grammars. Two particular configurations in Mboshi (A3-B6-C3-D1+ and A1-B6-C1-D1) did not reach 2,000 iterations within the maximum wall clock time allowed by the cluster used for these experiments (2 weeks), and are left out of the discussion.

[12]The differences between C3 and C2, two very similar hypotheses, are hardly significant.

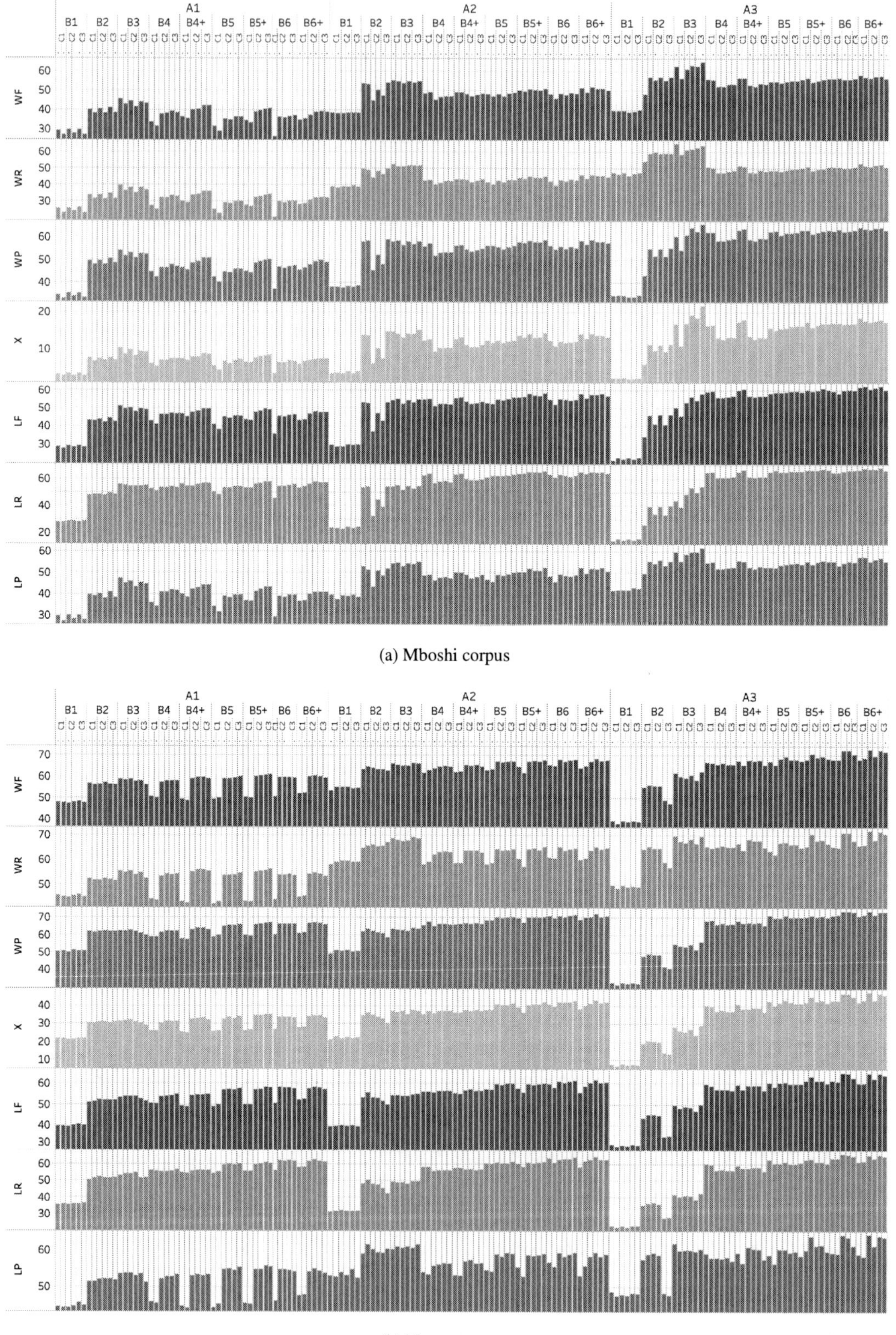

(a) Mboshi corpus

(b) Myene corpus

Figure 3: Word segmentation performance evaluated with token metrics (WP, WR, WF), type metrics (LP, LR, LF), and sentence exact-match (X) for Mboshi (top) and Myene (bottom). All grammars are broken down by A, B, C, and D levels (D1 shown before D1+).

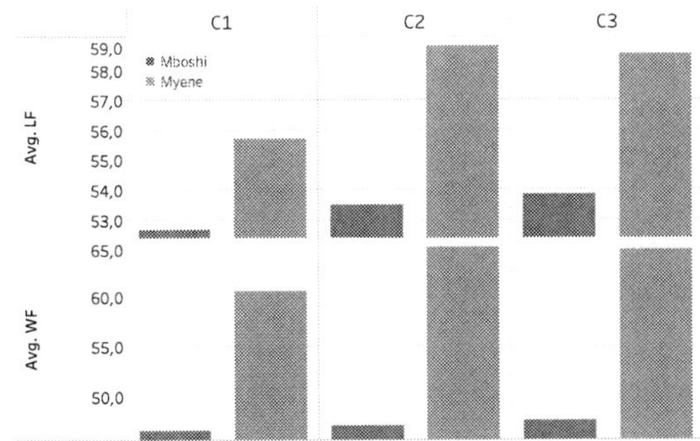

Figure 4: Impact of C variants on Mboshi and Myene. Token F-measure (WF) and type F-measure (LF) are averaged over hypotheses B4, B4+, B5, B5+, B6, and B6+.

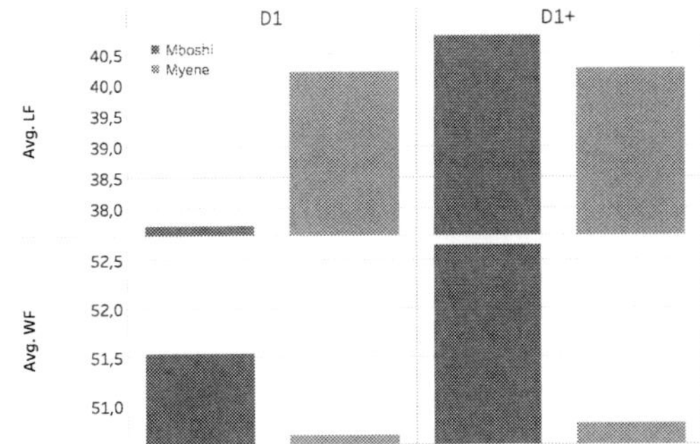

Figure 5: Impact of D variants on Mboshi and Myene. Token F-measure (WF) and type F-measure (LF) are averaged over hypotheses with A level set to A3 and B level set to B1, B2, or B3.

to the consonant inventory. Averaging over all hypotheses at the A, B, and C levels do not exhibit any clearer impact. It is likely that refined models at the syllable level (C) compensate for a less accurate consonant inventory through the adaptation of their non-terminals, and do learn some phonotactics. This would explain the weak contribution of D1+. To test this hypothesis, we set the sentence level to A3 (the best compromise for Mboshi and Myene) and the word level to B1, B2, or B3 (levels without a Syllable non-terminal, which cancels the effect of the syllable level C). The token and type F-measures averaged over the considered hypotheses are shown Figure 5. We do observe a benefit in using the D1+ character variant in Mboshi, but not in Myene. This is not surprising, as the digraph and trigraph rules added by the D1+ variant are specific to Mboshi and do not cover the inventory for Myene.

**Stronger results in Myene** Segmentation performance is globally superior in Myene. This can probably be explained by corpus statistics (see Table 1), as the average number of words per sentence is 3.94 in Myene, and 5.96 in Mboshi. Since sentence boundaries are also word boundaries, the proportion of already known word boundaries is higher in Myene, which makes word segmentation a harder task in Mboshi. Figure 3 also reveals an interesting contrast: token results are higher than type results in Myene, while the converse is true in Mboshi. The token/type ratio (5.75 tokens for one type in Mboshi, and 4.30 in Myene) indicates a higher lexical diversity in Myene, which might explain weaker results on types. Strong results on types for Mboshi, on the other hand, show the ca-

pacity of AGs to generalize well on low-frequency events, a property of particular interest in the low-resource scenario.

**Comparison to an existing baseline** Overall, our best performing grammars are A3-B3-C3-D1+ for Mboshi (64.78% token F-measure) and A3-B6+-C2-D1 for Myene (72.62% token F-measure). This result is about 30 points higher than a strong Bayesian baseline, the Dirichlet process-based bigram word segmentation system of Goldwater et al. (2006, 2009), [13] which yields 34.34% token F-score on Mboshi and 44.48% on Myene.

### 5.2 How Can This Help a Linguist?

Our second goal is to understand more precisely how such experiments can be useful for linguists, beyond the benefit of having access to better automatic word segmentation tools for their data.

**Phonological status of complex consonants** In the analysis of the results (Section 5.1 above) we showed the benefit of integrating digraphs or trigraphs in the consonants inventory for Mboshi. This result is of special interest for linguists, since it is in line with the most recent phonological analyses of Mboshi (Embanga Aborobongui, 2013; Kouarata, 2014; Amboulou, 1998) which agree in recognizing complex consonants (represented by digraphs or trigraphs) in the phonological inventory of this language. The analysis of complex consonants, in particular prenasalized consonants, generated many debates in Bantu linguistics

---

[13] `https://homepages.inf.ed.ac.uk/sgwater/resources.html`.

(Odden, 2015; Herbert, 1986; Downing, 2005). The present experiments provide more substance to support the integration of complex consonants in the phonological inventory of Mboshi.

**Learning prefixes without supervision** Since parses are produced to segment sentences into words, it is possible to extract the most frequent prefixes or suffixes (for B variants introducing such a concept). The precision on the 20 most frequently found prefixes for grammars without prefix-supervision (B3, B4, B5 and B6)[14] reaches 58.21% in Mboshi, and 61.21% in Myene. The capacity of AGs to learn true prefixes without supervision could thus help linguists in the process of documenting a new language. On the supervised variants (B4+, B5+, and B6+), the precision achieved in Mboshi is 61.11%, and 63.07% in Myene: the benefit of the supervision is limited; token measures for Mboshi with these variants (Figure 3) nevertheless indicate a benefit for word segmentation.

## 6 Related Work

AGs have been used to infer the structure of unsegmented sequences of symbols, offering a plausible modeling of language acquisition (Johnson, 2008b; Johnson and Goldwater, 2009); they have also been used for the unsupervised discovery of word structure, applied to the Sesotho language by Johnson (2008a). One notable outcome of this latter study was to demonstrate the effectiveness of having an explicit hierarchical model of word internal structure ; an observation that was one of our primary motivations for using AGs in our language documentation work. In this series of studies, AGs are shown to generalize models of unsupervised word segmentations such as the Bayesian nonparametric model of Goldwater (2006), delivering hierarchical (rather than flat) decompositions for words or sentences.

While AGs are essentially viewed as an unsupervised grammatical inference tool, several authors have also tried to better inform grammar inference with external knowledge sources. This is the case of Sirts and Goldwater (2013), who study a semi-supervised learning scheme combining annotated data (parse trees) with raw sentences. The linguistic knowledge considered in (Johnson et al., 2014) aims to better model function words in a

---

[14] We include B3 variant, interpreting its non-terminal Prefixes as a prefix.

language acquisition setting: explicitly representing the occurrence of these short (typically monosyllabic) tokens in front of content-bearing words was shown to improve the resulting word segmentations. The work of Eskander et al. (2016) considers the use of additional dictionaries, storing partial lists of prefixes or suffixes collected either on the Internet, or discovered during a first round of training. We study similar complementary information, which are collected in close collaboration with linguistic experts.

Various other extensions or applications of AGs are worth mentioning, such as O'Donnell et al. (2009), which generalizes AGs so as to adapt fragments of subtrees (rather than entire subtrees). Botha and Blunsom (2013) consider the adaptation of grammars from a more general class than context-free grammars (mildly context-sensitive grammars), in order to model discontinuous fragments in non-concatenative morphology. Finally, Börschinger and Johnson (2014) propose to model the role of stress cues in language learning.

## 7 Conclusion

This paper had two main goals: (1) improve upon a strong baseline for the unsupervised discovery of words in two very low-resource Bantu languages; (2) explore the Adaptor Grammar framework as an analysis and prediction tool for linguists studying a new language.

Systematic experiments with 162 grammar configurations for each language have shown that using AGs for word segmentation is a way to test linguistic hypotheses during a language documentation process. Conversely, we have also shown that specializing a generic grammar with language specific knowledge greatly improves word segmentation performance. In addition, our paper reports word segmentation results that are way higher than a Bayesian baseline. These results invite us to further this collaboration, and to analyze more thoroughly the usability of output parses in speeding up the documentation process.

**Acknowledgments**

We thank the anonymous reviewers for their insightful comments. We also thank Ramy Eskander for his help in the early stages of this research. This work was partly funded by French ANR and German DFG under grant ANR-14-CE35-0002 (BULB project).

## References

Oliver Adams, Trevor Cohn, Graham Neubig, and Alexis Michaud. 2017. Phonemic transcription of low-resource tonal languages. In *Proceedings of the Australasian Language Technology Association Workshop 2017*, pages 53–60.

Gilles Adda, Sebastian Stüker, Martine Adda-Decker, Odette Ambouroue, Laurent Besacier, David Blachon, Hélène Bonneau-Maynard, Pierre Godard, Fatima Hamlaoui, Dmitri Idiatov, Guy-Noël Kouarata, Lori Lamel, Emmanuel-Moselly Makasso, Annie Rialland, Mark Van de Velde, François Yvon, and Sabine Zerbian. 2016. Breaking the unwritten language barrier: The Bulb project. In *Proceedings of SLTU (Spoken Language Technologies for Under-Resourced Languages)*, Yogyakarta, Indonesia.

Célestin Amboulou. 1998. *Le Mbochi: Langue Bantu Du Congo-Brazzaville (Zone C, Groupe C20)*. Ph.D. thesis, INALCO, Paris.

Odette Ambouroue. 2007. *Éléments de description de l'orungu, langue bantu du Gabon (B11b)*. Ph.D. thesis, Université Libre de Bruxelles.

Antonios Anastasopoulos and David Chiang. 2017. A case study on using speech-to-translation alignments for language documentation. In *Proceedings of the 2nd Workshop on the Use of Computational Methods in the Study of Endangered Languages*, pages 170–178, Honolulu. Association for Computational Linguistics.

Steven Bird, Florian R. Hanke, Oliver Adams, and Haejoong Lee. 2014. Aikuma: A mobile app for collaborative language documentation. *ACL 2014*.

David Blachon, Élodie Gauthier, Laurent Besacier, Guy-Noël Kouarata, Martine Adda-Decker, and Annie Rialland. 2016. Parallel speech collection for under-resourced language studies using the LIG-Aikuma mobile device app. *Procedia Computer Science*, 81:61–66.

Benjamin Börschinger and Mark Johnson. 2014. Exploring the Role of Stress in Bayesian Word Segmentation using Adaptor Grammars. *Transactions of the Association of Computational Linguistics*, 2:93–104.

Jan A. Botha and Phil Blunsom. 2013. Adaptor Grammars for Learning Non-Concatenative Morphology. In *EMNLP*, pages 345–356.

Zhiyi Chi. 1999. Statistical properties of probabilistic context-free grammars. *Comput. Linguist.*, 25(1):131–160.

David Crystal. 2002. *Language Death*. Cambridge University Press. Cambridge Books Online.

Laura J. Downing. 2005. On the ambiguous segmental status of nasals in homorganic NC sequences. In *The Internal Organization of Phonological Segments*, pages 183–216.

Georges Martial Embanga Aborobongui. 2013. *Processus segmentaux et tonals en Mbondzi – (variété de la langue embosi C25)*. Ph.D. thesis, Université Paris 3 Sorbonne Nouvelle.

Ramy Eskander, Owen Rambow, and Tianchun Yang. 2016. Extending the Use of Adaptor Grammars for Unsupervised Morphological Segmentation of Unseen Languages. In *Proceedings of COLING 2016, the 26th International Conference on Computational Linguistics: Technical Papers*, pages 900–910, Osaka, Japan. The COLING 2016 Organizing Committee.

Pierre Godard, Gilles Adda, Martine Adda-Decker, Juan Benjumea, Laurent Besacier, Jamison Cooper-Leavitt, Guy-Noël Kouarata, Lori Lamel, Hélène Maynard, Markus Müller, Annie Rialland, Sebastian Stüker, François Yvon, and Marcely Zanon Boito. 2018a. A Very Low Resource Language Speech Corpus for Computational Language Documentation Experiments. In *Proceedings of LREC*, Miyazaki, Japan.

Pierre Godard, Kevin Loser, Alexandre Allauzen, Laurent Besacier, and Francois Yvon. 2018b. Unsupervised learning of word segmentation: Does tone matter ? In *Proceedings of the 19th International Conference on Computational Linguistics and Intelligent Text Processing (CICLING), Hanoi, Vietnam*.

Sharon Goldwater. 2006. *Nonparametric Bayesian Models of Lexical Acquisition*. Ph.D. thesis, Brown University.

Sharon Goldwater, Thomas L. Griffiths, and Mark Johnson. 2006. Contextual Dependencies in Unsupervised Word Segmentation. In *Proceedings of the 21st International Conference on Computational Linguistics and 44th Annual Meeting of the Association for Computational Linguistics*, pages 673–680, Sydney, Australia. Association for Computational Linguistics.

Sharon Goldwater, Thomas L. Griffiths, and Mark Johnson. 2009. A Bayesian framework for word segmentation: Exploring the effects of context. *Cognition*, 112(1):21–54.

Fatima Hamlaoui and Emmanuel-Moselly Makasso. 2015. Focus marking and the unavailability of inversion structures in the Bantu language Bàsàá. *Lingua*, 154:35–64.

Robert K. Herbert. 1986. *Language Universals, Markedness Theory, and Natural Phonetic Processes*. De Gruyter Mouton, Berlin, Boston.

Tore Janson. 2003. *Speak: A Short History of Languages*. Oxford University Press.

Mark Johnson. 1998. PCFG models of linguistic tree representations. *Comput. Linguist.*, 24(4):613–632.

Mark Johnson. 2008a. Unsupervised Word Segmentation for Sesotho Using Adaptor Grammars. In *Proceedings of the Tenth Meeting of ACL Special Interest Group on Computational Morphology and Phonology*, pages 20–27, Columbus, Ohio. Association for Computational Linguistics.

Mark Johnson. 2008b. Using Adaptor Grammars to Identify Synergies in the Unsupervised Acquisition of Linguistic Structure. In *Proceedings of ACL-08: HLT*, pages 398–406, Columbus, Ohio. Association for Computational Linguistics.

Mark Johnson, Anne Christophe, Emmanuel Dupoux, and Katherine Demuth. 2014. Modelling function words improves unsupervised word segmentation. In *Proceedings of the 52nd Annual Meeting of the Association for Computational Linguistics (Volume 1: Long Papers)*, pages 282–292, Baltimore, Maryland. Association for Computational Linguistics.

Mark Johnson and Sharon Goldwater. 2009. Improving nonparameteric Bayesian inference: Experiments on unsupervised word segmentation with adaptor grammars. In *Proceedings of Human Language Technologies: The 2009 Annual Conference of the North American Chapter of the Association for Computational Linguistics*, pages 317–325, Boulder, Colorado. Association for Computational Linguistics.

Mark Johnson, Thomas L. Griffiths, and Sharon Goldwater. 2007. Adaptor Grammars: A Framework for Specifying Compositional Nonparametric Bayesian Models. In *Advances in Neural Information Processing Systems 19*, pages 641–648, Cambridge, MA. MIT Press.

Guy-Noël Kouarata. 2014. *Variations de formes dans la langue mbochi (Bantu C25)*. Ph.D. thesis, Université Lumière Lyon 2.

Kamran Lari and Steve J. Young. 1990. The estimation of stochastic context-free grammars using the inside-outside algorithm. *Computer Speech and Language*, 4:35–56.

David Odden. 2015. Bantu Phonology. *Oxford Handbooks Online*.

Timothy J. O'Donnell, Joshua B. Tenenbaum, and Noah D. Goodman. 2009. Fragment grammars: Exploring computation and reuse in language. Technical report, Massachusetts Institute of Technology.

Annie Rialland, Georges Martial Embanga Aborobongui, Martine Adda-Decker, and Lori Lamel. 2015. Dropping of the class-prefix consonant, vowel elision and automatic phonological mining in Embosi. In *Proceedings of the 44th ACAL meeting*, pages 221–230, Somerville. Cascadilla.

Kairit Sirts and Sharon Goldwater. 2013. Minimally-supervised morphological segmentation using adaptor grammars. *Transactions of the Association for Computational Linguistics*, 1:255–266.

# String Transduction with Target Language Models and Insertion Handling


**Garrett Nicolai**[†]  and  **Saeed Najafi**[‡]  and  **Grzegorz Kondrak**[‡]

[†]Department of Computer Science
Johns Hopkins University
gnicola2@jhu.edu

[‡]Department of Computing Science
University of Alberta
{snajafi, gkondrak}@ualberta.ca



## Abstract

Many character-level tasks can be framed as sequence-to-sequence transduction, where the target is a word from a natural language. We show that leveraging target language models derived from unannotated target corpora, combined with a precise alignment of the training data, yields state-of-the art results on cognate projection, inflection generation, and phoneme-to-grapheme conversion.


## 1 Introduction

Many natural language tasks, particularly those involving character-level operations, can be viewed as sequence-to-sequence transduction (Figure 1). Although these tasks are often addressed in isolation, they share a common objective — in each case, the output is a word in the target language.

The hypothesis that we investigate in this paper is that a single task- and language-independent system can achieve state-of-the-art results by leveraging unannotated target language corpora that contain thousands of valid target word types. We focus on low-data scenarios, which present a challenge to neural sequence-to-sequence models because sufficiently large parallel datasets are often difficult to obtain. To reinforce transduction models trained on modest-sized collections of source-target pairs, we leverage monolingual text corpora that are freely available for hundreds of languages.

Our approach is based on discriminative string transduction, where a learning algorithm assigns weights to features defined on aligned source and target pairs. At test time, an input sequence is converted into the highest-scoring output sequence. Advantages of discriminative transduction include an aptitude to derive effective models from small training sets, as wells as the capability to incorporate diverse sets of features. Specifically, we build

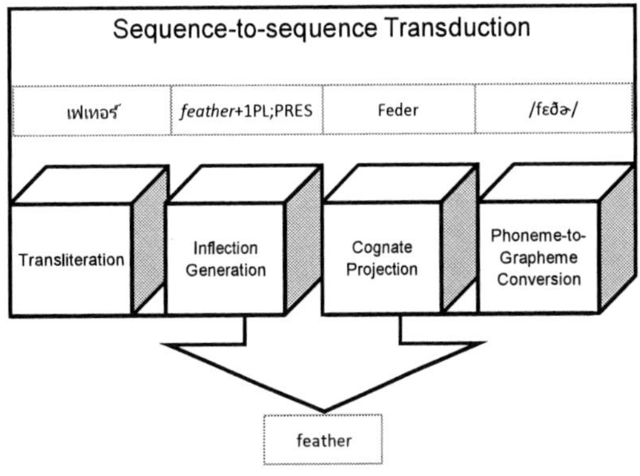



Figure 1: Illustration of four character-level sequence-to-sequence prediction tasks. In each case, the output is a word in the target language.

upon DIRECTL+ (Jiampojamarn et al., 2010), a string transduction tool which was originally designed for grapheme-to-phoneme conversion.

We present a new system, DTLM, that combines discriminative transduction with character and word language models (LMs) derived from large unannotated corpora. Target language modeling is particularly important in low-data scenarios, where the limited transduction models often produce many ill-formed output candidates. We avoid the error propagation problem which is inherent in pipeline approaches by incorporating the LM feature sets directly into the transducer.

In addition, we bolster the quality of transduction by employing a novel alignment method, which we refer to as *precision alignment*. The idea is to allow null substrings (*nulls*) on the source side during the alignment of the training data, and then apply a separate aggregation algorithm to merge them nulls with adjacent non-empty substrings. This method yields precise many-to-many alignment links that lead to improved transduction accuracy.




*Proceedings of the 15th SIGMORPHON Workshop on Computational Research in Phonetics, Phonology, and Morphology*, pages 43–53
Brussels, Belgium, October 31, 2018. ©2018 The Special Interest Group on Computational Morphology and Phonology
https://doi.org/10.18653/v1/P17

The contributions of this paper include the following. (1) A novel method of incorporating strong target language models directly into discriminative transduction. (2) A novel approach to unsupervised alignment that is particularly beneficial in low-resource settings. (3) An extensive experimental comparison to previous models on multiple tasks and languages, which includes state-of-the-art results on inflection generation, cognate projection, and phoneme-to-grapheme generation. (4) Publicly available implementation of the proposed methods. (5) Three new datasets for cognate projection.

## 2 Baseline methods

In this section, we describe the baseline methods, including the alignment of the training data, the feature sets of DirecTL+ (henceforth DTL), and reranking as a way of incorporating corpus statistics.

### 2.1 Alignment

Before a transduction model can be derived from the training data, the pairs of source and target strings need to be aligned, in order to identify atomic substring transformations. The unsupervised M2M aligner (Jiampojamarn et al., 2007) employs the Expectation-Maximization (EM) algorithm with the objective of maximizing the joint likelihood of its aligned source and target pairs. The alignment involves every source and target character. The pairs of aligned substrings may contain multiple characters on both the source and target sides, yielding *many-to-many* (M-M) alignment links.

DTL excludes insertions from its set of edit operations because they greatly increase the complexity of the generation process, to the point of making it computationally intractable (Barton, 1986). Therefore, the M2M aligner is forced to avoid nulls on the source side by incorporating them into many-to-many links during the alignment of the training data. Although many-to-many alignment models are more flexible than 1-1 models, they also generally require larger parallel datasets to produce correct alignments. In low-data scenarios, especially when the target strings tend to be longer than the source strings, this approach often yields sub-optimal alignments (e.g., the leftmost alignment in Figure 2).

Figure 2: Examples of different alignments in phoneme-to-letter conversion. The underscore denotes a null substring.

### 2.2 Features

DTL is a feature-rich, discriminative character transducer, which searches for a model-optimal sequence of character transformation operations for its input. The core of the engine is a dynamic programming algorithm capable of transducing many consecutive characters in a single operation, also known as a semi-Markov model. Using a structured version of the MIRA algorithm (McDonald et al., 2005), the training process assigns weights to each feature, in order to achieve maximum separation of the gold-standard output from all others in the search space.

DTL uses a number of feature templates to assess the quality of an operation: source context, target $n$-gram, and joint $n$-gram features. Context features conjoin the rule with indicators for all source character $n$-grams within a fixed window of where the rule is being applied. Target n-grams provide indicators on target character sequences, describing the shape of the target as it is being produced, and may also be conjoined with the source context features. Joint $n$-grams build indicators on rule sequences, combining source and target context, and memorizing frequently-used rule patterns. An additional copy feature generalizes the identity function from source to target, which is useful if there is an overlap between the input and output symbol sets.

### 2.3 Reranking

The target language modeling of DTL is limited to a set of binary $n$-gram features, which are based exclusively on the target sequences from the parallel training data. This shortcoming can be remedied by taking advantage of large unannotated corpora that contain thousands of examples of valid target words.

Nicolai et al. (2015) propose to leverage corpus statistics by reranking the $n$-best list of candidates generated by the transducer. They report consistent modest gains by applying an SVM-based reranker, with features including a word unigram corpus presence indicator, a normalized character language model score, and the rank and normalized confidence score generated by DTL. However, such a pipeline approach suffers from error propagation, and is unable to produce output forms that are not already present in the $n$-best list. In addition, training a reranker requires a held-out set that substantially reduces the amount of training data in low-data scenarios.

## 3  Methods

In this section, we describe our novel extensions: precision alignment, character-level target language modeling, and corpus frequency. We make the new implementation publicly available.[1]

### 3.1  Precision Alignment

We propose a novel alignment method that produces accurate many-to-many alignments in two stages. The first step consists of a standard 1-1 alignment, with nulls allowed on either side of the parallel training data. The second step removes the undesirable nulls on the source side by merging the corresponding 0-1 links with adjacent 1-1 links. This alignment approach is superior to the one described in Section 2.1, especially in low-data scenarios when there is not enough evidence for many-to-many links.[2]

Our precision alignment is essentially a 1-1 alignment with 1-M links added when necessary. In a low-resource setting, an aligner is often unable to distinguish valid M-M links from spurious ones, as both types will have minimal support in the training data. On the other hand, good 1-1 links are much more likely to have been observed. By limiting our first pass to 1-1 links, we ensure that only good 1-1 links are posited; otherwise, an insertion is predicted instead. On the second pass, the aligner only needs to choose between a small number of alternatives for merging the insertions, increasing the likelihood of a good alignment, and, subsequently, correct transduction.

Consider the example in Figure 2 where 5 source phonemes need to be aligned to 7 target letters. The baseline approach incorrectly links the

---

[1] http://github.com/GarrettNicolai/DTLM and /M2MP

[2] The improvement in the alignment quality is relative to the performance of our transduction system, as we demonstrate in Section 4.6 — the alignments are not necessarily optimal from the linguistic point of view.

---

1: **Algorithm:ForwardInsertionMerging**
2: **Input:** $(x^T, y^V)$
3: **Output:** $(\alpha^{T+1,V+1})$
4: $CI = 0, PI = 0$
5: **for** $t = 0; t \leq T$ **do**
6:    **if** $t > 0$ **and** $x_t == \_$ **then**
7:       $CI += 1$
8:    **else**
9:       $PI = CI$
10:       $CI = 0$
11:    **for** $v = 0; v \leq V$ **do**
12:       **if** $t - CI == 0$ **then**
13:          $\alpha_{t,v} = 1$
14:          $continue$ {insertions at the start of the word}
15:       **if** $t > 0$ **or** $v > 0$ **then**
16:          $\alpha_{t,v} = 0$
17:       **if** $t > 0$ **and** $v > 0$ **then**
18:          **for** $k = 0; k \leq PI$ **do**
19:             $\alpha_{t,v} += \delta(x^t_{t-CI-k}, y^v_{v-CI-k}) * \alpha_{t-CI-k-1, v-CI-k-1}$

Figure 3: The forward step of M2M, modified to merge insertions to adjacent characters.

letter 'a' with the phoneme /w/ (the leftmost alignment in the diagram). Our first-pass 1-1 alignment (in the middle), correctly matches /ɔ/ to 'a', while 'l' is treated as an insertion. On the second pass, our algorithm merges the null with the preceding 1-1 link. By contrast, the second insertion, which involves /ə/, is merged with the substitution that follows it (the rightmost alignment).

Figure 3 demonstrates how we modify the forward step to merge insertions with adjacent substituions; similar modifications are made for the backward step, expectation, and decoder. The input consists of a source string **x** of length $T$, and a target string **y** of length $V$. Both **x** and **y** may contain underscores, which represent nulls from the first alignment pass. The $\alpha$ score represents the sum of the likelihoods of all paths that have been traversed through source character $t$ and target character $v$. In a 1-1 alignment, all $\alpha$ scores accumulate along the diagonal, while in a many-to-many alignment, other cells of the $\alpha$ matrix may be filled. Our precision alignment is a compromise between these two methods: we consider adjacent characters, but force the $\alpha$ score to accumulate on the diagonal. By allowing insertions and deletions in the first pass, we force **x** and **y** to be of equal length. We then perform a 1-1 alignment, expanding the alignment size only when the source character is a null.

We supplement the forward algorithm of M2M with two counters: PI is the number of adjacent insertions immediately to the left of the current character, while CI is the number of insertions that have been encountered since the last substitution. The loop at line 18 executes the $\alpha$ score accumulation, where $\delta$ is the likelihood of a specific sequence alignment, effectively merging insertions with adjacent substitutions. An extended example that illustrates the operation of the algorithm is included in the Appendix.

## 3.2 Character-level language model

In order to incorporate a stronger character language model into DTL, we propose an additional set of features that directly reflect the probability of the generated subsequences. We train a character-level language model on a list of types extracted from a raw corpus in the target language, applying Witten-Bell smoothing and back-off for unseen $n$-grams. During the generation process, the transducer incrementally constructs target sequences character-by-character. The normalized log-likelihood score of the current output sequence is computed according to the character language model.

For consistency with other sets of features, we convert these real-valued scores into binary indicators by means of binning. Development experiments led to the creation of bins that represent a normal distribution around the mean likelihood of words. Features fire in a cumulative manner, and a final feature fires only if no bin threshold is met. For example, if a sequence has a log-likelihood of -0.85, the feature for -0.9 fires, as does the one for -0.975, and -1.05, etc.

## 3.3 Corpus frequency counts

We also extend DTL with a feature set that can be described as a unigram word-level language model. The objective is to bias the model towards generating output sequences that correspond to words observed in a large corpus. Since an output sequence can only be matched against a word list after the generation process is complete, we propose to estimate the final frequency count for each prefix considered during the generation process. Following Cherry and Suzuki (2009) we use a prefix trie to store partial words for reference in the generation phase. We modify their solution by also storing the count of each prefix, calculated as the sum of all of the words in which the prefix occurs.

As with our language model features, unigram features are binned. A unigram feature fires if the

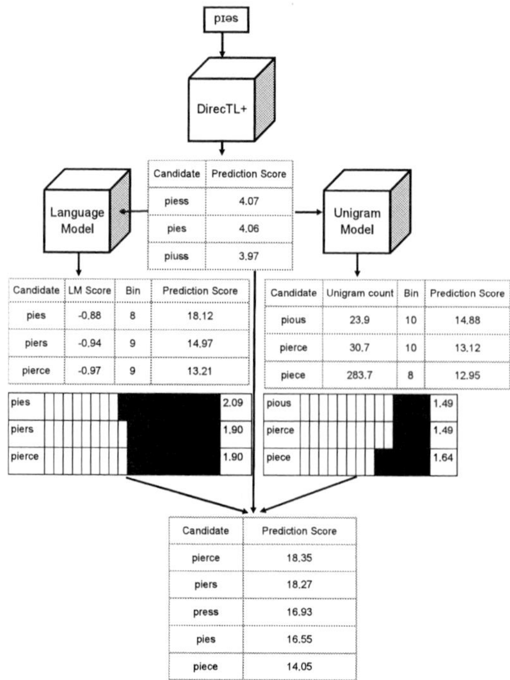


| Candidate | Prediction Score |
| --- | --- |
| piess | 4.07 |
| pies | 4.06 |
| piuss | 3.97 |

| Candidate | LM Score | Bin | Prediction Score |
| --- | --- | --- | --- |
| pies | -0.88 | 8 | 18.12 |
| piers | -0.94 | 9 | 14.97 |
| pierce | -0.97 | 9 | 13.21 |

| Candidate | Unigram count | Bin | Prediction Score |
| --- | --- | --- | --- |
| pious | 23.9 | 10 | 14.88 |
| pierce | 30.7 | 10 | 13.12 |
| piece | 283.7 | 8 | 12.95 |

| Candidate | | Score |
| --- | --- | --- |
| pies | | 2.09 |
| piers | | 1.90 |
| pierce | | 1.90 |

| Candidate | | Score |
| --- | --- | --- |
| pious | | 1.49 |
| pierce | | 1.49 |
| piece | | 1.64 |

| Candidate | Prediction Score |
| --- | --- |
| pierce | 18.35 |
| piers | 18.27 |
| press | 16.93 |
| pies | 16.55 |
| piece | 14.05 |

Figure 4: An example of transduction with target language models. Black cells represent firing features.

count of the generated sequence surpasses the bin threshold, in a cumulative manner.

We found that the quality of the target unigram set can be greatly improved by language-based corpus pruning. Although unannotated corpora are more readily available than parallel ones, they are often noisier. Specifically, crowd-sourced corpora such as Wikipedia contain many English words that can unduly influence our unigram features. In order to mitigate this problem, we preprocess our corpora by removing all word unigrams that have a higher probability in an English corpus than in a target-language corpus.

Consider an example of how our new features benefit a transduction model, shown in Figure 4. Note that although we portray the extensions as part of a pipeline, their scores are incorporated jointly with DTL's other features. The top-$n$ list produced by the baseline DTL for the input phoneme sequence /pɪəs/ fails to include the correct output *pierce*. However, after the new language model features are added, the correct form makes its way to the top predictions. The new features combine with the original features of DTL, so that the high unigram count of *piece* is not sufficient to make it the top prediction on the right side of the diagram. Only when both sets of new features are incorporated does the system manage to produce the correct form, as seen at the bottom of the diagram.

## 4 Experiments

In this section, we present the results of our experiments on four different character-level sequence-to-sequence tasks: transliteration, inflection generation, cognate projection, and phoneme-to-grapheme conversion (P2G). In order to demonstrate the generality of our approach, the experiments involve multiple systems and datasets, in both low-data and high-data scenarios.

Where low-data resources do not already exist, we simulate a low-data environment by sampling an existing larger training set. Low-data training sets consist of 100 training examples, 1000 development examples, and 1000 held-out examples, except for cognate projection, where we limit the development set to 100 training examples, and the held-out set to the remaining examples. An output is considered correct if it exactly matches any of the targets in the reference data.

### 4.1 Systems

We evaluate DTLM, our new system, against two strong baselines and two competitive tools. Parameter tuning was performed on the same development sets for all systems.

We compare against two baselines. The first is the standard DTL, as described in Section 2.2. The second follows the methodology of Nicolai et al. (2015), augmenting DTL with a reranker (DTL+RR), as described in Section 2.3. Both baselines use the default 2-2 alignment with deletions produced by the M2M aligner. We train the reranker using 10-fold cross validation on the training set, using the reranking method of Joachims (2002). Due to the complexity of its setup on large datasets, we omit DTL+RR in such scenarios. Except where noted otherwise, we train 4-gram character language models using the CMU toolkit[3] with Witten-Bell smoothing on the Uni-Morph corpora of inflected word forms.[4] Word counts are determined from the first one million lines of the corresponding Wikipedia dumps.

We also compare against Sequitur (SEQ), a generative string transduction tool based on joint source and target $n$-grams (Bisani and Ney, 2008), and a character-level neural model (RNN). The neural model uses the encoder-decoder architecture typically used for NMT (Sutskever et al., 2014). The encoder is a bi-directional RNN applied to randomly initialized character embeddings; we employ a soft-attention mechanism to learn an aligner within the model. The RNN is trained for a fixed random seed using the Adam optimizer, embeddings of 128 dimensions, and hidden units of size 256. We use a beam of size 10 to generate the final predictions. We experimented with the alternative neural approach of Makarov et al. (2017), but found that it only outperforms our RNN when the source and target sides are largely composed of the same set of symbols; therefore, we only use it for inflection generation.

### 4.2 Transliteration

Transliteration is the task of converting a word from a source to a target script on the basis of the word's pronunciation.

Our low-resource data consists of three back-transliteration pairs from the 2018 NEWS Shared Task: Hebrew to English (HeEn), Thai to English (ThEn), and Persian to English (PeEn). These languages were chosen because they represent back-transliteration into English. Since the original forms were originally English, they are much more likely to appear in an English corpus than if the words originated in the source language. We report the results on the task's 1000-instance development sets.

Since transliteration is mostly used for named entities, our language model and unigram counts are obtained from a corpus of named entities. We query DBPedia[5] for a list of proper names, discarding names that contain non-English characters. The resulting list of 1M names is used to train the character language model and inform the word unigram features.

The results in Table 1 show that our proposed extensions have a dramatic impact on low-resource transliteration. In particular, the seamless incorporation of the target language model not only simplifies the model but also greatly improves the results with respect to the reranking approach. On the other hand, the RNN struggles to learn an adequate model with only 100 training examples.

---

[3] http://www.speech.cs.cmu.edu/SLM
[4] unimorph.org

[5] https://wiki.dbpedia.org

| System | HeEn | ThEn | PeEn |
|--------|------|------|------|
| DTL | 13.2 | 1.1 | 8.7 |
| DTL+RR | 19.0 | 2.7 | 13.6 |
| DTLM | **36.7** | **9.6** | **26.1** |
| RNN | 5.4 | 1.3 | 2.6 |
| SEQ | 7.8 | 4.4 | 8.5 |

Table 1: Word-level accuracy on transliteration (in %) with 100 training instances.

| System | HeEn | ThEn | PeEn |
|--------|------|------|------|
| DTL | 21.9 | 37.0 | 23.6 |
| DTLM | **38.7** | **48.0** | **36.8** |
| RNN | 25.8 | 43.8 | 26.7 |
| SEQ | 25.5 | 44.9 | 31.2 |

Table 2: Word-level accuracy on transliteration (in %) with complete training sets.

We also evaluate a larger-data scenario. Using the same three languages, we replace the 100 instance training sets with the official training sets from the 2018 shared task, which contain 9,447, 27,273, and 15,677 examples for HeEn, TnEn, and PeEn, respectively. The language model and frequency lists are the same as for the low-resource experiments. Table 2 shows that DTLM outperforms the other systems by a large margin thanks to its ability to leverage a target word list. Additional results are reported by Najafi et al. (2018b).

### 4.3 Inflection generation

Inflection generation is the task of producing an inflected word-form, given a citation form and a set of morphological features. For example, given the Spanish infinitive `liberar`, with the tag `V;IND;FUT;2;SG`, the word-form *liberarás* should be produced.

In recent years, inflection generation has attracted much interest (Dreyer and Eisner, 2011; Durrett and DeNero, 2013; Nicolai et al., 2015; Ahlberg et al., 2015). Aharoni and Goldberg (2017) propose an RNN augmented with hard attention and explicit alignments for inflection, but have difficulty consistently improving upon the results of DTL, even on larger datasets. Furthermore, their system cannot be applied to tasks where the source and target are different languages, due to shared embeddings between the encoder and decoder. Ruzsics and Samardzic (2017) incorporate a language model into the decoder of

| System | Average |
|--------|---------|
| DTL | 40.7 |
| DTLM | **49.0** |
| CLUZH | 40.9 |

Table 3: Word-level accuracy (in %) on inflection generation with 100 training instances.

a canonical segmentation system. Our model differs in that we learn the influence of the language model during training, in conjunction with DTL's other features. Deutsch et al. (2018) place a hard constraint on the decoder, so that it only produces observed derivational forms. We instead implement a soft constraint, encouraging candidates that look like real words, but allowing the model to generalize to unseen forms.

Our inflection data comes from the 2017 CoNLL–SIGMORPHON Shared Task on Reinflection (Cotterell et al., 2017). We use the datasets from the low-resource setting of the inflection generation sub-task, in which the training sets are composed of 100 source lemmas with inflection tags and the corresponding inflected forms. We supplement the training data with 100 synthetic "copy" instances that simply transform the target string into itself. This modification, which is known to help in transduction tasks where the source and target are nearly identical, is used for the inflection generation experiments only. Along with the training sets from the shared task, we also use the task's development and test sets, each consisting of 1000 instances.

Since Sequitur is ill-suited for this type of transduction, we instead train a model using the method of the CLUZH team (Makarov et al., 2017), a state-of-the-art neural system that was the winner of the 2017 shared task. Their primary submission in the shared task was an ensemble of 20 individual systems. For our experiments, we selected their best individual system, as reported in their system paper. For each language, we train models with 3 separate seeds, and select the model that achieves the highest accuracy on the development set.

Table 3 shows that DTLM improves upon CLUZH by a significant margin. The Appendix contains the detailed results for individual languages. DTLM outperforms CLUZH on 46 of the 52 languages. Even for languages with large morphological inventories, such as Basque and Polish, with the sparse corpora that such inventories supply, we see notable gains over DTL. We also see large gains for languages such as Northern Sami and Navajo that have relatively small Wikipedias (fewer than 10,000 articles).

DTLM was also evaluated as a non-standard submission in the low-data track of the 2018 Shared Task on Universal Morphological Inflection (Cotterell et al., 2018). The results reported by Najafi et al. (2018a) confirm that DTLM substantially outperforms DTL on average. Furthermore, a linear combination of DTLM and a neural system achieved the highest accuracy among all submissions on 34 out of 103 tested languages.

### 4.4 Cognate projection

Cognate projection, also referred to as cognate production, is the task of predicting the spelling of a hypothetical cognate in another language. For example, given the English word *difficulty*, the Spanish word *dificultad* should be produced. Previously proposed cognate projection systems have been based on SVM taggers (Mulloni, 2007), character-level SMT models (Beinborn et al., 2013), and sequence labeling combined with a maximum-entropy reranker (Ciobanu, 2016).

In this section, we evaluate DTLM in both low- and high-resource settings. Our low-resource data consists of three diverse language pairs. The first set corresponds to a mother-daughter historical relationship between reconstructed Vulgar Latin and Italian (VL-IT) and contains 601 word pairs manually compiled from the textbook of Boyd-Bowman (1980). English and German (EN-DE), close siblings from the Germanic family, are represented by 1013 pairs extracted from Wiktionary. From the same source, we also obtain 438 Slavic word pairs from Russian and Polish (RU-PL), which are written in different scripts (Cyrillic vs. Latin). We make the new datasets publicly available.[6]

The results are shown in Table 4. Of the systems that have no recourse to corpus statistics, the RNN appears crippled by the small training size, while SEQ is competitive with DTL, especially on the difficult EN-DE dataset. On the other hand, the other two systems obtain substantial improvements over DTL, but the gains obtained by DTLM are 2-3 times greater than those obtained by DTL+RR. This demonstrates the advantage of incorporating the language model features directly

---

6http://github.com/GarrettNicolai/CognateData

| System | EN-DE | RU-PL | VL-IT |
|--------|-------|-------|-------|
| DTL | 4.3 | 23.5 | 39.2 |
| DTL+RR | 7.1 | 32.8 | 43.6 |
| DTLM | **17.7** | **43.9** | **52.5** |
| RNN | 2.2 | 1.7 | 15.7 |
| SEQ | 9.2 | 22.3 | 36.9 |

Table 4: Word-level accuracy (in %) on cognate projection with 100 training instances.

| System | EN-ES | EN-DE | EN-RU |
|--------|-------|-------|-------|
| BZG-13 | 45.7 | 17.2 | 8.3 |
| DTL | 30.3 | 24.3 | 13.3 |
| DTLM | **56.8** | **33.5** | **45.9** |
| RNN | 34.3 | 20.5 | 15.0 |

Table 5: Word-level accuracy (in %) on large-scale cognate projection.

into the training phase over simple reranking.

Our high-resource data comes from a previous study of Beinborn et al. (2013). The datasets were created by applying romanization scripts and string similarity filters to translation pairs extracted from Bing. We find that the datasets are noisy, consisting mostly of lexical loans from Latin, Greek, and English, and include many compound words that share only a single morpheme (i.e., *informatics* and *informationswissenschaft*). In order to alleviate the noise, we found it beneficial to disregard all training pairs that could not be aligned by M2M under the default 2-2 link setting.

Another problem in the data is the overlap between the training and test sets, which ranges from 40% in EN-ES to 94% in EN-EL. Since we believe it would be inappropriate to report results on contaminated sets, we decided to ignore all test instances that occur in the training data. (Unfortunately, this makes some of the test sets too small for a meaningful evaluation.) The resulting dataset sizes are included in the Appendix. Along with the datasets, Beinborn et al. (2013) provide the predictions made by their system. We re-calculate the accuracy of their predictions (BZG-13), discarding any forms that were present in the training set, and compare against DTL and DTLM, as well as the RNN.

Table 5 shows striking gains. While DTL and the RNN generally improve upon BZG-13, DTLM vastly outstrips either alternative. On EN-RU,

DTLM correctly produces nearly half of potential cognates, 3 times more than any of the other systems. We conclude that our results constitute a new state of the art for cognate projection.

### 4.5 Phoneme-to-grapheme conversion

Phoneme-to-grapheme (P2G) conversion is the task of predicting the spelling of a word from a sequence of phonemes that represent its pronunciation (Rentzepopoulos and Kokkinakis, 1996). For example, a P2G system should convert [t r ae n z d ah k sh ah n] into *transduction*. Unlike the opposite task of grapheme-to-phoneme (G2P) conversion, large target corpora are widely available. To the best of our knowledge, the state of the art on P2G is the joint $n$-gram approach of Bisani and Ney (2008), who report improvements on the results of Galescu and Allen (2002) on the NetTalk and CMUDict datasets.

Our low-resource dataset consists of three languages: English (EN), Dutch (NL), and German (DE), extracted from the CELEX lexical database (Baayen et al., 1995).

Table 6 shows that our modifications yield substantial gains for all three languages, with consistent error reductions of 15-20% over the reranking approach. Despite only training on 100 words, the system is able to convert phonetic transcriptions into completely correct spellings for a large fraction of words, even in English, which is notorious for its idiosyncratic orthography. Once again, the RNN is hampered by the small training size.

We also evaluate DTLM in a large-data scenario. We attempt to replicate the P2G experiments reported by (Bisani and Ney, 2008). The data comes from three lexicons on which we conduct 10-fold cross validation: English NetTalk (Sejnowski and Rosenberg, 1993), French Brulex (Mousty and Radeau, 1990), and English CMUDict (Weide, 2005). These corpora contain 20,008, 24,726, and 113,438 words, respectively, in both orthographic and phonetic notations. We note that CMUDict differs from the other two lexicons in that it is much larger, and contains predominantly names, as well as alternative pronunciations. When the training data is that abundant, there is less to be gained from improving the alignment or the target language models, as they are already adequate in the baseline approach.

Table 7 shows the comparison of the results. The P2G results obtained by Sequitur in our exper-

| System | EN | NL | DE |
|--------|------|------|------|
| DTL | 13.9 | 30.6 | 33.5 |
| DTL+RR | 25.3 | 32.6 | 51.5 |
| DTLM | **39.6** | **43.7** | **60.5** |
| RNN | 2.7 | 6.6 | 14.1 |
| SEQ | 15.9 | 30.5 | 28.6 |

Table 6: Word-level accuracy (in %) on phoneme-to-grapheme conversion with 100 training instances.

| | NetTalk | Brulex | CMU |
|------|------|------|------|
| DTL | 61.0 | 68.0 | 48.3 |
| DTLM | **75.2** | **76.8** | **49.0** |
| RNN | 55.8 | 67.1 | 48.0 |
| SEQ | 62.7 | 71.5 | 48.6 |

Table 7: Word-level accuracy (in %) on phoneme-to-grapheme conversion with large training sets.

iments are slightly lower than those reported in the original paper, which is attributable to differences in data splits, tuned hyper-parameters, and/or the presence of stress markers in the data. Sequitur still outperforms the baseline DTL, but DTLM substantially outperforms both Sequitur and the RNN on both the NetTalk and Brulex datasets, with smaller gains on the much larger CMUDict. We conclude that our results advance the state of the art on phoneme-to-grapheme conversion.

### 4.6 Ablation

Table 8 shows the results of disabling individual components in the low-resource setting of the P2G task. The top row reproduces the full DTLM system results reported in Table 6. The remaining three show the results without the character-level LM, word unigram, and precision alignment, respectively. We observe that the accuracy substantially decreases in almost every case, which demonstrates the contribution of all three components.

In a separate experiment on the English G2P dataset, we investigate the impact of the alignment quality by applying several different alignment approaches to the training sets. When M2M aligner uses unconstrained alignment, it favors long alignments that are too sparse to learn a transduction model, achieving less than 1% accuracy. Kubo et al. (2011)'s MPALIGNER, which employs a length penalty to discourage such overlong substring matches, improves moderately, achiev-

| System | EN | NL | DE |
|---|---|---|---|
| DTLM | **39.6** | **43.7** | **60.5** |
| -Language model | 37.8 | 38.2 | 48.5 |
| -Freq | 22.0 | 37.1 | 56.7 |
| -Precision | 34.9 | 43.7 | 46.7 |

Table 8: Ablation test on P2G data with 100 training instances.

ing 27.5% accuracy, while constraining M2M to 2-2 improves further, to 34.9%. The accuracy increases to 39.6% when the precision alignment is employed. We conclude that in the low-resource setting, our proposed precision alignment is preferable to both MPALIGNER and the standard M2M alignment.

### 4.7 Error Analysis

The following error examples from three different tasks demonstrate the advantages of incorporating the character-level LM, word frequency, and precision alignment, respectively. For the purpose of insightful analysis, we selected test instances for which DTLM produces markedly better output than DTL.

In inflection generation, the second person plural form of *knechten* is correctly predicted as *knechtetet*, instead of *knechttet*. In this case, our character language model derived from a large text corpus rightly assigns very low probability to the unlikely 4-gram sequence `chtt`, which violates German phonotactic constraints.

In the phoneme-to-grapheme conversion task, [tɪlɛmətri] is transduced to *telemetry*, instead of *tilemetry*. In English, a reduced vowel phoneme such as [ɪ] may correspond to any vowel letter. In this example, DTLM is able to successfully leverage the occurrence of the correct word-form in a raw corpus.

In cognate projection, the actual cognate of *Kenyan* is *kenianisch*, rather than *kenyisch*. This prediction can be traced to the alignment of the adjectival suffix *-an* to *-anisch* in the training data. The match, which involves a target substring of considerable length, is achieved through a merger of multiple insertion operations.

The errors made by DTLM fall into a few different categories. Occasionally, DTLM produces an incorrect form that is more frequent in the corpus. For example, DTLM incorrectly guesses a subjunctive form of the verb *versetzen* to be the high-

frequency *versetzt*, rather than the unseen *versetzet*. More important, the transducer is incapable of generalizing beyond source-target pairs seen in training. For example, consider the doubling of consonants in English orthography (e.g. *betting*). Unlike the RNN, DTLM incorrectly predicts the present participle of *rug* as **ruging*, because there is no instance of the doubling of 'g' in the training data.

## 5 Conclusion

We have presented DTLM: a powerful language- and task-independent transduction system that can leverage raw target corpora. DTLM is particularly effective in low-resource settings, but is also successful when larger training sets are available. The results of our experiments on four varied transduction tasks show large gains over alternative approaches.

## Acknowledgments

The first author was supported in part by the Defense Advanced Research Projects Agency's (DARPA) Low Resource Emergent Incidents (LORELEI) program, under contract No. HR0011-15-C0113. Any opinions and conclusions expressed in this material are those of the authors, and do not necessarily reflect the views of the Defense Advanced Research Projects Agency (DARPA).

The second and third authors were supported by the Natural Sciences and Engineering Research Council of Canada (NSERC).

We thank the members of the University of Alberta teams who collaborated with us in the context of the 2018 shared tasks on transliteration and morphological reinflection: Bradley Hauer, Rashed Rubby Riyadh, and Leyuan Yu.

## References

Roee Aharoni and Yoav Goldberg. 2017. Morphological inflection generation with hard monotonic attention. In *Proceedings of the 55th Annual Meeting of the Association for Computational Linguistics (Volume 1: Long Papers)*, pages 2004–2015, Vancouver, Canada. Association for Computational Linguistics.

Malin Ahlberg, Markus Forsberg, and Mans Hulden. 2015. Paradigm classification in supervised learning of morphology. In *Proceedings of the 2015 Conference of the North American Chapter of the Association for Computational Linguistics: Human Lan-*

*guage Technologies*, pages 1024–1029. Association for Computational Linguistics.

Harald R. Baayen, Richard Piepenbrock, and Leon Gulikers. 1995. *The CELEX Lexical Database. Release 2 (CD-ROM)*. Linguistic Data Consortium, University of Pennsylvania, Philadelphia, Pennsylvania.

G. Edward Barton. 1986. Computational complexity in two-level morphology. In *Proceedings of the 24th Annual Meeting of the Association for Computational Linguistics*, pages 53–59, New York, New York, USA. Association for Computational Linguistics.

Lisa Beinborn, Torsten Zesch, and Iryna Gurevych. 2013. Cognate production using character-based machine translation. In *Proceedings of the Sixth International Joint Conference on Natural Language Processing*, pages 883–891, Nagoya, Japan. Asian Federation of Natural Language Processing.

Maximilian Bisani and Hermann Ney. 2008. Joint-sequence models for grapheme-to-phoneme conversion. *Speech communication*, 50(5):434–451.

Peter Boyd-Bowman. 1980. *From Latin to Romance in sound charts*. Georgetown University Press.

Colin Cherry and Hisami Suzuki. 2009. Discriminative substring decoding for transliteration. In *Proceedings of the 2009 Conference on Empirical Methods in Natural Language Processing*, pages 1066–1075. Association for Computational Linguistics.

Alina Maria Ciobanu. 2016. Sequence labeling for cognate production. In *Knowledge-Based and Intelligent Information and Engineering Systems: Proceedings of the 20th International Conference KES-2016*, pages 1391–1399.

Ryan Cotterell, Christo Kirov, John Sylak-Glassman, Géraldine Walther, Ekaterina Vylomova, Arya D. McCarthy, Katharina Kann, Sebastian Mielke, Garrett Nicolai, Miikka Silfverberg, David Yarowsky, Jason Eisner, and Mans Hulden. 2018. The CoNLL–SIGMORPHON 2018 shared task: Universal morphological reinflection. In *Proceedings of the CoNLL–SIGMORPHON 2018 Shared Task: Universal Morphological Reinflection*, Brussels, Belgium. Association for Computational Linguistics.

Ryan Cotterell, Christo Kirov, John Sylak-Glassman, Géraldine Walther, Ekaterina Vylomova, Patrick Xia, Manaal Faruqui, Sandra Kübler, David Yarowsky, Jason Eisner, and Mans Hulden. 2017. CoNLL–SIGMORPHON 2017 shared task: Universal morphological reinflection in 52 languages. In *Proceedings of the CoNLL–SIGMORPHON 2017 Shared Task: Universal Morphological Reinflection*, pages 1–30, Vancouver. Association for Computational Linguistics.

Daniel Deutsch, John Hewitt, and Dan Roth. 2018. A distributional and orthographic aggregation model for english derivational morphology. In *Proceedings of the 56th Annual Meeting of the Association for Computational Linguistics (Volume 1: Long Papers)*, pages 1938–1947. Association for Computational Linguistics.

Markus Dreyer and Jason Eisner. 2011. Discovering morphological paradigms from plain text using a Dirichlet process mixture model. In *Proceedings of the Conference on Empirical Methods in Natural Language Processing*, pages 616–627. Association for Computational Linguistics.

Greg Durrett and John DeNero. 2013. Supervised learning of complete morphological paradigms. In *HLT-NAACL*, pages 1185–1195.

Lucian Galescu and James F. Allen. 2002. Pronunciation of proper names with a joint n-gram model for bi-directional grapheme-to-phoneme conversion. In *Seventh International Conference on Spoken Language Processing*.

Sittichai Jiampojamarn, Colin Cherry, and Grzegorz Kondrak. 2010. Integrating joint n-gram features into a discriminative training network. In *NAACL-HLT*, pages 697–700, Los Angeles, CA. Association for Computational Linguistics.

Sittichai Jiampojamarn, Grzegorz Kondrak, and Tarek Sherif. 2007. Applying many-to-many alignments and hidden markov models to letter-to-phoneme conversion. In *Human Language Technologies 2007: The Conference of the North American Chapter of the Association for Computational Linguistics; Proceedings of the Main Conference*, pages 372–379. Association for Computational Linguistics.

Thorsten Joachims. 2002. Optimizing search engines using clickthrough data. In *Proceedings of the eighth ACM SIGKDD international conference on Knowledge discovery and data mining*, pages 133–142. ACM.

Keigo Kubo, Hiromichi Kawanami, Hiroshi Saruwatari, and Kiyohiro Shikano. 2011. Unconstraned many-to-many alignment for automatic pronunciation annotation. In *Proceedings of the Asia-Pacific Signal and Information Processing Association Annual Summit and Conference*.

Peter Makarov, Tatiana Ruzsics, and Simon Clematide. 2017. Align and copy: UZH at SIGMORPHON 2017 shared task for morphological reinflection. *arXiv preprint arXiv:1707.01355*.

Ryan McDonald, Koby Crammer, and Fernando Pereira. 2005. Online large-margin training of dependency parsers. In *ACL*.

Philippe Mousty and Monique Radeau. 1990. Brulex. Une base de données lexicales informatisée pour le français écrit et parlé. *L'année Psychologique*, 90(4):551–566.

Andrea Mulloni. 2007. Automatic prediction of cognate orthography using support vector machines. In *Proceedings of the ACL 2007 Student Research Workshop*, pages 25–30, Prague, Czech Republic. Association for Computational Linguistics.

Saeed Najafi, Bradley Hauer, Rashed Rubby Riyadh, Leyuan Yu, and Grzegorz Kondrak. 2018a. Combining neural and non-neural methods for low-resource morphological reinflection. In *Proceedings of the CoNLL–SIGMORPHON 2018 Shared Task: Universal Morphological Reinflection*, Brussels, Belgium. Association for Computational Linguistics.

Saeed Najafi, Bradley Hauer, Rashed Rubby Riyadh, Leyuan Yu, and Grzegorz Kondrak. 2018b. Comparison of assorted models for transliteration. In *Proceedings of the Seventh Named Entities Workshop*, pages 84–88. Association for Computational Linguistics.

Garrett Nicolai, Colin Cherry, and Grzegorz Kondrak. 2015. Inflection generation as discriminative string transduction. In *Proceedings of the 2015 Conference of the North American Chapter of the Association for Computational Linguistics: Human Language Technologies*, pages 922–931. Association for Computational Linguistics.

Panagiotis A. Rentzepopoulos and George K. Kokkinakis. 1996. Efficient multilingual phoneme-to-grapheme conversion based on HMM. *Computational Linguistics*, 22(3):351–375.

Tatyana Ruzsics and Tanja Samardzic. 2017. Neural sequence-to-sequence learning of internal word structure. In *Proceedings of the 21st Conference on Computational Natural Language Learning (CoNLL 2017)*, pages 184–194, Vancouver, Canada. Association for Computational Linguistics.

TJ Sejnowski and CR Rosenberg. 1993. NETtalk corpus. *URL< ftp://svrftp. eng. cam. ac. uk/pub/comp. speech/dictionaries.*

Ilya Sutskever, Oriol Vinyals, and Quoc V Le. 2014. Sequence to sequence learning with neural networks. In *Advances in neural information processing systems*, pages 3104–3112.

Robert Weide. 2005. The Carnegie Mellon pronouncing dictionary [cmudict. 0.6].

# Complementary Strategies for Low Resourced Morphological Modeling

**Alexander Erdmann and Nizar Habash**
Computational Approaches to Modeling Language Lab
New York University Abu Dhabi
United Arab Emirates
{ae1541,nizar.habash}@nyu.edu

## Abstract

Morphologically rich languages are challenging for natural language processing tasks due to data sparsity. This can be addressed either by introducing out-of-context morphological knowledge, or by developing machine learning architectures that specifically target data sparsity and/or morphological information. We find these approaches to complement each other in a morphological paradigm modeling task in Modern Standard Arabic, which, in addition to being morphologically complex, features ubiquitous ambiguity, exacerbating sparsity with noise. Given a small number of out-of-context rules describing closed class morphology, we combine them with word embeddings leveraging subword strings and noise reduction techniques. The combination outperforms both approaches individually by about 20% absolute. While morphological resources already exist for Modern Standard Arabic, our results inform how comparable resources might be constructed for non-standard dialects or any morphologically rich, low resourced language, given scarcity of time and funding.

## 1 Introduction

Morphologically rich languages pose many challenges for natural language processing tasks. This often takes the shape of data sparsity, as the increase in the number of possible inflections for any given core concept leads to a lower average word frequency of individual (i.e., unique) word types. Hence, models have fewer chances to learn about types based on their in-context behavior. One common, albeit time consuming response to this challenge is to introduce out-of-context morphological knowledge, hand crafting rules to relate forms inflected from the same lemma. The other common response is to adopt machine learning architectures specifically targeting data sparsity and/or morphological informa-

tion. We find these two responses to be complementary in a paradigm modeling task for Modern Standard Arabic (MSA).

MSA is characterized by morphological richness and extreme orthographic ambiguity, compounding the issue of data sparsity with noise (Habash, 2010). Despite its challenges, MSA is relatively well resourced, with many solutions for morphological analysis and disambiguation leveraging large amounts of annotated data, hand crafted rules, and/or sophisticated neural architectures (Khoja and Garside, 1999; Habash and Rambow, 2006; Smrž, 2007; Graff et al., 2009; Pasha et al., 2014; Abdelali et al., 2016; Inoue et al., 2017; Zalmout and Habash, 2017). Such resources and techniques, however, are not available or not viable for the many under resourced and often mutually unintelligible dialects of Arabic (DA), which are similarly morphologically rich and highly ambiguous (Chiang et al., 2006; Erdmann et al., 2017). Many recent efforts seek to develop morphological resources for DA, but most are under developed or specific to one dialect (Habash et al., 2012; Eskander et al., 2013; Jarrar et al., 2014; Al-Shargi et al., 2016; Eskander et al., 2016a; Khalifa et al., 2016, 2017; Zribi et al., 2017; Zalmout et al., 2018; Khalifa et al., 2018).

This work does not aim to develop a full morphological analysis and disambiguation resource, but to inform how one might be most efficiently developed for any DA variety or similarly low resourced language, given scarcity of time and funding. For such a resource to be practical and easily extendable to new DA varieties, it must take as input the natural, highly ambiguous orthography. Thus, we do not rely on constructed phonological representations to clarify ambiguities, as is common practice when modeling morphology for its own sake (Cotterell et al., 2016, 2017). To in-

54

*Proceedings of the 15th SIGMORPHON Workshop on Computational Research in Phonetics, Phonology, and Morphology*, pages 54–65
Brussels, Belgium, October 31, 2018. ©2018 The Special Interest Group on Computational Morphology and Phonology
https://doi.org/10.18653/v1/P17

form how such a resource should be developed, we evaluate minimally rule based and unsupervised techniques for clustering words that belong to the same paradigm in MSA. We primarily use pre-existing MSA resources only for evaluation, constraining resource availability to emulate DA settings during training, as we lack the resources to evaluate our techniques in DA. Our best system combines a minimal set of rules describing closed class morphology with word embeddings that leverage subword strings and noise reduction strategies. The former, despite being cheaper and easier to produce than other rule-based systems, provides valuable out-of-context morphological knowledge, which the latter complements by modeling the in-context behavior of words and morphemes. Combining the techniques outperforms either individually by about 20% absolute.

## 2 Morphology and Ambiguity

Arabic morphology is structurally and functionally complex. Structurally, paradigms are relatively large. Component cells convey morphosyntactic properties at a much finer granularity than English. Functionally, many morphological processes are non-concatenative, or *templatic*. Arabic roots are lists of de-lexicalized radicals, which must be mapped onto a template to derive a word. The derived word will then exhibit some predictable semantic and morpho-syntactic relationship to the root, based on its template. For example, the root د د ر *r d d*,[1] having to do with *responding*, could take a singular nominal template where geminates are collapsed, becoming رد *rd*, 'response', or a so-called *broken plural* template, separating the geminate with a long vowel to become ردود *rdwd*, 'responses'. Arabic orthography complicates the issue further, as diacritics marking short vowels, gemination, and case endings are typically not written. In addition to causing frequent lexical ambiguity among forms that are pronounced differently, this also causes templatic processes to appear to be concatenative or completely disappear. For example, deriving 'to cool' برد *brd* (*fully diacritized,* بَرَّد *bar~ad*) from 'coldness' برد *brd* (*fully diacritized,* بَرد *bar.d*) involves doubling the second root letter and adding a short vowel before the third, yet these templatic changes usually disappear in the orthography.

Most templatic processes are derivational, deriving new core meanings with separate paradigms from a shared root. Inflectional processes generally concatenate affixes to a shared stem to realize different cells in the same paradigm. Broken plurals however, like ردود *rdwd*, are a notable exception, resulting from a templatic inflectional process. Approximately 55% of all plurals are broken (Alkuhlani and Habash, 2011).

Arabic is further characterized by frequent cliticization of prepositions, conjunctions, and object pronouns. Thus, a single syntactic word can take many cliticized forms, potentially becoming homonymous with inflections of unrelated lemmas or distinct cells in the same paradigm. The برد *brd*, 'response'–'coldness' ambiguity exemplifies this. The 'response' meaning interprets ب *b* as a cliticized preposition meaning 'with', while the 'coldness' meaning interprets ب *b* as the first root radical. To investigate how these morphological traits affect our ability to model paradigms, we define the following morphological structures.

**Paradigm** All words that share a certain lemma comprise a paradigm, e.g., in Figure 1, the paradigm of verbal lemma رَدّ *rad~*, 'to respond', contains the four words connected to it by a solid line. Ambiguity within the paradigm is referred to as *syncretism*, and is very common in Arabic. For example, the present tense second person masculine singular form is syncretic with the third person feminine singular in verbs, as shown by ترد *trd*, 'you[masc.sing]/she respond(s)'. Additionally, orthography normalizes short vowel distinctions between past tense second person masculine, second person feminine, and first person forms (and sometimes third person feminine), thus causing رَدَدتَ *radadta*, رَدَدتِ *radadti*, and رَدَدتُ *radadtu*, respectively, to be orthographically syncretic. Cliticized forms can also cause unique syncretisms, e.g., بردنا *brdnA* has two possible interpretations from the same lemma بَرَّد *bar~ad*, 'to cool'. If the final suffix نا *nA* is interpreted as a past tense verbal exponent, it means 'we cooled', whereas if it is interpreted as a cliticized personal pronoun, it becomes 'he/it cooled us'.

**Subparadigm** At or below the paradigm level, subparadigms are comprised of all words that share the same *lemma ambiguity*. Lemma ambiguity refers to the set of all lemmas a word could have been derived from out of context. Hence, برد

---

[1] Arabic transliteration is presented in the Habash-Soudi-Buckwalter scheme (Habash et al., 2007).

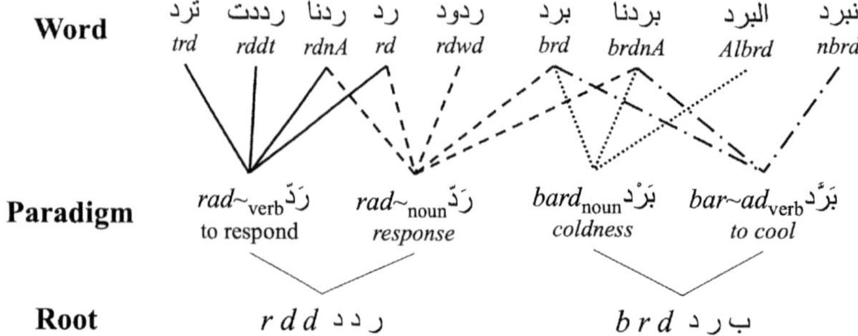

Figure 1: A clan of two families with two paradigms each, connected by both derivational and coincidental ambiguities. Line dotting style is only used to visually distinguish paradigm membership.

*brd* and بردنا *brdnA* form a subparadigm, being the only words in Figure 1 which can all be derived exclusively from lemmas, رَدّ *rad~*, 'response', بَرد *bard*, 'coldness', and بَرَّد *bar~ad*, 'to cool'.

**Family**  At or above the paradigm level, a family is comprised of all paradigms which can be linked via *derivational ambiguity*, such that all paradigms are derived from the same root. Thus, all forms mapping to the two paradigms which in turn map to the root ب ر د *b r d*, relating to *cold*, constitute a single family. The subparadigm of برد *brd* and بردنا *brdnA* link the two component paradigms via derivational ambiguity.[2]

**Clan**  At or above the family level, a clan is comprised of all families which can be linked by *coincidental ambiguity*. Thus, the subparadigm of برد *brd* and بردنا *brdnA*, whose derivational ambiguity joins the paradigms of the ب ر د *b r d* family, also connects that family to the unrelated ر د د *r d d* family via coincidental ambiguity. This is caused by the multiple possible analyses of ب *b* as either a cliticized preposition or a root letter.

## 3  Experiments

In this section, we describe the data, design, and models used in our experiments.

### 3.1  Data

To train word embedding models, we use a corpus of 500,000 Arabic sentences (13 million words) randomly selected from the corpus used in Almahairi et al. (2016). This makes our findings more generalizable to DA, as many dialects have similar amounts of available data (Erdmann et al., 2018). We clean our corpus via standard preprocessing[3] and analyze each word out of context with SAMA (Graff et al., 2009) to get the set of possible fully diacritized lemmas from which it could be derived.[4]

To build an evaluation set, we sum the frequencies of all types within each paradigm and bucket paradigms based on frequency. We randomly select evaluation paradigms such that all 10 buckets contribute at least 10 paradigms each. For all selected paradigms, any paradigms from the same clan are also selected, allowing us to assume that the paradigms included in the evaluation set are independent of those that are not included. Paradigms with only a single type are discarded, as these are not interesting for analysis. Our resulting EVAL set contains 1,036 words from 91 paradigms and a great deal of ambiguity at all levels of abstraction (see Table 1). Because we prohibit paradigms from entering EVAL without the rest of their clan, EVAL also exhibits the desirable property of reflecting a generally realistic distribution of ambiguity: 36% of its vocabulary are lemma ambiguous as compared to 39% for the entire corpus.

---

[2]The linguistic concept of derivational family differs from ours in that it does not require any ambiguous forms to be shared by derivationally related paradigms. However, identifying such derivational families automatically is non-trivial. Even if the shared root can be identified, it can be difficult to determine whether the root is mono or polysemous, e.g., ش ع ر *š ς r* could refer to *hair*, *poetry*, or *feeling*. Regardless, our definition of family better serves our investigation into the effects of ambiguity.

[3]We remove the rarely used diacritics and *Alif/Ya* normalize (El Kholy and Habash, 2012).

[4]We exclude words from the embedding model and evaluation set if they either cannot be analyzed by SAMA, only receive proper noun analyses, or if they do not also occur in the larger Arabic Gigaword corpus (Parker et al., 2011). This controls for many idiosyncrasies.

| | Count | Ambiguous | Non-derivationally Ambiguous |
|---|---|---|---|
| Clan | 49 | 18 | 5 |
| Family | 55 | 24 | 11 |
| Paradigm | 91 | 60 | 14 |
| Subparadigm | 116 | 48 | 6 |
| Word | 1,036 | 372 | 85 |

Table 1: Statistics from the EVAL set. Morphological structures by level of abstraction. Ambiguous structures contain at least one lemma ambiguous form. Non-derivationally ambiguous structures contain at least one coincidentally lemma ambiguous form.

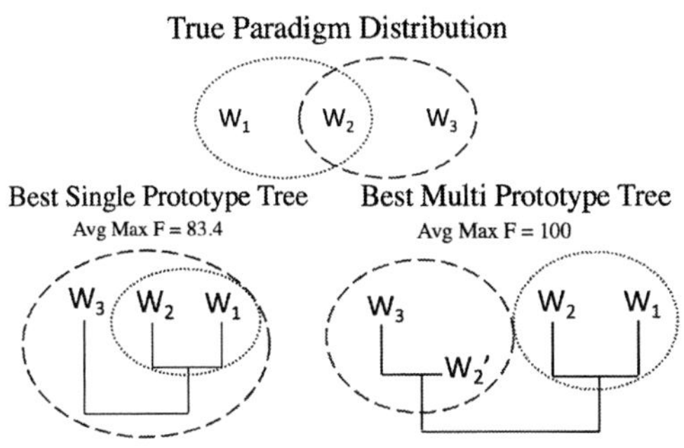


Figure 2: Best clustering strategies for two paradigms–dotted versus dashed ovals–given single or multi prototype vocabulary representations.

## 3.2 Approach and Evaluation Metric

We build single and multi prototype representations of the entire vocabulary, then examine how well they reflect the paradigms in EVAL. Each representation can be thought of as a tree where each word is a leaf at depth 0, i.e., $W_1$, $W_2$, and $W_3$ in Figure 2. Descending down the tree, words are clustered with other words' branches at subsequent depths until the clustering algorithm finishes or the root is reached where all words in the vocabulary are clustered together. All trees use some model of word similarity to guide clustering. In multi prototype representations, a word's leaf prototype at depth 0 can be copied and grafted onto other words' branches at non-zero depths before those branches are clustered to its own. Such is the case of $W_2$, which is copied as $W_2'$ at depth 1 of $W_3$'s branch before $W_3$'s branch connects to $W_2$'s. This enables partially overlapping paradigms to be modeled, like those in Figure 2.

We evaluate the trees via average maximum F-score. For each word in EVAL, we descend from its leaf, at each depth calculating an F-score for the overlap between the words that have been clustered to the leaf's branch so far and the leaf word's known paradigm mates, i.e., the set of words sharing at least one lemma with the leaf. Thus, paradigms are soft clusters in our representation, in that, for each word in a paradigm, its set of proposed paradigm mates need not be consistent with any of its proposed paradigm mates' sets of proposed paradigm mates. We then take the best F-score for each leaf word in EVAL, regardless of the depth level at which it was achieved, and average these maximum F-scores. This reflects how cohesively paradigms are represented in the tree.[5] Additionally, we report the average depth at which templatic and concatenatively related paradigm mates are added.

Because we evaluate via average maximum F-score, this metric represents the potential performance of any given model. Future work will address predicting the depth level where average maximum F-score is achieved for a given leaf word via rule-based and/or empirical techniques that have proven successful for related tasks (Narasimhan et al., 2015; Soricut and Och, 2015; Cao and Rei, 2016; Bergmanis and Goldwater, 2017; Sakakini et al., 2017).

## 3.3 Word Similarity Models

We use the following word similarity models for clustering words in single and multi prototype tree representations.

**LEVENSHTEIN** The LEVENSHTEIN baseline uses only orthographic edit distances to form a multi prototype tree. At each depth level $i$, the branch will include every word which has an edit distance of $i$ when compared to the leaf. Transitivity does not hold in this model, as words $x$ and $y$ could be in each other's depth 1 branch, but the fact that $z$ is in $y$'s depth 1 branch does not imply its inclusion in $x$'s depth 1 branch. If the edit distance between $x$ and $z$ is greater than 1, copies, or additional prototypes must be made of $x$ and $y$. Because morphology involves complicated processes that cannot be explained merely via orthographic similarity, we predict this model will perform poorly. Still, this baseline is useful to ensure that other models are learning something

---

[5] To control for idiosyncratic paradigms, we calculated a macro F-score averaged over the average maximum F-scores of individual paradigms, though we do not report this as results were not significantly different.

from words' in-context behavior or out-of-context morphological knowledge beyond what can be superficially induced from edit distances.

**DELEX** We use a de-lexicalized (DELEX) morphological analyzer to predict morphological relatedness. The analyzer covers all MSA closed-class affixes and clitics and their allowed combinations in open class parts-of-speech (POS); however there is no information about stems and lemmas in the model.[6] The affixes and clitics and their compatibility rules were extracted from SAMA (Graff et al., 2009). They are relatively cheap to create for any DA or other languages. The independent, expensive component of SAMA is the information regarding stems and lemmas, which we used to form our evaluation set. We are inspired by Darwish (2002), who demonstrated the creation of an Arabic shallow analyzer in one day. Our approach can be easily extended to DA at least in a similar manner to Salloum and Habash (2014).

To determine if two MSA words are possibly in the same paradigm, we do the following: (1) we use the analyzer to identify all potential stems with corresponding POS for each word (these stems are simply the leftover string after removing any prefixal and suffixal strings which match a prefix-suffix combination deemed compatible by SAMA); (2) each stem is deterministically converted into an orthographic root as per Eskander et al. (2013) by removing Hamzas (the set of letters representing the glottal stop phoneme, i.e., ء ', أ $\hat{A}$, إ $\check{A}$, آ $\bar{A}$, ؤ $\hat{w}$, ئ $\hat{y}$), long vowels (ا $A$, ي $y$, و $w$, ى $\hat{y}$), and reducing geminate consonants (e.g., ردد $rdd$ → رد $rd$); (3) two words are determined to be possibly from the same paradigm if there exists a possible orthographic root–POS analysis shared by both words.

DELEX builds a multi prototype tree with a maximum depth of 1. For each leaf word, it uses the above algorithm to identify all words in the vocabulary which can possibly share a paradigm with the leaf word, and grafts them into the branch. Hence, a word can belong to more than one hypothesized paradigm. Because DELEX has access

to valuable morphological knowledge, we predict it will be a competitive baseline. Furthermore, it should produce nearly perfect recall, only missing rare exceptional forms, e.g., broken plurals that introduce new consonants such as برامج $brAmj$, 'programs', the plural of برنامج $brnAmj$, 'program'. We expect its precision to be weak because it lacks lexical or stem-pattern information, leading to rampant clustering of derivationally related and unrelated forms. For example, a word like جائزة $jA\hat{y}z\hbar$, 'prize' (true root ج و ز $j$ $w$ $z$) receives the orthographic root ج ز $j$ $z$ (long vowel, hamza letter, and suffix are dropped), which clusters it with unrelated forms such as جزء $jz$', 'part' (true root ج ز ء $j$ $z$ '), and جز $jz$, 'shearing' (true root ج ز ز $j$ $z$ $z$).

**Word Embedding Models (W2V, FT, and FT+)** We use different word embedding models to build single prototype representations of the vocabulary via binary hierarchical clustering (Müllner et al., 2013). In order to analyze the effects of data sparsity, we do not impose a minimum word frequency count, but learn vectors for the entire vocabulary. At depth 0, we consider each leaf word to be its own branch. Descending down the tree, we iteratively join the closest two branches based on Ward distance (Ward Jr, 1963). Joined branches are represented by the centroid of their component words' vectors (though, as in other models, we do not include the leaf word as a match when calculating average maximum F-score). We continue iterating until only a single root remains containing the entire vocabulary.

These trees are single prototype because the input embeddings only provide one vector for each word, regardless of whether or not it is ambiguous in any way. While this is a limitation for these models,[7] existing multi prototype word embeddings generally model sense ambiguity, which is easier to capture (though harder to evaluate) given the unsupervised settings in which embeddings are typically trained (Reisinger and Mooney, 2010; Huang et al., 2012; Chen et al., 2014; Bartunov et al., 2016). Adapting multi prototype embed-

---

[6]The system includes 15 basic prefixes/proclitics (ا $A$, ال $Al$, ب $b$, ف $f$, في $fy$, ك $k$, ل $l$, لا $lA$, ما $mA$, ن $n$, س $s$, ت $t$, و $w$, ي $y$, and $\phi$) in 84 unique combinations; and 30 suffixes/enclitics (ا $A$, ان $An$, ات $At$, ه $h$, ها $hA$, هم $hm$, هما $hmA$, هن $hn$, ك $k$, كم $km$, كما $kmA$, كن $kn$, ن $n$, نا $nA$, ني $ny$, ة $\hbar$, ت $t$, تا $tA$, تان $tAn$, تم $tm$, تما $tmA$, تن $tn$, تي $ty$, تين $tyn$, و $w$, وا $wA$, ون $wn$, ي $y$, ين $yn$ and $\phi$) in 193 unique combinations.

[7]A single prototype oracle that always correctly maps non-lemma ambiguous words to their paradigm and maps lemma ambiguous words only to their largest possible paradigm scores 97% (92% specifically on lemma ambiguous types). This represents the best possible performance for single prototype models.

dings to model lemma ambiguities is non-trivial, especially without lots of supervision. We leave this for future work.

Because trees built from word embeddings are all constructed via the same binary clustering algorithm, the depths at which templatic and concatenatively inflected paradigm mates are joined in Table 2 are comparable vertically across W2V, FT, and FT+ as well as horizontally. However, the multi prototype trees are shorter and fatter, such that the templatic and concatenative average join depths are only comparable horizontally with each other, i.e., within the same model.

**W2V** The Gensim implementation of WORD2VEC (Mikolov et al., 2013a; Řehůřek and Sojka, 2010) uses the SkipGram algorithm with 200 dimensions and a context window of 5 tokens on either side of the target word. As this does not have access to any subword information and is specifically designed for semantics, not morphology, we predict that it will not perform well in our evaluation.

**FT** We train a FASTTEXT (Bojanowski et al., 2016) implementation with the same parameters as W2V, except a word's vector is the sum of its SkipGram vector and that of all its component character n-grams between length 2 and 6. Since short vowels are not written, many Arabic affixes are only one character. With FASTTEXT bookending words with start/end symbols in its internal representation, outermost single-letter affixes are functionally two characters. By inducing knowledge of such affixes, these character n-gram parameters outperform the language agnostic range of 3 to 6 proposed by Bojanowski et al. (2016).

With the ability to model how subword strings behave in context, FT should outperform both LEVENSHTEIN and W2V, though without access to scholar seeded knowledge of morphological structures, it is difficult to predict how FT will compare with DELEX. Errors may arise from clustering words based on affixes indicative of syntactic behavior instead of the stem, which indicates paradigm membership. Also, if the word is infrequent and contains no semantically distinct subword string with higher frequency, the embeddings will be noisy. Frequency and noise also interact with the *hubbiness*, or crowdedness of the embedding region, as rural regions will require less precision in the vectors to cluster well, whereas there is little room for noise in crowded urban regions where many similar but morphologically unrelated words could interfere.

**FT+** We build another FT model by concatenating the vectors learned from two variant FT models, one with the normal window size of 5 and one with a narrow window size of 1. Both are trained on a preprocessed corpus where phrases have been probabilistically identified in potentially unique distributions over multiple copies of each sentence, as described in Erdmann et al. (2018).[8] This technique attempts to better model syntactic cues–which are better encoded with narrow context windows (Pennington et al., 2014; Trask et al., 2015; Goldberg, 2016; Tu et al., 2017)–while avoiding treating non-compositional phrases as compositional, and also learning from multiple, potentially complementary phrase-chunkings of every sentence. By combining these sources of information, FT+ is designed to learn more meaningful vectors without requiring additional data. We predict it will uniformly outperform FT by reducing noise in the handling of sparse forms like infrequent inflections–a hallmark of morphologically rich languages.

**FT+&DELEX** We make unique copies for each leaf word's branch extending all the way to the root in the single prototype FT+ tree. Then, for each leaf word, at every depth of its branch copy, we use DELEX to prune any words which could not share an orthographic root with the leaf word. Pruning is local to that branch copy, and does not affect the branch copies of paradigm mates which had originally been proposed by FT+ before making branch copies. This makes FT+&DELEX a multi-prototype model. After pruning, the F-score is recalculated for each depth of each leaf word's branch and a new average maximum F-score is reported. Because FT+ encodes information regarding the in-context behavior of words, it is quite complementary to the out-of-context morphological knowledge supplied by DELEX. We predict this model will outperform all others.

---

[8]For control, we compared every possible combination of narrow and wide window sizes (1 or 5), dimension sizes (200 or 400), and techniques for phrase identification (none, deterministic (Mikolov et al., 2013b), and probabilistic (Erdmann et al., 2018)), but none approached the performance achieved with the parameters used in FT+.

| Word Similarity Model | Multi Prototype | Averaged Scores | | | Join Depth | |
|---|---|---|---|---|---|---|
| | | Max F-Score | Precision | Recall | Concat | Temp |
| LEVENSHTEIN | ✓ | 22.0 | 35.5 | 23.4 | 3.5 | 4.1 |
| DELEX | ✓ | 52.9 | 41.6 | 99.3 | 1.0 | 1.0 |
| W2V | | 2.1 | 6.7 | 28.1 | 17.1 | 17.4 |
| FT | | 39.2 | 66.0 | 44.2 | 13.7 | 16.8 |
| FT+ | | 50.2 | 71.8 | 52.9 | 13.3 | 16.4 |
| **FT+&DELEX** | ✓ | **71.5** | **74.0** | **81.3** | **13.3** | **16.4** |

Table 2: Scores for clustering words with their paradigm mates in tree representations built from different models of word similarity. Scores are calculated as described in Section 3.2, with precision and recall extracted from the depth that maximizes F and then averaged over all words in EVAL. Join depths refer to the average depth at which templatic or concatenatively related paradigm mates are added to the branch.

## 4 Results and Discussion

The results in Table 2 provide strong evidence in support of our hypotheses. The only model performing worse than the LEVENSHTEIN edit distance baseline is W2V, which only understands the in-context, semantic behavior of words. By being able to learn morphological knowledge from in-context behavior of subword strings, FT greatly improves over both W2V and LEVENSHTEIN, demonstrating that it learns far more than can be inferred from out-of-context subword strings, i.e., edit distance, or in-context distributional semantic knowledge without any morphology, i.e., W2V. As predicted, FT+ improves uniformly over FT in all categories, presumably by reducing noise in the vectors of infrequent inflections. Interestingly, with no access to subword information, W2V performs equally poorly on both templatic and concatenatively related paradigm mates, whereas FT and FT+ greatly improve on concatenative mates, but not templatic ones. This is likely because FT and FT+ can identify patterns in subword strings, but not in non-adjacent characters.

DELEX's strong baseline performance demonstrates that simple, out-of-context, de-lexicalized knowledge of morphology is sufficient to outperform the best word embedding model that only learns from words' in-context behaviors. However, given the complementarity between DELEX's knowledge and the information FT+ can learn, it is not surprising that the combination of these techniques, FT+&DELEX, far outperforms either system individually.

**Specific Examples** We discuss a number of examples that illustrate the variety in the behavior and complementarity of rule-based DELEX, embedding-based FT+, and the combined FT+&DELEX models. For each

example, we specify the strength of the maximum F-score for the three models as such:[9] $strength^{\text{DELEX}} + strength^{\text{FT+}} \rightarrow strength^{\text{FT+&DELEX}}$, e.g., LOW+MID→HI denotes poor DELEX and mediocre FT+ performance on a word, yielding high performance in the combined model.

- جائزة *jAŷzħ*, 'prize' (LOW+HI→HI)
  This word has high orthographic root ambiguity since its second morphological root radical is a Hamza. This results in matching words with unrelated true roots like جزء *jz'*, 'part' and جز *jz*, 'shearing' under DELEX. It also has high root fertility, in that different paradigms can come from the same true root, like جائز *jAŷz*, 'permissible', further challenging DELEX. FT+ does relatively better, capturing the word's other inflections, even the broken plural جوائز *jwAŷz*, as their in-context behavior is similar to جائزة *jAŷzħ*. Interesting recall errors by FT+ include semantically and orthographically similar فائزة *fAŷzħ*, 'winner[fem.sing]'. The combination yields a perfect F-score.

- يهرعون *yhrʕwn*, 'they rush' (HI+LOW→HI)
  This word has an unambiguous orthographic root with no root fertility, resulting in a perfect F-score for DELEX. However, FT+ misses several inflections such as نهرع *nhrʕ*, 'we rush', and وهرعت *whrʕt*, 'and I/you/she rushed'. FT+ also makes many semantically and/or syntactically similar precision errors: يسرعون *ysrʕwn*, 'they hurry', يصارعون *ySArʕwn*, 'they wrestle', and يقرعون *yqrʕwn*, 'they ring (a bell)'. The combination leads to a perfect F-score.

- ديناميكي *dynAmyky*, 'dynamic' (HI+HI→HI)
  This word has an unambiguous orthographic

---

[9]The strength designation HI is used for F-scores above 75%, LOW for scores below 25%, and MID for the rest.

root based on a foreign borrowing and relatively unique semantics and subword strings. Thus, it achieves a perfect F-score in all three models.

- انتشروا *AntšrwA*, 'they spread out' (MID+MID→HI)
  This word has high orthographic root ambiguity (and, incidentally, fertility) due to the presence of ن *n* and ت *t*, which could belong to a root, template, or prefix. This leads to a 63% F-score under DELEX with many precision errors: انتشاره *AntšArh*, 'his spreading out', ونتشاور *wntšAwr*, 'we discuss', and نتشارك *ntšArk*, 'we collaborate'. FT+ scores only 47%, proposing semantically related but morphologically unrelated or only derivationally related forms: e.g., منتشر *mntšr*, 'spread out' (adjective), and تمركزوا *tmrkzwA*, 'they centralized' (antonym). This semantic knowledge however, complements DELEX's knowledge, such that the combination is almost perfect (98%).

- كفء *kf'*, 'efficient' (LOW+LOW→LOW)
  While 17% of words are LOW in DELEX and 28% in FT+, only 4% are LOW in FT+&DELEX. This word exemplifies that 4%, occupying the gap between DELEX's knowledge and FT+'s. It has an extremely ambiguous orthographic root due to the true root containing a Hamza and the first letter being interpretable as a proclitic or root radical. Thus, DELEX achieves 2% F. FT+ is only slightly better (5%). It is likely that this word's low frequency is the main contributor to its noisy embedding, as it only appears once in our corpus. The combination F-score is thus, only 11%.

## 5 Related Work

This work builds on several others addressing word embeddings and computational morphology.

**Word Embeddings** Word embeddings are trained by predicting either a target word given its context (Continuous Bag of Words) or elements of the context given a target (SkipGram) in unannotated corpora (Mikolov et al., 2013a), with the learned vectors modeling how words relate to each other. Embeddings have been adapted to incorporate word order (Trask et al., 2015) or subword information (Bojanowski et al., 2016) to motivate the learned vectors to specifically capture syntactic, morphological, or other similarities.

Word embeddings are generally *single prototype* models, in that they learn one vector for each word, which can be problematic for ambiguous forms (Reisinger and Mooney, 2010; Huang et al., 2012; Chen et al., 2014). Bartunov et al. (2016) propose a *multi prototype* model that learns distinct vectors for distinct meanings of types based on variation in the contexts within which they appear. Gyllensten and Sahlgren (2015), argue that single prototype embeddings actually can model ambiguity because the defining characteristics of a word's different meanings typically manifest in different dimensions of the highly dimensional vector space. They find ambiguous words' relative nearest neighbors in a relative neighborhood graph often correlate with distinct meanings. Such works however, deal with sense ambiguity, or abstract semantic distinctions between different usages of a word with potentially the same morphosyntactic properties and core meaning. Evaluation usually requires linking to large semantic databases which, for Arabic, are still underdeveloped (Black et al., 2006; Badaro et al., 2014; Elrazzaz et al., 2017).

**Computational Morphology** This field of study includes rule-based, machine learning, and hybrid approaches to modeling morphology. The traditional approach is to hand write rules to identify the morphological properties of words (Beesley, 1998; Khoja and Garside, 1999; Habash and Rambow, 2006; Smrž, 2007; Graff et al., 2009; Habash, 2010). These can be used for out-of-context analysis–which SAMA (Graff et al., 2009) performs for MSA–or they can be combined with machine learning approaches that leverage information from the context in which a word appears. MADAMIRA (Pasha et al., 2014), for example, is trained on an annotated corpus to disambiguate SAMA's analyses based on the surrounding sentence.

Other systems use machine learning without rules. They can train on annotated data, like Faruqui et al. (2016) who learn morpho-syntactic lexica from a small seed, or they can learn without supervision, like Luo et al. (2017) who induce "morphological forests" of derivationally related words by predicting suffixes and prefixes based on the vocabulary alone. Some approaches seek to be language independent. MORFESSOR (Creutz and Lagus, 2005), for instance, segments words based on unannotated text. However, it deterministically produces context-irrelevant segmentations, causing error propagation in languages like Arabic, characterized by high lexical ambiguity (Saleh and Habash, 2009; Pasha et al., 2014). A few systems have incorporated word embeddings to perform segmentation (Narasimhan et al., 2015; Soricut and Och, 2015; Cao and Rei, 2016), with some attempting to model and analyze relations between underlying morphemes as well (Bergmanis and Goldwater, 2017; Sakakini et al., 2017), though none of these distinguish between inflectional and derivational morphology. Eskander et al. (2016b) propose another segmentation system using Adaptor Grammars for six typologically distinct languages. Snyder and Barzilay (2010) actually use multiple languages simultaneously, finding the parallels between them useful for disambiguation in morphological and syntactic tasks.

Our work is closely related to Avraham and Goldberg (2017), who train embeddings on a Hebrew corpus with disambiguated morphosyntactic information appended to each token. Similarly, Cotterell and Schütze (2015) "guide" German word embeddings with morphological annotation, and Gieske (2017) use morphological information encoded in word embeddings to inflect German verbs. For Arabic, Rasooli et al. (2014) induce paradigmatic knowledge from raw text to produce unseen inflections, and Eskander et al. (2013) identify *orthographic roots* and use them to extract features for paradigm completion given annotated data. While we adopt the concept of approximating the linguistic root with an orthographic root, we do not use annotated data where the stem has already been determined as in Eskander et al. (2013). Thus, we generate all possible orthographic roots for a given word instead of just one, as discussed in Section 3.3.

Sakakini et al. (2017) provide an alternative unsupervised technique for extracting roots in Semitic languages, however, we chose to adopt the orthographic root concept instead for several reasons. Firstly, despite performing comparably with other empirical techniques, Sakakini et al. (2017)'s root extractor is not extremely accurate. While our implementation generates potentially multiple orthographic roots with imperfect precision, the near perfect recall is useful for pruning without propogating error. A major reason why we find DELEX and FT+ to complement one another is the independence of the orthographic root extraction rules and the distributional statistics leveraged by word embeddings. Sakakini et al. (2017)'s root extractor however, depends on embeddings to identify roots. Furthermore, their root extractor cannot be used to generate multi prototype models as it only produces one root per word. Finally, despite orthographic roots' dependance on hand written rules, we show that these rules are very few, such that adapting Sakakini et al. (2017)'s root extractor to a new language or dialect would not necessarily require any less effort than writing new rules.

## 6 Conclusion and Future Work

In this work, we demonstrated that out-of-context, rule-based knowledge of morphological structure, even in minimal supply, greatly complements what word embeddings can learn about morphology from words' in-context behaviors. We discussed how Arabic's morphological richness and many forms of ambiguity interact with different word similarity models' ability to represent morphological structure in a paradigm clustering task. Our work quantifies the value of leveraging subword information when learning embeddings and the further value of noise reduction techniques targeting the sparsity caused by complex morphology. Our best performing model uses out-of-context rules to prune unlikely paradigm mates suggested by our best embedding model, achieving an F-score of 71.5% averaged over our evaluation vocabulary. Our results inform how one would most cost effectively construct morphological resources for DA or similarly under resourced, morphologically complex languages.

Our future work will target templatic morphological processes which still challenge our best model, requiring knowledge of patterns realized over non-adjacent characters. We will also address errors due to ambiguity, either by adapting multi prototype embedding models to capture morphological ambiguity, including knowledge of paradigm structure in our de-lexicalized rules, or by using disambiguated lemma frequencies to model ambiguity probabilistically. In applying this work to DA, we will additionally need to address the issue of noisy, unstandardized spelling. We will also investigate different knowledge transfer techniques to leverage the many resources available for MSA.

# References


Ahmed Abdelali, Kareem Darwish, Nadir Durrani, and Hamdy Mubarak. 2016. Farasa: A fast and furious segmenter for Arabic. In *Proceedings of the 2016 Conference of the North American Chapter of the Association for Computational Linguistics: Demonstrations*, pages 11–16.

Faisal Al-Shargi, Aidan Kaplan, Ramy Eskander, Nizar Habash, and Owen Rambow. 2016. Morphologically annotated corpora and morphological analyzers for Moroccan and Sanaani Yemeni Arabic. In *10th Language Resources and Evaluation Conference (LREC 2016)*.

Sarah Alkuhlani and Nizar Habash. 2011. A Corpus for Modeling Morpho-Syntactic Agreement in Arabic: Gender, Number and Rationality. In *Proceedings of the 49th Annual Meeting of the Association for Computational Linguistics (ACL'11)*, Portland, Oregon, USA.

Amjad Almahairi, Kyunghyun Cho, Nizar Habash, and Aaron C. Courville. 2016. First result on Arabic neural machine translation. *CoRR*, abs/1606.02680.

Oded Avraham and Yoav Goldberg. 2017. The interplay of semantics and morphology in word embeddings. *arXiv preprint arXiv:1704.01938*.

Gilbert Badaro, Ramy Baly, Hazem Hajj, Nizar Habash, and Wassim El-Hajj. 2014. A large scale Arabic sentiment lexicon for Arabic opinion mining. In *Proceedings of the EMNLP 2014 Workshop on Arabic Natural Language Processing (ANLP)*, pages 165–173.

Sergey Bartunov, Dmitry Kondrashkin, Anton Osokin, and Dmitry Vetrov. 2016. Breaking sticks and ambiguities with adaptive skip-gram. In *Artificial Intelligence and Statistics*, pages 130–138.

Kenneth Beesley. 1998. Arabic morphology using only finite-state operations. In *Proceedings of the Workshop on Computational Approaches to Semitic Languages*, pages 50–7, Montereal.

Toms Bergmanis and Sharon Goldwater. 2017. From segmentation to analyses: A probabilistic model for unsupervised morphology induction. In *Proceedings of the 15th Conference of the European Chapter of the Association for Computational Linguistics: Volume 1, Long Papers*, volume 1, pages 337–346.

William Black, Sabri Elkateb, Horacio Rodriguez, Musa Alkhalifa, Piek Vossen, Adam Pease, and Christiane Fellbaum. 2006. Introducing the Arabic wordnet project. In *Proceedings of the third international WordNet conference*, pages 295–300. Citeseer.

Piotr Bojanowski, Edouard Grave, Armand Joulin, and Tomas Mikolov. 2016. Enriching word vectors with subword information. *arXiv preprint arXiv:1607.04606*.

Kris Cao and Marek Rei. 2016. A joint model for word embedding and word morphology. *arXiv preprint arXiv:1606.02601*.

Xinxiong Chen, Zhiyuan Liu, and Maosong Sun. 2014. A unified model for word sense representation and disambiguation. In *Proceedings of the 2014 Conference on Empirical Methods in Natural Language Processing (EMNLP)*, pages 1025–1035.

David Chiang, Mona Diab, Nizar Habash, Owen Rambow, and Safiullah Shareef. 2006. Parsing Arabic Dialects. In *Proceedings of EACL*, Trento, Italy. EACL.

Ryan Cotterell, Christo Kirov, John Sylak-Glassman, Géraldine Walther, Ekaterina Vylomova, Patrick Xia, Manaal Faruqui, Sandra Kübler, David Yarowsky, Jason Eisner, and Mans Hulden. 2017. CoNLL-SIGMORPHON 2017 shared task: Universal morphological reinflection in 52 languages. *CoRR*, abs/1706.09031.

Ryan Cotterell, Christo Kirov, John Sylak-Glassman, David Yarowsky, Jason Eisner, and Mans Hulden. 2016. The SIGMORPHON 2016 shared task—morphological reinflection. In *Proceedings of the 2016 Meeting of SIGMORPHON*, Berlin, Germany. Association for Computational Linguistics.

Ryan Cotterell and Hinrich Schütze. 2015. Morphological word-embeddings. In *Proceedings of the 2015 Conference of the North American Chapter of the Association for Computational Linguistics: Human Language Technologies*, pages 1287–1292.

Mathias Creutz and Krista Lagus. 2005. *Unsupervised morpheme segmentation and morphology induction from text corpora using Morfessor 1.0*. Helsinki University of Technology.

Kareem Darwish. 2002. Building a shallow Arabic morphological analyzer in one day. In *Computational Approaches to Semitic Languages, an ACL'02 Workshop*, pages 47–54, Philadelphia, PA.

Ahmed El Kholy and Nizar Habash. 2012. Orthographic and morphological processing for English–Arabic statistical machine translation. *Machine Translation*, 26(1-2):25–45.

Mohammed Elrazzaz, Shady Elbassuoni, Khaled Shaban, and Chadi Helwe. 2017. Methodical evaluation of Arabic word embeddings. In *Proceedings of the 55th Annual Meeting of the Association for Computational Linguistics (Volume 2: Short Papers)*, pages 454–458, Vancouver, Canada.

Alexander Erdmann, Nizar Habash, Dima Taji, and Houda Bouamor. 2017. Low resourced machine translation via morpho-syntactic modeling: The case of dialectal arabic. In *Proceedings of MT Summit 2017*, Nagoya, Japan.

Alexander Erdmann, Nasser Zalmout, and Nizar Habash. 2018. Addressing noise in multidialectal word embeddings. In *Proceedings of the 56th Annual Meeting of the Association for Computational Linguistics (Volume 2: Short Papers)*, volume 2, pages 558–565.

Ramy Eskander, Nizar Habash, and Owen Rambow. 2013. Automatic extraction of morphological lexicons from morphologically annotated corpora. In

*Proceedings of the 2013 conference on empirical methods in natural language processing*, pages 1032–1043.

Ramy Eskander, Nizar Habash, Owen Rambow, and Arfath Pasha. 2016a. Creating resources for Dialectal Arabic from a single annotation: A case study on Egyptian and Levantine. In *Proceedings of COLING 2016, the 26th International Conference on Computational Linguistics: Technical Papers*, pages 3455–3465, Osaka, Japan.

Ramy Eskander, Owen Rambow, and Tianchun Yang. 2016b. Extending the use of adaptor grammars for unsupervised morphological segmentation of unseen languages. In *Proceedings of COLING 2016, the 26th International Conference on Computational Linguistics: Technical Papers*, pages 900–910.

Manaal Faruqui, Ryan McDonald, and Radu Soricut. 2016. Morpho-syntactic lexicon generation using graph-based semi-supervised learning. *Transactions of the Association for Computational Linguistics*, 4:1–16.

Sharon Gieske. 2017. Inflecting verbs with word embeddings: A systematic investigation of morphological information captured by German verb embeddings. Master's thesis, University of Amsterdam.

Yoav Goldberg. 2016. A primer on neural network models for natural language processing. *J. Artif. Intell. Res.(JAIR)*, 57:345–420.

David Graff, Mohamed Maamouri, Basma Bouziri, Sondos Krouna, Seth Kulick, and Tim Buckwalter. 2009. Standard Arabic morphological analyzer (SAMA) version 3.1. *Linguistic Data Consortium LDC2009E73*.

Amaru Cuba Gyllensten and Magnus Sahlgren. 2015. Navigating the semantic horizon using relative neighborhood graphs. *arXiv preprint arXiv:1501.02670*.

Nizar Habash, Ramy Eskander, and Abdelati Hawwari. 2012. A morphological analyzer for Egyptian Arabic. In *Proceedings of the twelfth meeting of the special interest group on computational morphology and phonology*, pages 1–9. Association for Computational Linguistics.

Nizar Habash and Owen Rambow. 2006. MAGEAD: a morphological analyzer and generator for the Arabic dialects. In *Proceedings of the 21st International Conference on Computational Linguistics and the 44th annual meeting of the Association for Computational Linguistics*, pages 681–688. Association for Computational Linguistics.

Nizar Habash, Abdelhadi Soudi, and Tim Buckwalter. 2007. On Arabic Transliteration. In A. van den Bosch and A. Soudi, editors, *Arabic Computational Morphology: Knowledge-based and Empirical Methods*. Springer.

Nizar Y Habash. 2010. *Introduction to Arabic natural language processing*, volume 3. Morgan & Claypool Publishers.

Eric H Huang, Richard Socher, Christopher D Manning, and Andrew Y Ng. 2012. Improving word representations via global context and multiple word prototypes. In *Proceedings of the 50th Annual Meeting of the Association for Computational Linguistics: Long Papers-Volume 1*, pages 873–882. Association for Computational Linguistics.

Go Inoue, Hiroyuki Shindo, and Yuji Matsumoto. 2017. Joint prediction of morphosyntactic categories for fine-grained Arabic part-of-speech tagging exploiting tag dictionary information. In *Proceedings of the 21st Conference on Computational Natural Language Learning (CoNLL 2017)*, pages 421–431, Vancouver, Canada. Association for Computational Linguistics.

Mustafa Jarrar, Nizar Habash, Diyam Akra, and Nasser Zalmout. 2014. Building a corpus for Palestinian Arabic: a preliminary study. In *Proceedings of the EMNLP 2014 Workshop on Arabic Natural Language Processing (ANLP)*, pages 18–27.

Salam Khalifa, Nizar Habash, Fadhl Eryani, Ossama Obeid, Dana Abdulrahim, and Meera Al Kaabi. 2018. A Morphologically Annotated Corpus of Emirati Arabic. In *Proceedings of the Eleventh International Conference on Language Resources and Evaluation (LREC 2018)*, Miyazaki, Japan.

Salam Khalifa, Sara Hassan, and Nizar Habash. 2017. A morphological analyzer for Gulf Arabic verbs. *WANLP 2017 (co-located with EACL 2017)*, page 35.

Salam Khalifa, Nasser Zalmout, and Nizar Habash. 2016. Yamama: Yet another multi-dialect Arabic morphological analyzer. In *Proceedings of COLING 2016, the 26th International Conference on Computational Linguistics: System Demonstrations*, pages 223–227.

Shereen Khoja and Roger Garside. 1999. Stemming Arabic text. *Lancaster, UK, Computing Department, Lancaster University*.

Jiaming Luo, Karthik Narasimhan, and Regina Barzilay. 2017. Unsupervised learning of morphological forests. *arXiv preprint arXiv:1702.07015*.

Tomas Mikolov, Kai Chen, Greg Corrado, and Jeffrey Dean. 2013a. Efficient estimation of word representations in vector space. *arXiv preprint arXiv:1301.3781*.

Tomas Mikolov, Ilya Sutskever, Kai Chen, Greg S Corrado, and Jeff Dean. 2013b. Distributed representations of words and phrases and their compositionality. In *Advances in neural information processing systems*, pages 3111–3119.

Daniel Müllner et al. 2013. fastcluster: Fast hierarchical, agglomerative clustering routines for R and Python. *Journal of Statistical Software*, 53(9):1–18.

Karthik Narasimhan, Regina Barzilay, and Tommi Jaakkola. 2015. An unsupervised method for uncovering morphological chains. *arXiv preprint arXiv:1503.02335*.

Robert Parker, David Graff, Ke Chen, Junbo Kong, and Kazuaki Maeda. 2011. Arabic Gigaword Fifth Edition. LDC catalog number No. LDC2011T11, ISBN 1-58563-595-2.

Arfath Pasha, Mohamed Al-Badrashiny, Ahmed El Kholy, Ramy Eskander, Mona Diab, Nizar Habash, Manoj Pooleery, Owen Rambow, and Ryan Roth. 2014. MADAMIRA: A Fast, Comprehensive Tool for Morphological Analysis and Disambiguation of Arabic. In *In Proceedings of LREC*, Reykjavik, Iceland.

Jeffrey Pennington, Richard Socher, and Christopher Manning. 2014. Glove: Global vectors for word representation. In *Proceedings of the 2014 conference on empirical methods in natural language processing (EMNLP)*, pages 1532–1543.

Mohammad Sadegh Rasooli, Thomas Lippincott, Nizar Habash, and Owen Rambow. 2014. Unsupervised morphology-based vocabulary expansion. In *Proceedings of the 52nd Annual Meeting of the Association for Computational Linguistics (Volume 1: Long Papers)*, volume 1, pages 1349–1359.

Radim Řehůřek and Petr Sojka. 2010. Software Framework for Topic Modelling with Large Corpora. In *Proceedings of the LREC 2010 Workshop on New Challenges for NLP Frameworks*, pages 45–50, Valletta, Malta. ELRA. `http://is.muni.cz/publication/884893/en`.

Joseph Reisinger and Raymond J Mooney. 2010. Multi-prototype vector-space models of word meaning. In *Human Language Technologies: The 2010 Annual Conference of the North American Chapter of the Association for Computational Linguistics*, pages 109–117. Association for Computational Linguistics.

Tarek Sakakini, Suma Bhat, and Pramod Viswanath. 2017. Fixing the infix: Unsupervised discovery of root-and-pattern morphology. *arXiv preprint arXiv:1702.02211*.

Ibrahim M. Saleh and Nizar Habash. 2009. Automatic extraction of lemma-based bilingual dictionaries for morphologically rich languages. In *Proceedings of MT Summit*, Ottawa, Canada.

Wael Salloum and Nizar Habash. 2014. ADAM: Analyzer for Dialectal Arabic Morphology. *Journal of King Saud University-Computer and Information Sciences*, 26(4):372–378.

Otakar Smrž. 2007. *Functional Arabic Morphology. Formal System and Implementation.* Ph.D. thesis, Charles University, Prague.

Benjamin Snyder and Regina Barzilay. 2010. Climbing the tower of Babel: Unsupervised multilingual learning. In *Proceedings of the International Conference on Machine Learning (ICML-10)*, Haifa, Israel.

Radu Soricut and Franz Och. 2015. Unsupervised morphology induction using word embeddings. In *Proceedings of the 2015 Conference of the North American Chapter of the Association for Computational Linguistics: Human Language Technologies*, pages 1627–1637.

Andrew Trask, David Gilmore, and Matthew Russell. 2015. Modeling order in neural word embeddings at scale. *arXiv preprint arXiv:1506.02338*.

Lifu Tu, Kevin Gimpel, and Karen Livescu. 2017. Learning to embed words in context for syntactic tasks. *arXiv preprint arXiv:1706.02807*.

Joe H Ward Jr. 1963. Hierarchical grouping to optimize an objective function. *Journal of the American statistical association*, 58(301):236–244.

Nasser Zalmout, Alexander Erdmann, and Nizar Habash. 2018. Noise-robust morphological disambiguation for dialectal Arabic. In *Proceedings of the 16th Meeting of the North American Chapter of the Association for Computational Linguistics/Human Language Technologies Conference (HLT-NAACL18)*, New Orleans, Louisiana, USA.

Nasser Zalmout and Nizar Habash. 2017. Don't throw those morphological analyzers away just yet: Neural morphological disambiguation for Arabic. In *Proceedings of the 2017 Conference on Empirical Methods in Natural Language Processing*, pages 715–724.

Inès Zribi, Mariem Ellouze, Lamia Hadrich Belguith, and Philippe Blache. 2017. Morphological disambiguation of Tunisian dialect. *Journal of King Saud University-Computer and Information Sciences*, 29(2):147–155.

# Modeling reduplication with 2-way finite-state transducers


**Hossep Dolatian, Jeffrey Heinz**
Department of Linguistics
Institute for Advanced Computational Science
Stony Brook University
`hossep.dolatian,jeffrey.heinz@stonybrook.edu`



## Abstract

This article describes a novel approach to the computational modeling of reduplication. Reduplication is a well-studied linguistic phenomenon. However, it is often treated as a stumbling block within finite-state treatments of morphology. Most finite-state implementations of computational morphology cannot adequately capture the productivity of unbounded copying in reduplication, nor can they adequately capture bounded copying. We show that an understudied type of finite-state machines, two-way finite-state transducers (2-way FSTs), captures virtually all reduplicative processes, including total reduplication. 2-way FSTs can model reduplicative typology in a way which is convenient, easy to design and debug in practice, and linguistically-motivated. By virtue of being finite-state, 2-way FSTs are likewise incorporable into existing finite-state systems and programs. A small but representative typology of reduplicative processes is described in this article, alongside their corresponding 2-way FST models.


## 1 Introduction

Reduplication is a cross-linguistically common word-formation process. Reduplication is roughly divided into two categories, total reduplication where an unbounded number of segments are copied (1) vs. partial reduplication where a bounded number of segments are copied (2). In spoken language, reduplication usually involves making at most two copies, though making three copies is attested in spoken language (3) and is common in sign language (Wilbur, 2005).

1) wanita→wanita~wanita
 'woman' → 'women'
 Indonesian (Cohn, 1989, 308)

2) takki→tak~takki
 'leg' → 'legs' Agta (Moravcsik, 1978, 311)

3) roar→ roar~roar~roar
 'give a shudder' →'continue to shudder'
 Mokilese (Moravcsik, 1978, 301)

Most of the world's languages include at least one reduplicative process, with the most common reduplicative process being total reduplication. The WALS database documents that 278 out of 368 (75%) languages use both partial reduplication and total reduplication as productive morphological operations (Rubino, 2013). An extra 35 (10%) use only total reduplication as a productive morphological operation. The 55 (15%) remaining languages with no reduplicative processes include most Indo-European languages.[1]

Although reduplication has a rich history in morpho-phonology, it continues to present challenges for computational and mathematical linguistics (Sproat, 1992; Roark and Sproat, 2007). Within computational linguistics, most of morphology and phonology have been analyzed with finite-state calculus as rational languages and transductions (Kaplan and Kay, 1994; Beesley and Karttunen, 2003). However, reduplication cannot be easily modeled with the same finite-state systems used to model the rest of morpho-phonology. In the case of total reduplication, this is because those finite-state systems cannot express unbounded copying in the first place (Culy, 1985). As for partial reduplication, those finite-state systems are often discussed as being burdensome models because of the state explosion that partial reduplication causes (Roark and Sproat, 2007). This has lead some researchers to develop finite-state *approximations* of total reduplication (Walther, 2000; Beesley and Karttunen, 2000; Cohen-Sygal and Wintner, 2006; Hulden,

---

[1]This 15% is debatable because some argue that total reduplication is still used in those languages in one way or another (Stolz et al., 2011).




*Proceedings of the 15th SIGMORPHON Workshop on Computational Research in Phonetics, Phonology, and Morphology*, pages 66–77
Brussels, Belgium, October 31, 2018. ©2018 The Special Interest Group on Computational Morphology and Phonology
https://doi.org/10.18653/v1/P17

2009a; Hulden and Bischoff, 2009). These are approximations because they cannot model the productivity of total reduplication, the most common reduplicative process. Another alternative is to use formalisms that are beyond finite-state, e.g. queue-based CFGs (Savitch, 1989), MCFGs (Albro, 2000, 2005), and HPSG (Crysmann, 2017).

This article shows how a specific understudied type of finite-state technology actually <u>can</u> account for virtually all forms of bounded and unbounded reduplication as they are found in typological studies (Moravcsik, 1978; Rubino, 2005). This finite-state technology not only describes reduplication as a process which applies to infinitely many words of unbounded size, but it does so without the state-space explosion. The type of transducer which accomplishes this is known as a 2-way Finite-State Transducer or 2-way FST (Savitch, 1982; Engelfriet and Hoogeboom, 2001; Filiot and Reynier, 2016). While these computer scientists are well aware that 2-way FSTS can model unbounded copying, this is the first use of 2-way FSTs within computational linguisticst to our knowledge.[2]

2-way FSTs are distinguished from the more well-known (1-way) finite-state transducers or 1-way FSTs by allowing the machine to move back and forth on the input tape, but not on the output tape. It is this increased power of 2-way FSTs that allows them to adequately model reduplication without the difficulties of using 1-way FSTs.

In this paper, we focus on *deterministic* 2-way FSTs. Like 1-way FSTs, 2-way FSTs can be either deterministic or non-deterministic on the input. Deterministic 1-way FSTs are less expressive than non-deterministic 1-way FSTs (Elgot and Mezei, 1965; Schützenberger, 1975; Choffrut, 1977; Mohri, 1997; Heinz and Lai, 2013). Similarly, deterministic 2-way FSTs are less expressive than non-deterministic 2-way FSTs (Culik and Karhumäki, 1986). For the typology of reduplication studied in this article, *deterministic* 2-way FSTs are sufficient. This result is in line with work showing that various phonological and morphological processes can be described with deterministic finite-state technology (Chandlee et al., 2012; Gainor et al., 2012; Chandlee and Heinz, 2012; Heinz and Lai, 2013; Chandlee, 2014; Luo, 2017; Payne, 2014, 2017).

<hr>

<sup>2</sup>2-way finite-state automata (2-way FSAs) have been used to model non-concatenative Semitic morphology (Narayanan and Hashem, 1993).

This article is organized as follows. 2-way finite-state transducers (2-way FSTs) are introduced in section §2, where we provide a formal definition (§2.1), discuss their computational properties (§2.2), and discuss their computational complexity (§2.3). In §3, we illustrate how 2-way FSTs can model reduplication, notably total reduplication (§3.1) and partial reduplication (§3.2). In section §4, we contrast 2-way FSTs with 1-way FSTs and show how the former are empirically adequate, practically convenient or useful, and linguistically-motivated for modeling reduplication. To illustrate this, we briefly discuss how we have used 2-way FSTs to develop the RedTyp database, a database of reduplicative processes with corresponding 2-way FSTs. Conclusions and directions for future research are in §5.

## 2 Two-way finite-state transducers: definition and properties

### 2.1 Definition

It is useful to imagine a 2-way FST as a machine operating on an input tape and writing to an output tape. The symbols on the input tape are drawn from an alphabet $\Sigma$ and the symbols written to the output tape are drawn from an alphabet $\Gamma$. For an input string $w = \sigma_1 \ldots \sigma_n$, the initial configuration is that the FST is in some internal state $q_0$, the read head. The FST begins at the first position of the tape reading $\sigma_1$, and the writing head of the FST is positioned at the beginning of an empty output tape. After the FST reads the symbol under the read head, three things occur:

- The internal state of the FST changes.
- The FST writes some string, possibly empty, to the output tape.
- The read head may move in one of three ways: it can either move to the left (-1), move to the right (+1), or stay (0).

This process repeats until the read head "falls off" one of the edges of the input tape. If for some input string $w$, the FST falls off the right edge of the input tape when the FST is in an accepting state after writing $u$ on the output tape, we say the FST transduces, transforms, or maps, $w$ to $u$. If for some input string $w$, the FST falls off the left edge, falls off the right edge while in a non-accepting state, or never falls off an edge, then the FST is undefined at $w$. Note the writing head of the FST can never move back along the output tape. It only ever advances as strings are written.

Below is a formalization of 2-way FSTs based on Filiot and Reynier (2016) and Shallit (2008). We adopt the convention that inputs to a 2-way FST are flanked with the start ($\rtimes$) and end boundaries ($\ltimes$). This larger alphabet is denoted by $\Sigma_{\ltimes}$.

4) **Definition:** A 2-way, deterministic FST is a six-tuple $(Q, \Sigma_{\ltimes}, \Gamma, q_0, F, \delta)$ such that:

$Q$ is a finite set of states,

$\Sigma_{\ltimes} = \Sigma \cup \{\rtimes, \ltimes\}$ is the input alphabet,

$\Gamma$ is the output alphabet,

$q_0 \in Q$ is the initial state,

$F \subseteq Q$ is the set of final states,

$\delta : Q \times \Sigma \rightarrow Q \times \Gamma^* \times D$ is the transition function where the direction $D = \{-1, 0, +1\}$.

A *configuration* of a 2-way FST $T$ is an element of $\Sigma_{\ltimes}^* Q \Sigma_{\ltimes}^* \times \Gamma^*$. The meaning of the configuration $(wqx, u)$ is that the input to $T$ is $wx$ and the machine is currently in state $q$ with the read head on the first symbol of $x$ (or has fallen off the right edge of the input tape if $x = \lambda$) and that $u$ is currently written on the output tape.

If the current configuration is $(wqax, u)$ and $\delta(q, a) = (r, v, 0)$ then the next configuration is $(wrax, uv)$, in which case we write $(wqax, u) \rightarrow (wrax, uv)$. If the current configuration is $(wqax, u)$ and $\delta(q, a) = (r, v, +1)$ then the next configuration is $(warx, uv)$. In this case, we write $(wqax, u) \rightarrow (warx, uv)$. If the current configuration is $(waqx, u)$ and $\delta(q, a) = (r, v, -1)$ then the next configuration is $(wrax, uv)$. We write $(waqx, u) \rightarrow (wrax, uv)$.

The transitive closure of $\rightarrow$ is denoted with $\rightarrow^+$. Thus, if $c \rightarrow^+ c'$ then there exists a finite sequence of configurations $c_1, c_2 \ldots c_n$ with $n > 1$ such that $c = c_1 \rightarrow c_2 \rightarrow \ldots \rightarrow c_n = c'$.

Next we define the function that a 2-way FST $T = (Q, \Sigma_{\ltimes}, \Gamma, q_0, F, \delta)$ computes. For each string $w \in \Sigma^*$, $f_T(w) = u \in \Gamma^*$ provided there exists $q_f \in F$ such that $(q_0 \rtimes w \ltimes, \lambda) \rightarrow^+ (\rtimes w \ltimes q_f, u)$. Note that since a 2-way FST is deterministic, it follows that if $f_T(w)$ is defined then $u$ is unique.

There are situations where a 2-way FST $T$ crashes on some input $w$ and hence $f_T(w)$ is undefined. If the configuration is $(qax, u)$ and $\delta(q, a) = (r, -1, v)$ then the derivation crashes and the transduction $f_T(ax)$ is undefined. Likewise, if the configuration is $(wq, u)$ and $q \notin F$ then the transducer crashes and the transduction $f_T$ is undefined on input $w$.

There is one more way in which $f_T$ may be undefined for some input. The input may cause the transducer to go into an infinite loop.[3] This occurs for input $wx \in \Sigma_{\ltimes}^*$ whenever there exist $q \in Q$ and $u, v \in \Gamma^*$ such that $(q_0 wx, \lambda) \rightarrow^+ (wqx, u) \rightarrow^+ (wqx, uv)$.

## 2.2 Computational properties

With respect to acceptors, 1-way and 2-way finite-state acceptors are equivalent in expressive power. Both define the regular languages (Hopcroft and Ullman, 1969; Shallit, 2008). However, with respect to transducers, 1-way FSTs are strictly less expressive than 2-way FSTs (Savitch, 1982; Aho et al., 1969). For a 1-way FST, both the input language and the output language must be regular languages. A 1-way FST thus cannot have its output language be the non-regular copy language $L_{ww} = \{ww | w \in \Sigma^*\}$. In contrast, as we will see, the output language of a 2-way FST can be a non-regular language such as $L_{ww}$. The next section will show that this additional power allows 2-way FSTs to productively model reduplication.

2-way FSTs are equivalent in expressivity to MSO-definable string transductions (Engelfriet and Hoogeboom, 2001) and to streaming string transducers (1-way FSTs with registers) (Alur, 2010). They are closed under composition (Chytil and Jákl, 1977) and their non-deterministic variants are invertible (Courcelle and Engelfriet, 2012). 2-way FSTs are less powerful than Turing machines because they cannot move back and forth over the output tape.

Note that given the difference in expressive power between 1-way and 2-way FSTs, it makes sense to give the classes of functions that they compute different names. We follow Filiot and Reynier (2016) who identify the class of functions describable with a 1-way deterministic FST as 'rational functions', and they reserve the term 'regular functions' for functions describable with 2-way deterministic FSTs.

---

[3]Infinite loops can be prevented through carefully designing the 2-way FST. The 2-way FSTs which we have made do not suffer from infinite loops. Infinite loops can likewise be checked and stopped during run-time.

## 2.3 Computational complexity

Deterministic 1-way FSTs run in time linear to the length of the input string. Since 2-way FSTs can reread the input string, is this still the case? One useful metric for measuring the complexity of deterministic 2-way FSTs is in terms of the number of times the 2-way FST passes through the input (Baschenis et al., 2016). In the case of the reduplication examples in §3, a deterministic 2-way FST can be designed with only two passes through the input per copy. Thus, the run time for a deterministic 2-way FST modeling reduplication which makes at most $n$ copies of an input string of length $m$ is $2n \cdot m$. Since $n$ is fixed by the reduplicative morpheme, the run time is still linear in the size of the input string.

Also, to our knowledge existing applications of regular functions have been efficient (Alur and Černý, 2011; Alur et al., 2014).

## 3 Illustrative use of two-way transducers for reduplication

Having established what 2-way FSTs are and how they behave, this section illustrates how they can be used model reduplication. We provide two illustrative examples: total reduplication (§3.1) and partial reduplication (§3.2).

### 3.1 Total reduplication

Total reduplication is cross-linguistically the most common reduplicative process (Rubino, 2005), and it is used in an estimated 85% of the world's languages (Rubino, 2013). A canonical example is total reduplication in Indonesian which marks plurality (Cohn, 1989). Examples are in Table 1.

| input | gloss | output | gloss |
|---|---|---|---|
| buku | 'book' | buku~buku | 'books' |
| wanita | 'woman' | wanita~wanita | 'women' |
| hak | 'right' | hak~hak | 'right' |
| kəra | 'donkey' | kəra~kəra | 'donkeys' |

Table 1: Total reduplication in Indonesian.

Figure 1 shows a 2-way FST that captures this total reduplication process. Basically, the 2-way FST in Figure 1 operates by:

1. reading the input tape once from left to right in order to output the first copy,
2. going back to the start of the input tape by moving left until the start boundary $\ltimes$ is reached,

3. reading the input tape once more from left to right in order to output the second copy.

Specifically, this figure is interpreted as follows. The symbol $\Sigma$ stands for any segment in the alphabet except for $\{\ltimes, \rtimes\}$. The arrow from $q_1$ to itself means this 2-way FST reads $\Sigma$, writes $\Sigma$, and advances the read head one step to the right on the input tape. The boundary symbol $\sim$ is a symbol in the output alphabet $\Gamma$, and is not necessary. We include it only for illustration.

We show an example derivation in Figure 2 of /buku/→[buku~buku] using the 2-way FST in Figure 1. The derivation shows the configurations of the computation for the input /buku/ and is step by step. Each tuple consists of four parts: *input string, output string, current state, transition*. In the *input string*, we underline the input symbol which FST will read next. The *output string* is what the 2-way FST has outputted up to that point. The symbol $\lambda$ marks the empty string. The *current state* is what state the FST is currently in. The *transition* represents the used transition arc from input to output. In the first tuple, there is no transition arc used (N/A). But for other tuples, the form of the arc is:

$$input\ state\ \xrightarrow[\text{direction}]{\text{input symbol:output string}} output\ state$$

### 3.2 Partial reduplication

Partial reduplication processes are also very common. A canonical example is initial-CV reduplication found in many Austronesian languages (Rubino, 2005). This section presents a simplified version of initial-CV reduplication from Bikol that is used to mark imperfective aspect (Mattes, 2007).[4] Examples are in Table 2.

| input | gloss | output | gloss |
|---|---|---|---|
| ŋirit | 'to laugh' | ŋi~ŋirit | 'laughing' |
| diretsjo | 'to continue' | di~diretsjo | 'continuing' |
| trabaho | 'to work' | ta~trabaho | 'working' |
| draɪf | 'to drive' | da~draɪf | 'driving' |

Table 2: Initial-CV reduplication in Bikol.

Initial-CV reduplication in Bikol has two phonological modifications processes[5] apply to the reduplicant, i.e. the smaller copy:

---

[4] Initial-CV reduplication in Bikol targets the root and is triggered by the addition of certain prefixes. For illustrative purposes, we set aside these prefixes.

[5] These modifications effects are often called TETU (or *the emergence of the unmarked*) effects in the linguistics literature (McCarthy and Prince, 1994, 1995).

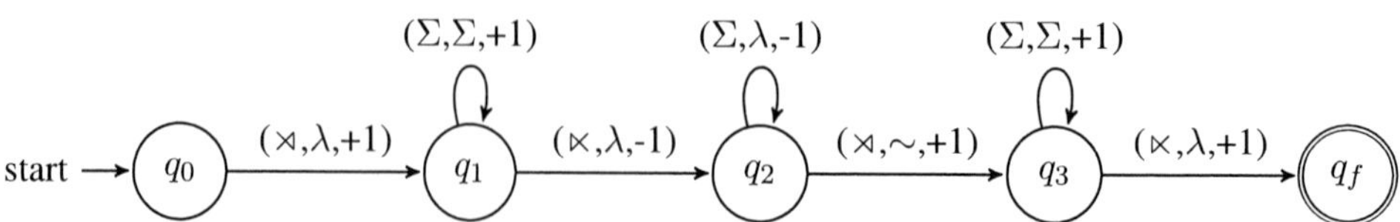

Figure 1: 2-way FST for total reduplication in Indonesian.

| Outputting the first copy | | | | |
|---|---|---|---|---|
| 1. (⋊buku⋉, | λ, | $q_0$, | N/A) | |
| 2. (⋊buku⋉, | λ, | $q_1$, | $q_0 \xrightarrow[+1]{⋊:λ} q_1$) | |
| 3. (⋊buku⋉, | b, | $q_1$, | $q_1 \xrightarrow[+1]{Σ:Σ} q_1$) | |
| 4. (⋊buku⋉, | bu, | $q_1$, | $q_1 \xrightarrow[+1]{Σ:Σ} q_1$) | |
| 5. (⋊buku⋉, | buk, | $q_1$, | $q_1 \xrightarrow[+1]{Σ:Σ} q_1$) | |
| 6. (⋊buku⋉, | buku, | $q_1$, | $q_1 \xrightarrow[+1]{Σ:Σ} q_1$) | |
| 7. (⋊buku⋉, | buku~, | $q_2$, | $q_1 \xrightarrow[-1]{⋉:\sim} q_2$) | |
| 8. (⋊buku⋉, | buku~, | $q_2$, | $q_2 \xrightarrow[-1]{Σ:λ} q_2$) | |
| 9. (⋊buku⋉, | buku~, | $q_2$, | $q_2 \xrightarrow[-1]{Σ:λ} q_2$) | |
| 10. (⋊buku⋉, | buku~, | $q_2$, | $q_2 \xrightarrow[-1]{Σ:λ} q_2$) | |
| 11. (⋊buku⋉, | buku~, | $q_2$, | $q_2 \xrightarrow[-1]{Σ:λ} q_2$) | |
| Outputting the second copy | | | | |
| 12. (⋊buku⋉, | buku~, | $q_3$, | $q_2 \xrightarrow[+1]{⋊:λ} q_3$) | |
| 13. (⋊buku⋉, | buku~b, | $q_3$, | $q_3 \xrightarrow[+1]{Σ:Σ} q_3$) | |
| 14. (⋊buku⋉, | buku~bu, | $q_3$, | $q_3 \xrightarrow[+1]{Σ:Σ} q_3$) | |
| 15. (⋊buku⋉, | buku~buk, | $q_3$, | $q_3 \xrightarrow[+1]{Σ:Σ} q_3$) | |
| 16. (⋊buku⋉, | buku~buku, | $q_3$, | $q_3 \xrightarrow[+1]{Σ:Σ} q_3$) | |
| 17. (⋊buku⋉, | buku~buku, | $q_f$, | $q_3 \xrightarrow[+1]{⋉:⋉} q_f$) | |

Figure 2: Derivation of /buku/→[buku~buku].

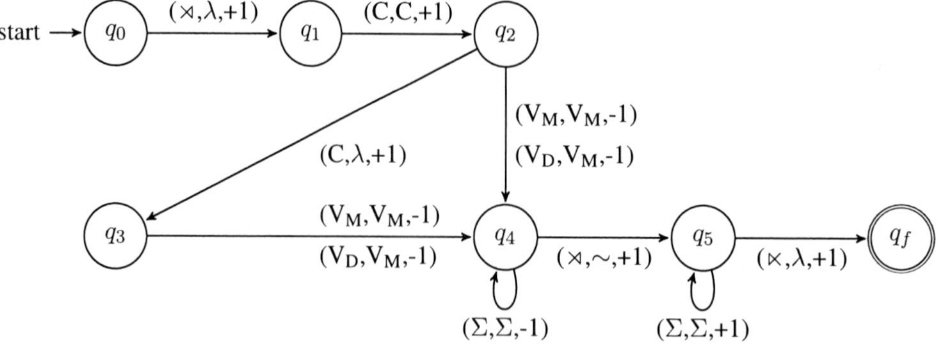

Figure 3: 2-way FST for initial-CV reduplication in Bikol.

- complex onsets are reduced to simple onsets, e.g. /trabaho/→[ta~trabaho] 'working'
- diphthongs are reduced to monophthongs, e.g. /draɪf/→[da~draɪf] 'driving'

The 2-way FST in Figure 3 captures the partial reduplication pattern and its modifications. The symbol $V_M$ stands for monophthongs, $V_D$ for diphthongs, and C for consonants. An example derivation of /draɪf/→[da~draɪf] using our 2-way FST is provided in Figure 4.[6]

## 4 Contrasting 2-way FSTs with 1-way FSTs

Having illustrated how 2-way FSTs can model reduplication, here we contrast 2-way FSTs with 1-way FSTs on three criteria: empirical coverage, practical utility, and intensional description.

We do not contrast 2-way FSTs with more powerful formalisms like pushdown transducers (Allauzen and Riley, 2012). We do not assume the former are superior to other such formalisms. Our goal is to show 2-way FSTs have practical and scientific utility in computational linguistics; thus, they merit further study.

### 4.1 Empirical coverage

In terms of empirical coverage, 2-way FSTs can model *virtually* the entire typology of reduplication (Moravcsik, 1978; Hurch, 2005; Inkelas and Zoll, 2005; Rubino, 2005; Samuels, 2010). This includes both local reduplication (as in the two examples from §3), but likewise non-local or 'wrong-side' reduplication (Riggle, 2004), internal reduplication (Broselow and McCarthy, 1983), multiple reduplication (Urbanczyk, 1999), sub-constituent reduplication (Downing, 1998), and cases of interactions between reduplication and opaque phonological processes (overapplication, underapplication, backcopying) (McCarthy and Prince, 1995). This is especially the case for total reduplication which is the most widespread reduplicative process (Rubino, 2013) but which cannot be modeled with 1-way FSTs. In most cases, this will be inadequate because total reduplication is a productive grammatical process (Rubino, 2005, 2013).

We emphasize the term *virtually* because in our investigation we have found only two marginal cases of reduplication in the literature which cannot be modeled by 2-way FSTs unless certain plausible assumptions are made. These two cases involve reduplication producing suppletive allomorphs of morphemes as in Sye (Inkelas and Zoll, 2005, 52), and reduplication being blocked by homophony or haplology as in Kanuri (Moravcsik, 1978, 313). These two cases of 'under-generation' can be solved if we assume the language contains a finite number of suppletive allomorphs, and if we assume that there's either a finite number of banned identical sequences or a separate linguistic mechanism that filters out ill-formed homophonies.

Of course there are cases where 2-way FSTs can 'over-generate' and model unattested types of reduplication, e.g. reduplicate a word $n$ times for some natural number $n$ or reduplicate a word by reversing it. This over-generation can be addressed by either restricting the class of 2-way FSTs used (Dolatian and Heinz, 2018) or by not treating 2-way FSTs as having to be exact models of human cognition (Potts and Pullum, 2002). For further discussion and solutions on how 2-way FSTs can over- and under-generate, see Dolatian and Heinz (In press.).

### 4.2 Practical utility

To showcase empirical coverage of 2-way FSTs and their practical utility, we have constructed the RedTyp database[7] which contains entries for 138 reduplicative processes from 91 languages gleaned from various surveys (Rubino, 2005; Inkelas and Downing, 2015). 50 of these processes were from Moravcsik (1978), an early survey which is representative of the cross-linguistically most common reduplicative patterns. RedTyp contains 57 distinct 2-way FSTs that model the 138 processes.[8] Each 2-way FST was designed manually, implemented in Python, and checked for correctness. On average, these 2-way FSTs had 8.8 states. This shows that 2-way FSTs are concise and convenient computational descriptions and models for reduplicative morphology. This is in contrast to 1-way FSTs which suffer from an explosion of states when modeling partial redupli-

---

[6]The FST treats the diphthong /aɪ/ as a single segment.

[7]A copy of RedTyp can be found online at our GitHub page https://github.com/jhdeov/RedTyp.

[8]To our knowledge, the only other database on reduplication is the Graz Database on Reduplication (Hurch, 2005 ff.). However, RedTyp differs from the Graz Database because the latter does not include computational representations or implementations of its entries.

| Outputting reduplicant | | |
|---|---|---|
| 1. (⋊draɪf⋉,    λ,    $q_0$,    N/A) | 4. (⋊draɪf⋉,    d,    $q_3$,    $q_2 \xrightarrow[+1]{C:C} q_3$) |
| 2. (⋊draɪf⋉,    λ,    $q_1$,    $q_0 \xrightarrow[+1]{⋊:λ} q_1$) | 5. (⋊draɪf⋉,    da,    $q_4$,    $q_3 \xrightarrow[-1]{V_D:V_M} q_4$) |
| 3. (⋊draɪf⋉,    d,    $q_2$,    $q_1 \xrightarrow[+1]{C:C} q_2$) | |

| Going back to the start of the tape | |
|---|---|
| 6. (⋊draɪf⋉,    da,    $q_4$,    $q_4 \xrightarrow[-1]{\Sigma:λ} q_4$) | 7. (⋊draɪf⋉,    da,    $q_4$,    $q_4 \xrightarrow[-1]{\Sigma:λ} q_4$) |

| Outputting the base | |
|---|---|
| 8. (⋊draɪf⋉,    da~,    $q_5$,    $q_4 \xrightarrow[+1]{⋊:\sim} q_5$) | 11. (⋊draɪf⋉,    da~draɪ,    $q_5$,    $q_5 \xrightarrow[+1]{\Sigma:\Sigma} q_5$) |
| 9. (⋊draɪf⋉,    da~d,    $q_5$,    $q_5 \xrightarrow[+1]{\Sigma:\Sigma} q_5$) | 12. (⋊draɪf⋉,    da~draɪf,    $q_5$,    $q_5 \xrightarrow[+1]{\Sigma:\Sigma} q_5$) |
| 10. (⋊draɪf⋉,    da~dr,    $q_5$,    $q_5 \xrightarrow[+1]{\Sigma:\Sigma} q_5$) | 13. (⋊draɪf⋉,    da~draɪf,    $q_f$,    $q_5 \xrightarrow[+1]{⋉:λ} q_5$) |

Figure 4: Derivation of /draɪf/→[da~draɪf].

cation.[9] On average, a language's phoneme inventory would include 22 consonants and 5 vowels (Maddieson, 2013a,b). In order to handle initial-CV, initial-CVC, or initial-CVCV reduplication with a 1-way FST, the FST would require at least an estimated 22, 110, and 2420 states respectively.

### 4.3 Linguistic motivation and origin semantics

Finally, using 2-way FSTs for reduplication is linguistically motivated and matches the intensional descriptions behind the linguistic generalizations on reduplication. 2-way FSTs do not approximate reduplication like 1-way FSTs do. They can fully and productively model reduplicative processes as they appear in the typology, including both partial and total reduplication. As said, this is because 1-way FSTs simply *remember* the possible shapes for a reduplicant when the number of possible shapes is (large yet) finite as in partial reduplication. When the number of possible shapes to remember is unbounded as in total reduplication, a 1-way FST cannot productively model reduplication. In contrast, a 2-way FST does not need to remember strings of segments in order to copy them, but *actively copies* them.

This contrast between copying and remembering can be formalized with the notion of the *origin semantics* of a transduction (Bojańczyk, 2014).

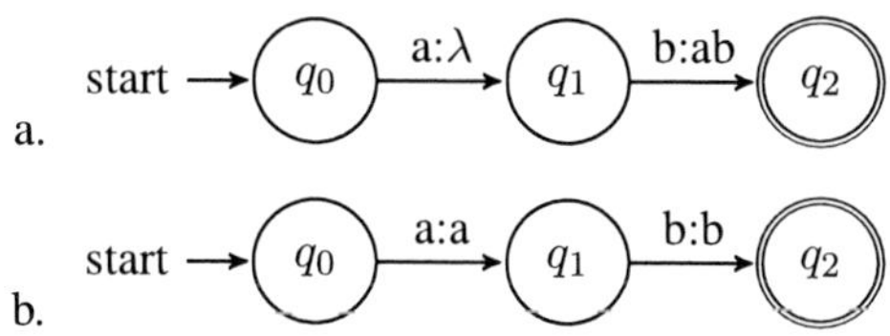



Figure 5: Pair of 1-way FSTs for the function $f_{ab}$.

Given a string-to-string function, the origin semantics of a function is the origin information of each symbol $o_n$ in the output string. This is the position $i_m$ of the read head on the input tape when the transducer had outputted $o_n$.

To illustrate, consider a string-to-string function $f_{ab}$ which maps $ab$ to itself, and every other string to the empty string: $f(x) = \{(ab, ab), (a, λ), (b, λ), ...\}$. This function can be modeled with at least two different 1-way FSTs as in Figure 5 which differ in when they output the output symbols $a$ and $b$. In Figure 6, we show the origin information created by the two 1-way FSTs from Figure 5 for the mapping $(ab, ab)$. The two FSTs model the same function and are equivalent in their general semantics of what they output; however, they are not equivalent in their origin semantics because they create differ origin information for their output.

This notion of origin semantics can be used to contrast how 1-way FSTs and 2-way FSTs model reduplication. Consider the case of Bikol initial-CV reduplication from section §3.2 and assume a smaller alphabet $\Sigma = \{p,a,t\}$. This function can

---

[9] The largest 2-way FST in RedTyp is for verbal reduplication in Kinande (Downing, 2000) with 29 states. This pattern depends on the size of the root and the number and type of suffixes and prefixes around it. In contrast, we estimate a deterministic 1-way FST would require over 1,000 states for this pattern of partial reduplication.

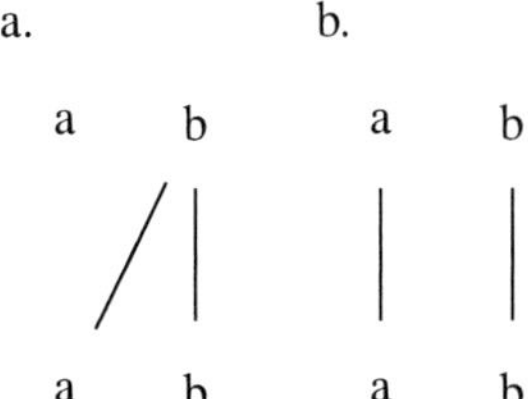

Figure 6: Origin information created by the 1-way FSTs (5) for the mapping *ab*→*ab*.

be modeled by the same 2-way FST in Figure 3. Because of the bound on the size of the reduplicant, this function can also be modeled with the 1-way FST in Figure 7.

The two transducers in Figures 3,7 are equivalent in their general semantics because they can output the same string. For example, given the input /pat/, both FSTs will output [pa~pat]. However, the two FSTs differ in their origin semantics. Given the mapping /pat/→[pa~pat], the two FSTs will create different origin information. Setting aside the word boundaries and reduplicant boundary ~, the 1-way FST associates the second *pa* string of the output with the vowel *a* of the input as in Figure 8a. This is because the second *pa* was outputted when the 1-way FST was reading the *a* in the input. In contrast, the 2-way FST associates each segment in the output with an identical segment in the input as in Figure 8b.

The origin information created by the 2-way FST matches theoretical treatments of how the reduplicant's segments are individually associated with identical segments in the input (Marantz, 1982; Inkelas and Zoll, 2005). In contrast, the origin information created by the 1-way FST does not match any linguistic intuitions of reduplication because non-identical segments are associated. This difference in the origin semantics of the 1-way FST and 2-way FST formalizes their difference in behavior: the 1-way FST simply remembers what strings of segments to output twice, while the 2-way FST actively copies.

In Base-Reduplicant correspondence theory (BRCT), what matters for reduplication is not the relationship or correspondence between input and output segments in the reduplication, but between the two copies in the output (McCarthy and Prince, 1995). Origin semantics might be able to formalize the intuition behind BRCT with finite-state technology (output symbols with the same origin

are in correspondence). The only computational implementation of BRCT to our knowledge (Albro, 2000, 2005) uses MCFGs to do so. Note however that the empirical validity of BRCT is questionable (Inkelas and Zoll, 2005; McCarthy et al., 2012).

## 5 Conclusion

In summary, finite-state technology has often been argued to be incapable of adequately and efficiently capturing productive reduplication as used in natural language. However, this article shows that an understudied type of finite-state machinery—2-way finite-state transducers—can exactly model reduplication and its wide typology.

2-way FSTs can model the virtually entire typology of reduplication, without needing to approximate any processes (unlike 1-way FSTs). They likewise do not suffer from a state explosion for partial reduplication because the size of the 2-way FST is not dependent on the size of the alphabet. This allows 2-way FSTs to directly capture the copying aspect of reduplication instead of remembering all potential reduplicants. This makes 2-way FSTs be a practical, convenient, and concise tool to model reduplication. As a sign of their empirical coverage and utility, we developed the RedTyp database of reduplicative processes that contains 57 distinct 2-way FSTs which model common and uncommon reduplicative processes covered in the literature (Moravcsik, 1978).

Having showcased their utility, several avenues of future research remain, of which we highlight three. First, we have approached reduplication from the perspective of morphological generation. Given an input /buku/, a 2-way can generate the output [buku~buku] easily. On the other hand, it is an open question as to how to do morphological *analysis* with 2-way FSTs to get the inverse relation of [buku~buku→buku].[10]

A second, more practical, area of research is the integration of 2-way FSTs into natural language processing. This obviously has many aspects. A first step may be the integration of 2-way FSTs into existing platforms such as `xfst` (Beesley and Karttunen, 2003), `foma` (Hulden, 2009b), `open-fst` (Allauzen et al., 2007), and `pynini` (Gorman, 2016).

---

[10]One potential route may be the use of non-deterministic 2-way FSTs (Alur and Deshmukh, 2011).

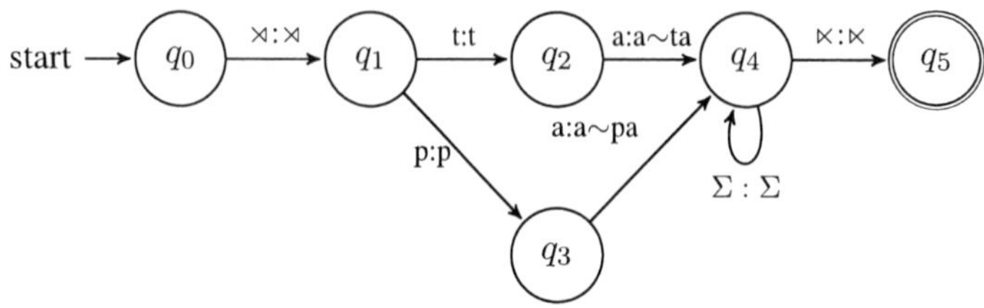


Figure 7: 1-way FST for partial reduplication.

a. Origin information of the 1-way FST

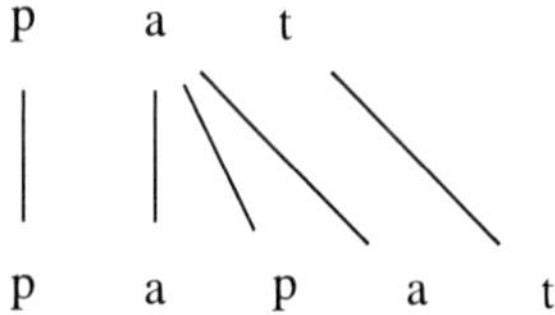


b. Origin information of the 2-way FST

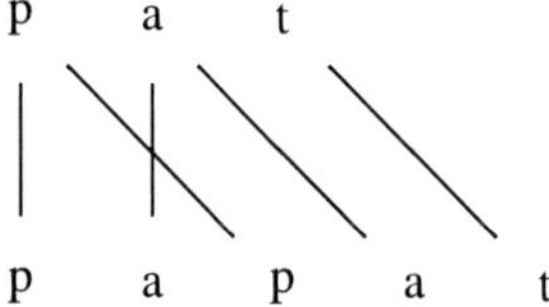


Figure 8: Origin information of /pat/→[pa∼pat] created by the 1-way FST (Figure 7) vs. the 2-way FST (Figure 3).

Third, it is theoretically interesting that within morpho-phonology, only reduplication requires the bidirectional power of 2-way FSTs. The bulk of morphology and phonology can be modeled with non-deterministic 1-way finite-state transducers (Beesley and Karttunen, 2003; Jardine, 2016) or subclasses of them (Chandlee, 2017). As a copying process, reduplication requires more than just 1-way finite-state technology. This may be a sign that it is of a different nature than the rest of morpho-phonology (Inkelas and Zoll, 2005; Urbanczyk, 2017). It is an open question if 2-way FSTs can likewise be used to model copying in other areas of natural language, including syntactic copying (Kobele, 2006).

Fourth, in the same way that Chandlee 2014; 2017 and Chandlee et al. (2014, 2015) have studied subclasses of 1-way FSTs and shown how they map to subclasses of morpho-phonology, we are currently investigating what proper subclasses of 2-way FSTs can be designed in order to make a tighter fit with reduplicative typology. This would

open doors to not only better understanding the computational properties of reduplication, but to likewise develop learning algorithms for reduplication. As of now, we hypothesize that a large majority of reduplicative fall under a sub-class of 2-way FSTs (that we have discovered) based on a 2-way extension of the Output-Strictly Local subclass of 1-way FSTs (Chandlee et al., 2015). For more discussion of this subclass for reduplication and its learnability, see Dolatian and Heinz (2018).

In sum, the present study is the initial step in formalizing the wide typology of reduplicative processes into mathematically sound, yet expressively adequate, formal-language theoretic terms. Future work will include incorporating this technology into existing platforms and NLP systems, and further bridging the gaps between computational and theoretical morpho-phonology.

## Acknowledgments


This research is supported by NIH grant #R01-HD087133 to JH. We thank the reviewers and audiences at CLS53, NAPhCX, the University of Delaware, and Stony Brook University.


## References


Alfred V. Aho, John E. Hopcroft, and Jeffrey D. Ullman. 1969. A general theory of translation. *Mathematical Systems Theory*, 3(3):193–221.

Daniel M. Albro. 2000. Taking primitive Optimality Theory beyond the finite state. In *Finite-state phonology: proceedings of the 5th Workshop of SIGPHON*, pages 57–67.

Daniel M. Albro. 2005. *Studies in Computational Optimality Theory, with Special Reference to the Phonological System of Malagasy*. Ph.D. thesis, University of California, Los Angeles, Los Angeles.

Cyril Allauzen and Michael Riley. 2012. A pushdown transducer extension for the OpenFst library. In *Implementation and Application of Automata*, pages 66–77, Berlin, Heidelberg. Springer.

Cyril Allauzen, Michael Riley, Johan Schalkwyk, Wojciech Skut, and Mehryar Mohri. 2007. OpenFst: A general and efficient weighted finite-state transducer library. In *Implementation and Application of Automata*, pages 11–23, Berlin, Heidelberg. Springer.

Rajeev Alur. 2010. Expressiveness of streaming string transducers. In *Proceedings of the 30th Annual Conference on Foundations of Software Technology and Theoretical Computer Science,*, volume 8, page 112.

Rajeev Alur and Jyotirmoy V. Deshmukh. 2011. Nondeterministic streaming string transducers. In *Automata, Languages and Programming*, pages 1–20, Berlin, Heidelberg. Springer.

Rajeev Alur, Adam Freilich, and Mukund Raghothaman. 2014. Regular combinators for string transformations. In *Proceedings of the Joint Meeting of the Twenty-Third EACSL Annual Conference on Computer Science Logic (CSL) and the Twenty-Ninth Annual ACM/IEEE Symposium on Logic in Computer Science (LICS)*, CSL-LICS '14, pages 9:1–9:10, New York, NY, USA. ACM.

Rajeev Alur and Pavol Černý. 2011. Streaming transducers for algorithmic verification of single-pass list-processing programs. In *Proceedings of the 38th Annual ACM SIGPLAN-SIGACT Symposium on Principles of Programming Languages*, POPL '11, pages 599–610, New York, NY, USA. ACM.

Félix Baschenis, Olivier Gauwin, Anca Muscholl, and Gabriele Puppis. 2016. Minimizing Resources of Sweeping and Streaming String Transducers. In *43rd International Colloquium on Automata, Languages, and Programming (ICALP 2016)*, volume 55 of *Leibniz International Proceedings in Informatics (LIPIcs)*, pages 114:1–114:14, Dagstuhl, Germany. Schloss Dagstuhl–Leibniz-Zentrum fuer Informatik.

Kenneth R. Beesley and Lauri Karttunen. 2000. Finite-state non-concatenative morphotactics. In *Proceedings of the 38th Annual Meeting on Association for Computational Linguistics*, ACL '00, pages 191–198, Stroudsburg, PA, USA. Association for Computational Linguistics.

Kenneth R. Beesley and Lauri Karttunen. 2003. *Finite-state morphology: Xerox tools and techniques*. CSLI Publications.

Mikołaj Bojańczyk. 2014. Transducers with origin information. In *Automata, Languages, and Programming*, pages 26–37, Berlin, Heidelberg. Springer.

Ellen Broselow and John McCarthy. 1983. A theory of internal reduplication. *The Linguistic Review*, 3(1):25–88.

Jane Chandlee. 2014. *Strictly Local Phonological Processes*. Ph.D. thesis, University of Delaware, Newark, DE.

Jane Chandlee. 2017. Computational locality in morphological maps. *Morphology*, pages 1–43.

Jane Chandlee, Angeliki Athanasopoulou, and Jeffrey Heinz. 2012. Evidence for classifying metathesis patterns as subsequential. In *The Proceedings of the 29th West Coast Conference on Formal Linguistics*, pages 303–309, Somerville, MA. Cascillida Press.

Jane Chandlee, Rémi Eyraud, and Jeffrey Heinz. 2014. Learning strictly local subsequential functions. *Transactions of the Association for Computational Linguistics*, 2:491–503.

Jane Chandlee, Rémi Eyraud, and Jeffrey Heinz. 2015. Output strictly local functions. In *Proceedings of the 14th Meeting on the Mathematics of Language (MoL 2015)*, pages 112–125, Chicago, USA.

Jane Chandlee and Jeffrey Heinz. 2012. Bounded copying is subsequential: Implications for metathesis and reduplication. In *Proceedings of the 12th Meeting of the ACL Special Interest Group on Computational Morphology and Phonology*, SIGMORPHON '12, pages 42–51, Montreal, Canada. Association for Computational Linguistics.

Christian Choffrut. 1977. Une caractérisation des fonctions séquentielles et des fonctions sousséquentielles en tant que relations rationnelles. *Theoretical Computer Science*, 5(3):325–337.

Michal P. Chytil and Vojtěch Jákl. 1977. Serial composition of 2-way finite-state transducers and simple programs on strings. In *Automata, Languages and Programming*, pages 135–147, Berlin, Heidelberg. Springer.

Yael Cohen-Sygal and Shuly Wintner. 2006. Finite-state registered automata for non-concatenative morphology. *Computational Linguistics*, 32(1):49–82.

Abigail C Cohn. 1989. Stress in Indonesian and bracketing paradoxes. *Natural language & linguistic theory*, 7(2):167–216.

Bruno Courcelle and Joost Engelfriet. 2012. *Graph Structure and Monadic Second-Order Logic, a Language Theoretic Approach*. Cambridge University Press.

Berthold Crysmann. 2017. Reduplication in a computational HPSG of Hausa. *Morphology*, 27(4):527–561.

Karel Culik and Juhani Karhumäki. 1986. The equivalence of finite valued transducers (on HDT0L languages) is decidable. *Theoretical Computer Science*, 47:71 – 84.

Christopher Culy. 1985. The complexity of the vocabulary of Bambara. *Linguistics and philosophy*, 8:345–351.

Hossep Dolatian and Jeffrey Heinz. 2018. Learning reduplication with 2-way finite-state transducers. In *Proceedings of Machine Learning Research: International Conference on Grammatical Inference*, volume 93 of *Proceedings of Machine Learning Research*, pages 67–80, Wroclaw, Poland.

Hossep Dolatian and Jeffrey Heinz. In press. Reduplication with finite-state technology. In *Proceedings of the 53rd Annual Meeting of the Chicago Linguistics Society*.

Laura J Downing. 1998. Prosodic misalignment and reduplication. In Geert Booij and Jaap van Marle, editors, *Yearbook of Morphology 1997*, pages 83–120. Kluwer Academic Publishers, Dordrecht.

Laura J Downing. 2000. Morphological and prosodic constraints on Kinande verbal reduplication. *Phonology*, 17(01):1–38.

C. C. Elgot and J. E. Mezei. 1965. On relations defined by generalized finite automata. *IBM Journal of Research and Development*, 9(1):47–68.

Joost Engelfriet and Hendrik Jan Hoogeboom. 2001. MSO definable string transductions and two-way finite-state transducers. *ACM Trans. Comput. Logic*, 2(2):216–254.

Emmanuel Filiot and Pierre-Alain Reynier. 2016. Transducers, logic and algebra for functions of finite words. *ACM SIGLOG News*, 3(3):4–19.

Brian Gainor, Regine Lai, and Jeffrey Heinz. 2012. Computational characterizations of vowel harmony patterns and pathologies. In *The Proceedings of the 29th West Coast Conference on Formal Linguistics*, pages 63–71, Somerville, MA. Cascillida Press.

Kyle Gorman. 2016. Pynini: A python library for weighted finite-state grammar compilation. In *Proceedings of the SIGFSM Workshop on Statistical NLP and Weighted Automata*, pages 75–80. Association for Computational Linguistics.

Jeffrey Heinz and Regine Lai. 2013. Vowel harmony and subsequentiality. In *Proceedings of the 13th Meeting on the Mathematics of Language (MoL 13)*, pages 52–63, Sofia, Bulgaria. Association for Computational Linguistics.

John E Hopcroft and Jeffrey D Ullman. 1969. *Formal languages and their relation to automata*. Addison-Wesley Longman Publishing Co., Inc., Boston:MA.

Mans Hulden. 2009a. *Finite-state machine construction methods and algorithms for phonology and morphology*. Ph.D. thesis, The University of Arizona, Tucson, AZ.

Mans Hulden. 2009b. Foma: a finite-state compiler and library. In *Proceedings of the Demonstrations Session at EACL 2009*, pages 29–32. Association for Computational Linguistics.

Mans Hulden and Shannon T Bischoff. 2009. A simple formalism for capturing reduplication in finite-state morphology. In *Proceedings of the 2009 conference on Finite-State Methods and Natural Language Processing: Post-proceedings of the 7th International Workshop FSMNLP 2008*, pages 207–214, Amsterdam. IOS Press.

Bernhard Hurch, editor. 2005. *Studies on reduplication*. 28. Walter de Gruyter, Berlin.

Bernhard Hurch. 2005 ff. Graz database on reduplication. Last accessed 10-26-2017 from `http://reduplication.uni-graz.at/redup/`.

Sharon Inkelas and Laura J Downing. 2015. What is reduplication? Typology and analysis part 1/2: The typology of reduplication. *Language and Linguistics Compass*, 9(12):502–515.

Sharon Inkelas and Cheryl Zoll. 2005. *Reduplication: Doubling in Morphology*. Cambridge University Press, Cambridge.

Adam Jardine. 2016. Computationally, tone is different. *Phonology*, 33(2):247–283.

Ronald Kaplan and Martin Kay. 1994. Regular models of phonological rule systems. *Computational Linguistics*, 20(3):331–378.

Gregory Michael Kobele. 2006. *Generating Copies: An investigation into structural identity in language and grammar*. Ph.D. thesis, University of California, Los Angeles.

Huan Luo. 2017. Long-distance consonant agreement and subsequentiality. *Glossa: a journal of general linguistics*, 2(1):125.

Ian Maddieson. 2013a. *Consonant Inventories*. Max Planck Institute for Evolutionary Anthropology, Leipzig.

Ian Maddieson. 2013b. *Vowel Quality Inventories*. Max Planck Institute for Evolutionary Anthropology, Leipzig.

Alec Marantz. 1982. Re reduplication. *Linguistic inquiry*, 13(3):435–482.

Veronika Mattes. 2007. *Reduplication in Bikol*. Ph.D. thesis, University of Graz, Graz, Austria.

John J McCarthy, Wendell Kimper, and Kevin Mullin. 2012. Reduplication in harmonic serialism. *Morphology*, 22(2):173–232.

John J McCarthy and Alan Prince. 1995. Faithfulness and reduplicative identity. In Jill N. Beckman, Laura Walsh Dickey, and Suzanne Urbanczyk, editors, *Papers in Optimality Theory*. Graduate Linguistic Student Association, University of Massachusetts, Amherst, MA.

John J McCarthy and Alan S Prince. 1994. The emergence of the unmarked: Optimality in prosodic morphology. In *Proceedings of the North East Linguistic Society 24*, page 33379, Amherst, MA. Graduate Linguistic Student Association, University of Massachusetts.

Mehryar Mohri. 1997. Finite-state transducers in language and speech processing. *Computational Linguistics*, 23(2):269–311.

Edith Moravcsik. 1978. Reduplicative constructions. In Joseph Greenberg, editor, *Universals of Human Language*, volume 1, pages 297–334. Stanford University Press, Stanford, California.

Ajit Narayanan and Lama Hashem. 1993. On abstract finite-state morphology. In *Proceedings of the Sixth Conference on European Chapter of the Association for Computational Linguistics*, EACL '93, pages 297–304, Stroudsburg, PA, USA. Association for Computational Linguistics.

Amanda Payne. 2014. Dissimilation as a subsequential process. In *NELS 44: Proceedings of the 44th Meeting of the North East Linguistic Society*, volume 2, pages 79–90, Amherst, MA. Graduate Linguistic Student Association, University of Massachusetts.

Amanda Payne. 2017. All dissimilation is computationally subsequential. *Language: Phonological Analysis*, 93(4):e353–e371.

Christopher Potts and Geoffrey K Pullum. 2002. Model theory and the content of OT constraints. *Phonology*, 19(3):361–393.

Jason Riggle. 2004. Nonlocal reduplication. In *Proceedings of the 34th meeting of the North Eastern Einguistics Society*. Graduate Linguistic Student Association, University of Massachusetts.

Brian Roark and Richard Sproat. 2007. *Computational Approaches to Morphology and Syntax*. Oxford University Press, Oxford.

Carl Rubino. 2005. Reduplication: Form, function and distribution. In *Studies on reduplication*, pages 11–29. Mouton de Gruyter, Berlin.

Carl Rubino. 2013. *Reduplication*. Max Planck Institute for Evolutionary Anthropology, Leipzig.

Bridget Samuels. 2010. The topology of infixation and reduplication. *The Linguistic Review*, 27(2):131–176.

Walter J Savitch. 1982. *Abstract machines and grammars*. Little Brown and Company, Boston.

Walter J Savitch. 1989. A formal model for context-free languages augmented with reduplication. *Computational Linguistics*, 15(4):250–261.

Marcel-Paul Schützenberger. 1975. Sur certaines opérations de fermeture dans les langages rationnels. In *Symposia Mathematica*, volume 15, pages 245–253.

Jeffrey Shallit. 2008. *A Second Course in Formal Languages and Automata Theory*, 1 edition. Cambridge University Press, New York, NY, USA.

Richard William Sproat. 1992. *Morphology and computation*. MIT press, Cambridge:MA.

Thomas Stolz, Cornelia Stroh, and Aina Urdze. 2011. *Total reduplication: The areal linguistics of a potential universal*, volume 8. Walter de Gruyter, Berlin.

Suzanne Urbanczyk. 1999. Double reduplications in parallel. In René Kager, Harry vn der Hulst, and Wim Zonneveld, editors, *The prosody-morphology interface*, pages 390–428. Cambridge University Press, Cambridge.

Suzanne Urbanczyk. 2017. Phonological and morphological aspects of reduplication.

Markus Walther. 2000. Finite-state reduplication in one-level prosodic morphology. In *Proceedings of the 1st North American chapter of the Association for Computational Linguistics conference*, NAACL 2000, pages 296–302, Stroudsburg, PA. Association for Computational Linguistics.

Ronnie B Wilbur. 2005. A reanalysis of reduplication in american sign language. In *Studies on reduplication*, pages 595–623. Berlin: Mouton de Gruyter.

# Automatically Tailoring Unsupervised Morphological Segmentation to the Language


**Ramy Eskander**[†]     **Owen Rambow**[♯]     **Smaranda Muresan**[†‡]

[†]Department of Computer Science, Columbia University
[‡]Data Science Institute, Columbia University
`{rnd2110,smara}@columbia.edu`
[♯]Elemental Cognition, Inc.
`owenr@elementalcognition.com`



## Abstract

Morphological segmentation is beneficial for several natural language processing tasks dealing with large vocabularies. Unsupervised methods for morphological segmentation are essential for handling a diverse set of languages, including low-resource languages. Eskander et al. (2016) introduced a Language Independent Morphological Segmenter (LIMS) using Adaptor Grammars (AG) based on the best-on-average performing AG configuration. However, while LIMS worked best on average and outperforms other state-of-the-art unsupervised morphological segmentation approaches, it did not provide the optimal AG configuration for five out of the six languages. We propose two language-independent classifiers that enable the selection of the optimal or nearly-optimal configuration for the morphological segmentation of unseen languages.


## 1 Introduction

As natural language processing becomes more interested in many languages, including low-resource languages, unsupervised morphological segmentation remains an important area of study. For most of the languages of the world, we do not have morphologically annotated resources. However, many human language technologies profit from morphological segmentation, for example machine translation (Nguyen et al., 2010; Ataman et al., 2017) and speech recognition (Narasimhan et al., 2014).

In this paper, we build on previous work on unsupervised morphological segmentation using Adaptor Grammars (AGs) (Johnson, 2008; Sirts and Goldwater, 2013; Eskander et al., 2016), a type of nonparametric Bayesian models that generalize probabilistic context-free grammars (PCFGs) (Johnson et al., 2007), where the PCFG is typically a morphological grammar that spec-

ifies the word structure. Specifically, we extend the research proposed by Eskander et al. (2016), who investigate a large space of parameters when using Adaptor Grammars related to (i) the underlying context-free grammar and (ii) the use of a "Cascaded" system in which one grammar chooses affixes to be seeded into another in order to simulate the situation where scholar-knowledge is available. Their results on a development set of 6 languages (English, German, Finish, Turkish, Estonian and Zulu) show that the best performing AG-based configuration (grammar and learning setup) differ from language to language. For processing unseen languages, Eskander et al. (2016) proposed the Language-Independent Morphological Segmenter (LIMS) based on the best-on-average performing configuration when running leave-one-out cross validation on the development languages.

However, while LIMS works best on average and has been shown to outperform other state-of-the-art unsupervised morphological segmentation systems (Eskander et al., 2016), it is not the optimal configuration for any of the development languages except Zulu. Thus, in this paper we propose an approach to automatically select the optimal or nearly-optimal language-independent configuration for the morphological segmentation of unseen languages. We train two classifiers on the development languages used by Eskander et al. (2016) to make choices for unseen languages (Section 3). We show that we can choose the best parameter settings for the six development languages in a leave-one-out cross validation, and also on an unseen test language (Arabic).

## 2 Problem Definition and Dataset

Adaptor Grammars (AGs) have been used successfully for unsupervised morphological seg-




*Proceedings of the 15th SIGMORPHON Workshop on Computational Research in Phonetics, Phonology, and Morphology*, pages 78–83
Brussels, Belgium, October 31, 2018. ©2018 The Special Interest Group on Computational Morphology and Phonology
https://doi.org/10.18653/v1/P17

| Grammar | Main Representation | Compound | Morph | SubMorph | Segmentation Level |
|---|---|---|---|---|---|
| Morph+SM | Morph+ | No | Yes | Yes | Morph |
| Simple | Prefix?+Stem+Suffix? | No | No | No | Prefix-Stem-Suffix |
| Simple+SM | Prefix?+Stem+Suffix? | No | No | Yes | Prefix-Stem-Suffix |
| PrStSu | Prefix+Stem+Suffix | No | Yes | No | Prefix-Stem-Suffix |
| PrStSu+SM | Prefix+Stem+Suffix | No | Yes | Yes | Prefix-Stem-Suffix |
| PrStSu+Co+SM | Prefix+Stem+Suffix | Yes | Yes | Yes | Prefix-Stem-Suffix |
| PrStSu2a+SM | Prefix?+(Stem+Suffix) | No | Yes | Yes | Prefix-Stem-Suffix |
| PrStSu2b+SM | (Prefix-Stem)+Suffix? | No | Yes | Yes | Prefix-Stem-Suffix |
| PrStSu2b++Co+SM | (Prefix-Stem)+Suffix? | Yes | Yes | Yes | Prefix-Stem-Suffix |

Table 1: Grammar Representations. Compound = Upper level representation of the word as a sequence of compounds; Morph = Affix/Morph representation as a sequence of morphs. SubMorph (SM) = Lower level representation of characters as a sequence of sub-morphs. "+" denotes *one or more* and "?" denotes *optional.*

mentation (Johnson, 2008; Sirts and Goldwater, 2013; Eskander et al., 2016), which is the task of breaking down words in a language into a sequence of morphs. An AG model typically has two main components: a PCFG and an adaptor that adapts the probabilities assigned to individual subtrees in the grammar. For the task of morphological segmentation, a PCFG is typically a morphological grammar that specifies word structure. Given a list of input strings, AGs can learn latent tree structures.

Eskander et al. (2016) developed several AG models based on different underlying context-free grammars and learning settings, which we briefly introduce below.

**Grammars.** Eskander et al. (2016) introduce a set of 9 grammars (see Table 1) designed based on three dimensions: 1) how the grammar generates the prefix, stem and suffix (morph vs. tripartite), 2) the levels which are represented in nonterminals (e.g., compounds, morphs and sub-morphs) and 3) the levels at which the segmentation into output morphs is produced. For example, in the PrStSu+SM grammar a word is modeled as a prefix, a stem and a suffix, where the prefix and suffix are sequences of zero or more morphs, while a morph is a sequence of sub-morphs, and the segmentation is based on the prefix, suffix and stem level. The PrStSu2a+SM grammar is similar, but a word is modeled as a prefix and stem-suffix sequence, where the prefix is optional, and stem-suffix is either a stem or a stem and a suffix (see Eskander et al. (2016) for more details). Figure 1 shows the trees for segmenting the word *replayings* using the PrStSu+SM and PrStSu2a+SM grammars.

**Learning Settings.** Eskander et al. (2016) consider three learning settings: Standard (Std), Scholar-Seeded Knowledge (Sch) and Cascaded (Casc). In the Standard setting, no scholar knowledge is introduced in the grammars, while in the Scholar-Seeded Knowledge setting the grammars are augmented with scholar knowledge in the form of information about affixes gathered from grammar books (before learning happens). The Cascaded setting approximates the effect of scholar-seeded knowledge by first using a high-precision AG to derive a set of affixes and then insert those affixes into the grammars used in a second learning step.

Eskander et al. (2016) show that the segmentation performance differs significantly across the different grammars, learning settings and languages. For instance, the best performance for German is obtained by running the Standard PrStSu+SM configuration, while the Cascaded PrStSu2a+SM configuration produces the best segmentation for Finnish. That means, there is no setup that yields the optimal segmentation for all languages. For the processing of an unseen language (i.e., not part of the development), Eskander et al. (2016) recommend using the Cascaded PrStSu+SM configuration (referred to as LIMS: Language-Independent Morphological Segmenter), as it is the best-on-average performing one when running leave-one-out cross validation on the development languages.

**Problem definition.** While LIMS works best on average, it is not the optimal configuration for any of the development languages except Zulu. Thus, in this paper, we address the problem of automatically selecting the optimal or nearly-optimal language-independent (Standard or Cascaded) configuration for the morphological segmentation of unseen languages.

We use the 6 development languages used by Eskander et al. (2016) as well as Arabic as a fully unseen language. The data for English, German, Finnish, Turkish and Estonian is from Morpho Challenge[1], and the data for Zulu is from the Ukwabelana corpus (Spiegler et al., 2010). For the

---

[1] http://research.ics.aalto.fi/events/morphochallenge/

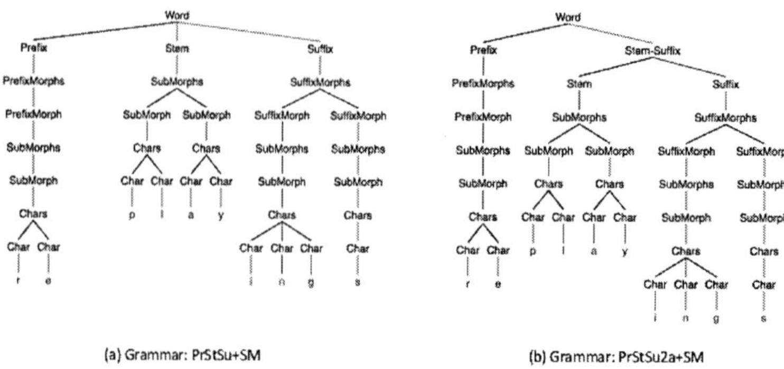

Figure 1: Grammar trees for the word *replayings*: (a) PrStSu+SM, (b) PrStSu2a+SM

| Lang. | Source | TRAIN | DEV | TEST |
|---|---|---|---|---|
| English | Morpho Challenge | 50,046 | 1,212 | – |
| German | Morpho Challenge | 50,086 | 540 | – |
| Finnish | Morpho Challenge | 49,909 | 1,494 | – |
| Turkish | Morpho Challenge | 49,765 | 1,531 | – |
| Estonian | Morpho Challenge | 49,909 | 1,500 | – |
| Zulu | Ukwabelana | 50,000 | 1,000 | – |
| Arabic | PATB | 50,000 | – | 1,000 |

Table 2: Data source and size information. TRAIN = training corpus, DEV = development corpus and TEST = test corpus.

unseen language we choose Arabic as it belongs to the Semitic family, while none of the development languages does. We obtain the Arabic data by randomly selecting 50K words from the PATB corpus (Maamourio et al., 2004). Table 2 lists the sources and sizes of our corpora.

## 3 Method

Since we have nine grammars to choose from (see Table 1) with two possible learning setting (Standard and Cascaded), for a total of 18 possible configurations, we restrict our pool of selection to the four configurations that yield the best-on-average performance across the development languages, namely Cascaded PrStSu+SM, Cascaded PrStSu2a+SM, Standard PrStSu+SM and Standard PrStSu2a+SM, with average EMMA F-scores (Spiegler and Monson, 2010) of 0.720, 0.695, 0.684 and 0.683, respectively (see Section 2 and Table 1 for grammar descriptions). EMMA stands for the Evaluation Metric for Morphological Analysis (Spiegler and

Monson, 2010), and is a metric that has been shown to be particularly adequate for evaluating unsupervised methods for morphological segmentation and superior to the metric used in the Morpho Challenge competition series.

We use a supervised machine learning approach to select the best configuration. Since we only have six development languages, we split the classification task into two binary classification ones: Approach Classification (Standard (Std) vs. Cascaded (Casc)) and Grammar Classification (PrStSu+SM vs. PrStSu2a+SM), and run leave-one-out cross validation on the development languages for both tasks. Table 3 lists the best configurations and the gold class labels (for both Approach and Grammar) for the six development languages.

| Language | Best Configuration | Approach class | Grammar class |
|---|---|---|---|
| English | Std PrStSu+SM | Std | PrStSu+SM |
| German | Std PrStSu+SM | Std | PrStSu+SM |
| Finnish | Casc PrStSu2a+SM | Casc | PrStSu2a+SM |
| Turkish | Std PrStSu+SM | Std | PrStSu+SM |
| Estonian | Casc PrStSu2a+SM | Casc | PrStSu2a+SM |
| Zulu | Casc PrStSu+SM | Casc | PrStSu+SM |

Table 3: The best configurations and the gold class labels for both the Approach classification and Grammar classification for the six development languages.

### 3.1 Feature Generation

In order to generate morphological features for the classification tasks, we run a phase of AG segmentation using the Standard PrStSu+SM configuration, where we only run 50 optimization iterations (i.e., one tenth of the number of iterations in a complete segmentation process as

| Feature ID | Description |
|---|---|
| F01 | Average no. of simple affixes per word |
| F02 | Average no. of simple prefixes per word |
| F03 | Average no. of simple suffixes per word |
| F04 | Average no. of characters per affix |
| F05 | No. of distinct simple affixes |
| F06 | No. of distinct simple prefixes |
| F07 | No. of distinct simple suffixes |
| F08 | Average no. of complex affixes per word |
| F09 | Average no. of complex prefixes per word |
| F10 | Average no. of complex suffixes per word |
| F11 | Average no. of characters per affix |
| F12 | No. of distinct complex affixes |
| F13 | No. of distinct complex prefixes |
| F14 | No. of distinct complex suffixes |

Table 4: Classification features

| Language | KNN | NB | RF |
|---|---|---|---|
| English | Std PrStSu+SM | Std PrStSu+SM | Std PrStSu+SM |
| German | Std PrStSu+SM | Std PrStSu+SM | Casc PrStSu+SM |
| Finnish | Casc PrStSu2a+SM | Casc PrStSu+SM (x) | Casc PrStSu2a+SM |
| Turkish | Std PrStSu+SM | Std PrStSu+SM | Std PrStSu+SM |
| Estonian | Casc PrStSu2a+SM | Casc PrStSu+SM (x) | Std PrStSu2a+SM (x) |
| Zulu | Casc PrStSu+SM | Casc PrStSu+SM | Casc PrStSu+SM |
| Accuracy | 100.0% | 66.7% | 88.3% |

Table 5: Overall system output. KNN = K-Nearest Neighbors, NB = Naive Bayes and RF = Random Forest. Wrong predictions are denoted by (x).

reported by Eskander et al. (2016)), as the purpose is to quickly generate morphological clues that help the classification rather than to obtain highly optimized segmentation. We choose this particular configuration due to its high efficiency across all languages in addition to its relatively small execution time. Upon generating the initial segmentation, we extract 14 morphological features for classification. The features are listed in Table 4. We only consider affixes that appear more than 10 times in the segmentation output, where a simple affix contains only one morpheme, while a complex affix contains one or more simple affixes.

### 3.2 Classification

We experiment with three classification methods; K-Nearest Neighbors (KNN), Naive Bayes (NB) and Random Forest (RF) for both the Approach (Std vs. Casc) and Grammar (PrStSu+SM vs. PrStSu2a+SM) classification tasks. We conduct the two classification tasks separately, and then we combine the outcome to obtain the best configuration.

In the training phase, we perform leave-one-out cross validation on the six development languages. In each of the six folds of the cross validation, we choose one language in turn as the test language. We use the training and development corpora listed in table 2 for training the models and evaluating the classifiers, respectively.

Table 5 shows the final system output after combining the outcomes from the Approach classification and Grammar Classification. KNN predicts the right configuration consistently, while NB picks the wrong grammars for Finnish and Estonian, and RF predicts the wrong approach and grammar for Estonian. Thus, the overall accuracies of KNN, NB and RF are 100%, 66.7% and 88.3%, respectively, which suggests using KNN for classification. So for an unseen language, we first run the Standard PrTuSu+SM configuration for 50 optimization iterations to obtain the morphological features. We then run the KNN classifier on those features in order to obtain the final AG configuration.

Studying the correlation between the morphological features and the output shows that features F14, F07, F11 and F03 in table 4, are the most significant ones for the selection of the best configuration. This illustrates the high reliance on information about suffixes as three out of the four features, namely F14, F07 and F03, are suffix-related.

## 4  Evaluation

We report results using the EMMA F-measure score (Spiegler and Monson, 2010).

**Results on an unseen language.** We evaluate our system on Arabic, a language that is not part of the development of the system. Arabic also belongs to the Semitic family, where none of the development languages does. For an unseen language, we first run the Standard PrStSu+SM configuration for 50 optimization iterations to obtain the morphological features. We then run the KNN classifier on those features in order to obtain the final AG configuration. Table 6 lists the EMMA F-scores for Arabic for all grammars in both the Standard and Cascaded setups. Our KNN classifier picks the Standard PrStSu+SM configuration, which yields the best segmentation among all the configurations with an EMMA F-score of 0.701.

**Comparison with existing unsupervised approaches.** Table 7 compares the performance of the selected configurations of our system (Table 5) to three other systems; Morfessor (Creutz and Lagus, 2007), MorphoChain (Narasimhan et al., 2015) and LIMS (Eskander et al., 2016) (where the cascaded PrStSu+SM configuration is

| Grammar | Standard | Cascaded |
|---|---|---|
| Morph+SM | 0.647 | 0.642 |
| Simple | 0.651 | 0.593 |
| Simple+SM | 0.680 | 0.631 |
| PrStSu | 0.642 | 0.646 |
| **PrStSu+SM** | **0.701** | 0.692 |
| PrStSu+Co+SM | 0.648 | 0.628 |
| PrStSu2a+SM | 0.676 | 0.682 |
| PrStSu2b+SM | 0.682 | 0.688 |
| PrStSu2b+Co+SM | 0.532 | 0.532 |

Table 6: Adaptor-grammar results (Emma F-scores) for the Standard and Cascaded setups for Arabic. Boldface indicates the best configuration and the choice of our system.

| Grammar | Morfessor | MorphoChain | LIMS | Ours | Best |
|---|---|---|---|---|---|
| English | 0.805 | 0.746 | 0.809 | 0.821 | 0.826 |
| German | 0.740 | 0.625 | 0.777 | 0.790 | 0.790 |
| Finnish | 0.675 | 0.621 | 0.727 | 0.733 | 0.733 |
| Turkish | 0.551 | 0.551 | 0.591 | 0.647 | 0.647 |
| Zulu | 0.414 | 0.390 | 0.611 | 0.611 | 0.611 |
| Estonian | 0.779 | 0.679 | 0.805 | 0.828 | 0.847 |
| Arabic | 0.779 | 0.751 | 0.682 | 0.701 | 0.701 |
| Avg. | 0.678 | 0.623 | 0.715 | 0.733 | 0.736 |

Table 7: The performance of our system (Ours) compared to Morfessor, MorphoChain, LIMS and an upper-bound system (Best), using EMMA F-scores.

chosen). Our system has EMMA F-score error reductions of 17.1%, 29.2% and 6.3% over Morfessor, MorphoChain[2] and LIMS, respectively, on average across the development languages and Arabic. It is also only 0.003 of average EMMA F-score behind an oracle system, where the best configuration is always selected (indicated as *Best*). We are not able to compare versus the system presented by Wang et al. (2016) as neither their system nor their data is currently available.

## 5   Related Work

The first work that utilizes AGs for unsupervised morphological segmentation is introduced by Johnson (2008), while Sirts and Goldwater (2013) propose minimally supervised AG models of different tree structures for morphological segmentation. The most recent work on using AGs for morphological segmentation is proposed by Eskander et al. (2016), where they experiment with several AG models based on different underlying grammars and learning settings. They also research the use of scholar knowledge seeded in the grammar trees. This knowledge could be gathered from grammar books or automatically generated via bootstrapping. This paper extends their work by proposing a machine learning approach to select the best language-independent model for each language.

In addition to the use of AGs, several models have been successfully used for unsupervised morphological segmentation such as generative probabilistic models (utilized by Morfessor (Creutz and Lagus, 2007)), and log-linear models using contextual and global features (Poon et al., 2009). Narasimhan et al. (2015) use a discriminative model for unsupervised morphological segmentation that integrates orthographic and semantic properties of words. The model learns morphological chains, where a chain extends a base form available in the lexicon.

Another recent notable work is introduced by Wang et al. (2016), who use neural networks for unsupervised segmentation, where they build LSTM (Hochreiter and Schmidhuber, 1997) architectures to learn word structures in order to predict morphological boundaries. Another variation of the this approach is presented by Yang et al. (2017), where they use partial-word information as character bigram embeddings and evaluate their work on Chinese.

## 6   Conclusion and Future Work

We have shown that our language-independent classifiers improve the state-of-the-art unsupervised morphological segmentation proposed by Eskander et al. (2016) by making choices that optimize for a given language, rather than choosing parameters for all languages based on averages on the development languages.

In future work, we plan to conduct an extrinsic evaluation on tasks that could benefit from morphological segmentation such as machine translation, information retrieval and summarization. We also plan to optimize the segmentation models for those specific tasks.

## Acknowledgements

This research is based upon work supported in part by the Office of the Director of National Intelligence (ODNI), Intelligence Advanced Research Projects Activity (IARPA), via contract # FA8650-17-C-9117. The views and conclusions contained herein are those of the authors and should not be interpreted as necessarily representing the official policies, either expressed or implied, of ODNI, IARPA, or the U.S. Government. The U.S. Government is authorized to reproduce and distribute reprints for governmental purposes notwithstanding any copyright annotation therein.

---

[2]Since MorphoChain expects large corpora in order to learn the morphological chains, it does not perform well on the small corpora we use in our setup, where we experiment with real conditions of low-resource languages.

## References

Duygu Ataman, Matteo Negri, Marco Turchi, and Marcello Federico. 2017. Linguistically motivated vocabulary reduction for neural machine translation from turkish to english. 108.

Mathias Creutz and Krista Lagus. 2007. Unsupervised models for morpheme segmentation and morphology learning. *ACM Trans. Speech Lang. Process.*, 4(1):3:1–3:34.

Ramy Eskander, Owen Rambow, and Tianchun Yang. 2016. Extending the use of adaptor grammars for unsupervised morphological segmentation of unseen languages. In *Proceedings of he Twenty-Sixth International Conference on Computational Linguistics (COLING)*, Osaka, Japan.

Sepp Hochreiter and Jürgen Schmidhuber. 1997. Long short-term memory. *Neural computation*, 9(8):1735–1780.

Mark Johnson. 2008. Unsupervised word segmentation for Sesotho using adaptor grammars. In *Proceedings of the Tenth Meeting of ACL Special Interest Group on Computational Morphology and Phonology*, pages 20–27, Columbus, Ohio. Association for Computational Linguistics.

Mark Johnson, Thomas L. Griffiths, and Sharon Goldwater. 2007. Adaptor grammars: a framework for specifying compositional nonparametric bayesian models. In *Advances in Neural Information Processing Systems 19*, pages 641–648, Cambridge, MA. MIT Press.

Mohamed Maamourio, Ann Bies, Tim Buckwalter, and Wigdan Mekki. 2004. Arabic treebank: Building a large-scale annotated arabic corpus. In *Proceedings of the NEMLAR Conference on Arabic Language Resources and Tools*, Cairo, Egypt.

Karthik Narasimhan, Regina Barzilay, and Tommi Jaakkola. 2015. An unsupervised method for uncovering morphological chains. In *Twelfth AAAI Conference on Artificial Intelligence*.

Karthik Narasimhan, Damianos Karakos, Richard M. Schwartz, Stavros Tsakalidis, and Regina Barzilay. 2014. Morphological segmentation for keyword spotting. In *EMNLP*.

ThuyLinh Nguyen, Stephan Vogel, and Noah A. Smith. 2010. Nonparametric word segmentation for machine translation. In *Proceedings of the 23rd International Conference on Computational Linguistics*, COLING '10, pages 815–823, Stroudsburg, PA, USA. Association for Computational Linguistics.

Hoifung Poon, Colin Cherry, and Kristina Toutanova. 2009. Unsupervised morphological segmentation with log-linear models. In *Proceedings of Human Language Technologies: The 2009 Annual Conference of the North American Chapter of the Association for Computational Linguistics*, pages 209–217, Boulder, Colorado. Association for Computational Linguistics.

Kairit Sirts and Sharon Goldwater. 2013. Minimally-supervised morphological segmentation using adaptor grammars. *Transactions of the Association for Computational Linguistics*, 1(May):231–242.

Sebastian Spiegler and Christian Monson. 2010. Emma: A novel evaluation metric for morphological analysis. In *Proceedings of the 23rd International Conference on Computational Linguistics (Coling 2010)*, pages 1029–1037, Beijing, China. Coling 2010 Organizing Committee.

Sebastian Spiegler, Andrew van der Spuy, and Peter A. Flach. 2010. Ukwabelana - an open-source morphological zulu corpus. In *Proceedings of the 23rd International Conference on Computational Linguistics (Coling 2010)*, pages 1020–1028, Beijing, China. Coling 2010 Organizing Committee.

Linlin Wang, Zhu Cao, Yu Xia, and Gerard de Melo. 2016. Morphological segmentation with window LSTM neural networks. In *Thirtieth AAAI Conference on Artificial Intelligence*.

Jie Yang, Yue Zhang, and Fei Dong. 2017. Neural word segmentation with rich pretraining. In *Proceedings of the 55th Annual Meeting of the Association for Computational Linguistics, ACL*, Vancouver, Canada.

# A Comparison of Entity Matching Methods
## between English and Japanese Katakana


**Michiharu Yamashita**        **Hideki Awashima**        **Hidekazu Oiwa**[*]

Recruit Co., Ltd. / Megagon Labs

Tokyo, Japan

{chewgen, awashima}@r.recruit.co.jp, hidekazu.oiwa@gmail.com



## Abstract

Japanese Katakana is one component of the Japanese writing system and is used to express English terms, loanwords, and onomatopoeia in Japanese characters based on the phonemes. The main purpose of this research is to find the best entity matching methods between English and Katakana. We built two research questions to clarify which types of entity matching systems works better than others. The first question is what transliteration should be used for conversion. We need to transliterate English or Katakana terms into the same form in order to compute the string similarity. We consider five conversions that transliterate English to Katakana directly, Katakana to English directly, English to Katakana via phoneme, Katakana to English via phoneme, and both English and Katakana to phoneme. The second question is what should be used for the similarity measure at entity matching. To investigate the problem, we choose six methods, which are Overlap Coefficient, Cosine, Jaccard, Jaro-Winkler, Levenshtein, and the similarity of the phoneme probability predicted by RNN. Our results show that 1) matching using phonemes and conversion of Katakana to English works better than other methods, and 2) the similarity of phonemes outperforms other methods while other similarity score is changed depending on data and models.


## 1 Introduction

Cleansing and preprocessing data is one of the essential tasks in data analysis such as natural language processing (Witten et al., 2016). In particular, finding the same entity from multiple datasets is a important task. For example, when the same entities are expressed by different languages, you need to convert them to the same writing format before entity matching.

The Japanese language has three kinds of character types, and they are used for different purposes (Nagata, 1998). One of the character types is Katakana, which is used to convert English words, foreign languages, and alphabet letters into Japanese characters (Martin, 2004). Katakana is often transliterated by phonemes unique to Japanese and that is similar but different from English pronunciation. In addition, whether terms are expressed in English or Katakana is dependent on sites. For example, on Japanese web pages, there are many restaurants written in English and Japanese even if they are the same stores such as "Wendy' s" and "ウェンディーズ". If it is the same type of character, it is easier to identify the entity simply by calculating the similarity of the string, but in the case of different writing systems like English and Katakana, it is difficult to identify the entity.

In this research, we clarify the problem by exploring the following two research questions.

**(1) What transliteration should be used for conversion?**

In order to change the same string form, the following method can be considered.

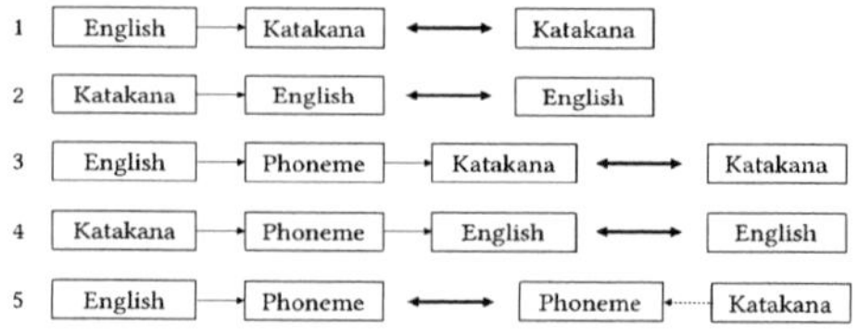


Figure 1: Method to Convert the Entity Name.

The first and second methods are to convert English to Katakana or Katakana to English and then match the entities.

The third and fourth methods are to use pronunciation information. Katakana is based on phonemes and is a syllable system, where each




*Proceedings of the 15th SIGMORPHON Workshop on Computational Research in Phonetics, Phonology, and Morphology*, pages 84–92

Brussels, Belgium, October 31, 2018. ©2018 The Special Interest Group on Computational Morphology and Phonology

https://doi.org/10.18653/v1/P17


---

[*]The author is now at Google Inc.

syllabogram corresponds to one sound in the Japanese language. Therefore, the methods match the entities after converting English or Katakana into phonemes and converting the transliterated phonemes to Katakana or English.

The fifth method also uses phonemes. This method matches the entities based on the transliterated phoneme from both English and Katakana.

**(2) What should be used for the similarity measure?**

In order to calculate the similarity of a character string for entity matching, it is necessary to select measures from many similarity measures. In this research, as commonly used similarity measures, we use the similarity of Overlap Coefficient, Cosine, Jaccard, Jaro-Winkler, and Levenshtein (Cohen et al., 2003). Moreover, we propose a similarity method using the probability of the phonemes by prediction model. We clarify which of the six similarity methods should be used to compare the accuracy.

## 2 Related Work

Entity matching is a crucial task, and there is a lot of research on entity matching (Shen et al., 2015; Cai et al., 2013; Carmel et al., 2014; Mudgal et al., 2018). In these studies, the attribute information of an entity is used. In the case where there is no attribute and there is only the entity name, the character name information must be used. Different from general entity linking tasks, some works match entities only on entries in tables (Muñoz et al., 2014; Sekhavat et al., 2014). Although these studies match entities by collecting additional information on the entity, pronunciation information is not used.

In addition to studies of entity matching, transliteration is also studied. Transliteration is a task that converts a word in a language into a character of a different language and makes it as closely as possible to the native pronunciation. Many studies on transliteration are also conducted such as those on Hindi and Myanmar (Pandey and Roy, 2017; Thu et al., 2016). Some studies consider pronunciation information in transliteration (Yao and Zweig, 2015; Toshniwal and Livescu, 2016; Rao et al., 2015). Transliteration differs from entity matching itself in the purpose of the task, but it is applicable to entity matching because transliteration can extend the information of the entity. Therefore, we use transliteration to solve the task of entity matching.

There are some transliteration and entity matching studies, but there is little research that solves entity matching using transliteration information. Our motivation is to extend our database from external data by entity matching because we have relations of many types of clients such as restaurants, beauty salons, and companies and extension of data is essential for discovery of new clients. Therefore, we need to transform the name of the entities and to find which methods are the best for entity matching between English and Katakana.

## 3 Japanese Characters

Japanese characters are normally written in a combination of three character types. One type is ideographic characters, Kanji, from China, and the other two types, Hiragana and Katakana, are phonetic characters. Kanji is mainly used for nouns and stems of adjectives and verbs, and Hiragana is used for helpful markings of adjectives, verbs and Japanese words that are not expressed in Kanji. On the other hand, Katakana is used to write sound effects and transcribe foreign words (Martin, 2004). When we try entity matching with Japanese data, we usually face English expressed in Japanese Katakana in restaurants, companies, books, electrical items, and so on. We usually cannot find two names where one is written in English and the other is written in Katakana within enormous data because Japanese speakers use both English and Katakana to write foreign words.

Dictionaries already exist for English words with Japanese meanings, but few dictionaries also exist for English with Katakana. The report (Benson et al., 2009) mentions that the Japanese language is based on morae rather than syllables. A mora is a unit of sound that contributes to a syllable's weight. Katakana is more accurately described as a way to write the set of Japanese morae rather than the set of Japanese syllables, as each symbol represents not a syllable but a unit of sound of Japanese speech. A mora-based writing system in Japanese represents a dimension of the language that has no corresponding representation in English. This challenges the transliteration task of English and Katakana. Therefore, it is not easy to convert English into Katakana.

The Japanese language also has a method to transliterate Katakana into alphabet characters, and this transliterated alphabet is called Romaji, which is a phoneme of Japanese characters (Smith, 1996). Romaji is used in any context for non-Japanese speakers who cannot read Japanese characters, such as for names, passports, and any Japanese entities. Romaji is the most common way to input Japanese into computers and to display Japanese on devices that do not support Japanese characters (DeFrancis, 1984), and almost all Japanese people learn Romaji and are able to read and write Japanese using Romaji. Therefore, generally speaking, Japanese people who do not write in English usually use Romaji to express Katakana or foreign terms without Japanese characters.

## 4 Methods

To solve the task of entity matching between English and Katakana, the entity name must somehow be transliterated. Figure 2 shows the frame of the task. For example, the word "angel" has four features which are English, phonemes of English, Japanese Katakana and Romaji. We state how to convert the entity name, how to calculate the similarity, and what the baseline is below.

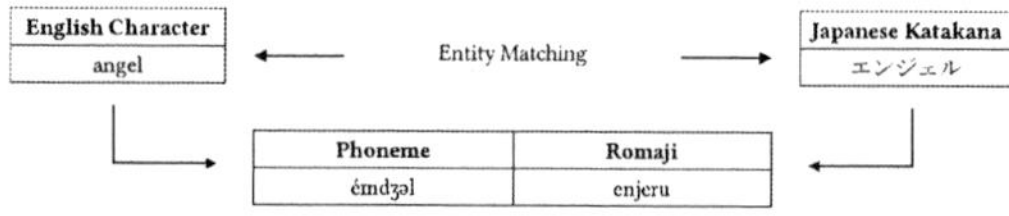


Figure 2: Entity Matching Task between English and Japanese Katakana.

### 4.1 Baseline

As the baseline, we used Romaji transliteration, which is characters used to transliterate Katakana to an alphabet sequence (DeFrancis, 1984). We converted Katakana to English using Romaji and then perform entity matching using both alphabets. There are many different popular ways of romanizing Katakana, and we use the Hepburn romanization because the romanization of a Katakana word generally faithfully represents the pronunciation of that Japanese word and many Japanese speakers use it to express Katakana and foreign terms without Japanese characteres. We used the module romkan[1] for this method. For example, in terms of "Japan", the Romaji transliteration is "ジャパン" and the actual Katakana is also "ジャパン". As another example, in terms of "Orange", the Romaji transliteration is "オランゲ"

---

[1] https://pypi.python.org/pypi/romkan

but the actual Katakana is "オレンジ". In addition, we also used Soundex[2] as a benchmark of entity matching between phoneme pairs. Soundex is a phonetic algorithm for indexing names by sound, as pronounced in English.

### 4.2 Predictive Model

We used a sequence to sequence model for transliteration. For example, the input is the sequence of English characters $(x_1, ..., x_n)$, and the output is the sequence of phoneme characters $(y_1, ..., y_m)$. In our model, we estimated the conditional probability $p$ of an output sequence $(y_1, ..., y_m)$ given an input sequence $(x_1, ..., x_n)$ as follows:

$$p(y_1, ..., y_m | x_1, ..., x_n) \qquad (1)$$

Given an input sequence $(x_1, ..., x_n)$, LSTM computes a sequence of hidden states $(h_1, ..., h_n)$. During decoding, it defines a distribution over the output sequence $(y_1, ..., y_m)$ given the input sequence $p(y_1, ..., y_m | x_1, ..., x_n)$ is:

$$p(y_1, ..., y_m | x_1, ..., x_n) = \prod_{t=1}^{m} p(y_t | h_{n+t-1}, y_{l-1})$$

$$(2)$$

We also used a bi-directional recurrent neural network (Schuster and Paliwal, 1997). In our architecture, one RNN processes the input from left to right, while another processes it right to left. The outputs of the two subnetworks are then combined. This model has been applied to machine translation and, in this case, the phoneme prediction depends on the whole character sequence. Figure 3 shows an architecture of our models in this research. The combinations of input and output are English-Katakana, Katakana-English, English-Phoneme, Katakana-Phoneme, Phoneme-English, and Phoneme-Katakana. The input and the output of Figure 3 shows English-Phoneme as an example, and our other models were created in the same manner.

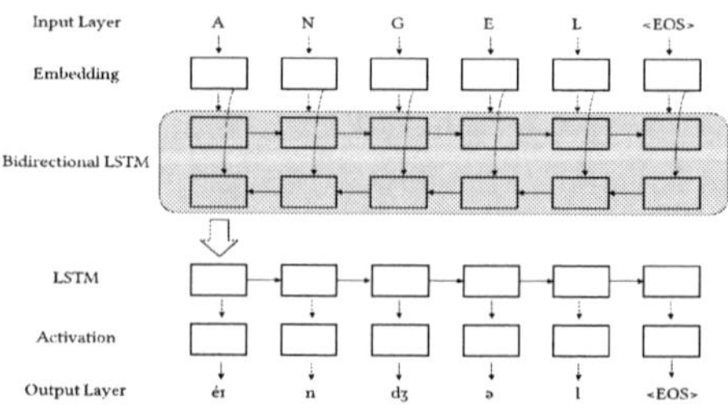


Figure 3: Architecture of the Predictive Model.

---

[2] https://www.archives.gov/research/census/soundex.html

### 4.3 Model Settings

We chose each hyper parameter of the model by grid search. Targets of the hyper parameter were word embedding, hidden layers, and input reverse. Input of embedding and hidden layers was set to 256, 512, or 1024, and input of reverse is True or False. In the experiment, we chose the best model that has the lowest loss value for validation data and applied the model for validation data. We used categorical cross entropy as the loss value and the optimizer was Adam (Kingma and Ba, 2014). The hyper parameters used are shown in Table 1. Regarding the six models with RNN, we tried to match the entities of the transliterated word as shown in Figure 1.

At last, we created all word combinations with the dataset and then calculated their similarity score. Each model was trained by 80% of train dataset and 20% was used as test data. Test data was also used as an experiment for this research.

### 4.4 Similarity Metric

We implemented the module "py_stringmatching"[3] that consists of a comprehensive and scalable set of string tokenizers such as alphabetical tokenizers, whitespace tokenizers, and string similarity measures. We used this module to calculate the string similarity. We chose Overlap Coefficient, Cosine, Jacquard, Jaro-Winkler, and Levenshtein from the modules. In addition to these similarities, we also proposed a new method that uses a probability of predicted phonemes from a term and compares each string similarity in the tasks of matching entity names. Definitions of each method are as follows.

Overlap coefficient measures the overlap between two sets, and is defined as the size of the intersection divided by the smaller of the size of the two sets. For two sets X and Y, the overlap coefficient is:

$$\frac{|X \cap Y|}{\min(|X|, |Y|)} \tag{3}$$

Cosine similarity measures the cosine of the angle between two non-zero vectors, and we use Ochiai coefficient as the angular cosine similarity and the normalized angle. This measure computes:

---

$^3$https://pypi.python.org/pypi/py_stringmatching

$$\frac{|X \cap Y|}{\sqrt{(|X||Y|)}} \tag{4}$$

Jaccard similarity measures the similarity between finite sample sets, and is defined as the size of the intersection divided by the size of the union of the sample sets. For two sets X and Y, Jaccard similarity score is:

$$\frac{|X \cap Y|}{|X \cup Y|} \tag{5}$$

Jaro-Winkler similarity (Winkler, 1999) measures the edit distance between two sequences. It uses a prefix scale which gives weights to strings that match from the beginning for a set prefix length. For two sets X and Y, when $s_i$ is the length of the string $s_i$, $m$ is the number of matching characters, $t$ is half the number of transpositions, and $l$ is the length of the common prefix at the start of a string up to a maximum of four characters, Jaro-Winkler similarity $sim_w$ is:

$$sim_w = sim_j + (l \cdot 0.1(1 - sim_j))$$
$$sim_j = \frac{1}{3}\left(\frac{m}{|s_X|} + \frac{m}{|s_Y|} + \frac{m-t}{m}\right) \tag{6}$$

Levenshtein distance measures the edit distance between two sequences. It computes the minimum cost to transform all edit procedures. Transforming a string is to delete a character, insert a character, and substitute one character for another.

The last similarity metric is the similarity of the probability of a predicted phoneme for a term, which we proposed. RNN model predicts phoneme probability, and we applied this metric for English-Phoneme and Katakana-Phoneme models. The output layer is the sequence, and the output of a predicted phoneme at the time $t$ in our model are calculated as {"ei" :0.37, "e" :0.31, "æ" :0.23, ⋯} using the vector of the hidden layer of the decoder at time $t$. In this metric, we calculate the distance of dynamic time warping (Müller, 2007) between two temporal sequences. Dynamic time warping calculates an optimal match between two-time series sequences with certain restrictions. We regard the probability vector as a time point and use cosine similarity as a distance between two vectors. We computed all of the probability vectors from English and Katakana, and measured the distance of dynamic time warping.

Table 1: Hyper Parameters of the Best Model (Acc is accuracy for validation data of train data.)

| Input | Output | Embedding | Hidden Layers | Input Reverse | Acc |
|---|---|---|---|---|---|
| English | Katakana | 512 | 512 | False | 0.765 |
| Katakana | English | 1024 | 512 | True | 0.785 |
| English | Phoneme | 1024 | 512 | True | 0.826 |
| Katakana | Phoneme | 512 | 512 | True | 0.811 |
| Phoneme | English | 512 | 512 | True | 0.815 |
| Phoneme | Katakana | 1024 | 512 | False | 0.764 |

## 5  Experiments

### 5.1  Dictionary Data

We prepared corpora of English, Katakana, and phonemes for training and creating models. We found a corpus of English and phonemes, and a corpus of English and Katakana. We created the data by merging each dictionary and made the original data ourselves as Japanese speakers.

At first, we used the dataset consisting of English, Katakana, and phonemes of English from Benson's dictionary[4], which is made from JMDict dictionary (Breen, 1995) and the sum of entries is 17798. However, in this dataset, there are a lot of mistakes because the creators are not native Japanese speakers, and they made it automatically. So, we removed the noise by hand as native Japanese speakers and then succeeded in cleansing the data of which 20% was occupied by noise.

Second, we used the CMU Pronouncing Dictionary[5] that includes a large amount of English terms and pronunciation signs but not Japanese Katakana. We combined them with Katakana by mecab-ipadic-NEologd[6]. mecab-ipadic-NEologd is a customized dictionary-system for MeCab (Kudo, 2006) that is an open-source text segmentation library for text written in the Japanese language, and some terms have both expression of English and Katakana. We merged the CMU Pronouncing Dictionary and mecab-ipadic-NEologd where both of the dictionaries had terms.

At last, we created an original dictionary by randomly extracting 3000 terms from the CMU Pronouncing Dictionary and attached each Katakana term by hand. We eventually concatenated those dictionaries and deleted duplicates. The total number of entries is 26815.

### 5.2  Experimental Methodology

For the experiment, we prepared three validation datasets. One was test data that comprised 20% of the dictionary. Another was city names in the U.S. from Google Maps API[7]. Google Maps provide a city name and we were able to find the same U.S. city expressed by English and Japanese. We collected 1110 terms from Google Maps. The last is the restaurant store names in Japan from HOT PEPPER GOURMET[8], which is called HPG. HPG is one of the most famous search services that provides information and discount coupons for restaurants, cafes, bars, and any place to eat in Japan. We know some restaurants that have both names in alphabet characters and Katakana from HPG, and built a validation dataset. Table 2 shows all of the data we used.

In terms of measuring accuracy, we used a top-five precision. We calculated the similarity scores of all combinations of entities in the experiment data and evaluated the precision of the entities included in the top-five entities, and then compared the value of top-five's precision for each model and similarity measure. The procedure of transliterating and measuring was as follows:

**(1) En2Kana**

We transliterated the sequence of alphabet characters into Katakana through RNN model and computed the similarity between the transliterated Katakana and Katakana terms.

**(2) Kana2En**

We transliterated the sequence of Katakana into English through RNN model and computed the similarity between the transliterated English and English terms.

**(3) Both2Ph**

We transliterated the sequence of alphabet characters into phonemes through RNN model, transliterated the sequence of Katakana into

---

[4]https://github.com/eob/englishjapanese-transliteration/blob/master/data/dictionary.txt

[5]http://www.speech.cs.cmu.edu/cgi-bin/cmudict

[6]https://github.com/neologd/mecab-ipadic-neologd

[7]https://developers.google.com/maps

[8]https://www.hotpepper-gourmet.com/en

Table 2: Dataset for Experiment

| Dataset | Numbers of Entities | Data Source | Example |
| --- | --- | --- | --- |
| Train and Test Data | Total: 26815<br>Train: 21452<br>Test: 5363 | Modified E. Benson's dictionary<br>CMU Pronouncing Dictionary and mecab-ipadic-NEologd<br>Our original dictionary | English: artist<br>Katakana: アーティスト<br>Phoneme: AA R T IX S T AX |
| City Names in the U.S. | 1110 | Google Maps | English: Phoenix<br>Katakana: フェニックス |
| Restaurant Names | 2458 | HOT PEPPER GOURMET | English: ### Cafe<br>Katakana: ###カフェ |

phonemes through RNN model, and computed the similarity between both of the transliterated phonemes to regard one phoneme character as one index. In addition, we also used the probability vector similarity in terms of this method as we stated the end of subsection 4.4.

### (4) En2Ph2Kana

We transliterated the sequence of alphabet characters into phonemes through RNN model, transliterated the transliterated phonemes into Katakana through RNN model, and computed the similarity between the transliterated Katakana and Katakana terms.

### (5) Kana2Ph2En

We transliterated the sequence of Katakana into phonemes through RNN model, transliterated the transliterated phonemes into English through RNN model, and computed the similarity between the transliterated English and English terms.

### (6) En2Romaji

We converted the sequence of alphabet characters into Katakana based on Romaji and computed the similarity between the Katakana of Romaji and Katakana terms.

### (7) Kana2Romaji

We converted the sequence of Katakana into alphabets based on Romaji and computed the similarity between the alphabets of the Romaji and English terms.

### (8)Both2Soundex

We transliterated the sequence of alphabet characters into Soundex as pronunciation, transliterated the sequence of Katakana based on Romaji into Soundex, and computed the score of both of the transliterated phonemes. We regarded one Soundex character as one index.

### 5.3  Results

Figure 4 shows the top-five precision graph of all methods and similarity metrics for each validation dataset, and Table 3 shows the top-five precision of predicted phoneme probability similarity.

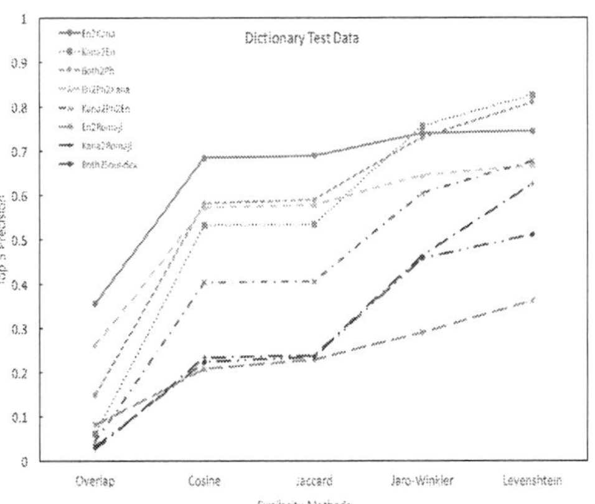

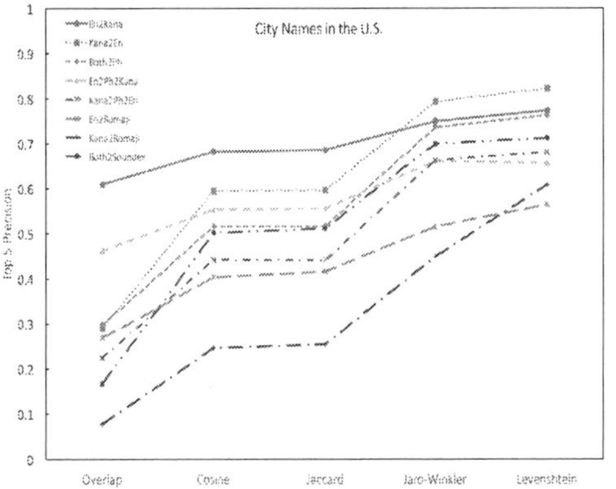

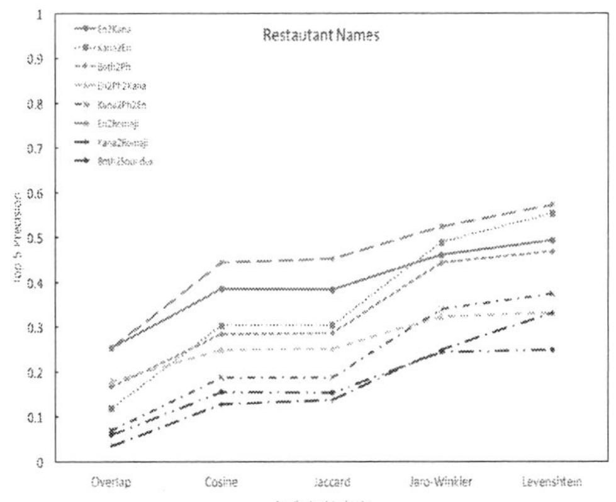

Figure 4: Top-Five Precision for Each Method and Similarity Measure.

First, we compared each of the eight methods with the similarity scores of Overlap coefficient, Cosine, Jacquard, Jaro-Winkler, and Levenshtein. The tendency of accuracy is similar in almost all methods in each dataset. In terms of the dictionary test data and the city name data, Kana2En and Both2Ph have the highest accuracy at 0.83 and 0.81 in Levenshtein distance. En2Kana was the next highest with an accuracy of 0.74 in Levenshtein. Regarding En2Ph2Kana, Kana2Ph2En, and Kana2Romaji, the accuracy was not high in any data. Likewise, even in the restaurant data, the accuracy of Kana2En and Both2Ph was relatively high at 0.55 and 0.46 in Levenshtein. However, regarding En2Romaji, it clarified that the accuracy was quite different depending on the dataset. In the dictionary test data, the accuracy was the lowest at 0.36 in Levenshtein distance, and in the city name data, the accuracy of En2Romaji is relatively low. On the other hand, in the restaurant data, En2Romaji was the highest accuracy at 0.57 in Levenshtein.

Second, focusing on the similarity measure, the accuracy trends are similar in almost all methods in each data set although the accuracy differs depending on the dataset. Levenshtein and Jaro-Winkler are the highest in almost all methods, and Overlap is the lowest. In other words, it shows that it is better to use the editing distance for word similarity in entity matching than other distance to compute the same character string.

Lastly, we considered the similarity of probability vectors. In fact, this similarity achieved the highest score. The test data of the dictionary and the data of city names' accuracy was over 0.9 and that is about 10% higher than the second highest score. The restaurant data accuracy was 0.62, which is 5% higher than the second highest score. These results insist that pronunciation is crucial for entity matching.

Table 3: Top 5 Precision of similarity of predicted Phoneme Probability Vector

| Test Data of Dict | City Names | Restaurant Names |
| --- | --- | --- |
| 0.91 | 0.92 | 0.62 |

### 5.4  Error Analysis and Discussion

Regarding the dictionary test data and the city name data, the accuracy was over 80%, whereas the accuracy of the restaurant data was under 70%.

Focusing on this phenomena, we analyzed how words were converted in each dataset. Table 4 shows some examples of each conversion.

While short words such as "switch" and "Benton" succeeded in being transformed cleanly, long words such as "coconut milk" and "South San Francisco" could not be predicted accurately. This is caused by the lack of long words in the training data. As the solution, it would be beneficial to adjust the algorithm to long terms and extend the dataset. However, in the case of Japanese, it is difficult to divide a long word into two or more words, because in comparison to English terms, Japanese terms are not separated by spaces.

Furthermore, in the restaurant data, we mined the reason why the accuracy was extremely low and found three considerable reasons in addition to the reason of word length. One reason is that there were many alphabetical representations of foreign languages other than English. For example, "Amore" is Italian, and "MAI-THAI" is Thai. Since our training data consisted only of pure English words, and the model was created for English, we can treat pure English terms as dictionary data or American city name data, but terms of other foreign languages cannot be converted accurately. To solve the problem, it is essential to create a model besides English for each language, and to create a model to recognize what language is written in words. The second is that there are some shops written in Romaji characters such as "AKICHI", which is not English but the Romaji representation of Katakana. Therefore, there should also be a model to determine whether the word is a foreign word or Romaji. Third is the mistakes of the datasets. In this study, we extracted both alphabetical and Katakana stores automatically from HPG database, but there was a pattern in which English and Katakana combinations did not correspond completely. One of them is an abbreviation such as "Cafe X" and "X". Prefixes are sometimes omitted in the data.

Considering similarities, the predicted phoneme probability had the highest score. Katakana is segmental scripts, and each term is based on sounds, but some exceptions are changed somehow by implicit Japanese rules. Therefore, we can not predict the pronunciation perfectly. However, because we can predict candidates of the pronunciation as phoneme probability vector like {"ei":0.37, "e":0.31, "æ":0.23, ⋯}, we could match enti-

| Dataset | English | Katakana | En2Ph | Kana2Ph | En2Kana | Kana2En | En2Ph2Kana | Kana2Ph2En | En2Romaji | Kana2Romaji |
|---|---|---|---|---|---|---|---|---|---|---|
| Dictionary Test Data | switch | スイッチ | s w ih ch | s w ih ch | スウィッチ | swicch | スイッチ | switch | sウイ tch | suicchi |
| | chicken | チキン | ch ih k ah n | ch ih k ah n | チェッンン | chicken | チカン | chickon | チcケン | chikin |
| | coconut milk | ココナッツミルク | k ax k y n t t ih ih k ax | k ax k ax k ax n t m m ih ax ax | ココトノミトックク | coconantliiii | コャントトトトッツ | cococononmmam | ココヌt ミk | kokonattsumiruku |
| | airport | エアポート | eh r p ao r t | eh r p ow r t | エアポート | airpott | エアポート | airooort | アイrポrt | eapoto |
| City Names in the U.S. | Phoenix | フェニックス | f iy n ih k s | t eh n ih k s | フェニックク | phenixs | フェニックス | phnix | pホエ ニx | fenikkusu |
| | Benton | ベントン | b eh n t ax n | b eh n t ah n | ベントン | benton | ベントン | benton | ベントン | benton |
| | Mountain View | マウンテン・ビュー | m aw n t t n n y uw | m aw n t ix n y uw | マウンンン ビイビー | mouttinnbwe | マウトトンニュー | mouttinveww | モ ウンタインヴィエw | mauntenbyu |
| | San Jose | サンノゼ | s ae n jh ow z | s ae n n ow z | サンジェス | sannoss | サンジジーズ | sannose | サンジョセ | sannoze |
| | South San Francisco | サウス・サンフランシスコ | s ow f f ae n s s s s k k k ax | s er s s ax s s ae n s ax k f s s | サススラランンンニカス | soussccnnnnssccoo | ファファスンフスククク | ssrssasaacancuctes | ソウth サンfランc イsc オ | saususanfuransisko |
| Restaurant Names | Adesso | アデッソ | ax d eh s ow | ae d eh s ow | アドッソ | adesso | アデッ | adeso | アデッノ | adesso |
| | Amore | アモーレ | ah m ao r | ah m ow r ey | アモー | amorel | アモー | amora | アモレ | amore |
| | MAI-THAI | マイタイ | m ey th ey | m ay t ay | メイア | mitite | メイイ | mithte | マイ-ティイ | maitai |
| | Ristorante | リストランテ | r ih s t ow t t | r ih s t r ax n t en ih eh r ow | リストラインアア | resteraattttooo | リトトトンシシアア | resternaaarr | リストランテ | risutorante |
| | AKICHI | アキチ- | ae k iy ch iy | ae k ch iy | アキチ- | aciih | アキチー | acchi | アキチ | akichi |

Table 4: Example Results of Transliteration.

ties using vector similarity more accurately. This is why the probability vector metric outperforms all other metrics. We also computed the other top-N precision, and the result was precision (N=10) at 67% and precision (N=30) at 74%. This opens the way for narrowing down by entity matching with the name alone.

For future work, in order to improve accuracy on restaurant data, we could implement a few procedures. The first would be cleaning the datasets because there are some pairs that do not correspond. This time we checked the non-matching pairs quickly but because of large volume of the datasets, there could remain some amount of noise. It could be solved by crowdsourcing of many Japanese speakers. The second would be polishing the transliteration model. We tried to use an attention mechanism for RNN model, but the accuracy was not good. We may polish the model by adjusting the best hyper parameter. Moreover, we could train pair data of English and Katakana at the same time instead of independently to create the model. In the entity matching task of the actual restaurant data, if we detect 60% through the top-five precision, entity matching would be easy through using additional data such as postal code level addresses.

## 6 CONCLUSION

In this paper we built two research questions to clarify how to solve heterogeneous entity matching. The first question was what should be used for conversion in entity matching between English and Japanese Katakana. We proposed an entity matching method that considers phoneme symbols, and compared models to convert a term into English, Katakana, and phonemes. The second question was what should be used for the similarity metric. We proposed a similarity method that uses a phoneme probability vector predicted by sequence to sequence models and compared six metrics, which are Overlap Coefficient, Cosine, Jacquard, Jaro-Winkler, Levenshtein, and the similarity of phonemes.

Our experiments in the three real datasets showed that 1) a phoneme matching system works better than other methods, and 2) the similarity of phoneme in the phoneme method and Levenshtein similarity in other methods suit the entity matching problems. We insist that phoneme information is crucial for heterogeneous entity matching.

Based on these results, we will build an entity matching system between English and Japanese Katakana, and publish a part of it as an open-source software. We can apply the system to extension of a dataset from a vast amount of data on the web and to rare query expansion on a search engine. Almost of our services have a search engine and in some services, we are using a part of the entity matching system to reduce outputs of 0 hits result. In the future, the model is expected to be polished and applied to other languages. In this paper it is tested on Japanese and English, but potentially could be used on other languages. We believe that our method could apply to any language that has phonetic characters.

## Acknowledgments

In this research, we would like to thank Wang-Chiew Tan and Akiko Ito for crucial advice and supports of this work. We also thank the reviewers for valuable feedbacks.

**References**

Edward Benson, Stephen Pueblo, Fuming Shih, and Robert Berwick. 2009. English-japanese transliteration.

Jim Breen. 1995. Building an electronic japanese-english dictionary. In *Japanese Studies Association of Australia Conference*. Citeseer.

Zhiyuan Cai, Kaiqi Zhao, Kenny Q Zhu, and Haixun Wang. 2013. Wikification via link co-occurrence. In *Proceedings of the 22nd ACM international conference on Conference on information & knowledge management*, pages 1087–1096. ACM.

David Carmel, Ming-Wei Chang, Evgeniy Gabrilovich, Bo-June Paul Hsu, and Kuansan Wang. 2014. Erd'14: entity recognition and disambiguation challenge. In *ACM SIGIR Forum*, volume 48, pages 63–77. ACM.

William Cohen, Pradeep Ravikumar, and Stephen Fienberg. 2003. A comparison of string metrics for matching names and records. In *Kdd workshop on data cleaning and object consolidation*, volume 3, pages 73–78.

John DeFrancis. 1984. Digraphia. *Word*, 35(1):59–66.

Diederik P Kingma and Jimmy Ba. 2014. Adam: A method for stochastic optimization. *arXiv preprint arXiv:1412.6980*.

Taku Kudo. 2006. Mecab: Yet another part-of-speech and morphological analyzer. *http://mecab.sourceforge.net*.

Assunta Martin. 2004. The 'katakana effect' and teaching english in japan. *English Today*, 20(1):50–55.

Sidharth Mudgal, Han Li, Theodoros Rekatsinas, An-Hai Doan, Youngchoon Park, Ganesh Krishnan, Rohit Deep, Esteban Arcaute, and Vijay Raghavendra. 2018. Deep learning for entity matching: A design space exploration. In *Proceedings of the 2018 International Conference on Management of Data*, pages 19–34. ACM.

Meinard Müller. 2007. Dynamic time warping. *Information retrieval for music and motion*, pages 69–84.

Emir Muñoz, Aidan Hogan, and Alessandra Mileo. 2014. Using linked data to mine rdf from wikipedia's tables. In *Proceedings of the 7th ACM international conference on Web search and data mining*, pages 533–542. ACM.

Noriko Nagata. 1998. Input vs. output practice in educational software for second language acquisition. *Language Learning and Technology*, 1:23–40.

Pramod Pandey and Somnath Roy. 2017. A generative model of a pronunciation lexicon for hindi. *arXiv preprint arXiv:1705.02452*.

Kanishka Rao, Fuchun Peng, Haşim Sak, and Françoise Beaufays. 2015. Grapheme-to-phoneme conversion using long short-term memory recurrent neural networks. In *Acoustics, Speech and Signal Processing (ICASSP), 2015 IEEE International Conference on*, pages 4225–4229. IEEE.

Mike Schuster and Kuldip K Paliwal. 1997. Bidirectional recurrent neural networks. *IEEE Transactions on Signal Processing*, 45(11):2673–2681.

Yoones A Sekhavat, Francesco Di Paolo, Denilson Barbosa, and Paolo Merialdo. 2014. Knowledge base augmentation using tabular data. In *LDOW*.

Wei Shen, Jianyong Wang, and Jiawei Han. 2015. Entity linking with a knowledge base: Issues, techniques, and solutions. *IEEE Transactions on Knowledge and Data Engineering*, 27(2):443–460.

Janet S Smith. 1996. Japanese writing. *The world's writing systems*, pages 209–217.

Ye Kyaw Thu, Win Pa Pa, Yoshinori Sagisaka, and Naoto Iwahashi. 2016. Comparison of grapheme-to-phoneme conversion methods on a myanmar pronunciation dictionary. In *Proceedings of the 6th Workshop on South and Southeast Asian Natural Language Processing (WSSANLP2016)*, pages 11–22.

Shubham Toshniwal and Karen Livescu. 2016. Jointly learning to align and convert graphemes to phonemes with neural attention models. In *Spoken Language Technology Workshop (SLT), 2016 IEEE*, pages 76–82. IEEE.

William E Winkler. 1999. The state of record linkage and current research problems. In *Statistical Research Division, US Census Bureau*. Citeseer.

Ian H Witten, Eibe Frank, Mark A Hall, and Christopher J Pal. 2016. *Data Mining: Practical machine learning tools and techniques*. Morgan Kaufmann.

Kaisheng Yao and Geoffrey Zweig. 2015. Sequence-to-sequence neural net models for grapheme-to-phoneme conversion. In *INTERSPEECH 2015*, pages 3330–3334. ISCA.

# Seq2Seq Models with Dropout can Learn Generalizable Reduplication


**Brandon Prickett, Aaron Traylor,** and **Joe Pater**
Linguistics Department
University of Massachusetts Amherst
bprickett@umass.edu, aaron_traylor@brown.edu,
pater@linguist.umass.edu



## Abstract

Natural language reduplication can pose a challenge to neural models of language, and has been argued to require variables (Marcus et al., 1999). Sequence-to-sequence neural networks have been shown to perform well at a number of other morphological tasks (Cotterell et al., 2016), and produce results that highly correlate with human behavior (Kirov, 2017; Kirov & Cotterell, 2018) but do not include any explicit variables in their architecture. We find that they can learn a reduplicative pattern that generalizes to novel segments if they are trained with dropout (Srivastava et al., 2014). We argue that this matches the scope of generalization observed in human reduplication.


## 1   Introduction

Reduplication is a common morphological process in which all or part of a word is copied and added to one side of the word's stem. An example of reduplication occurring in the language Karao is given in (1):

*(1) Reduplication in Karao*
*(from Ŝtekaurer et al. 2012):*

| man*ba*kal | → | man*baba*kal |
|---|---|---|
| 'fight each other' | | 'fight each other' |
| (2 people) | | (>2 people) |

In the example above, the stem *ba* is reduplicated to create the affixed form *baba*. Berent (2013) discusses four different possibilities for how speakers could represent reduplication in their

minds: (i) memorization of which reduplicated forms go with which stems, (ii) learning a function that copies all segments that undergo reduplication, (iii) learning a function that copies all feature values that undergo reduplication, or (iv) learning a function that uses algebraic symbols to copy the appropriate material, regardless of its segmental or featural content. She concludes that reduplication and similar processes in language involve the fourth possibility, which she labels an *identity function*. An identity function for reduplication is illustrated in (2), with $\alpha$ acting as a variable that represents the reduplicated sequence.

*(2) Reduplication as an algebraic rule*
$$\alpha \rightarrow \alpha\alpha$$

Marcus et al. (1999) came to a similar conclusion regarding reduplication and identity functions, after showing that infants could learn a reduplication-like pattern and generalize that pattern to novel segments. They used this as evidence against connectionist models of grammar, which do not typically include explicit variables[1] (see, for example, Elman, 1990; Rumelhart & McClelland, 1986). Both feed-forward and simple recurrent neural networks fail at learning generalizable identity functions (Berent, 2013; Marcus, 2001; Marcus et al., 1999; Tupper & Shahriari, 2016).

In this paper, we revisit these arguments against variable-free connectionist models in light of recent developments in neural network architecture and training techniques. Specifically, we test Sequence-to-Sequence models (Sutskever et al., 2014) with LTSM (Long Short-Term

---

[1] We use the term *explicit variable* to refer to the algebraic symbols that are often absent from connectionist theories of cognition. However, a number of connectionist models do incorporate explicit variables, such as the models in Marcus (2001), Smolensky and Legendre (2006), and Moreton (2012). See Pater (2018:§4) for a more detailed discussion of different hybrids of connectionist and symbolic approaches.




*Proceedings of the 15th SIGMORPHON Workshop on Computational Research in Phonetics, Phonology, and Morphology*, pages 93–100
Brussels, Belgium, October 31, 2018. ©2018 The Special Interest Group on Computational Morphology and Phonology
https://doi.org/10.18653/v1/P17

Memory; Hochreiter & Schmidhuber, 1997) and dropout (Srivastava et al., 2014). We find that the scope of generalization for the models is increased from copying segments to copying feature values when dropout is added. Additionally, we argue that variable-free feature copying is sufficient to model human generalization, contrary to Berent's (2013) claim that an algebraic identity function is necessary.

## 2 Background

The debate between connectionist and symbolic theories of grammar has largely been focused on the domain of morphology (for a review, see Pater, 2018). Reduplication was no exception, with standard connectionist models failing to learn the pattern (Gasser, 1993). Standard models also failed to generalize a reduplicative pattern in a way that mimicked human behavior (Marcus et al., 1999). Marcus (2001) argued that this was evidence of the need for variables in models of cognition. While supporters of connectionism pointed out issues with some of Marcus et al.'s (1999) conclusions (e.g. Seidenberg & Elman, 1999), they failed to show that a connectionist network with no variables could learn reduplication without being previously trained on a similar identity function (see Endress, Dehaene-Lambertz, & Mehler, 2007 for an overview of these studies).

Research in phonotactics has also supported the need for variables in models of language. Berent (2013) showed that Hebrew speakers generalized a phonotactic identity-based restriction in a way that she argued required variables. She presented various experimental results demonstrating that speakers would generalize the restriction to novel words, novel segments, and what she claimed to be novel feature values (for more on our interpretation of these findings, see §5.2). This ran contrary to the predictions of phonotactic learning models that did not include variables (Berent et al., 2012).

However, the models tested by Marcus et al. (1999) and Berent et al. (2012) were relatively simple compared to many modern neural network architectures. The modern model that we will examine is the Seq2Seq neural network (Sutskever et al., 2014), originally designed for machine translation. These models have been shown to perform well at learning a variety of morphological tasks (Cotterell et al., 2016), and produce results that highly correlate with human behavior (Kirov, 2017; Kirov & Cotterell, 2018).

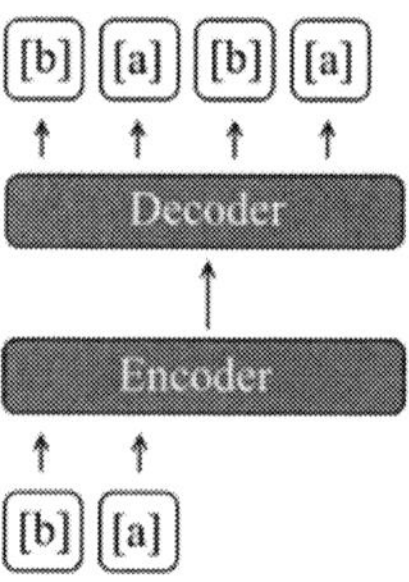


Figure 1: Illustration of Seq2Seq architecture modeling reduplication of the stem [ba].

Since these models include a number of recently-invented mechanisms, such as an encoder-decoder structure (Sutskever et al., 2014), Long Short-Term Memory layers instead of simple, recurrent ones (Hochreiter & Schmidhuber, 1997), and the possibility of dropout during training (Srivastava et al., 2014), it's unclear whether they will be limited in the same ways as their predecessors.

## 3 The Model

In this section, we will give a brief introduction to each of the mechanisms in our model that we consider to be relevant to the simulations presented in §4. For the documentation on the Python packages used to implement the model, see Chollet et al. (2015) and Rahman (2016). We chose to focus on Seq2Seq models because of their recent success in a number of linguistic tasks (summarized in §3.1). We leave exploring the differences between this architecture and its alternatives (such as simple recurrent networks) to future work.

### 3.1 The Seq2Seq Architecture

Seq2Seq neural networks have the ability to map from one string to another, without requiring a one-on-one mapping between the strings' elements (Sutskever et al., 2014). The model achieves this by using an architecture made up of an encoder and decoder pair. Each member in the pair is its own recurrent network, with the encoder processing the input string and the decoder transforming that processed data into an output string. The ability of these models' inputs and outputs to have independent lengths is useful for morphology, which usually involves adding or copying segments in a stem. An example of this for reduplication is shown in Figure 1.

In Figure 1, the encoder passes through the entire input string (i.e. the stem [ba]) before transferring information to the decoder. The decoder then unpacks this information, and gives a reduplicated form (i.e. [baba]) as output. In all of the simulations discussed in this paper, the encoder is *bidirectional*, meaning that it passes through the input string starting from both the left and right edges.

## 3.2 Long Short-Term Memory (LSTM)

LSTM (Hochreiter & Schmidhuber, 1997) is a kind of recurrent neural network layer which allows the model to store certain information in memory more easily than a simple recurrent layer could. While this architectural innovation was originally designed to address the problem of vanishing gradients (Bengio et al., 1994), it has been demonstrated that LSTM can also provide models with added representational power (Levy et al., 2018).

The way the model performs both of these tasks is by using *cell states*, bundles of interacting layers that can learn which features are important for the model to keep track of in a long-term way. During training, the network is not only keeping track of which information will allow it to predict the output from the input, but also which information at a given time step (i.e. at a given segment in the simulations presented here) will help it to predict the output at future time steps.

Vanishing gradients are not much of a concern in morphological learning, since input and output strings are relatively short in this domain of language. However, the effects of LSTM's added representational power on learning of reduplication have not yet been explored.

## 3.3 Dropout

Dropout is a method used in neural network training that helps models generalize correctly to items outside of their training data (Srivastava et al., 2014). It achieves this by having some units in the network "drop out" in each forward pass. This prevents the network from finding solutions that are too dependent on a small number of units. Practically speaking, this is implemented by setting a probability with which each unit will drop out (a hyper parameter set by the analyst) and then multiplying every unit's output by either a 0 or 1, depending on whether it has been randomly chosen to be dropped out or not. Which units are dropped

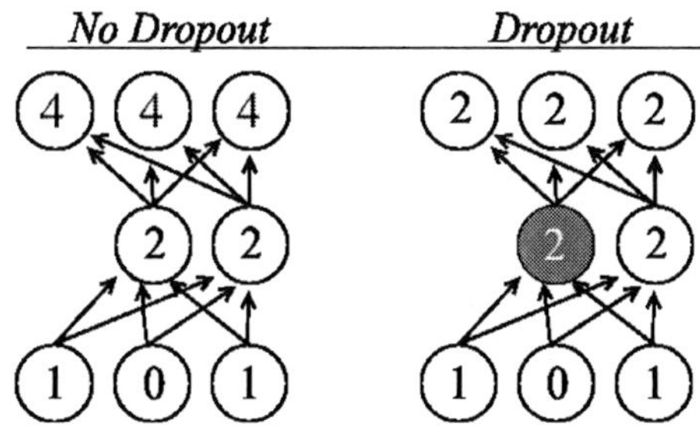



Figure 2: A simple, feed-forward network, with and without dropout. Each circle is a unit and each arrow is a connection. Dropped out units are in grey. Each unit's output (before dropout) is denoted by the number inside of it. All connections have a weight of 1 and all activation functions are f(x)=x.

out is resampled each forward pass, causing the network's solution to be more general than it might have been otherwise. This is illustrated for a single forward pass in a simple, feed-forward network on the right side of Figure 2. In this illustration, dropout causes the output units to have an activation of 2, instead of 4, because a unit in the middle layer is being dropped out and cannot contribute to the activations in the layer above it. For the simulations presented here that use dropout, it was applied with equal probability to all layers of the network.

## 4 Experiments

To test whether reduplication can be modeled by a neural network without explicit variables, we ran a number of simulations in which the model was trained on a reduplication pattern in a toy language and tested on how it generalized that pattern to novel data. To test what kind of generalization the model was performing, we set up different scenarios: one in which the model was tested on a novel syllable made up of segments it had seen reduplicating in its training data (§4.1), one in which the model was tested on a syllable made with a segment that it hadn't received in training (§4.2), and one in which the model was tested on a syllable with a novel segment containing a feature value that hadn't been presented in the training data (§4.3).

In the experiments presented here, a language's segments were each represented by a unique, randomly-produced vector of 6 features (excluding the simulations in §4.3), with feature values being either -1 or 1 (corresponding to the [-] and [+] used in standard phonological models). The inventory was divided into consonants and vowels by treating the first feature as [syllabic], i.e. any of the feature vectors that began with -1 were considered a consonant and any that began with 1 were considered a vowel. If an inventory had no vowels, one of its consonants was randomly chosen and its value for the feature [syllabic] was changed to 1.

The toy language for any given simulation consisted of all the possible CV syllables that could be made with that simulation's randomly created segment inventory. Crucially, before the data was given to the model, some portion of it was withheld for testing (see the subsections below for more information on what was withheld in each testing condition). The mapping that the model was trained on treated each stem (e.g. [ba]) as input and each reduplicated form (e.g. [baba]) as output. The model's input and output lengths were fixed to 2 and 4 segments, respectively (reflecting the fact that all the toy languages only had stems that were 2 segments long).

The models were trained for 1000 epochs, with training batches that included all of the learning data (i.e. learning was done in batch). The loss function that was being minimized was mean-squared error, and the minimization algorithm was RMSprop (Tieleman & Hinton, 2012). The models had 2 layers each in the encoder and decoder, with 18 units in each of these layers. All other parameters were the default values in the deep-learning Python package, Keras (Chollet et al. 2015).

To test whether the model generalized to withheld data, a relatively strict definition of success was used in testing. The model was given a withheld stem as input, and the output it predicted was compared to the correct output (i.e. the reduplicated form of the stem it was given). If every feature value in the predicted output had the same sign (positive/negative) as its counterpart in the correct output, the model was considered to be successfully generalizing the reduplication pattern. However, if any of the feature values did not have the same sign, that model was considered to be non-generalizing. While we only report the results from 25 runs in each condition, we ran many more while investigating various hyperparameter settings and possibilities about the construction of

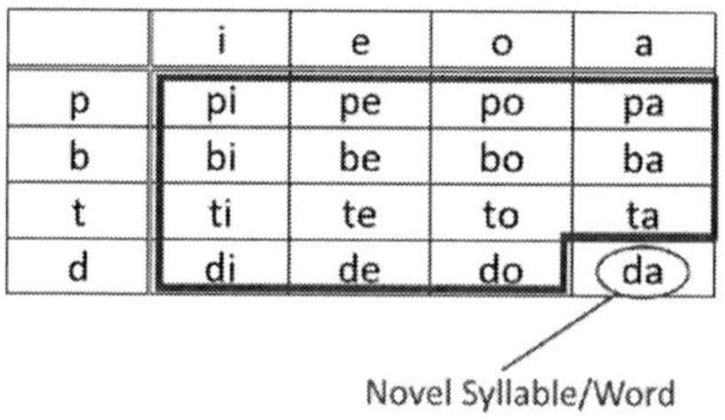

| | i | e | o | a |
|---|---|---|---|---|
| p | pi | pe | po | pa |
| b | bi | be | bo | ba |
| t | ti | te | to | ta |
| d | di | de | do | da |

Novel Syllable/Word

Figure 3: Illustration of generalization to a novel syllable/word in a language with only eight segments. Specific IPA labels are hypothetical. Syllables surrounded by the black box were presented in training, while the circled syllable was withheld for testing.

the training data. The results presented here are representative of the general pattern of results.

## 4.1 Generalizing to Novel Syllables

Our first set of simulations tested whether the model could generalize to novel syllables. If the model failed at this task, then it would mean that it was memorizing whole words in the training data, rather than learning an actual pattern. Figure 3 illustrates this.

In Figure 3, [da] is the syllable that was withheld from training. This means that the model never saw the mapping from [da]→[dada], but it did see the segments that make up [da]. For example, the training data [di] and [ba] would have demonstrated the behavior of [d] and [a] to the model, respectively.

For this condition, toy languages always contained 40 segments in their inventory, and the probability of a unit being dropped out was 0%.

The model successfully reduplicated syllables from training in all runs for this condition. Additionally, it generalized to novel syllables in 22 of the 25 simulations (88%). These results are summarized in Figure 6. This shows that a standard Seq2Seq model, with LSTM but no dropout, can perform generalization to novel syllables, and does so a majority of the time.

## 4.2 Generalizing to Novel Segments

The next scope of generalization described by Berent (2013) is generalization to novel segments. To test whether our model could achieve this, we created languages with inventories of 40 segments (as described above), but randomly chose a single consonant in each run to be withheld for testing. This is illustrated for a simplified example in Figure 4.

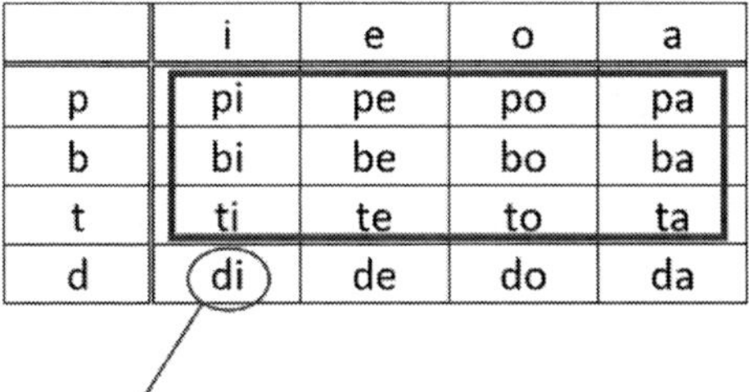

|   | i | e | o | a |
|---|---|---|---|---|
| p | pi | pe | po | pa |
| b | bi | be | bo | ba |
| t | ti | te | to | ta |
| d | di | de | do | da |



Figure 4: Illustration of generalization to a novel segments in a language with only eight sounds. Specific IPA labels are hypothetical. Syllables surrounded by the black box were presented in training, while the circled syllable was withheld for testing.

|   | i | e | o | a |
|---|---|---|---|---|
| p | pi | pe | po | pa |
| b | bi | be | bo | ba |
| t | ti | te | to | ta |
| d | di | de | do | da |
| n | ni | ne | no | na |



Figure 5: Illustration of generalization to a novel feature values in a language with only nine sounds. Specific IPA labels are hypothetical. Syllables surrounded by the black box were presented in training, while the circled syllable was withheld for testing.

In Figure 4, the consonant [d] is never shown to the model in training. This means that the model has no experience with reduplicating this vector of feature values before testing. The model would have been exposed to each of the feature values making up this segment, though. For example, [t] and [b] would have exposed the model to the place and voicing features of [d], respectively.

For the results reported in this section, toy languages always had inventories of 40 segments. Two conditions were tested in regards to dropout: one in which dropout never happened (0%) and one which it happened to the majority of units in any given forward pass (75%).

When no dropout was applied, the model was unable to reliably generalize—with only 6 of the 25 runs achieving success on novel segments (24 out of 25 for trained segments). However, when dropout was applied with a probability of 75%, the model successfully generalized to novel segments in 15 of the 25 runs (25 out of 25 for trained segments). These results are summarized in Figure 6. This demonstrates that without dropout, our model does not reliably generalize to novel syllables, but that with dropout it does.

### 4.3 Generalizing to Novel Feature Values

The most powerful form of generalization Berent (2013) discusses is generalization to novel feature values, which would signify the acquisition of a proper identity function. In the context of reduplication, this would involve correctly applying the process to a stem that includes feature values never seen in training. For example, if all of the consonants in training were oral, but the process generalized to nasal consonants, this would demonstrate generalization to the novel feature value [+nasal]. This is shown in Figure 5.

In the example above, the syllable [na] represents a novel feature value. If a model only learned a function that learned to copy individual feature values from the stem into the reduplicant, it wouldn't generalize to this kind of novel feature value correctly. This generalization can only occur if the model learns to copy the reduplicant irrespective of individual features.

For the results reported here, toy languages always contained 43 segments in their inventory, and these were not produced randomly (this made it easier to ensure that a particular feature value could be withheld). A variety of other segment inventories were tested, with no changes in the model's performance. Results are presented here for simulations using 0% and 75% dropout probability, although numerous other values for this were also tested.

Regardless of whether dropout occurred, the model never generalized to novel feature values. These results are summarized in Figure 6. This shows that a standard Seq2Seq model, regardless of whether it has dropout, cannot generalize to novel feature values. We discuss in §5.2 why we do not see this limitation as a flaw in terms of modeling human language learning.

## 5 Discussion

### 5.1 Summary of Results

The results for each simulation can be viewed side-by-side in Figure 6. The findings from this series of experiments showed that even without dropout, a Seq2Seq model is not simply learning to

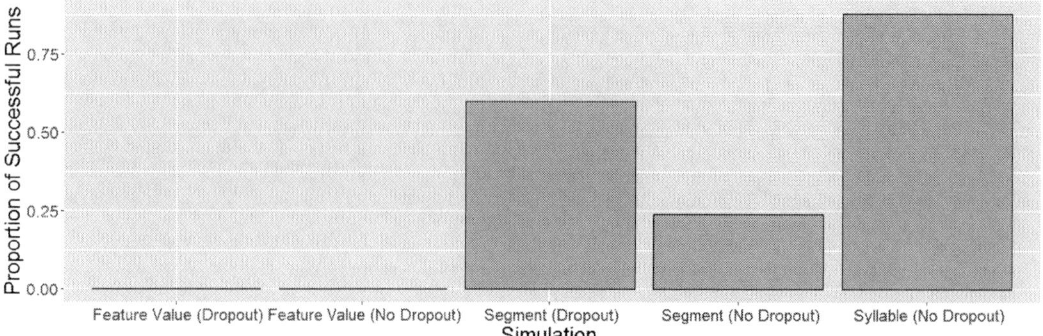


Figure 6: Full summary of results. Bars show the proportion of successful runs out of 25.

memorize <stem, reduplicant> pairs, since it was able to generalize reduplication to novel stems (i.e. novel syllables). We also showed that the model, when using dropout in training, can reliably generalize reduplication to novel segments.

## 5.2 Can humans generalize to novel feature values?

When discussing generalization, Berent (2013) used evidence from Hebrew speakers' phonotactic judgments to support the idea that they learn a true identity function when acquiring their native phonology. The judgments centered around a phonotactic restriction in Hebrew that prohibits the first two consonants in a stem from being identical. For example, the word *simem* 'he intoxicated' is grammatical, while the nonce word **sisem* is not. Berent (2013) showed that speakers generalized this pattern by having them rate the acceptability of various kinds of nonce forms.

The first results she discussed demonstrated Hebrew speakers generalizing to novel words. These words were made up of segments that were attested in Hebrew. Speakers in this experiment rated words with s-s-m stems (like **sisem* above) as significantly less acceptable than words with s-m-m and p-s-m stems. This demonstrated that Hebrew speakers were doing more than just memorizing the lexicon of their language (i.e. that they could extract phonotactic patterns).

The next results that Berent (2013) presented involved Hebrew speakers generalizing the pattern to novel segments. The segments of interest were /tʃ/, /dʒ/ and /w/, all of which are not present in native Hebrew stems. Even when these non-native phonemes were used, Hebrew speakers rated words whose first two consonants were identical (e.g. dʒ-dʒ-r) as worse than those that did not violate the phonotactic restriction (e.g. r-dʒ-dʒ).

This demonstrated that speakers had not just memorized a list of consonants that cannot cooccur (e.g. *pp, *ss, *mm, etc.) while acquiring their phonological grammar.

Finally, Berent (2013) showed that speakers can generalize the pattern to the segment [θ], which she claimed represented generalization to a novel feature value (which she referred to as *across the board generalization*). While we agree with her conclusions regarding the first two sets of results, we find her interpretation of this final result to be less convincing. The novel feature value that she claimed was represented by [θ] was the feature value [Wide]. However, this is a fairly non-standard phonological feature. Using a more standard featural representation for [θ], such as [+anterior, +continuant, -strident] (Chomsky & Halle, 1968), would mean that [θ] does not represent a novel feature value for Hebrew, since the language contains other, native, [+anterior], [+continuant], and [-strident] sounds.

Returning to reduplication, a relevant generalization experiment is Marcus et al. (1999). In that experiment, infants generalized a reduplication-like pattern to novel words with novel segments, but not with novel feature values. All of the words in Marcus et al.'s testing phase used feature values that would have been familiar to the infants from their native language of English.

To our knowledge, no experiment has shown humans generalizing to truly novel feature values. Because of this, we cannot conclude whether our model's results from §4.3 are human-like or not.

## 5.3 Why did dropout allow the model to generalize to novel segments?

While we've shown that dropout increases the Seq2Seq model's scope of generalization, it still remains unclear why this form of regularization succeeds for this task. One hypothesis is that dropout causes certain training data to be indistiguishable from crucial testing data. For example, if training includes the stems [pa] and [da], but [ta] is withheld, a model without dropout would not generalize to the novel item because it was never trained on reduplicating [t]. However, when dropout is applied, in a subset of epochs, the unit activations distinguishing [t] from [d] will be dropped out. This will allow the model to learn how to reduplicate a syllable that is ambiguous between [ta] and [da]. These ambiguous training epochs could provide enough information to the model for it to learn a function that generalizes correctly to withheld segments.

This explanation could suggest that other forms of regularization, such as an L2 prior, that don't create a similar kind of ambiguity, may not have the same effect on reduplication learning.

## 5.4 Future Work

A number of avenues exist for furthering this line of research. First of all, as mentioned in §5.2, the full picture of how humans behave in regards to generalizing reduplication-like patterns is still an open question. Additionally, more direct modeling of some of the experimental data that does exist on this subject (e.g. Marcus et al., 1999) could help to shed more light on how well a Seq2Seq network with no explicit variables can model such results.

The simulations outlined here could also be made to more realistically mimic natural language. Stems of varying lengths, and with various syllabic structures could pose an interesting challenge to any model of reduplication. A reduplication process that copies only part of the stem could also test whether the model is capable of learning a more complex identity function. Additionally, presenting the data in a way that mimics the exposure children receive could be useful, since infants are not directly presented with stem-reduplicant pairs in isolation.

Future research could also address the effects of dropout presented here. First of all, since dropout is one of many different regularization methods (Wager et al., 2013), testing its alternatives could be useful. And if it's the case that dropout allows a model to learn in a more human-like way, then adding dropout to models of other domains of language (such as phonotactics) should also be explored.

## 5.5 Conclusion

In summary, we found that a Seq2Seq model could learn a simple reduplication pattern and generalize that pattern to novel items. Dropout increased the model's scope of generalization from novel syllables to novel segments, demonstrating a human-like behavior that has been previously used as an argument against connectionist models with no explicit variables (for other alternatives to explicit variables in neural networks, see Garrido Alhama, 2017; Gu et al., 2016). These results weaken this line of argument against connectionism.

## Acknowledgments

The authors would like to thank the members of the UMass Sound Workshop, the members of the UMass NLP Reading Group, Tal Linzen, and Ryan Cotterell for helpful feedback and discussion. Additionally, we would like to thank the SIGMORPHON reviewers for their comments. This work was supported by NSF Grant #1650957.

## References

Bengio, Y., Simard, P., & Frasconi, P. (1994). Learning long-term dependencies with gradient descent is difficult. *IEEE Transactions on Neural Networks, 5*(2), 157–166.

Berent, I. (2013). The phonological mind. *Trends in Cognitive Sciences, 17*(7), 319–327.

Berent, I., Wilson, C., Marcus, G. F., & Bemis, D. K. (2012). On the role of variables in phonology: Remarks on Hayes and Wilson 2008. *Linguistic Inquiry, 43*(1), 97–119.

Chollet, F., & others. (2015). Keras. Retrieved January 18, 2018, from https://github.com/keras-team/keras

Chomsky, N., & Halle, M. (1968). *The sound pattern of English.* New York, NY: Harper & Row.

Cotterell, R., Kirov, C., Sylak-Glassman, J., Yarowsky, D., Eisner, J., & Hulden, M. (2016). The SIGMORPHON 2016 shared task— morphological reinflection. In *Proceedings of the 14th SIGMORPHON Workshop on Computational Research in Phonetics, Phonology, and Morphology* (pp. 10–22).

Elman, J. L. (1990). Finding structure in time. *Cognitive Science, 14*(2), 179–211.

Endress, A. D., Dehaene-Lambertz, G., & Mehler, J. (2007). Perceptual constraints and the learnability of simple grammars. *Cognition, 105*(3), 577–614.

Garrido Alhama, R. (2017). Computational modelling of Artificial Language Learning. *Dissertation*, Institute for Logic, Language and Computation (ILLC) at the University of Amsterdam.

Gasser, M. (1993). *Learning words in time: Towards a modular connectionist account of the acquisition of receptive morphology*. Indiana University, Department of Computer Science.

Gu, J., Lu, Z., Li, H., & Li, V. O. (2016). Incorporating copying mechanism in sequence-to-sequence learning. *ArXiv Preprint ArXiv:1603.06393*.

Hochreiter, S., & Schmidhuber, J. (1997). Long short-term memory. *Neural Computation, 9*(8), 1735–1780.

Kirov, C. (2017). Recurrent Neural Networks as a Strong Domain-General Baseline for Morpho-Phonological Learning. In *Poster presented at the 2017 Meeting of the Linguistic Society of America*.

Kirov, C., & Cotterell, R. (2018). *Recurrent Neural Networks in Linguistic Theory: Revisiting Pinker & Prince (1988) and the Past Tense Debate*.

Levy, O., Lee, K., FitzGerald, N., & Zettlemoyer, L. (2018). Long Short-Term Memory as a Dynamically Computed Element-wise Weighted Sum. *ArXiv Preprint ArXiv:1805.03716*.

Marcus, G. (2001). *The algebraic mind*. Cambridge, MA: MIT Press.

Marcus, G., Vijayan, S., Rao, S. B., & Vishton, P. M. (1999). Rule learning by seven-month-old infants. *Science, 283*(5398), 77–80.

Moreton, E. (2012). Inter-and intra-dimensional dependencies in implicit phonotactic learning. *Journal of Memory and Language, 67*(1), 165–183.

Pater, J. (2018). Generative linguistics and neural networks at 60: foundation, friction, and fusion. *Language*.

Rahman, F. (2016). *seq2seq: Sequence to Sequence Learning with Keras*. Python. Retrieved from https://github.com/farizrahman4u/seq2seq

Rumelhart, D., & McClelland, J. (1986). On learning the past tenses of English verbs. In J. McClelland & D. Rumelhart (Eds.), *Parallel Distributed Processing: Explorations in the Microstructure of Cognition* (Vol. 2: Psychological and Biological Models, pp. 216–271). The MIT Press.

Seidenberg, M. S., & Elman, J. L. (1999). Do infants learn grammar with algebra or statistics? *Science, 284*(5413), 433f–433f.

Smolensky, P., & Legendre, G. (2006). *The harmonic mind: From neural computation to optimality-theoretic grammar (Cognitive architecture), Vol. 1*. MIT press.

Srivastava, N., Hinton, G., Krizhevsky, A., Sutskever, I., & Salakhutdinov, R. (2014). Dropout: A simple way to prevent neural networks from overfitting. *The Journal of Machine Learning Research, 15*(1), 1929–1958.

Štekauer, P., Valera, S., & Körtvélyessy, L. (2012). *Word-formation in the world's languages: a typological survey*. Cambridge University Press.

Sutskever, I., Vinyals, O., & Le, Q. V. (2014). Sequence to sequence learning with neural networks. In *Advances in neural information processing systems* (pp. 3104–3112).

Tieleman, T., & Hinton, G. (2012). Lecture 6.5-rmsprop: Divide the gradient by a running average of its recent magnitude. *COURSERA: Neural Networks for Machine Learning, 4*(2), 26–31.

Tupper, P., & Shahriari, B. (2016). Which Learning Algorithms Can Generalize Identity-Based Rules to Novel Inputs? *ArXiv Preprint ArXiv:1605.04002*.

Wager, S., Wang, S., & Liang, P. S. (2013). Dropout training as adaptive regularization. *Advances in Neural Information Processing Systems*, 351–359.

# A Characterwise Windowed Approach to Hebrew Morphological Segmentation

**Amir Zeldes**

Department of Linguistics
Georgetown University
amir.zeldes@georgetown.edu

## Abstract

This paper presents a novel approach to the segmentation of orthographic word forms in contemporary Hebrew, focusing purely on splitting without carrying out morphological analysis or disambiguation. Casting the analysis task as character-wise binary classification and using adjacent character and word-based lexicon-lookup features, this approach achieves over 98% accuracy on the benchmark SPMRL shared task data for Hebrew, and 97% accuracy on a new out of domain Wikipedia dataset, an improvement of ≈4% and 5% over previous state of the art performance.

## 1 Introduction

Hebrew is a morphologically rich language in which, as in Arabic and other similar languages, space-delimited word forms contain multiple units corresponding to what other languages (and most POS tagging/parsing schemes) consider multiple words. This includes nouns fused with prepositions, articles and possessive pronouns, as in (1), or verbs fused with preceding conjunctions and object pronouns, as in (2), which uses one 'word' to mean "and that they found him", where the first two letters correspond to 'and' and 'that' respectively, while the last two letters after the verb mean 'him'.[1]

(1)    מהבית
     ⟨m.h.byt⟩ [me.ha.bayit]
     from.the.house

(2)    ושמצאוהו
     ⟨w.š.mc'w.hw⟩ [ve.še.mtsa'u.hu]
     and.that.found-3-PL.him

This complexity makes tokenization for Hebrew a challenging process, usually carried out in two steps: tokenization of large units, delimited by spaces or punctuation as in English, and a subsequent segmentation of the smaller units within each large unit. To avoid confusion, the rest of this paper will use the term 'super-token' for large units such as the entire contents of (1) and 'sub-token' for the smaller units.

Beyond this, three issues complicate Hebrew segmentation further. Firstly, much like Arabic and similar languages, Hebrew uses a consonantal script which disregards most vowels. For example in (2) the sub-tokens *ve* 'and' and *še* 'that' are spelled as single letters ⟨w⟩ and ⟨š⟩. While some vowels are represented (mainly word-final or etymologically long vowels), these are denoted by the same letters as consonants, e.g. the final -u in *vešemtsa'uhu*, spelled as ⟨w⟩, the same letter used for *ve* 'and'. This means that syllable structure, a crucial cue for segmentation, is obscured.

A second problem is that unlike Arabic, Hebrew has morpheme reductions creating segments which are pronounced, but not distinguished in the orthography.[2] This affects the definite article after some prepositions, as in (3) and (4), which mean 'in a house' and 'in the house' respectively.

(3)    בבית
     ⟨b.byt⟩ [be.bayit]
     in.house

(4)    בבית
     ⟨b..byt⟩ [b.a.bayit]
     in.the.house

---

[1] In all Hebrew examples below, angle brackets denote transliterated graphemes with dots separating morphemes, and square brackets represent standard Hebrew pronunciation. Dot-separated glosses correspond to the segments in the transliteration.

[2] A reviewer has mentioned that Arabic does have some reductions, e.g. in the fusion of articles with the preposition *li-* 'to' in *li.l-* 'to the'. This is certainly true and problematic for morphological segmentation of Arabic, however in these cases there is always some graphical trace of the existence of the article, whereas in the Hebrew cases discussed here, no trace of the article is found.



*Proceedings of the 15th SIGMORPHON Workshop on Computational Research in Phonetics, Phonology, and Morphology*, pages 101–110
Brussels, Belgium, October 31, 2018. ©2018 The Special Interest Group on Computational Morphology and Phonology
https://doi.org/10.18653/v1/P17

In (4), the definite article *ha* merges with the preposition *be* to produce the pronounced form *ba*; however the lack of vowel orthography means that both forms are spelled alike.

A final problem is the high degree of ambiguity in written Hebrew, which has often been exemplified by the following example, reproduced from Adler and Elhadad (2006), which has a large number of possible analyses.

(5)      בצלם
         ⟨b.cl.m⟩ be.cil.am - in.shadow.their
         ⟨b.clm⟩ (be./b.a.)celem - in.(a/the).image
         ⟨b.clm⟩ (be./b.a.)calam in.(a/the).photographer
         ⟨bcl.m⟩ bcal.am - onion.their
         ⟨bclm⟩ becelem - Betzelem (organization)

Because some options are likelier than others, information about possible segmentations, frequencies and surrounding words is crucial. We also note that although there are 7 distinct analyses in (5), in terms of segmenting the orthography, only two positions require a decision: either ⟨b⟩ is followed by a boundary or not, and either ⟨l⟩ is or not.

Unlike previous approaches which attempt a complete morphological analysis, in this paper the focus is on pure orthographic segmentation: deciding which characters should be followed by a boundary. Although it is clear that full morphological disambiguation is important, I will argue that a pure splitting task for Hebrew can be valuable if it produces substantially more accurate segmentations, which may be sufficient for some downstream applications (e.g. sequence-to-sequence MT)[3], but may also be fed into a morphological disambiguator. As will be shown here, this simpler task allows us to achieve very high accuracy on shared task data, substantially outperforming the pure segmentation accuracy of the previous state of the art while remaining robust against out-of-vocabulary (OOV) items and domain changes, a crucial weakness of existing tools.

The contributions of this work are threefold:

1. A robust, cross-domain state of the art model for pure Hebrew word segmentation, independent of morphological disambiguation, with an open source implementation and pretrained models

2. Introducing and evaluating a combination of shallow string-based features and ambiguous lexicon lookup features in a windowed approach to binary boundary classification

3. Providing new resources: a freely available, out-of-domain dataset from Wikipedia for evaluating pure segmentation; a converted version in the same format as the original Hebrew Treebank data used in previous work; and an expanded morphological lexicon based on Universal POS tags.

## 2   Previous Work

Earlier approaches to Hebrew morphological segmentation include finite-state analyzers (Yona and Wintner, 2005) and multiple classifiers for morphological properties feedings into a disambiguation step (Shacham and Wintner, 2007). Lattice based approaches have been used with variants of HMMs and the Viterbi algorithm (Adler and Elhadad, 2006) in order to generate all possible analyses supported by a broad coverage lexicon, and then disambiguate in a further step. The main difficulty encountered in all these approaches is the presence of items missing from the lexicon, either due to OOV lexical items or spelling variation, resulting in missing options for the disambiguator. Additionally, there have been issues in comparing results with different formats, datasets, and segmentation targets, especially before the creation of a standard shared task dataset (see below).

Differently from work on Arabic segmentation, where state of the art work operates as either a sequence tagging task (often using BIO-like encoding and CRF/RNN sequence models, Monroe et al. 2014), or a holistic character-wise segmentation ranking task (Abdelali et al., 2016), work on Hebrew segmentation has focused on segmentation in the context of complete morphological analysis, including categorical feature output (gender, tense, etc.). This is in part due to tasks requiring the reconstruction of orthographically unexpressed articles as in (4) and other orthographic changes which require morphological disambiguation, such as recovering base forms of inflected nouns and verbs, and inserting segments which cannot be aligned to any orthographic material, as in (6) below. In this example, an unexpressed possessive preposition *šel* is inserted, in contrast to segmentation practices for the same construction e.g. in Arabic and other languages,

---

[3]cf. Habash and Sadat (2006) on consequences of pure tokenization for Arabic MT.

where the pronoun sub-token is interpreted as inherently possessive.

(6)   ביתה
      ⟨byt.h⟩ [beyt.a] 'her house' (house.her)
      Target analysis:
      ⟨byt šl hy'⟩ [bayit šel hi] 'house of she'

Most recently, the shared task on Statistical Parsing of Morphologically Rich Languages (SPMRL 2013-2015, see Seddah et al. 2014) introduced a standard benchmark dataset for Hebrew morphological segmentation based on the Hebrew Treebank (Sima'an et al. 2001; the data has ≈94K super-tokens for training and ≈21K for testing and development), with a corresponding shared task scored in several scenarios. Systems were scored on segmentation, morphological analysis and syntactic parsing, while working from raw text, from gold segmentation (for morphological analysis and parsing), or from gold segmentation and morphology (for parsing).

The current state of the art is the open source system *yap* ('yet another parser', More and Tsarfaty 2016), based on joint morphological and syntactic disambiguation in a lattice-based parsing approach with a rich morphological lexicon. This will be the main system for comparison in Section 5. Although yap was designed for a fundamentally different task than the current system, i.e. canonical rather than surface segmentation (cf. Cotterell et al. 2016), it is nevertheless currently also the best performing Hebrew segmenter overall and widely used, making it a good point for comparison. Conversely, while the approach in this paper cannot address morphological disambiguation as *yap* and similar systems do, it will be shown that substantially better segmentation accuracy can be achieved using local features, evaluated character-wise, which are much more robustly attested in the limited training data available.

## 3   Character-wise Classification

In this paper we cast the segmentation task as character-wise binary classification, similarly to approaches in other languages, such as Chinese (Lee and Huang, 2013). The goal is to predict for each character in a super-token (except the last) whether it should be followed by a boundary. Although the character-wise setup prevents a truly global analysis of word formation in the way that a lattice-based model allows, it turns out to be more robust than previous approaches, in large part because it does not require a coherent full analysis in the case of OOV items (see Section 5).

### 3.1   Feature Extraction

Our features target a window of $n$ characters around the character being considered for a following boundary (the 'target' character), as well as characters in the preceding and following super-tokens. In practice we set $n$ to $\pm 2$, meaning each classification mainly includes information about the preceding and following two characters.

The extracted features for each window can be divided into three categories: character identity features (i.e. which letters are observed), numerical position/length features and lexicon lookup features. The lexicon is based on the fully inflected form lexicon created by the MILA center, also used by More and Tsarfaty (2016), but POS tags have been converted into much less sparse Universal POS tags (cf. Petrov et al. 2012) matching the Hebrew Treebank data set. Entries not corresponding to tags in the data (e.g. compound items that would not be a single unit, or additional POS categories) receive the tag X, while complex entries (e.g. NOUN + possessive) receive a tag affixed with 'CPLX'. Multiple entries per word form are possible (see Section 4.2).

**Character features** For each target character and the surrounding 2 characters in either direction, we consider the identity of the letter or punctuation sign from the set {",-,%,',.,?,!,/} as a categorical feature (using native Hebrew characters, not transliteration). Unavailable characters (less than 2 characters from beginning/end of word) and OOV characters are substituted by the underscore. We also encode the first and last letter of the preceding and following super-tokens in the same way. The rationale for choosing these letters is that any super-token always has a first and last character, and in Hebrew these will also encode definite article congruence and clitic pronouns in adjacent super-tokens, which are important for segmenting units. Finally, for each of the five character positions within the target super-token itself, we also encode a boolean feature indicating whether the character could be 'vocalic', i.e. whether it is one of the letters sometimes used to represent a vowel: {',h,w,y}. Though this is ostensibly redundant with letter identity, it is actually helpful in the final model (see Section 7).

| location | substring | lexicon response |
|---|---|---|
| super token | [šmhpkny] | _ |
| str so far | [šmh]... | ADV\|NOUN\|VERB |
| str remaining | ..[pkny] | _ |
| str -1 remain | ..[hpkny] | _ |
| str -2 remain | .[mhpkny] | ADJ\|NOUN\|CPLXN |
| str from -4 | [__šmh].... | _ |
| str from -3 | [_šmh].... | _ |
| str from -2 | [šmh].... | ADV\|NOUN\|VERB |
| str from -1 | .[mh].... | ADP\|ADV |
| str to +1 | ..[hp]... | _ |
| str to +2 | ..[hpk].. | NOUN\|VERB |
| str to +3 | ..[hpkn]. | _ |
| str to +4 | ..[hpkny] | _ |
| prev string | [xšbnw] | VERB |
| next string | [hw'] | PRON\|COP |

Table 1: Lexicon lookup features for character 3 in the super-token *š.mhpkny*. Overflow positions (e.g. substring from char -4 for the third character) return '_'.

**Lexicon lookup** Lexicon lookup is performed for several substring ranges, chosen using the development data: the entire super-token, and characters up to the target inclusive and exclusive; the entire remaining super-token characters inclusive and exclusive; the remaining substrings starting at target positions -1 and -2; 1, 2, 3 and 4-grams around the window including the target character; and the entire preceding and following super-token strings. Table 1 illustrates this for character #3 in the middle super-token from the trigram in (7). The value of the lexicon lookup is a categorical variable consisting of all POS tags attested for the substring in the lexicon, concatenated with a separator into a single string.

(7) חשבנו שמהפכני הוא
 ⟨xšbnw š.mhpkny hw'⟩
 [xašavnu še.mahapxani hu]
 thought-1PL that.revolutionary is
 'we thought that it is revolutionary'

**Numerical features** To provide information about super-token shape independent of lexicon lookup, we also extract the super-token lengths of the current, previous and next super-token, and encode the numerical position of the character being classified as integers. We also experimented with a 'frequency' feature, representing the ratio of the product of frequencies of the substrings left and right of a split under consideration divided by the frequency of the whole super-token. Frequencies were taken from the IsraBlog dataset word counts provided by Linzen (2009).[4] While this fraction in no way represents the probability of a split, it does provide some information about the relative frequency of parts versus whole in a naive two-segment scenario, which can occasionally help the classifier decide whether to segment ambiguous cases (although this feature's contribution is small, it was retained in the final model, see Section 7).

**Word embeddings** For one of the learning approaches tested, a deep neural network (DNN) classifier, word embeddings from a Hebrew dump of Wikipedia were added for the current, preceding and following super-tokens, which were expected to help in identifying the kinds of super-tokens seen in OOV cases. However somewhat surprisingly, the approach using these features turned out not to deliver the best results despite outperforming the previous state of the art, and these features are not used in the final system (see Section 5).

Note that although we do not encode word identities for any super-token, and even less so for models not using word embeddings, length information in conjunction with lexicon lookup and first and last character can already give a strong indication of the surrounding context, at least for those words which turn out to be worth learning. For example, the frequent purpose conjunction ⟨kdy⟩ *kedey* 'in order to', which strongly signals a following infinitive whose leading ⟨l⟩ should not be segmented, is uniquely identifiable as a three letter conjunction (tag SCONJ) beginning with ⟨k⟩ and ending with ⟨y⟩. This combination, if relevant for segmentation, can be learned and assigned weights for each of the characters in adjacent words.

### 3.2 Learning Approach

Several learning approaches were tested for the boundary classification task, including decision tree based classifiers, such as a Random Forest classifier, the Extra Trees variant of the same algorithm (Geurts et al., 2006), and Gradient Boosting, all using the implementation in scikit-learn (Pedregosa et al., 2011), as well as a DNN classifier implemented in TensorFlow (Abadi et al., 2016). An initial attempt using sequence-to-sequence learning with an RNN was abandoned

---

[4]Online at http://tallinzen.net/frequency/

early as it underperformed other approaches, possibly due to the limited size of the training data.

For tree-based classifiers, letters and categorical lexicon lookup values were pseudo-ordinalized into integers (using a non-meaningful alphabetic ordering), and numerical features were retained as-is. For the DNN, the best feature representation based on the validation set was to encode characters and positions as one-hot vectors, lexicon lookup features as trainable dense embeddings, and to bucketize length features in single digit buckets up to a maximum of 15, above which all values are grouped together. Additionally, we prohibit segmentations between Latin letters and digits (using regular expressions), and forbid producing any prefix/suffix not attested in training data, ruling out rare spurious segmentations.

## 4 Experimental Setup

### 4.1 Data

Evaluation was done on two datasets. The benchmark SPMRL dataset was transformed by discarding all inserted sub-tokens not present in the input super-tokens (i.e. inserted articles). We revert alterations due to morphological analysis (de-inflection to base forms), and identify the segmentation point of all clitic pronouns, prepositions etc., marking them in the super-tokens.[5] Figure 1 illustrates the procedure, which was manually checked and automatically verified to reconstitute correctly back into the input data.

A second test set of 5,000 super-tokens (7,100 sub-tokens) was constructed from another domain to give a realistic idea of performance outside the training domain. While SPMRL data is taken from newswire material with highly standard orthography, this dataset was taken from Hebrew Wikipedia NER data made available by Al-Rfou et al. (2015). Since that dataset was not segmented into subtokens, manual segmentation of the first 5,000 tokens was carried out, which represent shuffled sentences from a wide range of topics. This data set is referred to below as 'Wiki5K'. Both datasets are provided along with the code for this paper via GitHub[6] as new test sets for future

evaluations of Hebrew segmentation.

### 4.2 Lexicon extension

A major problem in Hebrew word segmentation is dealing with OOV items, and especially those due not to regular morphological processes, but to foreign names. If a foreign name begins with a letter that can be construed as a prefix, and neither the full name nor the substring after the prefix is attested in the lexicon, the system must resort to purely contextual information for disambiguation. As a result, having a very complete list of possible foreign names is crucial.

The lexicon mentioned above has very extensive coverage of native items as well as many foreign items, and after tag-wise conversion to Universal POS tags, contains over 767,000 items, including multiple entries for the same string with different tags. However its coverage of foreign names is still partial. In order to give the system access to a broader range of foreign names, we expanded the lexicon with proper name data from three sources:

- WikiData persons with a Hebrew label, excluding names whose English labels contain determiners, prepositions or pronouns

- WikiData cities with a Hebrew label, again excluding items with determiners, prepositions or pronouns in English labels

- All named entities from the Wikipedia NER data found later than the initial 5K tokens used for the Wiki5K data set

These data sources were then white-space tokenized, and all items which could spuriously be interpreted as a Hebrew article/preposition + noun were removed. For example, a name 'Leal' $\langle l'l \rangle$ is excluded, since it can interfere with segmenting the sequence $\langle l.'l \rangle$ *la'el* 'to God'. This process added over 15,000 items, or $\approx 2\%$ of lexicon volume, all labeled PROPN. In Section 7 performance with and without this extension is compared.

### 4.3 Evaluation Setup

Since comparable segmentation systems, including the previous state of the art, do insert reconstructed articles and carry out base form transformations (i.e. they aim to produce the gold format in Figure 1), we do not report or compare results to

---

[5] For comparability with previous results, we use the exact dataset and splits used by More and Tsarfaty (2016), despite a known mid-document split issue that was corrected in version 2 of the Hebrew Treebank data. We thank the authors for providing the data and for help reproducing their setup.

[6] `https://github.com/amir-zeldes/RFTokenizer`

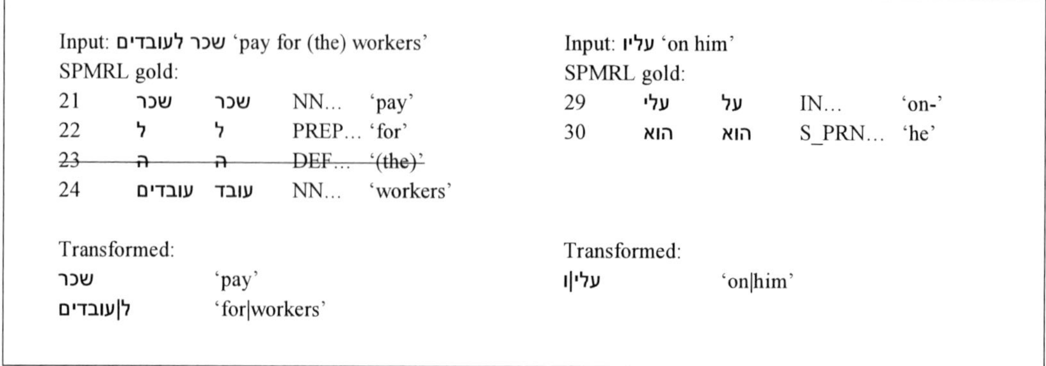

Figure 1: Transformation of SPMRL style data to pure segmentation information. Left: inserted article is deleted; right: a clitic pronoun form is restored.

previously published scores. All systems were re-run on both datasets, and no errors were counted where these resulted from data alterations. Specifically, other systems are never penalized for re-constructing or omitting inserted units such as articles, and when constructing clitics or alternate base forms of nouns or verbs, only the presence or absence of a split was checked, not whether inferred noun or verb lemmas are correct. This leads to higher scores than previously reported, but makes results comparable across systems on the pure segmentation task.

## 5   Results

Table 2 shows the results of several systems on both datasets.[7] The column '% perf' indicates the proportion of perfectly segmented super-tokens, while the next three columns indicate precision, recall and F-score for boundary detection, not including the trivial final position characters.

The first baseline strategy of not segmenting anything is given in the first row, and unsurprisingly gets many cases right, but performs badly overall. A more intelligent baseline is provided by UDPipe (Straka et al. 2016; retrained on the SPMRL data), which, for super-tokens in morphologically rich languages such as Hebrew, implements a 'most common segmentation' baseline

|  | % perf | P | R | F |
|---|---|---|---|---|
| **SPMRL** |  |  |  |  |
| *baseline* | 69.65 | – | – | – |
| *UDPipe* | 89.65 | 93.52 | 68.82 | 79.29 |
| *yap* | 94.25 | 86.33 | 96.33 | 91.05 |
| *RF* | **98.19** | **97.59** | **96.57** | **97.08** |
| *DNN* | 97.27 | 95.90 | 95.01 | 95.45 |
| **Wiki5K** |  |  |  |  |
| *baseline* | 67.61 | – | – | – |
| *UDPipe* | 87.39 | 92.03 | 64.88 | 76.11 |
| *yap* | 92.66 | 85.55 | 92.34 | 88.81 |
| *RF* | **97.63** | **97.41** | **95.31** | **96.35** |
| *DNN* | 95.72 | 94.95 | 92.22 | 93.56 |

Table 2: System performance on the SPMRL and Wiki5K datasets.

(i.e. each super-token is given its most common segmentation from training data, forgoing segmentation for OOV items).[8] Results for yap represent pure segmentation performance from the previous state of the art (More and Tsarfaty, 2016).

The best two approaches in the present paper are represented next: the Extra Trees Random Forest variant,[9] called RFTokenizer, is labeled *RF* and the DNN-based system is labeled *DNN*. Surprisingly, while the DNN is a close runner up, the best performance is achieved by the RFTokenizer, de-

---

[7] An anonymous reviewer suggested that it would also be interesting to add an unsupervised pure segmentation system such as Morfessor (Creutz and Lagus, 2002) to evaluate on this task. This would certainly be an interesting comparison, but due to the brief response period it was not possible to add this experiment before publication. It can however be expected that results would be substantially worse than yap, given the centrality of the lexicon representation to this task, which can be seen in detail in the ablation tests in Section 7.

[8] UDPipe also implements an RNN tokenizer to segment punctuation spelled together with super-tokens; however since the evaluation dataset already separates such punctuation symbols, this component can be ignored here.

[9] Extra Trees outperformed Gradient Boosting and Random Forest in hyperparameter selection tuned on the dev set. Using a grid search led to the choice of 250 estimators (tuned in increments of 10), with unlimited features and default scikit-learn values for all other parameters.

spite not having access to word embeddings. Its high performance on the SPMRL dataset makes it difficult to converge to a better solution using the DNN, though it is conceivable that substantially more data, a better feature representation and/or more hyperparameter tuning could equal or surpass the RFTokenizer's performance. Coupled with a lower cost in system resources and external dependencies, and the ability to forgo large model files to store word embeddings, we consider the RFTokenizer solution to be better given the current training data size.

Performance on the out of domain dataset is encouragingly nearly as good as on SPMRL, suggesting our features are robust. This is especially clear compared to UDPipe and yap, which degrade more substantially. A key advantage of the present approach is its comparatively high precision. While other approaches have good recall, and yap approaches RFTokenizer on recall for SPMRL, RFTokenizer's reduction in spurious segmentations boosts its F-score substantially. To see why, we examine some errors in the next section, and perform feature ablations in the following one.

## 6 Error Analysis

Looking at the SPMRL data, RFTokenizer makes relatively few errors, the large majority of which belong to two classes: morphologically ambiguous cases with known vocabulary, as in (8), and OOV items, as in (9). In (8), the sequence ⟨qch⟩ could be either the noun *katse* 'edge' (single supertoken and sub-token), or a possessed noun *kits.a* 'end of FEM-SG' with a final clitic pronoun possessor (two sub-tokens). The super-token coincidentally begins a sentence "The end of a year ...", meaning that the preceding unit is the relatively uninformative period, leaving little local context for disambiguating the nouns, both of which could be followed by *šel* 'of'.

(8) קצה של שנה
   Gold:    Pred:
   ⟨qc.h šl šnh⟩ ⟨qch šel šnh⟩
   [kits.a šel šana] [katse šel šana]
   end.SG-F of year edge of year
   "The end of a year" "An edge of a year"

A typical case of an OOV error can be seen in (9). In this example, the lexicon is missing the name ⟨w'r'lh⟩ 'Varela', but does contain a name ⟨'r'lh⟩ 'Arela'. As a result, given the context of a preceding name 'Maria', the tokenizer opts to recognize a shorter proper name and assigns the letter 'w' to be the word 'and'.

(9) מריה וראלה .
   Gold:    Pred:
   ⟨mryh w'r'lh .⟩ ⟨mryh w.'r'lh .⟩
   [mariya varela] [mariya ve.arela]
   'Maria Varela.' 'Maria and Arela.'

To understand the reasons for RFTokenizer's higher precision compared to other tools, it is useful to consider errors which RFTokenizer succeeds in avoiding, as in (10)-(11) (only a single bold-faced word is discussed in detail for space reasons; broader translations are given for context, keeping Hebrew word order). In (10), RF and yap both split *w* 'and' from the OOV item ⟨bwrmwr⟩ 'Barmore' correctly. The next possible boundary, 'b.w', is locally unlikely, as a spelling 'bw' makes a reading [bo] or [bu] likely, which is incompatible with the segmentation. However, yap considers global parsing likelihood, and the verb 'run into' takes the preposition *b* 'in'. It segments the 'b' in the OOV item, a decision which RFTokenizer avoids based on low local probabilities.

(10) "ran into Campbell and **Barmore**"
   RF:    yap:
   ⟨w.bwrmwr⟩ ⟨w.b.wrmwr⟩

(11) "meanwhile continues the player, who returned to practice last week, **to-train**"
   RF:    yap:
   ⟨lht'mn⟩ ⟨l.ht'm.n⟩

In (11), RF leaves the medium frequency verb 'to train' unsegmented. By contrast, yap considers the complex sentence structure and long distance to the fronted verb 'continues', and prefers a locally very improbable segmentation into the preposition *l* 'to', a noun *ht'm* 'congruence' and a 3rd person feminine plural possessive *n*: 'to their congruence'. Such an analysis is not likely to be guessed by a native speaker shown this word in isolation, but becomes likelier in the context of evaluating possible parse lattices with limited training data.

We speculate that lower reliance on complete parses makes RFTokenizer more robust to errors, since data for character-wise decisions is densely attested. In some cases, as in (10), it is possible to segment individual characters based on similarity to previously seen contexts, without requiring super-tokens to be segmentable using the lexicon. This is especially important for partially correct results, which affect recall, but not necessarily the percentage of perfectly segmented super-tokens.

In Wiki5K we find more errors, degrading performance ≈0.7%. Domain differences in this data lead not only to OOV items (esp. foreign names), but also distributional and spelling differences. In (12), heuristic segmentation based on a single character position backfires, and the tokenizer over-zealously segments. This is due to neither the place 'Hartberg', nor a hypothetical 'Retberg' being found in the lexicon, and the immediate context being uninformative surrounding commas.

(12)     , הרטברנ ,
         Gold:          Pred:
         ⟨hrtḅrg⟩       ⟨h.rtḅrg⟩
         [hartberg]     [ha.retberg]
         'Hartberg'     'the Retberg'

## 7 Ablation tests

Table 3 gives an overview of the impact on performance when specific features are removed: the entire lexicon, lexicon expansion, letter identity, 'vowel' features from Section 3.1, and both of the latter. Performance is high even in ablation scenarios, though we keep in mind that baselines for the task are high (e.g. 'most frequent lookup', the UDPipe strategy, achieves close to 90%).

The results show the centrality of the lexicon: removing lexicon lookup features degrades performance by about 3.5% perfect accuracy, or 5.5 F-score points. All other ablations impact performance by less than 1% or 1.5 F-score points. Expanding the lexicon using Wikipedia data offers a contribution of 0.3–0.4 points, confirming the original lexicon's incompleteness.[10]

Looking more closely at the other features, it is surprising that identity of the letters is not crucial, as long as we have access to dictionary lookup using the letters. Nevertheless, removing letter identity impacts especially boundary recall, perhaps

---

[10]An anonymous reviewer has asked whether the same resources from the NER dataset have been or could be made available to the competing systems. Unfortunately it was not possible to re-train yap using this data, since the lexicon used by that system has a much more complex structure compared to the simple PROPN tags used in our approach (i.e. we would need to codify much richer morphological information for the added words). However the ablations show that even without the expanded lexicon, RFTokenizer outperforms yap by a large margin. For UDPipe no lexicon is used, so that this issue does not arise.

|            | % perf | P     | R     | F     |
|------------|--------|-------|-------|-------|
| **SPMRL**  |        |       |       |       |
| FINAL      | 98.19  | 97.59 | 96.57 | 97.08 |
| -expansion | 98.01  | 97.25 | 96.35 | 96.80 |
| -vowels    | 97.99  | 97.55 | 95.97 | 96.75 |
| -letters   | 97.77  | 96.98 | 95.73 | 96.35 |
| -letr-vowl | 97.57  | 97.56 | 94.44 | 95.97 |
| -lexicon   | 94.79  | 92.08 | 91.46 | 91.77 |
| **Wiki5K** |        |       |       |       |
| FINAL      | 97.63  | 97.41 | 95.31 | 96.35 |
| -expansion | 97.33  | 96.64 | 95.31 | 95.97 |
| -vowels    | 97.51  | 97.56 | 94.87 | 96.19 |
| -letters   | 97.27  | 96.89 | 94.71 | 95.79 |
| -letr-vowl | 96.72  | 97.17 | 92.77 | 94.92 |
| -lexicon   | 94.72  | 92.53 | 91.51 | 92.01 |

Table 3: Effects of removing features on performance, ordered by descending F-score impact on SPMRL.

because some letters receive identical lookup values (e.g. single letter prepositions such as $b$ 'in', $l$ 'to') but have different segmentation likelihoods.

The 'vowel' features, though ostensibly redundant with letter identity, help a little, causing 0.33 SPMRL F-score point degradation if removed. A cursory inspection of differences with and without vowel features indicates that adding them allows for stronger generalizations in segmenting affixes, especially clitic pronouns (e.g. if a noun is attested with a 'vocalic' clitic like $h$ 'hers', it generalizes better to unseen cases with $w$ 'his'). In some cases, the features help identify phonotactically likely splits in a 'vowel' rich environment, as in (13) with the sequence ⟨hyy⟩ which is segmented correctly in the +vowels setting.

(13)     הייתכן
         +Vowels:        -Vowels:
         ⟨h.yytkn⟩        ⟨hyytkn⟩
         [ha.yitaxen]
         QUEST.possible
         'is it possible?'

Removing both letter and vowel features essentially reduces the system to using only the surrounding POS labels. However since classification is character-wise and a variety of common situations can nevertheless be memorized, performance does not break down drastically. The impact on Wiki5k is stronger, possibly because the necessary memorization of familiar contexts is less effective out of domain.

## 8 Discussion

This paper presented a character-wise approach to Hebrew segmentation, relying on a combination of shallow surface features and windowed lexicon lookup features, encoded as categorical variables concatenating possible POS tags for each window. Although the approach does not correspond to a manually created finite state morphology or a parsing-based approach, it can be conjectured that the sequence of possible POS tag combinations at each character position in a sequence of words gives a similar type of information about possible transitions at each potential boundary.

The character-wise approach turned out to be comparatively robust, possibly thanks to the dense training data available, when compared to the smaller order of magnitude if data is interpreted with each super-token, or even each sentence forming a single observation. Nevertheless, there are multiple limitations to the current approach.

Firstly, RFTokenizer does not reconstruct unexpressed articles. Although this is an important task in Hebrew NLP, it can be argued that definiteness annotation can be performed as part of morphological analysis after basic segmentation has been carried out. An advantage of this approach is that the segmented data corresponds perfectly to the input string, reducing processing efforts needed to keep track of the mapping of raw and tokenized data.

Secondly, there is still room for improvement, and it seems surprising that the DNN approach with embeddings could not outperform the RF approach. More training data is likely to make DNN/RNN approaches more effective, similarly to recent advances in tokenization for languages such as Chinese (cf. Cai and Zhao 2016, though we recognize Hebrew segmentation is much more ambiguous, and embeddings are likely more useful for ideographic scripts).[11] We are currently experimenting with word representations optimized to the segmentation task, including using embeddings or Brown clusters grouping super-tokens with different distributions. Finally, the frequency

data obtained from Linzen (2009) is relatively small (only 20K forms), and not error-free due to automatic processing, meaning that extending this data source may yield improvements as well.

## Acknowledgments

This work benefited from research on morphological segmentation for Coptic, funded by the National Endowment for the Humanities (NEH) and the German Research Foundation (DFG) (grants HG-229371 and HAA-261271). Thanks are also due to Shuly Wintner, Nathan Schneider and the anonymous reviewers for valuable comments on earlier versions of this paper, as well as to Amir More and Reut Tsarfaty for their help in reproducing the experimental setup for comparing yap and other systems with RFTokenizer.

## References

Martín Abadi, Paul Barham, Jianmin Chen, Zhifeng Chen, Andy Davis, Jeffrey Dean, Matthieu Devin, Sanjay Ghemawat, Geoffrey Irving, Michael Isard, Manjunath Kudlur, Josh Levenberg, Rajat Monga, Sherry Moore, Derek G. Murray, Benoit Steiner, Paul Tucker, Vijay Vasudevan, Pete Warden, Martin Wicke, Yuan Yu, and Xiaoqiang Zheng. 2016. TensorFlow: A system for large-scale machine learning. In *Proceedings of the 12th USENIX Conference on Operating Systems Design and Implementation*, pages 265–283, Savannah, GA.

Ahmed Abdelali, Kareem Darwish, Nadir Durrani, and Hamdy Mubarak. 2016. Farasa: A fast and furious segmenter for Arabic. In *Proceedings of the NAACL 2016: Demonstrations*, pages 11–16, San Diego, CA.

Meni Adler and Michael Elhadad. 2006. An unsupervised morpheme-based HMM for Hebrew morphological disambiguation. In *Proceedings of the 21st International Conference on Computational Linguistics and 44th Annual Meeting of the ACL*, pages 665–672, Sydney.

Rami Al-Rfou, Vivek Kulkarni, Bryan Perozzi, and Steven Skiena. 2015. Polyglot-NER: Massive multilingual named entity recognition. In *Proceedings of the 2015 SIAM International Conference on Data Mining*, Vancouver, Canada.

Deng Cai and Hai Zhao. 2016. Neural word segmentation learning for Chinese. In *Proceedings of ACL 2016*, pages 409–420, Berlin.

Ryan Cotterell, Tim Vieira, and Hinrich Schütze. 2016. A joint model of orthography and morphological segmentation. In *Proceedings of NAACL-HLT 2016*, pages 664–669, San Diego, CA.

---

[11]During the review period of this paper, a paper by Shao et al. (2018) appeared which nearly matches the performance of yap on Hebrew segmentation using an RNN approach. Achieving an F-score of 91.01 compared to yap's score of 91.05, but on a dataset with slightly different splits, this system gives a good baseline for a tuned RNN-based system. However comparing to RFTokenizer's score of 97.08, it is clear that while RNNs can also do well on the current task, there is still a substantial gap compared to the windowed, lexicon-based binary classification approach take here.

Mathias Creutz and Krista Lagus. 2002. Unsupervised discovery of morphemes. In *Proceedings of the Workshop on Morphological and Phonological Learning at ACL 2002*, pages 21–30, Philadelphia, PA.

Pierre Geurts, Damien Ernst, and Louis Wehenkel. 2006. Extremely randomized trees. *Machine Learning*, 63(1):3–42.

Nizar Habash and Fatiha Sadat. 2006. Arabic preprocessing schemes for statistical machine translation. In *Proceedings of NAACL 2006*, pages 49–52, New York.

Chia-Ming Lee and Chien-Kang Huang. 2013. Context-based Chinese word segmentation using SVM machine-learning algorithm without dictionary support. In *Sixth International Joint Conference on Natural Language Processing*, pages 614–622, Nagoya, Japan.

Tal Linzen. 2009. Corpus of blog postings collected from the Israblog website. Technical report, Tel Aviv University, Tel Aviv.

Will Monroe, Spence Green, and Christopher D. Manning. 2014. Word segmentation of informal Arabic with domain adaptation. In *Proceedings of the 52nd Annual Meeting of the Association for Computational Linguistics*, pages 206–211, Baltimore, MD.

Amir More and Reut Tsarfaty. 2016. Data-driven morphological analysis and disambiguation for morphologically-rich languages and universal dependencies. In *Proceedings of COLING 2016*, pages 337–348, Osaka, Japan.

Fabian Pedregosa, Gaël Varoquaux, Alexandre Gramfort, Vincent Michel, Bertrand Thirion, Olivier Grisel, Mathieu Blondel, Peter Prettenhofer, Ron Weiss, and Vincent Dubourg. 2011. Scikit-learn: Machine learning in Python. *Journal of machine learning research*, 12:2825–2830.

Slav Petrov, Dipanjan Das, and Ryan McDonald. 2012. A universal part-of-speech tagset. In *Proceedings of LREC 2012*, pages 2089–2096, Istanbul, Turkey.

Djamé Seddah, Sandra Kübler, and Reut Tsarfaty. 2014. Introducing the SPMRL 2014 shared task on parsing morphologically-rich languages. In *First Joint Workshop on Statistical Parsing of Morphologically Rich Languages and Syntactic Analysis of Non-Canonical Languages*, pages 103–109, Dublin, Ireland.

Danny Shacham and Shuly Wintner. 2007. Morphological disambiguation of Hebrew: A case study in classifier combination. In *Proceedings of EMNLP/CoNLL 2007*, pages 439–447, Prague.

Yan Shao, Christian Hardmeier, and Joakim Nivre. 2018. Universal word segmentation: Implementation and interpretation. *Transactions of the Association for Computational Linguistics*, 6:421–435.

Khalil Sima'an, Alon Itai, Yoad Winter, Alon Altman, and Noa Nativ. 2001. Building a tree-bank of Modern Hebrew text. *Traitement Automatique des Langues*, 42:347–380.

Milan Straka, Jan Hajič, and Jana Straková. 2016. UDPipe: Trainable pipeline for processing CoNLL-U files performing tokenization, morphological analysis, POS tagging and parsing. In *Proceedings of LREC 2016*, pages 4290–4297, Portorož, Slovenia.

Shlomo Yona and Shuly Wintner. 2005. A finite-state morphological grammar of Hebrew. In *Proceedings of ACL-05 Workshop on Computational Approaches to Semitic Languages*, pages 9–16, Ann Arbor, MI.

# Phonetic Vector Representations for Sound Sequence Alignment

**Pavel Sofroniev** and **Çağrı Çöltekin**
Department of Linguistics
University of Tübingen
`pavel.sofroniev@student.uni-tuebingen.de, ccoltekin@sfs.uni-tuebingen.de`

## Abstract

This study explores a number of data-driven vector representations of the IPA-encoded sound segments for the purpose of sound sequence alignment. We test the alternative representations based on the alignment accuracy in the context of computational historical linguistics. We show that the data-driven methods consistently do better than linguistically-motivated articulatory-acoustic features. The similarity scores obtained using the data-driven representations in a monolingual context, however, performs worse than the state-of-the-art distance (or similarity) scoring methods proposed in earlier studies of computational historical linguistics. We also show that adapting representations to the task at hand improves the results, yielding alignment accuracy comparable to the state of the art methods.

## 1 Introduction

Most studies in computational linguistics or natural language processing treat the phonetic segments as categorical units, which prevents analyzing or exploiting the similarities or differences between these units. Alignment of sound sequences, a crucial step in a number of different fields of inquiry, is one of the tasks that suffers if the segments are treated as distinct symbols with no notion of similarity. As a result, alignment algorithms commonly employed in practice (e.g., Needleman and Wunsch, 1970) use a scoring function based on similarity of the individual units.

The tasks that require or benefit from aligning sequences are prevalent in computational linguistics, as well as relatively unrelated fields such as bioinformatics. In this study, we focus on aligning phonetically transcribed parallel word lists in the context of computational historical linguistics, where alignment of sound sequences is interesting

either on its own (demonstrating differences between language varieties) or as a necessary step in a larger application, for example, for inferring the cognacy of these words or finding synchronic or diachronic sound correspondences.

The use of similarities between the sound segments has been common in computational studies of historical linguistics (Covington, 1996, 1998; Kondrak, 2000; Kondrak and Hirst, 2002; Kondrak, 2003; List, 2012; Jäger, 2013; Jäger and Sofroniev, 2016). These studies rely on scoring functions most of which are based on the linguistic knowledge about the sound changes that typically occur across languages. Another trend shared by all of the earlier studies is the use of a reduced alphabet for representing the sound segments. Even though the standard way to encode sound sequences is the International Phonetic Alphabet (IPA), using a smaller set of symbols, such as ASJP (Brown et al., 2013; Wichmann et al., 2016), seem to help creating scoring functions that are more useful for historical linguistics.

In the present study, we explore a number of methods that learn vector representations for IPA tokens from multi-lingual word-lists, either using the words in a monolingual context or making use of the fact that words represent the same concept in different languages. We use a standard similarity metric over vectors (cosine similarity) for determining the similarities between the segments, and, in turn, use these similarities for aligning IPA-transcribed sequences.

Besides providing a more principled method for measuring distances, compared to only distance information, vector representations are more useful for further analysis, and may yield better results in other computational tasks relying on supervised or unsupervised machine learning techniques. Vector representations for phonetic, phonological or orthographic units have been used successfully in



*Proceedings of the 15th SIGMORPHON Workshop on Computational Research in Phonetics, Phonology, and Morphology*, pages 111–116
Brussels, Belgium, October 31, 2018. ©2018 The Special Interest Group on Computational Morphology and Phonology
https://doi.org/10.18653/v1/P17

earlier research, e.g., for word segmentation (Ma et al., 2016), transfer learning of named entity recognition (Mortensen et al., 2016) and morphological inflection (Silfverberg et al., 2018).

We compare our methods to a one-hot-encoding baseline (which is equivalent to symbolic representations), linguistically-motivated vectors, and alignments produced using state-of-the-art scoring methods. We compare the alignment performance of these methods on a manually-annotated gold-standard corpus, using the same alignment algorithm and the same training data where applicable.

## 2 Methods

Our aim is to learn and use vector representations for the purposes of sound sequence alignment. Once we have vector representations, we align the two sequences with Needleman-Wunsch algorithm using the cosine similarity between the phonetic vectors as the similarity function.

### 2.1 Baseline Representations

**One-hot encoding** is a common method for representing categorical data. Under one-hot encoding, given a vocabulary of $N$ distinct segments, each segment would be represented as a distinct binary vector of size $N$, such that exactly one of its dimensions has value 1 and all other dimensions have value 0. The method does not yield useful distance measures as each segment is equidistant from all the others. We use one-hot encoding as a proxy for a purely symbolic baseline.

**PHOIBLE Online** is an ongoing project aiming to compile a comprehensive database of the world languages' phonological inventories (Moran et al., 2014). The project also maintains a table of phonological features, effectively mapping each segment encountered in the database to a unique ternary feature vector. Feature values are assigned based on Hayes (2009) and Moisik and Esling (2011), and indicate either the presence, absence, or non-applicability of an articulatory-acoustic feature for each IPA symbol. PHOIBLE feature vectors serve as a linguistically-informed baseline.

### 2.2 Data-driven Vector Representations

Our proposed methods include three data-driven methods to learn vector representations for IPA-encoded sound segments.

**phon2vec embeddings** are the well-known word2vec method (Mikolov et al., 2013) applied to IPA-encoded phonetic segments. The method learns dense vector representations that maximize the similarity of segments that appear in similar contexts. As in original word2vec models, the context is treated as a bag of words, ignoring the relative position of each context element.

**Position sensitive neural network embeddings** (NN embeddings) are obtained using a simple feed-forward neural network architecture. Similar to word2vec skip-gram method, the neural network tries to predict the context of a word from the word itself. The hidden layer representations are, then, used as the representations for the word. Unlike word2vec, however, the context is not treated as a bag of phonetic segments. The position of the elements in the context is significant.

**RNN embeddings** are obtained using a sequence-to-sequence recurrent neural network (Cho et al., 2014). Given a pair of sequences, the network encodes the first sequence into a vector which is then decoded into an output sequence. The first layer of the network is an embeddings layer which converts the input categories to dense vector representations with a smaller number of dimensions. The network is trained to 'translate' words (as sequences of IPA tokens) between the languages in the training set, while, in the process, learning useful representations for IPA tokens. Once the network is trained, we are interested in the representations build for each IPA-token by the embedding layer.

Unlike the other data-driven methods described above, the RNN embeddings require, and make use of, multi-lingual nature of the data. However, crucially, the method does not require any explicit alignment of the sequences in advance.

### 2.3 State-of-the-art Scoring Functions

We compare the alignment performance of our methods to two state-of-the-art scoring functions. The first one, the sound-class-based phonetic alignment (SCA, List, 2012) employs a set of 28 sound classes. It operates on IPA sequences by converting the segments into their respective sound classes, aligning the sound class tokens, and then converting these back into IPA. The scoring function is hand-crafted to reflect the perceived probabilities of sound change transforming a segment of one class into a segment of another.

We also compare our results with the alignments obtained using the method proposed by Jäger (2013), which uses the ASJP database (Wichmann et al., 2016) to calculate the pairwise mutual information (PMI) scores for each pair of ASJP segments. The method starts with an initial alignment, and re-aligns the corpus iteratively for obtaining the final PMI-based scores. The method is data-driven, but heavily optimized for the task. Since it does not work with IPA-encoded sequences, we first convert the IPA sequences to ASJP alphabet, and convert them back to IPA after alignment.[1]

## 3 Experiments and Results

### 3.1 Data

In order to evaluate the performance of the methods put forward in the previous section, we use the Benchmark Database for Phonetic Alignments (BDPA, List and Prokić, 2014). The database contains 7198 aligned pairs of IPA sequences collected from 12 source datasets, covering languages and dialects from 6 language families (detailed information about the data set is provided in the Appendix). The database also features the small set of 82 selected pairs used by Covington (1996) to evaluate his method, encoded in IPA.

Our training data is sourced from NorthEuraLex, a comprehensive lexicostatistical database that provides IPA-encoded lexical data for languages of, primarily but not exclusively, Northern Eurasia (Dellert and Jäger, 2017). At the time of writing the database covers 1016 concepts from 107 languages, resulting in 121 614 IPA transcriptions.

### 3.2 Experimental Setup

Obtaining vector representations with the phon2vec and neural network methods involves settings the models' hyperparameters and training on a data set of IPA sequences (or pairs thereof).

We tokenize the input sequences using an open source Python package developed during this study.[2] The phon2vec and NN embeddings are trained on the set of all tokenised transcriptions in the training set. For training the RNN, we need cognates, pairs of words in different languages that share a common root. As our training set does

not include cognacy information, the RNN embeddings are trained on the set of tokenised transcriptions of the word pairs constituting probable cognates — pairs in which the words belong to different languages, are linked to the same concept, and have normalised Levenshtein distance lower than 0.5. We have also experimented with thresholds of 0.4 and 0.6, but setting the cutoff at 0.5 yields better-performing embeddings.

For each method, we run the respective model with the Cartesian product of common values for each hyperparameter, practically performing a random search of the hyperparameter space. The values we have experimented with, as well as the best-performing combinations thereof, are summarized in the Appendix. Note that the models are optimized for the respective prediction task they perform, not for good alignment performance.

The implementation is realized in the Python programming language, and makes use of a number of libraries, including NumPy (Walt et al., 2011), SciPy (Jones et al., 2001), scikit-learn (Pedregosa et al., 2011), Gensim (Řehůřek and Sojka, 2010), and Keras (Chollet et al., 2015). The source code used for the experiments reported here is publicly available.[3]

### 3.3 Evaluation

In order to quantify the methods' performance, we employ an intuitive evaluation scheme similar to the one used by Kondrak and Hirst (2002): if, for a given word pair, $m$ is the number of alternative gold-standard alignments and $n$ is the number of correctly predicted alignments, the score for that pair would be $\frac{n}{m}$. In the common word pair case of a single gold-standard alignment and a single predicted alignment, the latter would yield 1 point if it is correct and 0 points otherwise; partially correct alignment do not yield points. The percentage scores are obtained by dividing the points by the total number of pairs.

### 3.4 Results and Discussion

The alignment performance of our baselines, proposed methods, as well as PMI and SCA on the BDPA data sets is summarized in Table 1.

The first point we would like to draw attention to is that the one-hot encoding scores are consistently lower than those in the other columns. This is expected because, unlike the other methods, one-

---

[1] The IPA to ASJP conversion is lossy. However, the alignments are not affected since the source IPA symbols are known during ASJP to IPA conversion.

[2] https://pypi.python.org/pypi/ipatok.

[3] https://github.com/pavelsof/ipavec.

|           | one-hot | phoible | phon2vec | nn    | rnn   | pmi   | sca   |
|-----------|---------|---------|----------|-------|-------|-------|-------|
| Andean    | 85.66   | 87.31   | 97.25    | 99.34 | 99.50 | 95.21 | 99.67 |
| Bai       | 52.55   | 62.77   | 61.25    | 74.72 | 75.52 | –     | 83.45 |
| Bulgarian | 60.54   | 80.54   | 77.98    | 82.55 | 86.70 | 81.70 | 89.34 |
| Dutch     | 14.16   | 25.65   | 26.00    | 32.50 | 32.50 | 36.67 | 42.20 |
| French    | 42.94   | 62.92   | 68.94    | 74.30 | 77.04 | 71.98 | 80.90 |
| Germanic  | 39.93   | 51.78   | 54.59    | 71.83 | 72.55 | 75.32 | 83.48 |
| Japanese  | 53.56   | 65.04   | 73.74    | 62.71 | 71.08 | 68.26 | 82.19 |
| Norwegian | 59.39   | 78.87   | 73.69    | 83.53 | 89.06 | 78.11 | 91.77 |
| Ob-Ugrian | 59.58   | 77.87   | 73.35    | 78.04 | 82.55 | 82.09 | 86.04 |
| Romance   | 40.48   | 71.28   | 63.16    | 76.37 | 77.55 | 84.51 | 95.62 |
| Sinitic   | 27.34   | 28.57   | 30.75    | 72.46 | 74.04 | –     | 98.95 |
| Slavic    | 76.96   | 90.73   | 84.22    | 89.89 | 96.81 | 89.36 | 94.15 |
| Global    | 51.83   | 66.64   | 66.99    | 75.88 | 78.45 | 77.36 | 84.84 |
| Covington | 60.61   | 82.42   | 80.18    | 82.52 | 82.52 | 87.80 | 90.24 |

Table 1: Scores, as percentage of total alignment pairs. Global scores does not include Covington. PMI method does not handle tonal languages, and its global score is based on the non-tonal language groups.

hot encoding cannot represent the degree of phonetic similarity between IPA segments. Viewing the one-hot encoding scores as a baseline, we conclude that the other methods' distance measures do indeed contribute to sequence alignment.

The PHOIBLE feature vectors are roughly on par with the phon2vec embeddings, yielding better results than the NN embeddings on two of the datasets (Japanese and Slavic), and are otherwise outperformed by the NN and the RNN embeddings, as well as PMI and SCA. Part of the low performance of the PHOIBLE's vectors can be due to the fact that PHOIBLE does not provide feature vectors for all IPA segments in the BDPA datasets. However, the similar performance between PHOIBLE vectors and phon2vec and, clearly better performance achieved by the NN embeddings indicates that we can learn (more) useful linguistic generalizations in a data-driven manner.

Of the data-driven methods, phon2vec yields the lowest scores, being outperformed by both neural network models in all datasets except Japanese. Given that both the phon2vec and the NN embeddings are trained on the same data, the consistent performance difference between phon2vec and NN embeddings points to usefulness of to the sequential order of IPA segments. The better performance of the RNN embeddings over other data driven methods is not surprising, as they capture useful information from the multi-lingual data set. Furthermore, the performance of RNN embeddings is similar to the PMI method, yielding better results in many data sets.

For all but the Slavic dataset, SCA yields higher scores than other methods compared in this study. The score differences exhibit considerable variance — from less than 1 percent point for the Andean dataset up to 26 percent points for the Sinitic dataset. A possible explanation for this variance is the fact that not all IPA segments found in the benchmark datasets are found in the training data. For example, NorthEuraLex includes a single tonal language, Mandarin Chinese, and the models cannot produce meaningful embeddings for most of the tones encountered in the Sinitic and Bai datasets. Arguably, a larger training dataset featuring a richer set of IPA segments would produce better-performing embeddings.

## 4 Conclusion

In this study we have proposed, implemented, and evaluated three methods for obtaining vector representations of IPA segments for the purposes of pairwise IPA sequence alignment. Our method outperforms a linguistically-informed baseline, as well as a trivial one-hot representation, performs comparably to a state-of-the-art data driven method. However, the performances of data driven methods, including ours, seem to be behind a linguistically-informed system, SCA. Nevertheless, the results of the data-driven methods are not too far off the mark, and we believe that they could be significantly improved by using larger and more diverse training data, and better tuning of the data-driven methods. This constitutes one direction for future experiments; another possibility is to train and use embeddings specific to a particular language family or macro-area. Further investigation is also needed with respect to comparing and evaluating the methods, especially in the context of a larger application, such as cognacy identification or phylogenetic inference.

## References

Bryan Allen. 2007. *Bai Dialect Survey*. SIL International.

Jørn Almberg and Kristian Skarbø. 2011. Nordavinden og sola. En norsk dialektprøvedatabase på nettet.

Cecil H. Brown, Eric W. Holman, and Søren Wichmann. 2013. Sound Correspondences in the World's Languages. *Language*, 89(1):4–29.

Kyunghyun Cho, Bart van Merrienboer, Caglar Gulcehre, Dzmitry Bahdanau, Fethi Bougares, Holger Schwenk, and Yoshua Bengio. 2014. Learning Phrase Representations using RNN Encoder-Decoder for Statistical Machine Translation. *arXiv:1406.1078 [cs, stat]*.

François Chollet et al. 2015. Keras.

Michael A. Covington. 1996. An Algorithm to Align Words for Historical Comparison. *Computational Linguistics*, 22(4):481–496.

Michael A. Covington. 1998. Alignment of Multiple Languages for Historical Comparison. In *Proceedings of the 17th International Conference on Computational Linguistics - Volume 1*, COLING '98, pages 275–279, Stroudsburg, PA, USA. Association for Computational Linguistics.

Johannes Dellert and Gerhard Jäger, editors. 2017. *NorthEuraLex (version 0.9)*. Eberhard Karls Universität Tübingen, Tübingen.

Rick Derksen, editor. 2008. *Etymological dictionary of the Slavic inherited lexicon*. Number 4 in Leiden Indo-European Etymological Dictionary Series. Brill, Leiden and Boston.

Louis Gauchat, Jules Jeanjaquet, and Ernest Tappolet, editors. 1925. *Tableaux phonétiques des patois suisses romands*. Attinger, Neuchâtel.

Harald Hammarström, Sebastian Bank, Robert Forkel, and Martin Haspelmath, editors. 2018. *Glottolog 3.2*. Max Planck Institute for the Science of Human History, Jena.

Bruce Hayes. 2009. *Introductory Phonology*. Blackwell.

Paul Heggarty. 2006. Sounds of the Andean languages.

Jīngyī Hóu, editor. 2004. *Xiàndài Hànyǔ fāngyán yīnkù*. Shànghǎi Jiàoyù, Shànghǎi.

Eric Jones, Travis Oliphant, Pearu Peterson, et al. 2001. SciPy: Open source scientific tools for Python.

Gerhard Jäger. 2013. Phylogenetic Inference from Word Lists Using Weighted Alignment with Empirically Determined Weights. *Language Dynamics and Change*, 3(2):245–291.

Gerhard Jäger and Pavel Sofroniev. 2016. Automatic cognate classification with a support vector machine. In *Proceedings of the 13th Conference on Natural Language Processing (KONVENS 2016)*, pages 128–134.

Grzegorz Kondrak. 2000. A New Algorithm for the Alignment of Phonetic Sequences. In *Proceedings of the 1st North American Chapter of the Association for Computational Linguistics Conference*, NAACL 2000, pages 288–295, Stroudsburg, PA, USA. Association for Computational Linguistics.

Grzegorz Kondrak. 2003. Phonetic alignment and similarity. *Computers and the Humanities*, 37(3):273–291.

Grzegorz Kondrak and Graeme Hirst. 2002. *Algorithms for language reconstruction*, volume 63. University of Toronto Toronto.

Johann-Mattis List. 2012. SCA: Phonetic Alignment based on sound classes. *New Directions in Logic, Language and Computation*, pages 32–51.

Johann-Mattis List and J Prokić. 2014. A benchmark database of phonetic alignments in historical linguistics and dialectology. In *Proceedings of the International Conference on Language Resources and Evaluation (LREC)*, pages 288–294.

Jianqiang Ma, Çağrı Çöltekin, and Erhard Hinrichs. 2016. Learning phone embeddings for word segmentation of child-directed speech. In *Proceedings Workshop on Cognitive Aspects of Computational Language Learning*, pages 53–63.

Tomas Mikolov, Kai Chen, Greg Corrado, and Jeffrey Dean. 2013. Efficient Estimation of Word Representations in Vector Space. *arXiv:1301.3781 [cs]*.

Scott R. Moisik and John H. Esling. 2011. The 'whole larynx' approach to laryngeal features. In *Proceedings of the International Congress of Phonetic Sciences (ICPhS XVII)*, pages 1406–1409.

Steven Moran, Daniel McCloy, and Richard Wright, editors. 2014. *PHOIBLE Online*. Max Planck Institute for Evolutionary Anthropology, Leipzig.

David R. Mortensen, Patrick Littell, Akash Bharadwaj, Kartik Goyal, Chris Dyer, and Lori S. Levin. 2016. PanPhon: A resource for mapping IPA segments to articulatory feature vectors. In *Proceedings of COLING 2016, the 26th International Conference on Computational Linguistics: Technical Papers*, pages 3475–3484. ACL.

Saul B Needleman and Christian D Wunsch. 1970. A general method applicable to the search for similarities in the amino acid sequence of two proteins. *Journal of molecular biology*, 48(3):443–453.

F. Pedregosa, G. Varoquaux, A. Gramfort, V. Michel, B. Thirion, O. Grisel, M. Blondel, P. Prettenhofer, R. Weiss, V. Dubourg, J. Vanderplas, A. Passos,

D. Cournapeau, M. Brucher, M. Perrot, and E. Duchesnay. 2011. Scikit-learn: Machine learning in Python. *Journal of Machine Learning Research*, 12:2825–2830.

Jelena Prokić, John Nerbonne, Vladimir Zhobov, Petya Osenova, Kiril Simov, Thomas Zastrow, and Erhard Hinrichs. 2009. The computational analysis of Bulgarian dialect pronunciation. *Serdica journal of computing*, 3(3):269–298.

Colin Renfrew and Paul Heggarty. 2009. Languages and origins in Europe.

Georges de Schutter, Boudewijn van den Berg, Ton Goeman, and Thera de Jong. 2005. Morfologische atlas van de Nederlandse dialecten.

Hattori Shirō. 1973. Japanese dialects. *Diachronic, areal and typological linguistics*, pages 368–400.

Miikka P. Silfverberg, Lingshuang Mao, and Mans Hulden. 2018. Sound Analogies with Phoneme Embeddings. In *Proceedings of the Society for Computation in Linguistics (SCiL) 2018*, pages 136–144.

Stefan van der Walt, S. Chris Colbert, and Gael Varoquaux. 2011. The NumPy array: A structure for efficient numerical computation. *Computing in Science and Engineering*, 13:22–30.

Feng Wang. 2006. *Comparison of languages in contact. The distillation method and the case of Bai*. Institute of Linguistics Academia Sinica, Taipei.

Søren Wichmann, Eric W. Holman, and Cecil H. Brown, editors. 2016. *The ASJP Database (version 17)*. Available at `http://asjp.clld.org/`.

M. Zhivlov. 2011. Annotated Swadesh wordlists for the Ob-Ugrian group (Uralic family). *The Global Lexicostatistical Database*.

Radim Řehůřek and Petr Sojka. 2010. Software Framework for Topic Modelling with Large Corpora. In *Proceedings of the LREC 2010 Workshop on New Challenges for NLP Frameworks*, pages 45–50, Valletta, Malta. ELRA.

# Sounds Wilde
### Phonetically extended embeddings for author-stylized poetry generation


**Alexey Tikhonov**
Yandex
Karl-Liebknecht strasse 1, Berlin
altsoph@gmail.com

**Ivan P. Yamshchikov**
Max Planck Institute
for Mathematics in the Sciences
Inselstrasse 22, Leipzig
ivan@yamshchikov.info



## Abstract

This paper addresses author-stylized text generation. Using a version of a language model with extended phonetic and semantic embeddings for poetry generation we show that phonetics has comparable contribution to the overall model performance as the information on the target author. Phonetic information is shown to be important for English and Russian language. Humans tend to attribute machine generated texts to the target author.


## 1  Introduction

Generative models for natural languages and for poetry specifically are discussed for more than fifty years (Wheatley, 1965). Lamb et al. (2017) provides a detailed overview of generative poetry techniques. This particular paper addresses the issue of author stylized poetry (Tikhonov and Yamshchikov, 2018a) and shows the importance of phonetics for the author-stylized poetry generation.

The structure of the poem can vary across different languages starting with highly specific and distinct structures of Chinese poems (Zhang et al., 2017) and finishing with poems where formal structure hardly exists, e.g. American poetry of the twentieth century (say, the lyrics of Charles Bukowski) or so-called *white poems* in Russian. The structure and standards of poems can depend on various factors primarily phonetic in thier nature. In the broadest sense, rhymes in a classical western sonnet, a structure of a Persian ruba'i, a sequence of tones in a Chinese quatrain or a structure within rap bars could be expressed as a set of phonetic rules based on a certain understanding of expressiveness and euphony shared across a given culture or, sometimes, an artistic community. Some cultures and styles also have particular semantic limitations or 'standards', for example, 'centrality' of certain topics in classical Japanese poetry, see (Maynard, 1994). We do not make attempts to address high-level semantic structure, however one can add some kind of pseudo-semantic rules to the model discussed further, say via some mechanism in line with (Ghazvininejad et al., 2016) or (Yi et al., 2017). The importance of phonetics in poetical texts was broadly discussed among Russian futuristic poets, see (Kruchenykh, 1923). Several Russian linguistic circles and art groups (particularly OPOJAZ) in the first quarter of 20th century were actively discussing the concept of the *abstruse* language, see (Shklovsky, 1919), stressing also that the form of a poem, and especially its acoustic structure, is a number one priority for the future of literature. In their recent paper (Blasi et al., 2016) have challenged the broadly accepted idea that sound and meaning are not interdependent: unrelated languages very often use (or avoid) the same sounds for specific referents. In (He et al., 2016) and (Ghannay et al., 2016) it was show that acoustic word embeddings improve algorithm performance on a number of NLP tasks. In line with these ideas, one of the key features of the model that we discuss below is its concatenated embedding that contains information on the phonetics of every word preprocessed by a bi-directional Long Short-Term Memory (LSTM) network alongside with its vectorized semantic representation.

In (Tikhonov and Yamshchikov, 2018a) a model for generation of texts resembling the writing style of a particular author within the training data set was proposed. In this paper we quantify the stylistic similarity of the generated texts and show the importance of extension of the word embeddings with phonetic information for the overall performance of the model. The proposed model might also be applicable to prose, but diverse phonetic structure of the poetry discussed above makes it

117


*Proceedings of the 15th SIGMORPHON Workshop on Computational Research in Phonetics, Phonology, and Morphology*, pages 117–124
Brussels, Belgium, October 31, 2018. ©2018 The Special Interest Group on Computational Morphology and Phonology
https://doi.org/10.18653/v1/P17

better suited for the purposes of this paper. Also, since one would like to incorporated human judgement of the generated text and measure how well a human reader can attribute generated text to the target author, poetry seems preferable to prose for its stylistic expressiveness.

The contribution of this paper is three-fold: (1) we propose an LSTM with extended phonetic and semantic embeddings and quantify the quality of the obtained stylized poems both subjectively through a survey and objectively with BLEU metrics; (2) we show that phonetic information plays key role in a author-stylized poetry generation (3) we demonstrate that the proposed approach works in a multilingual setting, providing examples in English and in Russian.

## 2   Related work

In (Lipton et al., 2015), (Kiddon et al., 2016), (Lebret et al., 2016), (Radford et al., 2017), (Tang et al., 2016), (Hu et al., 2017) a number of RNN-based generative or generative adversarial models for controlled text generation are developed. These papers took *content* and *semantics* of the output into consideration, yet did not work with the style of the generated texts. In (Li et al., 2016) the authors focused on the speaker consistency in a dialogue. In (Sutskever et al., 2011) and in (Graves, 2013) it is demonstrated that a character-based recurrent neural network with gated connections or LSTM networks respectively can generate texts that resemble news or Wikipedia articles. Chinese classical poetry due to its diverse and deeply studied structure is addressed in (He et al., 2012), (Yi et al., 2017), (Yan, 2016), (Yan et al., 2016), or (Zhang et al., 2017). In (Ghazvininejad et al., 2016) an algorithm generates a poem in line with a user-defined topic in (Potash et al., 2015) stylized rap lyrics are generated with LSTM trained on a rap poetry corpus.

There is a diverse understanding of literary style that lately became obvious due to the growing attention to the problems of automated style transfer. For a brief overview of the state-of-the-art style transfer problem see (Tikhonov and Yamshchikov, 2018b). Style is sometimes regarded as a sentiment of a text (see (Shen et al., 2017) or (Li et al., 2018)), it's politeness (Sennrich et al., 2016) or *style of the time* (see (Hughes et al., 2012)). In (Fu et al., 2017) authors generalize these ideas measuring the success of a particular style aspect with

a specifically trained classifier. In (Guu et al., 2017) it is shown that an existent human-written source used to control the saliency of the output can significantly improve the quality of the resulting texts. Generative models on the other hand often do not have such input and have to generate stylized texts from scratch, like in (Ficler and Goldberg, 2017).

## 3   Model

We use an LSTM-based language model that predicts the $w_{n+1}$ word based on $w_1, ..., w_n$ previous inputs and some other parameters of the modeled sequence. A schematic picture of the model is shown in Figure 1, document information projections obtained as a matrix multiplication of document embedding on a projection matrix the dimensionality of which differs according to the target dimensionality of a projection are highlighted with blue arrows. An LSTM with 1152-dimensional input and 512-dimensional state.

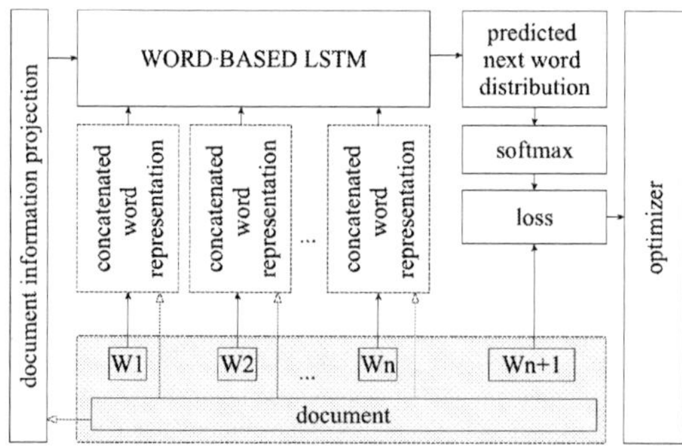


Figure 1: The scheme of the language model used. Document information projections are highlighted with blue arrows. The projections on a state space of the corresponding dimension is achieved with simple matrix multiplication of document embeddings.

Figure 2 shows a concatenated word representation of the model. The representation includes a 512-dimensional projection of a concatenated author and document embeddings at every step and two 128-dimensional vectors corresponding to finals states of two bidirectional LSTMs. The first LSTM works with a char-representation of the word and the second one uses phonemes of the International Phonetic Alphabet[1], employing an heuristics to transcribe words into phonemes. A somewhat similar idea, but with convolutional neural networks rather than with LSTMs, was pro-

---

[1] http://www.internationalphoneticalphabet.org

| | N. of documents | Size of vocab. | N. of authors | Size |
|---|---|---|---|---|
| English | 110000 | 165000 | 19000 | 150 Mb |
| Russian | 330000 | 400000 | 1700 | 140 Mb |

Table 1: Parameters of the training datasets.

| | N. of words | | N. of words |
|---|---|---|---|
| Shakespeare | 10 218 | Pushkin | 226 001 |
| Carroll | 19 632 | Esenin | 73 070 |
| Marley | 22 504 | Letov | 29 766 |
| MUSE | 7 031 | Zemfira | 23 099 |

Table 2: Number of words in the training datasets for human-peer tested lyrics.

posed in (Jozefowicz et al., 2016).

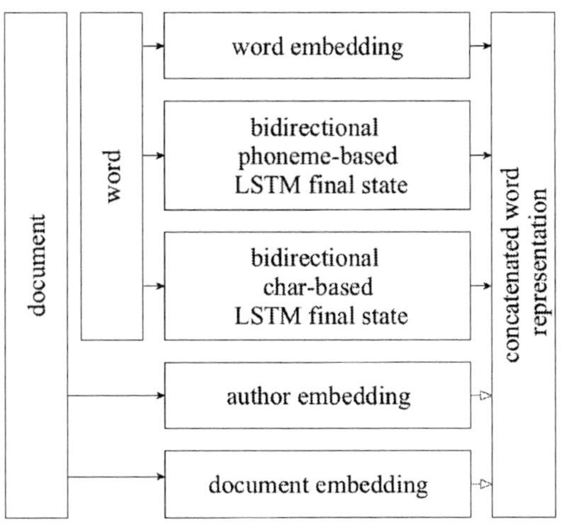


Figure 2: Concatenated word representation.

## 4 Datasets

Two proprietary datasets of English and Russian poetry were used for training. All punctuation was deleted, every character was transferred to a lower case. No other preprocessing was made. The datasets sizes can be found in Table 2. This allowed to have approximately 330 000 verses in train dataset and another 10 000 verses forming a test dataset for Russian poetry. For English poetry train data consisted of 360 000 verses with approximately 40 000 verses forming the test data.

The model was trained for English (William Shakespeare, Edgar Allan Poe, Lewis Carroll, Oscar Wilde and Bob Marley as well as lyrics of the American band Nirvana and UK band Muse) and Russian (Alexander Pushkin, Sergey Esenin,

Joseph Brodsky, Egor Letov and Zemfira Ramazanova).

The model produces results of comparable quality for both languages, so in order to make this paper shorter, we further address generative poems in English only and provide the experimental results for Russian in the Appendix. We want to emphasize that we do not see any excessive difficulties in implementation of the proposed model for other languages for which one can form a training corpus and provide a phonetically transcribed vocabulary.

Table 3 shows some generated stylized poetry examples. The model captures syntactic characteristics of the author (note the double negation in the first and the last line of Neuro-marley) alongside with the vocabulary ('burden', 'darkness', 'fears' could be subjectively associated with gothic lyrics of Poe, whereas 'sunshine', 'fun', 'fighting every rule' could be associated with positive yet rebellious reggae music). Author-specific vocabulary can technically imply specific phonetics that characterizes a given author, however this implication is not self evident and generally speaking does not have to hold. As we demonstrate later, phonetics does, indeed, contribute to the author stylization significantly.

## 5 Experiments

In (Tikhonov and Yamshchikov, 2018a) the detailed description of the experiments is provided alongside with a new metric for automated stylization quality estimation — *sample cross entropy*. In this submission we specifically address the results that deal with the phonetics of the generated texts.

### 5.1 BLEU

BLEU is a metric estimating the correspondence between a machine's output and that of a human and is usually mentioned in the context of machine translation. We suggest to adopt it for the task of stylized text generation in the following way: a random starting line is sampled out of the human-written poems and initializes the generation. Generative model 'finishes' the poem generating thee ending lines of the quatrain. Then one calculates BLEU between three actual lines that finished the human-written quatrain starting with a given first line and lines generated by the model when initialized with the same human-written line.

Table 4 shows BLEU calculated on the validation dataset for the plain vanilla LSTM, LSTM

| Neuro-Poe | Neuro-Marley |
| --- | --- |
| her beautiful eyes were bright | don t you know you ain t no fool |
| this day is a burden of tears | you r gonna make some fun |
| the darkness of the night | but she s fighting every rule |
| our dreams of hope and fears | ain t no sunshine when she s gone |

Table 3: Examples of the generated stylized quatrains. The punctuation is omitted since it was omitted in the training dataset.

with author information support but without bidirectional LSTMs for phonemes and characters included in the embeddings and the full model. The uniform random and weighted random give baselines to compare the model to.

| Model $G(A_i)$ | BLEU |
| --- | --- |
| Uniform Random | 0.35% |
| Weighted Random | 24.7% |
| Vanilla LSTM | 29.0% |
| Author LSTM | 29.3% (+1% to vanilla LSTM) |
| Full model | 29.5% (+1.7% to vanilla LSTM) |

Table 4: BLEU for uniform and weighted random random sampling, vanilla LSTM, LSTM with author embeddings but without phonetics, and for the full model. Phonetics is estimated to be almost as important for the task of stylization as the information on the target author.

Table 4 shows that extended phonetic embeddings play significant role in the overall quality of the generated stylized output. It is important to mention that phonetics in an implicit characteristic of an author and the training dataset (in line with the definition of style in (Tikhonov and Yamshchikov, 2018b)), humans do not have qualitative insights into phonetic of Wilde or Cobain, yet the information on it turns out to be important for the style attribution.

## 5.2 Survey data

Two quatrains from William Shakespeare, Lewis Carroll, Bob Marley and MUSE band were sampled. They were accompanied by two quatrains generated by the model conditioned on those four authors respectively. One hundred and forty fluent English-speakers were asked to read all 16 quatrains in randomized order and choose one option out of five offered for each quatrain, i.e. the author of this verse is William Shakespeare, Lewis Carroll, Bob Marley, MUSE or an Artificial Neural Network. The summary of the obtained results is shown in Table 5. Analogous results but for Russian language could be seen in Appendix in Table 8 alongside with more detailed description of the

methodology. It is important to note that the generated pieces for tests were human-filtered for mistakes, such as demonstrated in Table 6, whereas the automated metrics mentioned above were estimated on the whole sample of generated texts without any human-filtering.

Looking at Table 5 one can see the model has achieved good results in author stylization. Indeed the participants recognized Shakespeare more than 46% of the times (almost 2.5 times more often than compared with a random choice) and did slightly worse in their recognition of Bob Marley (40% of cases) and MUSE (39% of cases, still 2 times higher than a random choice). This shows that the human-written quatrains were, indeed, recognizable and the participants were fluent enough in the target language to attribute given texts to the correct author. At the same time, people were 'tricked' into believing that the text generated by the model was actually written by a target author in 37% of cases for Neuro-Shakespeare, 47% for Neuro-Marley, and 34% for Neuro-MUSE, respectively. Somehow, Lewis Carroll turned out to be less recognizable and was recognized in the survey only in 20% of cases (corresponds to a purely random guess). The subjective underperformance of the model on this author can therefore be explained with the difficulty experienced by the participants in determining his authorship.

Combining the results in Table 4 with the results of the survey shown in Table 5 one could conclude that phonetic structure of lyrics has impact on the correct author attribution of the stylized content. This impact is usually not acknowledged by a human reader but is highlighted with the proposed experiment.

## 6 Conclusion

In this paper we have addressed a problem of author-stylized text generation. It has been shown that the extending word embeddings with phonetic information has a comparable impact on the BLEU

| Model $G(A_i)$ or author | Shakespeare | Carroll | Marley | MUSE | LSTM |
|---|---|---|---|---|---|
| **Neuro-Shakespeare** | **0.37*** | 0.04 | 0.05 | 0.14 | **0.3**** |
| **Shakespeare** | **0.46*** | 0.05 | 0.04 | 0.07 | **0.3**** |
| **Neuro-Carroll** | 0.02 | 0.07 | **0.26**** | 0.18 | **0.41*** |
| **Carroll** | 0.05 | **0.2**** | 0.14 | 0.11 | **0.32*** |
| **Neuro-Marley** | 0.02 | 0.01 | **0.47*** | 0.2 | **0.29**** |
| **Marley** | 0.15 | 0.05 | **0.4*** | 0.1 | **0.24**** |
| **Neuro-MUSE** | 0.09 | 0 | 0.12 | **0.34**** | **0.39*** |
| **MUSE** | 0.03 | 0.05 | **0.28**** | **0.39*** | 0.2 |

Table 5: Results of a survey with 140 respondents. Shares of each out of 5 different answers given by people when reading an exempt of a poetic text by the author stated in the first column. The two biggest values in each row are marked with * and ** and a bold typeface.

of the generative model as the information on the authors of the text. It was also shown that, when faced with an author with a recognizable style (an author who is recognized approximately two times more frequently than at random), humans mistakenly recognize the output of the proposed generative model for the target author as often as they correctly attribute original texts to the author in question. The experiments were carried out in English and in Russian and there are no obvious obstacles for the application of the same approach to other languages.

## References


E Blasi, Damián, Søren Wichmann, Harald Hammarström, F. Stadler, Peter, and H. Christiansen, Morten. 2016. Sound − meaning association biases evidenced across thousands of languages. *Proceedings of the National Academy of Sciences*, 113(39):10818 − 10823.

Jessica Ficler and Yoav Goldberg. 2017. Controlling linguistic style aspects in neural language generation. In *Proceedings of the Workshop on Stylistic Variation*, pages 94 − 104.

Zhenxin Fu, Xiaoye Tan, Nanyun Peng, Dongyan Zhao, and Rui Yan. 2017. Style transfer in text: Exploration and evaluation. In *arXiv preprint:1711.06861*.

Sahar Ghannay, Yannick Estève, Nathalie Camelin, and Deléglise Paul. 2016. Evaluation of acoustic word embeddings. In *Proceedings of the 1st Workshop on Evaluating Vector-Space Representations for NLP 2016*, pages 62–66.

Marjan Ghazvininejad, Xing Shi, Yejin Choi, and Kevin Knight. 2016. Generating topical poetry. In *Proceedings of the 2016 Conference on Empirical Methods in Natural Language Processing*, pages 1183–1191. Association for Computational Linguistics.

Alex Graves. 2013. Generating sequences with recurrent neural networks. In *arXiv preprint:1308.0850*.

Kelvin Guu, Tatsunori B. Hashimoto, Yonatan Oren, and Percy Liang. 2017. Generating sentences by editing prototypes. In *arXiv preprint:1709.08878*.

Jing He, Ming Zhou, and Long Jiang. 2012. Generating chinese classical poems with statistical machine translation models. In *AAAI*.

Wanjia He, Weiran Wang, and Karen Livescu. 2016. Multi-view recurrent neural acoustic word embeddings. In *arXiv preprint:1611.04496*.

Zhiting Hu, Zichao Yang, Xiaodan Liang, Ruslan Salakhutdinov, and Eric P. Xing. 2017. Toward controlled generation of text. In *International Conference on Machine Learning*, pages 1587–1596.

James M. Hughes, Nicholas J. Foti, David C. Krakauer, and Daniel N. Rockmore. 2012. Quantitative patterns of stylistic influence in the evolution of literature. *Proceedings of the National Academy of Sciences*, 109(20):7682–7686.

Rafal Jozefowicz, Oriol Vinyals, Mike Schuster, Noam Shazeer, and Yonghui Wu. 2016. Exploring the limits of language modeling. In *arXiv preprint:1602.02410*.

Chloe Kiddon, Luke Zettlemoyer, and Yejin Choi. 2016. Globally coherent text generation with neural checklist models. *Proceedings of the 2016 Conference on Empirical Methods in Natural Language Processing*, pages 329–339.

Aleksei Kruchenykh. 1923. *Phonetics of theater*. M.:41, Moscow.

Carolyn Lamb, G. Brown, Daniel, and L. Clarke, Charles. 2017. A taxonomy of generative poetry techniques. *Journal of Mathematics and the Arts*, 11(3):159–179.

Remi Lebret, David Grangier, and Michael Auli. 2016. Neural text generation from structured data with application to the biography domain. In *Proceedings of the 2016 Conference on Empirical Methods in Natural Language Processing*, pages 1203–1213.

Jiwei Li, Michel Galley, Chris Brockett, Georgios P. Spithourakis, Jianfeng Gao, and William B. Dolan. 2016. A persona-based neural conversation model. *CoRR*, abs/1603.06155.

Juncen Li, Robin Jia, He He, and Percy Liang. 2018. Delete, retrieve, generate: A simple approach to sentiment and style transfer. In *Proceedings of the 2018 Conference of the North American Chapter of the Association for Computational Linguistics: Human Language Technologies*, volume 1, pages 1865–1874.

Zachary C. Lipton, Sharad Vikram, and Julian McAuley. 2015. Capturing meaning in product reviews with character-level generative text models. In *arXiv preprint:1511.03683*.

Senko K. Maynard. 1994. The centrality of thematic relations in japanese text. *Functions of language*, 1(2):229–260.

Peter Potash, Alexey Romanov, and Anna Rumshisky. 2015. Ghostwriter: Using an lstm for automatic rap lyric generation. In *Proceedings of the 2015 Conference on Empirical Methods in Natural Language Processing*, pages 1919–1924. Association for Computational Linguistics.

Alec Radford, Rafal Jozefowicz, and Ilya Sutskever. 2017. Learning to generate reviews and discovering sentiment. In *arXiv preprint:1704.01444*.

Rico Sennrich, Barry Haddow, and Alexandra Birch. 2016. Controlling politeness in neural machine translation via side constraints. *Proceedings of the 2016 Conference of the North American Chapter of the Association for Computational Linguistics: Human Language Technologies*, pages 35–40.

Tianxiao Shen, Tao Lei, Regina Barzilay, and Tommi Jaakkola. 2017. Style transfer from non-parallel text by cross-alignment. *31st Conference on Neural Information Processing Systems*, pages 6833–6844.

Boris Shklovsky. 1919. *Poetics: on the theory of poetic language.* 18 State typography, Petrograd.

Ilya Sutskever, James Martens, and Geoffrey Hinton. 2011. Generating text with recurrent neural networks. In *Proceedings of the 28th International Conference on Machine Learning*, pages 1017–1024.

Jian Tang, Yifan Yang, Sam Carton, Ming Zhang, and Qiaozhu Mei. 2016. Context-aware natural language generation with recurrent neural networks. In *arXiv preprint:1611.09900*.

Alexey Tikhonov and Ivan P. Yamshchikov. 2018a. Guess who? multilingual approach for the automated generation of author-stylized poetry. In *arXiv preprint:1807.07147*.

Alexey Tikhonov and Ivan P. Yamshchikov. 2018b. What is wrong with style transfer for texts? In *arXiv preprint:1808.04365*.

Jon Wheatley. 1965. The computer as poet. *Journal of Mathematics and the Arts*, 72(1):105.

Rui Yan. 2016. i, poet: Automatic poetry composition through recurrent neural networks with iterative polishing schema. In *Proceedings of the Twenty-Fifth International Joint Conference on Artificial Intelligence (IJCAI-16)*, pages 2238–2244.

Rui Yan, Cheng-Te Li, Xiaohua Hu, and Ming Zhang. 2016. Chinese couplet generation with neural network structures. In *Proceedings of the 54th Annual Meeting of the Association for Computational Linguistics*, pages 2347 – 2357.

Xiaoyuan Yi, Ruoyu Li, and Maosong Sun. 2017. Generating chinese classical poems with rnn encoder-decoder. In *Chinese Computational Linguistics and Natural Language Processing Based on Naturally Annotated Big Data*, pages 211–223.

Jiyuan Zhang, Yang Feng, Dong Wang, Yang Wang, Andrew Abel, Shiyue Zhang, and Andi Zhang. 2017. Flexible and creative chinese poetry generation using neural memory. In *Proceedings of the 55th Annual Meeting of the Association for Computational Linguistics*, volume 1, pages 1364–1373.

## A  Examples of output

Table 6 lists some illustrative mistakes of the model both for English and for Russian language. Reading the raw output we could see several types of recurring characteristic errors that are typical for LSTM-based text generation. They can be broadly classified into several different types:

- If the target author is underrepresented in the training dataset, model tends to make more mistakes, mostly, syntactic ones;

- Since generation is done in a word-by-word manner, model can deviate significantly when sampling a low-frequency word;

- Pronouns tend to cluster together, possibly due to the problem of anaphoras in the training dataset;

- The line can end abruptly, this problem also seems to occur more frequently for the authors that are underrepresented in the training dataset.

Table 7 lists some subjectively cherry-picked especially successful examples of the system outputs both for English and for Russian language. Since text is generated line by line and verses are obtained through random rhyme or rhythm filtering several types of serendipitous events occur. They can be broadly classified into four different types:

| Problem | English | Russain |
|---------|---------|---------|
| broken syntax | $Neuro - MUSE:$<br>every step inside on our faces<br>that i would stop my self going crazy | $Neuro - Zemfira:$<br>ты слышишь я слышу<br>шаги мои в душу дрожи |
| 'rare' word brakes the line | $Neuro - Shakespeare:$<br>o ho de profundis she says i am on her | $Neuro - Letov:$<br>иду гляжу в окно гляжу<br>мне вслед на небо |
| pronouns 'entangle' | $Neuro - Shakespeare:$<br>thou here shalt be and thine<br>who will have to my grave | $Neuro - Zemfira:$<br>тебе ли ты ль за |
| sentences don't end | $Neuro - Muse:$<br>at night i lay waiting for a | $Neuro - Brodsky:$<br>двух четырех десять лет за углом |
| nonsense | $Neuro - Shakespeare:$<br>do many a fair honour best of make or lose | $Neuro - Lenov:$<br>о о о о и о |

Table 6: Examples of several recurring types of mistakes that occur within generated lyrics.

- Wording of the verse that fits into the style of the target author;

- Pseudo-plot that is perceived by the reader due to a coincidental cross-reference between two lines;

- Pseudo-metaphor that is perceived by the reader due to a coincidental cross-reference between two lines;

- Sentiment and emotional ambience that correspond to the subjective perception of the target author.

## B  Survey design

The surveys were designed identically for English and Russian languages. We have recruited the respondents via social media, the only prerequisite was fluency in the target language. Respondents were asked to determine an authorship for 16 different 4-line verses. The verses for human-written text were chosen randomly out of the data for the given author. The generated verses were obtained through line-by-line automated rhyme and rhythm heuristic filtering. Since LSTMs are not perfect in text generation and tend to have clear problems illustrated in Table 6 we additionally filtered generative texts leaving the verses that do not contain obvious mistakes described above. Each of the 16 questions consisted of a text (in lower case with a stripped-off punctuation) and a multiple choice options listing five authors, namely, four human authors and an artificial neural network. Respondents were informed that they are to distinguish human- and machine-written texts. The correct answers were not shown to the respondents. Table 5 shows the results of the survey for English texts and Table 8 for Russian ones. Higher values in every row correspond to the options that were more popular among the respondents, when they were presented with the text written by the author listed in the first column of the table.

| Serendipity | English | Russain |
|---|---|---|
| **peculiar wording** | $Neuro - Shakespeare:$<br>a sense i may not comprehend<br>of whom i had not to defend | $Neuro - Pushkin:$<br>во славу вакха или тьмы<br>мы гордо пировали |
| **apophenic plot** | $Neuro - Marley:$<br>oh lord i know how long i d burn<br>take it and push it it s your turn | $Neuro - Esenin:$<br>ты под солнцем стоишь и в порфире<br>как в шелку беззаботно горишь |
| **apophenic metaphor** | $Neuro - Carroll:$<br>your laugh is bright with eyes that gleam<br>that might have seen a sudden dream | $Neuro - Zemfira:$<br>ветер в голове<br>с красной тенью шепчется |
| **peculiar sentiment** | $Neuro - Muse:$<br>i am the man of this universe<br>i remember i still am a curse | $Neuro - Letov:$<br>только в ушах отражается даль<br>только белая смерть превращается в ад |

Table 7: Cherry-picked examples of generated lyrics after either rhyme or rhythm filtering illustrating typical serendipities.

| Model $G(A_i)$ or author | Pushkin | Esenin | Letov | Zemfira | LSTM |
|---|---|---|---|---|---|
| **Neuro-Pushkin** | **0.31**** | 0.22 | 0.02 | 0.0 | **0.44*** |
| **Pushkin** | **0.62*** | 0.11 | 0.03 | 0.01 | **0.23**** |
| **Neuro-Esenin** | 0.02 | **0.61*** | 0.08 | 0.0 | **0.29**** |
| **Esenin** | 0.06 | **0.56*** | 0.07 | 0.02 | **0.29**** |
| **Neuro-Letov** | 0.0 | 0.02 | **0.40**** | 0.08 | **0.51*** |
| **Letov** | 0.0 | 0.01 | **0.61*** | 0.02 | **0.35**** |
| **Neuro-Zemfira** | 0.0 | 0.06 | 0.13 | **0.4**** | **0.41*** |
| **Zemfira** | 0.0 | 0.02 | 0.08 | **0.58*** | **0.31**** |

Table 8: Results of a survey with 178 respondents. Shares of each out of 5 different answers given by people when reading an exempt of a poetic text by the author stated in the first column. The two biggest values in each row are marked with * and ** and a bold typeface.

# On hapax legomena and morphological productivity


**Janet B. Pierrehumbert**
Dept. of Engineering Science
University of Oxford
`janet.pierrehumbert@`
`oerc.ox.ac.uk`

**Ramon Granell**
Dept. of Engineering Science
University of Oxford
`ramon.granell@`
`oerc.ox.ac.uk`



## Abstract

Quantifying and predicting morphological productivity is a long-standing challenge in corpus linguistics and psycholinguistics. The same challenge reappears in natural language processing in the context of handling words that were not seen in the training set (out-of-vocabulary, or OOV, words). Prior research showed that a good indicator of the productivity of a morpheme is the number of words involving it that occur exactly once (the *hapax legomena*). A technical connection was adduced between this result and Good-Turing smoothing, which assigns probability mass to unseen events on the basis of the simplifying assumption that word frequencies are stationary. In a large-scale study of 133 affixes in Wikipedia, we develop evidence that success in fact depends on tapping the frequency range in which the assumptions of Good-Turing are violated.


## 1 Introduction

The productivity of a morpheme is understood as the extent to which a language uses it actively in novel combinations. This vexed concept has multiple interpretations, of which two will concern us here. One views productivity as the cognitive propensity to create a new word involving a morpheme. The other infers productivity from the likelihood that new word types with a morpheme will be found when a corpus is expanded. The two can differ because the likelihood of finding a word depends not only on its creation, but also on the extent to which the word is learned and reused by others, and ultimately noted by an observer. One might suppose that a morpheme found in many different combinations would be more flexible in entering into novel ones, as in the rationale for Witten-Bell smoothing, (Jurafsky and Martin, 2000); if so, the type count of the morpheme

would be a good index of productivity. However, the type count correlates poorly with human intuitions about productivity and with the number of OOV words found in test sets (Baayen and Lieber, 1991; Baayen and Renouf, 1996; Anshen and Aronoff, 1999). Working with corpora that are small by current standards, corpus linguists in the 1990s observed that the number of *hapax legomena* (or *hapaxes*) that contain a given morpheme is a much better predictor (Baayen and Lieber, 1991; Baayen and Renouf, 1996). This finding is argued to follow from assumptions about the cognitive system that make Good-Turing smoothing applicable, which we explain in the following section.

This paper systematically explores hapax counts as an indicator of productivity for a set of 133 morphemes that meet objective inclusion criteria for a much larger corpus than was used previously. This is the August 2013 download of Wikipedia that has 1.24 billion word tokens. We address several questions: Is the measure successful when exercised at a larger scale? Are the simplifying assumptions put forward to justify the measure valid? What does the behaviour of the measure tell us about the lexical system? We address these questions with numerical experiments. We define "pseudohapax" sets as sets of words in the full corpus that would be expected to occur exactly once in five nominal corpora having sizes used in classic studies. We explore how well the pseudohapax sets predict the distribution of morphemes amongst extremely rare words. We also downsample the corpus to create hapax sets from subcorpora matching the nominal corpus sizes. This approach allows us to separate the influence of several factors: sparse sampling, variation across morphological families in the shape of the rank-frequency distribution, and the actual frequencies of words that appear as hapaxes in corpora of classic size.




*Proceedings of the 15th SIGMORPHON Workshop on Computational Research in Phonetics, Phonology, and Morphology*, pages 125–130
Brussels, Belgium, October 31, 2018. ©2018 The Special Interest Group on Computational Morphology and Phonology
https://doi.org/10.18653/v1/P17

## 2 Hapax Legomena and smoothing

Hapax counts are advanced as an indicator of productivity in Baayen & Lieber (1991). The article describes as "large" the 18-million word Cobuild corpus (Renouf, 1987) on which the study was based. Hay and Baayen (2002) used the same corpus. The indicator has been widely used for more than 25 years (Baayen and Renouf, 1996; Chitashvili and Baayen, 1993; Plag et al., 1999; Popescu and Altmann, 2008; Kenny, 2014; Aronoff and Lindsay, 2014; Stump, 2017, in press). Several different measures can be defined from the hapax count. Of particular interest is the hapax percentage $P*$ (the percentage of all hapaxes that contain the morpheme). Using $P*$, the number of unseen word types with any given morpheme is estimated as proportional to its representation amongst the hapaxes, and this supports predictions about the distributions of morphemes in OOV sets much bigger than the hapax sets.

A justification for the hapax-based measures is proposed in Baayen & Renouf (1996) and Hay and Baayen (2002). They assume that the text meets the assumptions for Good-Turing smoothing: each word is produced with a constant probability, or put differently, the word frequencies are stationary and the text results from a Poisson process (Church and Gale, 1991). They also assume that the hapaxes are so rare that they are very likely to have been created on the spot. Integrating these assumptions, the idea is that the probability of creating a rare word form like *zeitgeist+y* or *post+Sumerian* is constant and based on the mental representation of the parts. The hapax set is by definition a subset of the word types with a morpheme, but nonetheless supports better predictions. The authors suggest the hapax measure works well because it eliminates complex words that are not decomposed during lexical access, and therefore do not contribute to productivity. Our numerical experiments were designed to include only words that are decomposable.

It is well-known that word frequencies fluctuate with the topic of discussion. Such deviations from a Poisson process provide the foundation for modern document retrieval algorithms (Sparck Jones, 1972; Church and Gale, 1995). The effects can be as large as orders of magnitude in frequency, and impact all parts of speech, although the impact on proper nouns is generally greatest (Church, 2000; Altmann et al., 2009). Different corpora can thus yield different $P*$ values for the same affix, providing the grist for post-hoc interpretation as in Plagg et al. (1999). In interpreting our results, we will also be concerned with the possibility of variability across speakers, which is of similar magnitude (Altmann et al., 2011).

## 3 Materials

In selecting our materials, one goal was to compare all morphemes that met objective inclusion criteria (as opposed to using subjective judgment to make a selection). The inclusion criteria were designed to identify morphemes that are reasonably familiar and that are reliably identifiable within complex words with a minimum of false positives. We considered words to be potentially decomposable into Prefix+Stem or Stem+Suffix if removing the affix yielded a stem that also occurs independently as a word of higher frequency. This criterion is needed to eliminate many spurious decompositions, such as *season = sea+son*, as well as words that arc probably not decomposed into their parts in lexical processing (Hay, 2001). To select the target affixes, we began by considering all 184,499 words in Wikipedia that occur at least 100 times. Initial and final substrings of three or more letters were considered as potential affixes. The selected affixes occurred at least 50 times in the candidate list, and we also required that removing them reliably yield a valid stem. 68 prefixes and 65 suffixes met the criteria. The total set excludes many productive morphemes that coincidentally occur in many simplex words. It includes many true prefixes and suffixes, including combinations such as *+ingly, +ization, +ers*. Justification for treating these as units can be found in Stump (2017; in press). It also includes words that are used productively in compounding; the distinction between derivational morphology and compounding is a fuzzy one (Bauer, 2005). Detailed inclusion criteria and descriptive statistics, and a complete word list, are in the supplement (posted on the first author's web site).

Our outcome measure for productivity is the type frequencies for each morpheme family in the "far tail" of the distribution, defined as the set of words occurring 2 to 11 times. As is common in work on very large corpora, forms occurring only once are not considered because of problematic text normalization artifacts. The upper cutoff of 11 was selected to provide a large test set of words

| | Prefix | Example | Types |
|---|---|---|---|
| MOST | non+ | non-threat | 11360 |
| | anti+ | anti-badware | 4933 |
| | sub+ | subcritical | 3520 |
| | post+ | post-vulgate | 2854 |
| LEAST | north+ | northlands | 428 |
| | fore+ | forebrain | 410 |
| | south+ | southback | 400 |
| | second+ | second-degree | 365 |

| | Suffix | Example | Types |
|---|---|---|---|
| MOST | +ers | adopters | 6881 |
| | +man | beckman | 6639 |
| | +based | rock-based | 6169 |
| | +like | garlic-like | 5518 |
| LEAST | +ful | needful | 430 |
| | +water | floodwater | 399 |
| | +american | austral-american | 335 |
| | +shire | dorsetshire | 246 |

Table 1: Prefixes and suffixes having the most and least types in the far tail. Total types in the dataset.

| Size | PBand | PTypes | DB | HTypes |
|---|---|---|---|---|
| 0.25% | [200,600] | 5734 | 8 | 8196 |
| 0.5% | [100,300] | 8463 | 5 | 11769 |
| 1.0% | [50, 150] | 12709 | 2 | 16550 |
| 2.0% | [25,75] | 19051 | 1 | 22886 |
| 4.0% | [12, 37] | 29131 | 0 | 30650 |

Table 2: Banding scheme for five conditions, expressed as a percentage of the total corpus size. Frequency band for the pseudohapaxes (PBand), total number of pseudohapax types containing any of the prefixes or suffixes (PTypes), number of down-bands available before reaching the far tail (DB). Average number of hapaxes (HTypes).

with low frequencies (under 0.01 per million) that would be novel to many or most readers. The test set provides a much stronger mirror of underlying productivity than modest extensions of small corpora could. The far tail contains 129,714 complex word types that are relevant, in that they begin or end in one of the target affixes, and can be parsed into the affix plus a stem. Table 1 shows the most and least productive morphemes, as indicated by their counts in the far tail.

## 4  Frequency bands

We frame the calculations by considering nominal corpus sizes of 0.25%, 0.5%, 1.0%, 2.0%, 4.0% of the actual corpus size. Compared to classic corpus sizes, these range from rather small (3M words) to rather large (50M words). For each size, we take the "pseudohapaxes" to be words whose expected frequency in the nominal corpus would be 1.0, taking rounding into account. For example, for the 1.0% condition, the band is centered on words occurring 100 times. The 4.0% condition provides the largest possible pseudohapax set that has no overlap with the far tail (the test set).

The number of pseudohapaxes grows with the nominal corpus size. To evaluate the importance of sample size versus the absolute location in the frequency range, we also define down-bands, which have the same number of word types as a pseudohapax band but are simply shifted downwards in the frequency range by an integer multiple of the size of that band. Table 2 summarizes the banding scheme.

For the 4.0% condition, there is no down-band, because the pseudohapax band falls just above the far tail. It is also important to look at the set of words with higher frequencies than the pseudohapaxes. In this "up-band" we include all words up to the most frequent; the size of the up-band is always within 15% of the size of the pseudohapax set. It is never possible to define more than one up-band from each set of pseudohapaxes.

A real hapax set corresponding to one of our nominal sizes would have only a sparse sample of the pseudohapaxes, but would also include words of higher and lower frequency. For each of the five pseudohapax bands, we simulate a real hapax set by taking a random sample of sentences in the corpus and collating the hapaxes. For each corpus size, 10 different subcorpora were created. If the hapax set happened to include words from the far tail, these were removed from the far tail for testing.

## 5  Evaluating predictions

We use ordinary least squares regression (OLS) to predict the logarithm of type count for each morpheme in the tail as a function of the logarithm of type count in a pseudohapax band, treating prefixes and suffixes separately. To ensure that the observations are robust, we use a hold-one-out method. Each prefix (or suffix) is held out and the remaining prefixes (or suffixes) are used to predict its value. We make the same calculation for all conditions, all down-bands and up-bands, and all hapax sets. Predicted $R^2$ values are adjusted as described in Draper et al. (1998), yielding the measure $\bar{R}^2_{pred}$.

Table 3 summarizes the regression parameters. The slope is close to 1.0 for all fits (and closes in on 1.0 as the nominal corpus size increases), while the intercept varies. This means that the number of types in the far tail is approximately proportional to the number of types in the pseudohapax or hapax set, with the proportion decreasing as the nominal corpus size increases.

Figure 1 shows the results for $\bar{R}^2_{pred}$. For all conditions, the prediction from the pseudohapax band is better than the prediction from the up-band. Attempting predictions from words with frequencies over 600 (leftmost points in the figure) yields poor $\bar{R}^2_{pred}$ values of 0.4 and below. The pseudohapax bands for the 2.0%, and 4.0% conditions provide very good predictions with $\bar{R}^2_{pred} >$ 0.85. This outcome is not chiefly due to the large size of these two pseudohapax sets. Predictions are nearly as good from the down-bands falling in the same frequency range. Figure 1 also shows results for the same calculation for the hapax sets; the reported $\bar{R}^2_{pred}$ averages over the results for the 10 subcorpora of each size. For the smallest corpora, the prediction from the hapax set is better than the prediction from the corresponding pseudohapax set. The hapax set is dominated by rare words, because lexical rank-frequency distributions are heavy-tailed. The median word frequency for the 0.25% case is 88 (or 0.07 per million). As we go towards larger corpora, the difference between the hapax value and the pseudohapax value dwindles.

## 6    Interpretation

No matter whether the sample is obtained as a hapax set or a pseudohapax set, success in predicting word types in the far tail depends on having a sample that is dominated by rare words. Psycholinguists view words with frequencies of 1 to 3 per million as low-frequency words, as in Carreiras et al. (2006), but a median of 0.07 per million was needed to achieve $\bar{R}^2_{pred} > 0.8$. Why did this outcome occur? Figure 2 sheds light on this question. It shows a frequency-rank distribution on a log-log scale for the 5 most productive, and the 5 least productive, suffixes as measured by the count of word types in the far tail. This is a rotation of a Zipfian rank-frequency distribution, with a separate sub-lexicon for each morpheme.

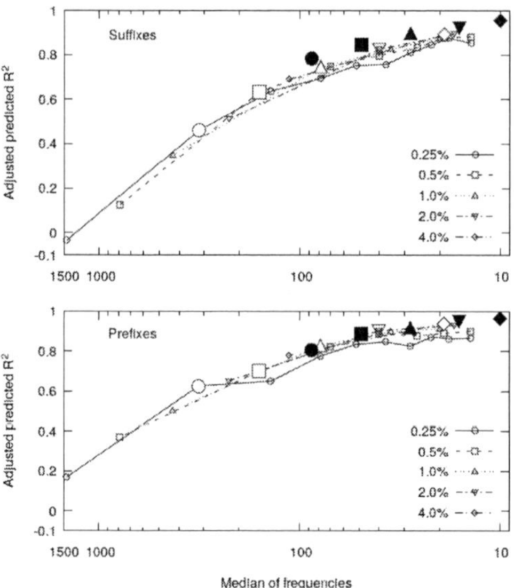


Figure 1:   $\bar{R}^2_{pred}$ for using type counts of the affixes in the indicated band to predict type counts in the far tail. The pseudohapax set for each condition is indicated with an enlarged plotting character. The hapax set for each condition is indicated with a filled plotting character.

If a frequency spectrum obeyed a power law (as proposed by Zipf) it would appear as a straight line on a log-log plot. All curves are concave downwards, as typically observed (Baayen, 2001). There are marked differences in how the spectra roll off. Words with frequencies above 600 (0.5 per million) provide little information about productivity, and two of the most productive suffixes (+*like*, +*related*) still have not pulled out of the bottom group by 600. The slope around 100 is, however, very indicative of the slope around 10.

With a frequency of 88, the median hapax in the 0.25% case has a rank of 187,474 in the rank-frequency distribution for the entire Wikipedia vocabulary (not shown). This number can be interpreted in the light of results on adult vocabularies. Based on a large crowdsourcing experiment, Brysbaert et al. (2016) estimate that a 60-year-old at the 95th percentile of vocabulary knowledge knows 56,400 lemmas, or 95,880 words including inflected forms. Thus, it seems that unlikely that even such a person knows all of the hapaxes. Brysbaert et al. (2016) however omit proper names. So it is also relevant to consider "alphabetic words", which are words spelled with alphabetic characters regardless of their morphological status. Brys-

|  | | Slope | | | Intercept | | |
|---|---|---|---|---|---|---|---|
|  | Size | Mean | Min | Max | Mean | Min | Max |
| Pseudohapaxes | 0.25% | 0.92 | 0.78 +based | 1.05 over+ | 3.32 | 2.96 over+ | 3.70 +based |
|  | 0.5% | 1.03 | 0.90, +based | 1.15 wiki+ | 2.53 | 2.15 wiki+ | 2.92 +based |
|  | 1.0% | 1.05 | 0.93 +based | 1.15 side+ | 2.06 | 1.69 side+ | 2.47 +based |
|  | 2.0% | 1.03 | 0.95 +like | 1.10 second+ | 1.73 | 1.50 second+ | 1.99 +like |
|  | 4.0% | 1.01 | 0.96 +based | 1.06 home+ | 1.41 | 1.22 home+ | 1.60 +based |
| Hapaxes | 0.25% | 1.05 | 0.95 +like | 1.16 self+ | 2.49 | 2.14 home+ | 2.78 non+ |
|  | 0.5% | 1.06 | 0.96 +like | 1.15 side+ | 2.06 | 1.68 side+ | 2.42 +like |
|  | 1.0% | 1.04 | 0.96 +like | 1.11 news+ | 1.78 | 1.49 news+ | 2.11 +like |
|  | 2.0% | 1.03 | 0.96 +based | 1.11 non+ | 1.45 | 1.09 non+ | 1.76 +based |
|  | 4.0% | 1.01 | 0.96 +based | 1.06 head+ | 1.20 | 0.99 +ful | 1.43 +based |

Table 3: Summary of regression parameters. For minimum and maximum values, the indicated affix is the one that was held out.

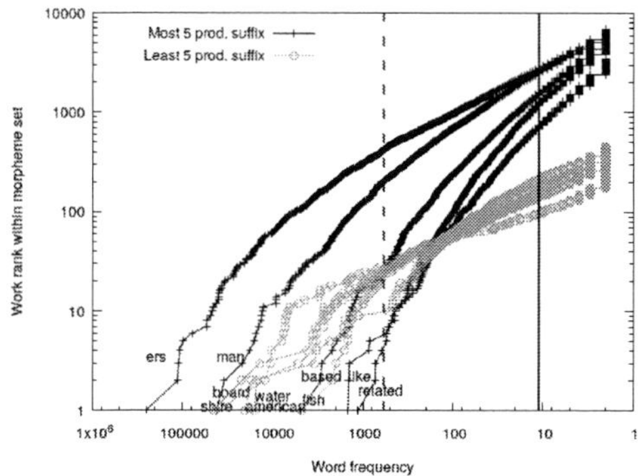


Figure 2: Frequency-rank distributions (on a log-log scale) for the most and least productive suffixes. Far tail to the right of the solid line at 11. 0.25% up-band to the left of the dashed line at 600. A comparable plot for prefixes is similar.

baert et al. (2016) apply the model fits in Gerlach & Altmann (2013) to estimate the number of distinct alphabetic words that a person has encountered, as a function of the total hours spent reading in their lifetime. For the Wikipedia editors, who had a median age of 25 in 2010 (Glott et al., 2010), reading 8 hours a day from age 5 yields a median estimated exposure to 146,000 alphabetic word types, which is still fewer than the median hapax rank. In short, the success of a hapax set as a predictor for words in the far tail depends on having words that are too rare to be known by everyone, and are therefore not constant in frequency across speakers.

We now consider the assumption that each word in the 0.25% hapax set was independently (and repeatedly) created with some probability. While this may be true for some words, it appears highly implausible for others. This frequency range includes many words that are not fully transparent and that recur many times within individual articles on specialized topics. Technical terms like *interaural* (audiology), *piquette* (oenology), *demand-side* (economics) are prototypical examples of words with non-stationary probabilities (Church and Gale, 1995; Curran and Osborne, 2002). For proper names, the suffix +*ville* is 17 times as productive as the suffix +*shire*. Given that Wikipedia asks all articles to be supported by secondary sources, few if any proper names would have been created on the spot.

We have seen that the hapaxes in a random sample of merely 3M words succeeded well in predicting the morphological profile in the tail of a corpus 400 times larger. The success seems to have occurred because the hapaxes provided a good slice of rare words that are not known to everyone, and that were not necessarily created on the spot. Pseudohapax sets that obtained a slice of similarly rare words worked just as well. Why are such rare words better indicators of productivity than more frequent words, even when these have been -filtered to be decomposable, as in this study? Possibly, rare words have a higher impact in ongoing learning of morphology because they are unexpected and salient. An alternative possibility brings in a social component. Different groups of editors in Wikipedia work on different topics. They may extend the morphological patterns that typify their field and distinguish it from other fields. In future research, we will evaluate such possibilities.

# References

Eduardo G Altmann, Janet B Pierrehumbert, and Adilson E Motter. 2009. Beyond word frequency: Bursts, lulls, and scaling in the temporal distributions of words. *PLOS one*, 4(11):e7678.

Eduardo G Altmann, Janet B Pierrehumbert, and Adilson E Motter. 2011. Niche as a determinant of word fate in online groups. *PloS one*, 6(5):e19009.

Frank Anshen and Mark Aronoff. 1999). Using dictionaries to study the mental lexicon. *Brain and Language*, 68:16– 26.

Mark Aronoff and Mark Lindsay. 2014. Productivity, blocking and lexicalization. *The Oxford handbook of derivational morphology*, pages 67–83.

Harald Baayen and Rochelle Lieber. 1991. Productivity and english derivation: A corpus-based study. *Linguistics*, 29(5):801–844.

R Harald Baayen. 2001. *Word frequency distributions*, volume 18. Springer Science & Business Media.

R Harald Baayen and Antoinette Renouf. 1996. Chronicling the Times: Productive lexical innovations in an English newspaper. *Language*, pages 69–96.

Laurie Bauer. 2005. The borderline between derivation and compounding. In *Morphology and its demarcations: Selected papers from the 11th Morphology meeting, Vienna, February 2004*, volume 264, page 97. John Benjamins Publishing.

Marc Brysbaert, Michaël Stevens, Paweł Mandera, and Emmanuel Keuleers. 2016. How many words do we know? practical estimates of vocabulary size dependent on word definition, the degree of language input and the participant?s age. *Frontiers in psychology*, 7.

Manuel Carreiras, Andrea Mechelli, and Cathy J Price. 2006. Effect of word and syllable frequency on activation during lexical decision and reading aloud. *Human Brain Mapping*, 27(12):963–972.

Revas J Chitashvili and R Harald Baayen. 1993. Word frequency distributions of texts and corpora as large number of rare event distributions. In *Quantitative text analysis*, pages 54–135. Wissenschaftlicher Verlag.

Kenneth W Church. 2000. Empirical estimates of adaptation: the chance of two noriegas is closer to p/2 than p 2. In *Proceedings of the 18th conference on Computational linguistics-Volume 1*, pages 180–186. Association for Computational Linguistics.

Kenneth W Church and William A Gale. 1991. A comparison of the enhanced Good-Turing and deleted estimation methods for estimating probabilities of English bigrams. *Computer Speech & Language*, 5(1):19–54.

Kenneth W Church and William A Gale. 1995. Poisson mixtures. *Natural Language Engineering*, 1(2):163–190.

James R Curran and Miles Osborne. 2002. A very very large corpus doesn't always yield reliable estimates. In *Proceedings of the 6th conference on Natural Language Learning-Volume 20*, pages 1–6. Association for Computational Linguistics.

Norman R Draper and Harry Smith. 1998. *Applied regression analysis*. Wiley series in probability and statistics: Texts and references section. Wiley, New York, NY.

Martin Gerlach and Eduardo G Altmann. 2013. Stochastic model for the vocabulary growth in natural languages. *Physical Review X*, 3(2):021006.

Ruediger Glott, Philipp Schmidt, and Rishab Ghosh. 2010. Wikipedia survey ? overview of results. *United Nations University*.

Jennifer Hay. 2001. Lexical frequency in morphology: Is everything relative? *Linguistics*, 39(6; ISSU 376):1041–1070.

Jennifer Hay and Harald Baayen. 2002. Parsing and productivity. In *Yearbook of Morphology 2001*, pages 203–235. Springer.

Daniel Jurafsky and James H Martin. 2000. *Speech and Language Processing*. Prentice-Hall, Upper Saddle River, NJ.

Dorothy Kenny. 2014. *Lexis and Creativity in Translation: A corpus-based approach*. Routledge.

Ingo Plag, Christiane Dalton-Puffer, and Harald Baayen. 1999. Morphological productivity across speech and writing. *English Language & Linguistics*, 3(2):209–228.

Ioan-Iovitz Popescu and Gabriel Altmann. 2008. Hapax legomena and language typology. *Journal of Quantitative Linguistics*, 15(4):370–378.

Antoinette Renouf. 1987. Corpus development. In John M. Sinclair, editor, *Looking up: An account of the COBUILD Project in lexical computing*, pages 1–40. William Collins Sons and Co. Ltd. London, England.

Karen Sparck Jones. 1972. A statistical interpretation of term specificity and its application in retrieval. *Journal of Documentation*, 28(1):11–21.

Gregory Stump. 2017. Rule conflation in an inferential-realizational theory of morphotactics. *Acta Linguistica Academica*, 64(1):79?124.

Gregory Stump. in press. Some sources of apparent gaps in derivational paradigms. *Morphology*.

# A Morphological Analyzer for Shipibo-Konibo


**Ronald Cardenas**
Charles University in Prague
Faculty of Mathematics and Physics
Inst. of Formal and Applied Linguistics
ronald.cardenas@matfyz.cz

**Daniel Zeman**
Charles University in Prague
Faculty of Mathematics and Physics
Inst. of Formal and Applied Linguistics
zeman@ufal.mff.cuni.cz



## Abstract

We present a fairly complete morphological analyzer for Shipibo-Konibo, a low-resourced native language spoken in the Amazonian region of Peru. We resort to the robustness of finite-state systems in order to model the complex morphosyntax of the language. Evaluation over raw corpora shows promising coverage of grammatical phenomena, limited only by the scarce lexicon. We make this tool freely available so as to aid the production of annotated corpora and impulse further research in native languages of Peru.


## 1 Introduction

Linguistic and language technology research on Peruvian native languages have experienced a revival in the last few years. The academic effort was accompanied by an ambitious long term initiative driven by the Peruvian government. This initiative has the objective of systematically documenting as many native languages as possible for preservation purposes (Acosta et al., 2013). So far, writing systems and standardization have been proposed for 19 language families and 47 languages.

In this paper, we focus on Shipibo-Konibo (henceforth, SK), also known in the literature as Shipibo or Shipibo-Conibo. SK is a member of the Panoan language family. This family is a well-established linguistic group of the South American Lowlands, alongside Arawak, Tupian, Cariban, and others. Currently, circa 28 Panoan languages are spoken in Western Amazonia in the regions between Peru, Bolivia, and Brazil. Nowadays, Shipibo is spoken by nearly 30,000 people mainly located in Peruvian lands.

The morphosyntax of SK in extensively analyzed by Valenzuela (2003). However, several phenomena such as discourse coherence marking

and ditransitive constructions still require deeper understanding, as pointed out by Biondi (2012).

We present the first finite-state morphological analyzer for SK, capable of performing POS tagging as well as morpheme segmentation and categorization. In order to impulse the development of downstream applications and corpora annotation, the tool is freely available[1] under the GPL license.

## 2 Related Work

The development of freely available basic language tools has proven to be of utmost importance for the development of downstream applications for native languages with low resources. Finite-state morphology systems constitute one type of such basic tools. Besides downstream applications, they are essential for the construction of annotated corpora, and consequently, for development of other tools. Such is the case of Quechua, a native language spoken in South America, for which the robust system developed by (Rios, 2010) paved the way to the proposal of a standard written system for the language (Acosta et al., 2013) and impulsed work in parsing, machine translation (Rios, 2016), and speech recognition (Zevallos and Camacho, 2018).

Initial research regarding SK has centered in the development of manual annotation tools (Mercado-Gonzales et al., 2018), lexical database creation (Valencia et al., 2018), Spanish-SK parallel corpora creation and initial machine translation experiments (Galarreta et al., 2017). Related to our line of research, work by Pereira-Noriega et al. (2017) addresses lemmatization but not morphological categorization. Alva and Oncevay-Marcos (2017) presents initial experiments on spell-checking using proximity of morphemes and syllable patterns extracted from anno-

---

[1] http://hdl.handle.net/11234/1-2857




*Proceedings of the 15th SIGMORPHON Workshop on Computational Research in Phonetics, Phonology, and Morphology*, pages 131–139
Brussels, Belgium, October 31, 2018. ©2018 The Special Interest Group on Computational Morphology and Phonology
https://doi.org/10.18653/v1/P17

tated corpora.

In this work, we take into account the morpho-tactics of all word categories and possible morpheme variations attested by Valenzuela (2003). We explored and included as many exceptions as found in the limited annotated corpora to which we got access. Hence, the tool presented is robust enough to leverage current efforts in the creation of basic language technologies for SK.

## 3 Shipibo-Konibo Morphosyntax

In terms of a syntactic profile, SK is a (mainly) post-positional and agglutinating language with highly synthetic verbal morphology, and a basic but quite flexible agent-object-verb (AOV) word order in transitive constructions and subject-verb (SV) order in intransitive ones, as summarized by (Fleck, 2013).

SK usually exhibits a biunique relationship between form and function, and in most cases morpheme boundaries are easily identifiable. It is common to have unmarked nominal and adjectival roots, and few instances of stem changes and suppletion are documented by (Valenzuela, 2003). In addition, the verb may carry one or more deictic-directive, adverb type suffixes, in what can be described as a polysynthetic tendency.

In addition, SK presents a rare instance of syntactic ergativity in an otherwise morphologically ergative but syntactically accusative language.

We proceed to comment about the most salient morpho-syntactic features relevant to the morphotactics argumentation in section 4.2. The examples presented in this section were taken from Valenzuela (2003).

### 3.1 Expression of Argument

Verb arguments are expressed through free lexical case-marked nominals, with no co-referential pronominal marking on the verb or auxiliary. That is, verbs and auxiliaries are not marked to agree with 1st, 2nd, or 3rd person of the subject or agent. Instead, verbs are marked to indicate that the action was carried out by the same participant of the previous clause or by another one. We explain this phenomena in section 3.4.

Omission of required subject and object is normally understood as zero third person singular form. There are no systematic morpho-syntactic means of distinguishing direct from indirect objects, or primary versus secondary objects.

### 3.2 Case Marking

Grammatical cases are always marked as suffixes, except for a couple of exceptions. SK exhibits a fairly rigid ergative-absolutive case-marking system. The ergative case is always marked, whereas the absolutive case is only marked on non-emphatic pronouns. All other grammatical cases are marked, except the vocative case. The vocative case is constructed by shifting the stress of a noun to the last syllable.

### 3.3 Participant Agreement

Certain adverbs, phrases, and clauses are semantically oriented towards one core participant or controller and receive a marking in accordance with the syntactic function this participant plays, namely *subject (S)* of a intransitive verb, *agent (A)* of a transitive verb, or *object (O)* of a transitive construction. This feature can be analyzed as a type of split-ergativity which might be exclusive to Panoan languages. The following example illustrates this phenomena for the adjunct *bochiki: high up* in S, O, and A orientation (ONOM refers to onomatopeic words).

(1) S orientation
*Bochiki-ra* e-a    oxa-i
up:S-Ev    1-Abs sleep-Inc
"I sleep high up (e.g., in a higher area inside the house)."

(2) O orientation
E-n-ra    yami kentí    *bochiki* a-ke
1-Erg-Ev metal pot:Abs up:O    do.T-Cmpl
"I placed the metal pot high up." (only the pot is high up)

(3) A orientation
E-n-ra    yami kentí    *bochiki-xon*
1-Erg-Ev metal pot:Abs up-A
tan    tan    a-ke.
ONOM ONOM do.T-Cmpl
"I hit the metal pot (being) high up." (I am high up with the pot)

### 3.4 Clause-Chaining and Switch-Reference System

Chained clauses present only one clause with fully finite verb inflection while the rest of them carry same- or switch-reference marking. Reference-marked clauses are strictly verb-final, carry no obvious nominalizing morphology and may precede, follow, or be embedded in their matrix clause.

Same-reference markers encode transitivity status of the matrix verb, co-referentiality or non co-referentiality of participant, and relative temporal or logical order of the two events. This is because most same-subject markers are identical to the participant agreement morphemes and hence correlate with the *subject (S)* or *agent (A)* function played by their controller in the matrix clause. The following example shows three chained clauses. Notice that the matrix verb is *chew*, and the subordinated clause's verbs carry the marker *xon* to indicate that the action was performed by the same agent prior to the action described in the main clause (PSSA: previous event, same subject, *A* orientation).

[ [ Jawen tapon    bi-xon ]    kobin-a-xon ]
　　Pos3   root:Abs get-PSSA boil-do.T-PSSA
*naka*-kati-kan-ai.
chew-Pst4-Pl-Inc
"After getting its (i.e., a plant's) root and boiling it, they chewed it."

Same- or switch- reference marking may also be used to encode different types of discourse (dis)continuity.

### 3.5 Pronouns and Split-Ergativity

The personal pronoun system in SK is composed of 6 basic forms corresponding to the combinations of three person (1,2,3) and two number (singular and plural) distinctions. SK does not differentiate gender or inclusive vs exclusive first person plural. There are no honorific pronouns either.

The ergative-absolutive alignment is used in all types of constructions, except for reflexive pronoun constructions. Reflexive pronouns are marked with the suffix *-n* when referring to both A and S arguments, but remain unmarked when referring to an O argument. Hence, reflexive pronouns constructions clearly present a nominative-accusative alignment.

### 3.5.1 Clitics

All clitics in SK are enclitics, i.e. they always function as suffixes, but most of them encode clause level features in which case they are attached to the last element of the phrase or clause they are modifying. SK clitics are categorized into case markers, *less-fixed clitics* and *second position clitics*, as proposed by Valenzuela (2003).

Case markers are attached to noun phrases preceding mood and evidentiality markers in its last constituent word.

Second position clitics are attached to the main clause in the sentence, and they encode evidentiality (+Ev:ra; +Hsy:ronki, ki; e.g. *it is said that ...*), reported speech (e.g. *he says/said that ...*), interrogative focus (+Int:ki,rin; +Em:bi), and dubitative voice.

Less-fixed clitics mark the specific element they are attached to, instead of the whole clause. These are endo-clitics, i.e. they can take any position other than the last morpheme slot in a construction. In this category we can find adverbial, adjectival, and dubitative suffixes.

## 4　Morphological Analyzer

The analyzer was implemented using the Foma (Hulden, 2009) toolkit, following the extensive morphological description provided by Valenzuela (2003). Besides segmenting and tagging all morphemes in a word form, the analyzer also categorizes the root and the final token in order to account for any sequence of derivational processes. The analysis is of the form

*[POS] root[POS.root] morpheme[+Tag] ...*
and it is illustrated with an example in Table 1.

The complete list of abbreviations and symbols used for morphological tagging can be found in the Appendix A of (Valenzuela, 2003). Language specific POS tagset was mapped to the Universal Dependencies (Nivre et al., 2016) v2 POS tagset.[2]

In the remaining of this section we provide a thorough explanation of the production rules for the main POS categories and the comment on the limitations of the analyzer.

### 4.1 The Lexicon

The lexicon was obtained from manually annotated corpus and a digitalized thesaurus kindly provided by the Artificial Intelligence Research Lab of the Pontifical Catholic University of Peru (GIPIAA-PUCP). The annotated corpus was built from folk tales documents and it consists of 12,250 tokens and 2,915 types. The thesaurus provides dictionary entries for 6,750 types.

The extensive work of (Valenzuela, 2003) provides a systematic encoding of morpho-syntactic information for SK. Similar guidelines were followed to design the encoding for Quechua (Rios, 2016), another agglutinative, ergative-absolutive

---

[2]http://universaldependencies.org/u/pos/

| Token | Translation | Analysis |
|---|---|---|
| Isábora | the birds | [NOUN] isá[NRoot] bo[+Pl] ra[+Ev] |
| noyai | are flying | [VERB] noy[VRoot.I] ai[+Inc] |

Table 1: Example of analysis produced.

| UPOS | Thesaurus | Annotated corpus |
|---|---|---|
| NOUN | 2557 | 719 |
| VERB | 2284 | 578 |
| ADJ | 601 | 107 |
| ADV | 223 | 112 |
| PROPN | - | 112 |
| PRON | 24 | 36 |
| NUM | - | 6 |
| SCONJ | - | 2 |
| CCONJ | - | 3 |
| AUX | - | 2 |
| DET | - | 28 |
| ADP | 46 | 19 |
| INTJ | - | 15 |
| PART | - | 9 |

Table 2: Number of roots per POS, for each lexicon source.

native language widely spoken in Peru and South America.

The annotated corpus, however, was not annotated following this encoding, and further manual annotation was required. With the help of a digitalized dictionary and an affix thesaurus we manually resolved the mappings and correspondences using the—now widely accepted—morphosyntactic encoding.

The following example illustrates the annotation. The first row shows the raw segmentation of the tokens; the second row, the original annotation (*Clit* stands for clitic, *VS stands for verbal suffix*); the third row, the new annotation following the morphosyntactic tagset proposed by Valenzuela (2003).

| Shoko-res | oxa-[a]i | / pi-ai. |
|---|---|---|
| a.little.bit-Clit | sleep-VS | eat-VS |
| a.little.bit-just | sleep-Inc | eat-Inc |

'I'm gonna sleep / eat just a little bit.'

Table 2 presents the number of roots per UD POS category for each lexicon source, for a total of 8,658 roots.

## 4.2 Morphotactics

Although SK presents a predominantly suffixed morphology, there exists a closed list of prefixes, almost all being body part derivatives shortened from the original noun (e.g. 'head' *mapo* → *ma*). These prefixes can be added to nouns, verbs, and adjectives to provide a locative signal.

### 4.2.1 Nouns

Nominal roots can occur in a bare form without any additional morphology or carry the following morphemes.

- Body part prefix (+Pref), to indicate location in the body.

- Plural marker (+Pl:bo), meaning more than one. Dual number distinction is not made in nouns, but in verbs.

- N-marker and other case markers. The suffix *-n* can mark the ergative (+Erg), genitive (+Gen), and interessive (+Intrss, to denote interest), and instrumental (+Inst) cases. Other marked cases in SK include absolutive (+Abs:a), dative (+Dat:ki), locative (+Loc:me,ke), allative (+All:n,nko), ablative (+Abl:a), and chezative (+Chez:iba). The allative case always follows a locative case marker, both of them presenting several allomorphs.

- Participant agreement marker (+S:x), to indicate the subject of a transitive verb.

- Distributive marker (+Distr:tibi), produces quantifier phrases, e.g. day+Distr > *every day*.

- Adjectival markers , such as diminutive (+Dim:shoko), deprecatory (+Deprec:isi), legitimate (+Good:kon, +Bad:koma), proprietive (+Prop:ya) and privative (+Priv:oma,nto).

- Adverbial markers.

- Postpositional markers.

- Second position clitics, exclusively the focus emphasizer (+Foc:kan).

It is worth mentioning that only the first plural morpheme has precedence over the others suffixes, and clitics are required to be last. Plural, cases, and adverbial markers can occur multiple times. There is no gender marking in SK. Instead, the words for woman (*ainbo*) and man (*benbo*) are used as noun modifiers. Consider the example

Títa-shoko-bicho-ra    oxa-ai
mom:Abs-Dim-Adv-Ev sleep-Inc
'Mommy sleeps alone.'

The diminutive *shoko* is denoting affection instead of size. Notice that the adverbial suffix *bicho* would have to be constructed as a separate adjunct in English and it is attached to the noun, not the verb.

**Derived Nominals**    Verbal roots can be nominalized by adding the suffix *-ti* or past participle suffixes *a, ai*. Zero nominalization is only possible over a closed set of verbs, e.g. *shinan-* 'to think, to remember / mind, thinking'.

On the other hand, adverbial expressions and adjectives may function as nominals and take the corresponding morphology directly without requiring any overt derivation.

### 4.2.2   Adjectives and Quantifiers

Adjectival roots can optionally bear the following morphemes.

- Negative (+Neg:ma), to encode the opposite feature of an adjective.

- Diminutive (+Dim:shoko), deprecatory (+Deprec:isi), intensifier (+Intens:yora).

- Adverbial markers.

- Interrogative clitics (+Int:ki,rin; +Em:bi).

**Derived Adjectives**    Nominal roots can be adjectivized when adding proprietive (+Prop:ya) or privative (+Priv:oma,nto) markers, e.g. *bene-ya* [husband+Prop] → *married (woman)*.

In regards to verbs, participial tense-marked verbs can function as adjectives. Transitive verbs and a closed set of intransitive verbs can take an agentive suffix (+Agtz:mis,yosma,kas) to express *one who always does that action*.

As with nominalization, adverbs take zero morphology to function as adjectives.

### 4.2.3   Verbs

Verbal morphology presents by far the most complex morphotactics in SK, allowing up to 3 prefixes and 18 suffixes following a relatively strict order of precedence, as follows.

- Prefixes related to body parts, providing locative information about the action.

- Plural marker (+Pl:kan).

- Up to 2 valency-changing suffixes, depending whether we are increasing or decreasing transitivity, whether the root is transitive or intransitive, or whether the root is bisyllabic or not.

- Interrogative intensifier (+Intens:shaman), to bring focus on the action in a question.

- Desiderative marker (+Des:kas), to indicate that the clause is desiderative (e.g. *I want to V*).

- Negative marker (+Neg:yama).

- Deictive-directive markers are identical or similar to motion verbs and encode a movement-action sequence, e.g. *V-ina* → 'go up the river and V'.

- Adverbial suffixes, depending whether the verb is marked as plural or not. Here in this slot we find the suffix *bekon* that indicates dual action.

- Habitual marker (+Hab:pao), to encode that the action is done as a habit.

- Tense markers.

- Adjectival (+Dim:shoko; +Deprec:isi; +Intens:yora) and adverbial suffixes.

- Preventive marker (+Prev:na), to express warning, a situation to be prevented.

- Final markers, including participial and reference markers depending whether the verb is finite or non-finite in the clause. Reference markers encode agreement with the agent or subject of the clause (S vs A agreement), whether it is even the same agent and the point in time the action was carried out.

- All second position clitics.

Verbal roots must always bear either a tense marker or at least one final marker. All other suffixes are optional. The following example illustrates how the deictive-directive marker can encode a whole subordinated clause.

Sani betan Tume bewa-kan-*inat*-pacho-ai
Sani and Tume sing-Pl-go.up.the.river-Adv-Inc
'Sani and Tume always sing while going up the river.'

**Derived Verbs** Nominal roots are turned into transitive verbs by adding the causativizer +Caus:n. The auxiliary marker +Aux:ak can be added to nominal, adjectival, and adverbial roots to form transitive verbs.

### 4.2.4 Pronouns

Personal pronouns can bear the following suffixes.

- Ergative (+Erg:n) and absolutive (+Abs:a) case marker. This last one is only used on singular forms and first person plural.

- Chezative (+Chez:iba), dative (+Dat:ki), and comitative (+Com:be) case markers.

- Post-positional suffixes.

- Interrogative and evidential clitics.

The ergative case construction also renders possessive modifiers, with the exception of the first and third singular form, which have a different form with no marking. Possessive pronouns are formed by adding the nominalizer +Nmlz:a to possessive modifiers.

Emphatic pronouns present the marker +S:x when agreeing with the S argument and no marker when agreeing with the A argument. Special attention was taken for the third person singular pronoun *ja-*, which presents a tripartite distribution: *ja-n-bi-x* for S, *ja-n-bi* for A, *ja-bi* for O.

Interrogative pronouns *who, what, where* can be marked for ergative, absolutive, genitive, chezative, and comitative cases. The participant agreement suffix for these pronouns presents a tripartite distribution: +S:x, +O:o, +A:xon for S, O, A agreement, respectively. The following example illustrates the behavior of pronoun *jawerano*: where.

(4) S orientation
   *Jawerano-a-x*-ki  mi-a   jo-a
   where:Abl-S-Int  2-Abs come-Pp2
   'From where did you come?'

(5) O orientation
   *Jawerano-a*-ki  mi-n paranta   be-a
   where:Abl-O-Int 2-Erg banana:Abs bring-Pp2
   'From where did you bring banana?'

(6) A orientation
   *Jawerano-xon*-ki  epa-n   pi-ai
   where-A-Int   uncle-Erg eat-Pp1
   'Where is uncle eating?'

Interrogative pronouns *how, how much, how many* are marked only for participant agreement using an ergative-absolutive distribution (+S:x, +A:xon). In addition, all interrogative pronouns can take interrogative, focus, and emphasis clitics.

Demonstrative roots can function both as pronouns and determiners. In the first case, they bear all proper pronoun morphology. In the second case, they can only bear the Plural nominal marker +Pl:bo.

### 4.2.5 Adverbs

Adverbs can be suffixed with evidential clitics. However, whenever an adverb is modifying an adjective, it takes participant agreement morphology (+S:x,ax,i; +A:xon) in order to agree with the syntactic function of the noun the adjective is modifying.

Adverbial roots can also function as suffixes and be attached to nouns, verbs, adjectives, and even other adverbial roots.

**Derived Adverbs** Adverbs can be derived from demonstrative roots by adding locative case markers depending of the proximity of the entity being referred to. Adjectival roots function as adverbs by receiving the +Advz:n morpheme. Nouns and quantifier roots take the locative case marker +Loc:ki in order to form adverbs.

### 4.3 Postpositions

There are only 20 postpositional roots in SK, all of them can take second position clitics. In the same fashion as adverbial roots, postpositional roots can also function as suffixes. Adverbial roots can function as postpositions by taking the locative marker sequence +Loc: ain-ko.

### 4.3.1 Conjunctions

All conjunction roots take participant agreement markers (+S:x, +A:xon), except coordinating conjunctions *betan* (and) and *itan* (and, or). These markers encode inter or intra-clausal participant agreement, often used as discourse discontinuity flags.

Subordinating conjunctions can take the following morphemes.

- Locative, ablative, and similitive (+Siml:ska) case markers.

- Completive aspect markers, also found as participials in verbs at the *final* slot.

- Reference agreement mark +P:ke, to encode discourse continuity.

- Second position clitics.

In the following example, we analyze the behavior of the conjunction root *ja*.

(7) *Ja-tian* jawen bene ka-a ik-á
    that-Temp Pos3 husband:Abs go-Pp2 be-Pp2

    iki jato onan-ma-i ...
    AUX 3p:Abs know-Caus-SSSI ...

    'By that moment her husband had gone to teach them (i.e. the Shipibo men) ...'

(8) Jo-xon jis-á-ronki ik-á iki
    come-PSSA notice-Pp2-Hsy be-Pp2 AUX

    Inka Ainbo wini wini-i.
    Inka woman:Abs cry cry-SSSI

    'When (he) returned, he saw the Inka Woman crying and crying.'

(9) *Ja-tian* jawen bene-n raté-xon
    3-Temp Pos3 husband-Erg scare:Mid-PSSA

    yokat-a iki: "Jawe-kopí-ki mi-a wini-ai?"
    ask-Pp2 AUX why-Int 2-Abs cry-Inc

    "Then her husband got scared and asked (her): 'Why are you crying?'"

While the first instance of *jatian* in (9) coincides with the introduction in subject function of the male Inka and hence with a change of subject, the second instance in (11) does not. In fact, the subjects in (10) and (11) have the same referent, but *jatian* is used to indicate a switch from narrative to direct quote in the chain. Note that in (11) the subject 'her husband' is overtly stated so that the hearer does not misinterpret *jatian* as indicating a change in subject.

## 4.4 Limitations

The analyzer processes token by token without considering context, restricting it from discarding hypothesis based on fairly rigid constructions, e.g. future tense with auxiliary verbs, modal verbs, nominal compounds, among others.

There exist a group of morphemes that present multiple possible functions in the same position of the construction template. Hence, they can be mapped to more than one morphological tag. Consider the case suffix *-n* in the following example. The square brackets indicate that even though *-n* is attached to *nonti*, it acts as a phrase suffix that modifies the whole phrase (*you canoe*).

E-n [ mi-n nonti]-n yomera-i ka-ai
1-Erg 2-Gen canoe-Ins get.fish-SSSS go-Inc
"I am going to fish with your canoe."

In this case, the analyzer outputs all possible tag combinations, such as +Erg:ergativo, +Inst:intrumental, +Gen:genitive, +Intrss:interessive, and +All:allative. Other suffixes with this kind of behavior are completive aspect suffixes and past tense suffixes in verbs. Disambiguation of these morphemes requires knowledge of the syntactic function of the word in the clause. Such sentence level disambiguation is out of the scope of the analyzer.

## 5  Evaluation

We evaluate the robustness of our analyzer by testing the coverage of word forms. A coverage per type of 94.99% was achieved for the training data (annotated corpus + thesaurus). A closer look into the remaining non-recognized types revealed that in all cases they contain an already covered root or affix but with different diacritization. This is to be expected since the only diacritization rules existent for SHK were proposed recently by Valenzuela (2003) and the text the annotated data was based in was written way before the proposal of the diacritization rules.

Table 3 shows type and token coverage over raw text not used during development. These corpora span several domains such as the bible, educational material, legal domain, and folk tales. This last domain—same as the domain of the annotated corpus—has the highest coverage.

As expected, the lowest coverage is obtained over the legal domain, a specialized domain with complex grammatical constructions and specialized vocabulary. For example, legal documents

|  | Number of Words | | Coverage (%) | |
| --- | --- | --- | --- | --- |
| Subset | Tokens | Types | Tokens | Types |
| Bible - New Testament | 210,828 | 20,504 | 79.11 | 49.49 |
| Elementary School Books | 31,127 | 4,395 | 76.59 | 45.12 |
| Kindergarten Text Material | 15,912 | 2,581 | 76.90 | 55.29 |
| Constitution of Peru | 12,319 | 2,645 | 70.83 | 40.57 |
| Folk tales | 10,934 | 2,737 | 94.38 | 85.42 |
| Total | 281,120 | 28,133 | 78.93 | 47.12 |

Table 3: Coverage on corpora from different domains of raw corpora.

| Error type | Count |
| --- | --- |
| Alternative spelling | 43 |
| Proper nouns | 20 |
| Common nouns | 4 |
| Other OOV | 25 |
| Foreign word | 8 |

Table 4: Error analysis of the 100 most frequent unanalyzed word types in raw corpora.

must be precise about semantic roles of the participants, information partially encoded through morphology in SK.

In contrast, educational material for kindergarten level presents the second highest coverage, quite possibly because only basic grammatical constructions are used at this level of education.

**Error Analysis:** We further analyze the unrecognized words in the raw corpora. We manually categorize the 100 most frequent unrecognized word types, as shown in Table 4. It can be noted that the most common error is due to alternative spelling of the final word form, mostly due to the absence—or presence—of diacritics or due to the presence of an unknown allomorph. Most of the errors of this kind can be traced back to tokens in the Bible domain. The Bible was translated to SK in the 17th century and it has remained almost intact since then. Hence, some constructions are considered nowadays ungrammatical (e.g. a verb must always carry either a participant agreement suffix or a tense suffix) or some suffixes are obsolete (e.g. the n-form +Erg:*sen*; the infinitive form +Inf:*ati*).

Furthermore, the high presence of OOV words other than nouns or proper nouns is an indicative that the root lexicon upon the analyzer is based is still limited and far more entries are needed.

## 6 Conclusion and Future Work

We presented a robust and fairly complete (in morphotactics, not in lexicon) finite-state morphological analyzer for Shipibo-Konibo, a low-resourced native language from Peru. The analyzer is capable of performing morphological segmentation and categorization, as well as part-of-speech tagging of the root and the whole final token.

Experiments over corpora from different domains show promising coverage given the limited root lexicon available. We performed a thorough analysis of errors over unrecognized words, finding that our analyzer cannot recognize certain obsolete constructions and spellings found in Biblical text, which was written centuries ago. However, for modern day Shipibo-Konibo in non-specialized domains (e.g. legal domain) the tool is quite robust and covers production rules for all word categories.

The work presented in this paper is part of a greater effort to provide the research community with basic language tools that would aid in the construction of treebanks. Future paths considered include the mapping of morphological tags into morphological features defined in Universal Dependencies [3], sentence-level tag disambiguation and parsing, among others.

## Acknowledgments

The work was partially supported by the grant 15-10472S of the Czech Science Foundation (GAČR). The authors would like to thank GR-PIAA Research Lab at the Pontifical Catholic University of Peru for kindly providing the annotated corpus, dictionaries, and raw corpora used in the experiments of this paper.

[3]`http://universaldependencies.org/u/feat/index.html`

# References

Sullón Acosta, Karina Natalia, Edinson Huamancayo Curi, Mabel Mori Clement, and Vidal Carbajal Solis. 2013. Documento nacional de lenguas originarias del Perú.

Carlo Alva and Arturo Oncevay-Marcos. 2017. Spellchecking based on syllabification and character-level graphs for a peruvian agglutinative language. In *Proceedings of the First Workshop on Subword and Character Level Models in NLP*, pages 109–116.

Roberto Zariquiey Biondi. 2012. Ditransitive constructions in Kashibo-Kakataibo and the non-distinguishable objects analysis. *Studies in Language. International Journal sponsored by the Foundation "Foundations of Language"*, 36(4):882–905.

David William Fleck. 2013. *Panoan languages and linguistics. (Anthropological papers of the American Museum of Natural History, no. 99)*. American Museum of Natural History.

Ana-Paula Galarreta, Andrés Melgar, and Arturo Oncevay-Marcos. 2017. Corpus creation and initial SMT experiments between Spanish and Shipibo-Konibo. In *Proceedings of RANLP*.

Mans Hulden. 2009. Foma: a finite-state compiler and library. In *Proceedings of the 12th Conference of the European Chapter of the Association for Computational Linguistics: Demonstrations Session*, pages 29–32. Association for Computational Linguistics.

Rodolfo Mercado-Gonzales, José Pereira-Noriega, Marco Antonio Sobrevilla Cabezudo, and Arturo Oncevay-Marcos. 2018. Chanot: An intelligent annotation tool for indigenous and highly agglutinative languages in Peru. In *LREC*.

Joakim Nivre, Marie-Catherine de Marneffe, Filip Ginter, Yoav Goldberg, Jan Hajič, Christopher Manning, Ryan McDonald, Slav Petrov, Sampo Pyysalo, Natalia Silveira, Reut Tsarfaty, and Daniel Zeman. 2016. Universal Dependencies v1: A multilingual treebank collection. In *Proceedings of the 10th International Conference on Language Resources and Evaluation (LREC 2016)*, pages 1659–1666, Portorož, Slovenia. European Language Resources Association.

José Pereira-Noriega, Rodolfo Mercado-Gonzales, Andrés Melgar, Marco Sobrevilla-Cabezudo, and Arturo Oncevay-Marcos. 2017. Ship-lemmatagger: Building an NLP toolkit for a peruvian native language. In *International Conference on Text, Speech, and Dialogue*, pages 473–481. Springer.

Annette Rios. 2010. Applying finite-state techniques to a native American language: Quechua. *Institut für Computerlinguistik, Universität Zürich*.

Annette Rios. 2016. A basic language technology toolkit for Quechua.

Diego Maguiño Valencia, Arturo Oncevay-Marcos, and Marco Antonio Sobrevilla Cabezudo. 2018. Wordnet-shp: Towards the building of a lexical database for a peruvian minority language. In *LREC*.

Pilar Valenzuela. 2003. *Transitivity in shipibo-konibo grammar*. Ph.D. thesis, University of Oregon.

Rodolfo Zevallos and Luis Camacho. 2018. Siminchik: A speech corpus for preservation of southern Quechua. In *Proceedings of the Eleventh International Conference on Language Resources and Evaluation (LREC 2018)*, Paris, France. European Language Resources Association (ELRA).

# An Arabic Morphological Analyzer and Generator with Copious Features

**Dima Taji, Salam Khalifa, Ossama Obeid, Fadhl Eryani, and Nizar Habash**
Computational Approaches to Modeling Languages Lab
New York University Abu Dhabi
{dima.taji, salamkhalifa, oobeid, fadhl.eryani, nizar.habash}@nyu.edu

## Abstract

We introduce CALIMA$_{Star}$, a very rich Arabic morphological analyzer and generator that provides functional and form-based morphological features as well as built-in tokenization, phonological representation, lexical rationality and much more. This tool includes a fast engine that can be easily integrated into other systems, as well as an easy-to-use API and a web interface. CALIMA$_{Star}$ also supports morphological reinflection. We evaluate CALIMA$_{Star}$ against four commonly used analyzers for Arabic in terms of speed and morphological content.

## 1 Introduction

Work on Modern Standard Arabic (MSA) morphological modeling has been ongoing for the past thirty years resulting in many resources with high degrees of accuracy for analysis, generation, and tokenization (Beesley et al., 1989; Al-Sughaiyer and Al-Kharashi, 2004; Habash, 2010; Pasha et al., 2014; Abdelali et al., 2016). These previous efforts addressed many of the important challenges of Arabic morphology such as its high degree of ambiguity resulting from optional diacritization and templatic morphemes. However, while there are several commonly used systems for Arabic morphology, we observe that there are still some unresolved challenges.

First, some aspects of Arabic's rich morphology are not fully or consistently modeled. Examples include the discrepancy between form and function (in gender, number, case and state) as well as the rationality feature. The commonly used Penn Arabic Treebank (PATB) (Maamouri et al., 2004) and Buckwalter Arabic Morphological Analyzer (BAMA) (Buckwalter, 2002) do not model nominal functional features or rationality. Some previous attempts did not cover all these phenomena or focused on limited data sets (Smrž, 2007; Alkuhlani and Habash, 2011).

Second, the different existing tools do not all provide the same kind of information, which often led researchers to improvise extensions to accommodate their downstream task needs. One example is the phonological representation mappings that Biadsy et al. (2009) devised on top of the MADA disambiguation system (Habash et al., 2009) instead of using Elixir-FM (Smrž, 2007), which already included phonology. This is partially because Elixir-FM was not connected to a disambiguation system. Another example is the work by Habash et al. (2009) to provide generation capability on top of the BAMA (Buckwalter, 2002) algorithm and databases because BAMA, which was used to annotate the PATB, was analysis focused, unlike the finite-state solutions to Arabic morphology (Beesley et al., 1989).

Third, many of the existing tools have different use requirements (operating system, programming language, etc.), and some have no easy-to-use APIs.

In this paper, we introduce CALIMA$_{Star}$,[1] a very rich Arabic morphological analyzer and generator that includes functional features, built-in tokenization, phonological representation, and numerous other features. CALIMA$_{Star}$ comes with a fast engine that can be easily integrated into other systems, and an easy-to-use web interface. CALIMA$_{Star}$ also supports morphological reinflection. While in this paper we focus on MSA only for the database discussion, the engine itself is independent of the variant choice. CALIMA$_{Star}$ will be made publicly available as part of a large suite of tools to support research on Arabic natural language processing (NLP).[2]

---

[1] In Arabic, كَلِمَة /kalima/ means 'word'. We follow and extend the naming convention from Habash et al. (2012) who developed CALIMA$_{EGY}$, and Khalifa et al. (2017) who developed CALIMA$_{GLF}$. The *Star* designation in CALIMA$_{Star}$ is intended to eventually represent all Arabic variants (MSA and dialects), and all possible features.

[2] `http://resources.camel-lab.com/`.



*Proceedings of the 15th SIGMORPHON Workshop on Computational Research in Phonetics, Phonology, and Morphology*, pages 140–150
Brussels, Belgium, October 31, 2018. ©2018 The Special Interest Group on Computational Morphology and Phonology
https://doi.org/10.18653/v1/P17

## 2   Related Work

In this section, we discuss previous work on Arabic morphological analysis and generation in terms of (a) algorithms and representations, (b) morphological knowledge, and (c) morphological disambiguation and tokenization. Table 1 compares the features supported by CALIMA$_{Star}$ and a number of analyzers discussed below.

### 2.1   Algorithms and Representations

There are a number of dimensions over which solutions to Arabic morphology modeling have varied (Beesley et al., 1989; Beesley, 1996; Habash and Rambow, 2006; Smrž, 2007; Altantawy et al., 2010, 2011). One important aspect is the degree of explicitness of representing morphological rules and their interactions. Some approaches use very abstract and linguistically rich representations and rules to derive surface forms of the words (Beesley et al., 1989; Beesley, 1996; Habash and Rambow, 2006; Smrž, 2007). Other approaches pre-compile representations of the different components needed by the system: BAMA (Buckwalter, 2002), SAMA (Graff et al., 2009), and ALMORGEANA (ALMOR for short) (Habash, 2007) are examples of such systems. They use a six-table representation consisting of three lexical tables (for prefixes, suffixes, and stems), and three compatibility tables (prefix-suffix, prefix-stem, and stem-suffix). Altantawy et al. (2011) described a method to bridge between these two types of solutions. The type of representation used naturally needs to synchronize with the appropriate algorithms for analysis and generation. CALIMA$_{Star}$ is of the second category (tabulated pre-compiled solutions), and it builds on the popularly used BAMA, SAMA, and ALMOR morphological analyzers.

### 2.2   Morphological Knowledge

Previous efforts show a wide range for the depth that morphological analyzers can produce. Some efforts include very shallow analyses such as in the Temple Translator's Workstation Project (Vanni and Zajac, 1996) which only provided English glossing. Others include a range of form-based features, functional features, and morpheme forms, in addition to lexical features (Buckwalter, 2002; Smrž, 2007; Boudlal et al., 2010; Alkuhlani and Habash, 2011; Boudchiche et al., 2017).

Alkuhlani and Habash (2011) extended part of the PATB to include functional gender and number, and rationality, but did not cover the entire database used by BAMA or SAMA. ElixirFM (Smrž, 2007) includes functional gender and number, as well as full case and state modeling, but not rationality. ElixirFM, MAGEAD (Altantawy et al., 2010; Habash and Rambow, 2006) and AlKhalil Morpho Sys (Boudlal et al., 2010; Boudchiche et al., 2017) include roots, with varying degrees of accuracy. ElixirFM includes phonological forms; but ALMOR does not. However, Biadsy et al. (2009) presented orthography-to-phonology rules that can be used on automatically diacritized text to generate pronunciation dictionaries.

Our goal is to make all these features be built-in as part of our CALIMA$_{Star}$ databases, and to fill in any gaps that were left by other efforts.

### 2.3   Analysis, Disambiguation and Tokenization

We distinguish between analysis and disambiguation: analysis refers to identifying all of the different readings (analyses) of a word out of context; while disambiguation is about identifying the specific analysis in context. Tokenization is the process of segmenting a word into different units for downstream applications. There are many possible tokenization *schemes* and techniques to apply them (Habash and Sadat, 2006). The tokenized form of a word varies depending on the specific analysis of the word. Systems such as MADA (Habash et al., 2009), AMIRA (Diab et al., 2004), and MADAMIRA (Pasha et al., 2014) handle disambiguation and tokenization differently. Both MADA and MADAMIRA disambiguate the analyses that are produced by a morphological analyzer. The chosen analyses are then used to tokenize the words using morphological regeneration. AMIRA, on the other hand, has a different two step process in which a toeknization component is followed by part-of-speech (POS) tagging.

The FARASA system (Abdelali et al., 2016) relies on probabilistic models of stems, prefixes, and suffixes, instead of using context information to produce high tokenization accuracy. YAMAMA (Khalifa et al., 2016) is a MADAMIRA-like (analysis/disambiguation) system that disambiguates using a maximum likelihood model inspired by FARASA.

CALIMA$_{Star}$ is primarily an out-of-context

| | BAMA | SAMA | ALMOR | MAGEAD | ElixirFM | AlKhalil | CALIMA$_{Star}$ |
|---|---|---|---|---|---|---|---|
| **Functional Gender and Number** | ✗ | ✗ | ✗ | partial | partial | partial | ✓ |
| **Case and State Modeling** | partial | partial | partial | ✓ | ✓ | partial | ✓ |
| **Rationality** | ✗ | ✗ | ✗ | ✗ | ✗ | ✗ | ✓ |
| **Roots and Patterns** | ✗ | ✗ | ✗ | ✓ | ✓ | ✓ | ✓ |
| **Phonological Representation** | ✗ | ✗ | ✗ | ✓ | ✓ | ✗ | ✓ |
| **Number of Tokenization Schemes** | 1 | 1 | 1 | 1 | 1 | 1 | 4 |
| **Number of POS Tag Sets** | 1 | 1 | 2 | 1 | 1 | 1 | 4 |
| **Out-of-Context Probabilities** | ✗ | ✗ | ✗ | ✗ | ✗ | ✗ | ✓ |
| **Functionalities** | Analysis | Analysis | Analysis | Analysis Generation | *Resolution Inflection Derivation Lookup* | Analysis | Analysis Generation Reinfletion |

Table 1: A comparison of the different features in a number of morphological tools. A ✓ denotes a feature that is present in the system, while an ✗ denotes a feature that is not. ElixirFM uses different terminology to denote the analysis, generation, and reinflection functionalities.

analysis and generation system. Its database includes pre-compiled out-of-context probabilities for POS and lemmas. In Section 6, we report on how well these probability features do in terms of disambiguation. CALIMA$_{Star}$ also produces tokenizations in different schemes from features that are pre-compiled in its database.

## 3 Baseline Arabic Morphology: Algorithm and Database

In this section, we describe the basic database and algorithm used in a number of morphological analyzers, all following the work of Buckwalter (2002), including our system CALIMA$_{Star}$.

### 3.1 Database Structure

The database we use has six tables. Three are lexicon tables for prefixes, suffixes, and stems. Each lexicon table entry has three columns: a lookup form, a compatibility category to control behavior and agreement, and a list of feature-value pairs. The lookup form is an orthographically normalized surface form, which can appear with multiple categories and feature-value pairs. The other three tables are compatibility tables: prefix-suffix, prefix-stem, and stem-suffix. These tables are used to ensure that any analysis that is produced by the system contains a prefix, a stem, and a suffix that are compatible with each other. This means, for example, that a nominal prefix will not be combined with a verbal stem. The compatibility tables are based on the compatibility categories appearing in the lexicon tables.

The differences among the many analyzers based on this model are mostly in features. BAMA and SAMA have four features: the diacritized sur-

face form, the lemma, the Buckwalter POS tag, and the English gloss (Buckwalter, 2002; Graff et al., 2009). ALMOR automatically extends these features with 17 others: MADA POS tag (Pasha et al., 2014), four possible proclitics, person, aspect, voice, mood, gender, number, state, case, enclitic, rationality, stem, and stem category. The ALMOR database also includes feature definitions specifying the values each feature can take, and default feature values for every POS tag. CALIMA$_{Star}$ extends on the ALMOR database feature list as will be discussed in Section 4.

### 3.2 Analysis Algorithm

The analyzer follows the algorithm description in Buckwalter (2002). The input of the algorithm is a word. The output is all the possible out-of-context analyses for this word. We match the input word using an orthographically normalized form of it that is consistent with the look up forms in the database. Orthographic normalization is necessary because, according to Habash (2010), the most common spelling errors in Arabic involve Hamzated Alifs and Alif-Maqsura/Ya confusion, affecting 11% of all words (or 4.5 errors per sentence) in the PATB. We normalize by removing diacritics, converting Hamzated Alif occurrences $\hat{A}$, $\check{A}$, $\bar{A}$,[3] to bare Alif $A$, Alif-Maqsura ى $\acute{y}$ to Ya ي $y$, and Ta-Marbuta ة $\hbar$ to Ha ه $h$.

The word is then segmented into all possible prefix-stem-suffix triplets. The segment validity is restricted by the minimum length of stem and the maximum lengths of the prefix and suffix which are inferred from the database, in addition to the

---

[3] Arabic transliteration is presented in the Habash-Soudi-Buckwalter scheme (Habash et al., 2007).

existence of all segments in their respective lexicon tables. Each segmentation triplet is tested for compatibility using the three-way compatibility tables in the database. For each valid triplet combination, the features from the prefix, stem and suffix are merged to produce a single featureset for the word. The merging process involves four operations depending on the feature: (i) concatenation of the Buckwalter POS tag; (ii) concatenation and rewriting of the final diacritized form; (iii) value overwrite for the remaining features, where, first, the suffix features overwrite the stem features, and then the prefix features overwrite all features; and (iv) producing the *source* feature by the analyzer depending on whether the analysis is from the lexicon, a backoff, or a default analysis of punctuation, digits, or foreign words. The result of this process is a unique set of out-of-context analyses for the input word. The first two operations above are used in BAMA and SAMA; and all are used in ALMOR. When no valid analysis is found, a backoff solution suspends the requirement for having a valid stem from the stem table. However, the prefixes and suffixes must still be compatible. We discuss the CALIMA$_{Star}$ algorithm extensions beyond ALMOR in Section 5.

### 3.3 Generation Algorithm

The generation algorithm follows the description of the generation component in ALMOR (Habash, 2007). It minimally expects a lemma and POS as input. The other features are handled in one of two ways. All inflectional features, such as person, gender and number, are considered obligatory, and as such, all their values are generated if no value was specified. Clitics, on the other hand, are considered optional, and are only generated when specified.

For the input lemma and POS, we retrieve all stems in the database. For each stem, the stem categories are then used to retrieve all stem-compatible prefixes and suffixes. Only compatible prefixes and suffixes (as per the prefix-suffix compatibility tables) are used, with the stem, to generate inflected words and corresponding full analyses. The same merging process used in the analysis component is used here also. The input feature-list is used in filtering which prefixes and suffixes to consider. For clitics, this is done before merging, but for inflectional features, this is done after merging.

## 4 CALIMA$_{Star}$ Database

In this section we detail our specific CALIMA$_{Star}$ database extensions to the basic ALMOR database structure presented in Section 3.

### 4.1 Gender and Number Functional Features

Smrž (2007) and Alkuhlani and Habash (2011) pointed out the common discrepancy between the form of some Arabic words and their function. A prime example is the very common *broken plural*[4] — almost 55% of all plurals look like singular words, but are functionally plural (Alkuhlani and Habash, 2011). For example, شرائح *šrAŷH* 'sections, slices, slivers' is the broken plural of the feminine singular word شريحة *šryHħ* 'section, slice, sliver'. ALMOR considers this (functionally feminine and plural) noun, masculine and singular because it has the form of a masculine singular noun. Alkuhlani and Habash (2011) modeled functional gender and number on a portion of the PATB, which is based on BAMA/SAMA. Smrž (2007) and Boudlal et al. (2010) modeled functional gender and number for part of their data.

Our contribution in CALIMA$_{Star}$ is that we extended all lexical databases, which are based on SAMA and ALMOR, with functional gender and number. We built on the work and guidelines by Alkuhlani and Habash (2011). While Alkuhlani and Habash (2011) only annotated the inflected words that appear in the PATB, we wanted to annotate our entire database. To do this properly, we inflected the 31,610 nominal lemmas[5] in the database for gender and number, making sure that each database stem is used at least once. Our dataset contained 77,023 inflected words, which were manually annotated by two annotators for functional gender and number. This effort took 130 hours to complete.

In our database, we renamed ALMOR's *gen* and *num* features as *form_gen* and *form_num*, and used *gen* and *num* as the names for the functional gender and number features, respectively. To operationalize the use of the functional gender and number features in the database, we assigned them the value - when the corresponding functional feature matches the form feature for all inflected forms of the stem. This value is then overwritten by the

---

[4] The 'broken' part of the name refers to the change in the template associated with forming these plurals.

[5] Verbs are regular and have no discrepancy between form and function gender and number.

form feature value coming from the suffix when producing an analysis. If the functional features does not match the form feature, then the functional feature is assigned an explicit value in the database, which can be *masculine* (*m*), or *feminine* (*f*) for gender, and *singular* (*s*), *plural* (*p*), or *dual* (*d*) for number. These explicit values in the stem are not overwritten by the suffix corresponding feature values.

## 4.2 State and Case Features

We follow the functional classification of the Arabic *state* feature into definite, indefinite, or construct values as described and implemented by Smrž (2007). Our contribution here is applying this classification to the latest SAMA/ALMOR database which we use in CALIMA$_{Star}$.

The ALMOR handling of state has two problems. First, the definite state is only assigned by the definite article proclitic +الـ *Al+*. This is linguistically incorrect, as there are nouns that can be definite without the definite article (e.g., directly addressed vocatives such as يا أولاد ادرسوا *yA ÂwlAd AdrswA* 'O children, study'); and the definite article can appear with construct state adjectives in what is called *false idafa* (e.g., الطويل القامة *AlTwyl AlqAmħ* 'The tall of stature'). Second, a number of nominal suffixes are ambiguous but that ambiguity is not represented. For example, the suffix +*u* indicating nominative case can appear with both definite and construct states, but ALMOR only assigns it the construct value. In CALIMA$_{Star}$ we address both of these issues: (i) we do not allow the definite article to assign a state value and relegate state specification to the suffixes completely; and (ii) we ensure all ambiguous suffix lexicon entries are duplicated and assigned explicit state analyses.

Case is properly handled for the most part in ALMOR, except for a few cases where it interacts with state, such as diptotes. Diptotes are nominals whose genitive case marker is the same as their accusative case marker when they are in an indefinite state (Habash, 2010). An example of a diptote is شرائح *šrAŷH* 'sections, slices, slivers'. When it is indefinite, the genitive diacritized form of this word is شَرائِح *šarAŷiHa*. The state feature extension that produces a definite analysis for the word without a definite article morpheme required an extension of the case feature to produce the definite genitive diacritized form شَرائِح *šarAŷiHi*.

## 4.3 Rationality

Rationality (or +Human) is a lexical feature in Arabic that affects noun-adjective and subject-verb agreement. Nouns that are exclusive to humans, such as موظف *mwĎf* 'employee' are considered rational, while others, such as شريحة *šryHħ* 'slice' are considered irrational. Rational nouns take adjectives and verbs that agree with them in gender and number. Irrational nouns, on the other hand, agree with their verbs and adjectives when they are singular, however they take the singular feminine form of a verb or adjective when they are plural, regardless of what the gender of the noun is. The plural word شرائح *šrAŷH* 'slices' is irrational and as such would take the adjective رفيعة *rfyÇħ* 'thin [feminine singular]' instead of رفيعات *rfyÇAt* 'thin [feminine plural]'.

Alkuhlani and Habash (2011) manually annotated a part of PATB for rationality. ALMOR and MAGEAD include a rationality feature, but it was automatically populated and not fully checked. Our contribution in CALIMA$_{Star}$ is fully annotating the SAMA/ALMOR database for rationality. We build on the work of Alkuhlani and Habash (2011), and use their manual annotation guidelines. We manually annotated all the noun and proper noun lemmas in the database (18,120 entries). This effort took approximately 60 hours.

## 4.4 Roots and Patterns

Arabic templatic morphology, or the use of roots and patterns, has been modeled successfully in a number of systems (Beesley et al., 1989; Smrž, 2007). MAGEAD (Habash and Rambow, 2006; Altantawy et al., 2010) made extensive use of the ElixirFM database. However, roots and patterns are not part of the SAMA/ALMOR database that we base our work on.

Our contribution is to fully specify the roots and patterns in the CALIMA$_{Star}$ database. This manual effort started from the MAGEAD and ElixirFM lemma root information when available. The roots are linked to the lemmas directly and specified in the lexicon stem entries. The patterns we include are concrete patterns (Habash and Rambow, 2006) that are generated automatically by subtracting the root from the diacritized stem.

## 4.5 Phonological Representation

The phonological form has been shown to be particularly useful for NLP applications, such as Arabic speech recognition (Biadsy et al., 2009). In MSA, most Arabic letters have a one-to-one mapping to phonemes. However, there are some exceptions. The Arabic definite article +ال Al+ assimilates to the first consonant in the nominal it modifies if this consonant is one of the so-called *Sun Letters* (Habash, 2010). For instance, the phonology of the noun الشَّرائِع *AlšarAŷiHa* is / a sh sh a r aa 2 i 7 a /,[6] as opposed to */ a l sh a r aa 2 i 7 a /, because the letter ش *š* is a Sun Letter. Another exception is the silent Alif in the suffix وا+ +*uwA*, which indicates a masculine plural conjugation in verbs. The phonology of the masculine plural verb كَتَبوا *katabuwA* 'they wrote' is / k a t a b uu /, as opposed to */ k a t a b uu aa /.

This feature does not exist in SAMA or AL-MOR. We extended our database entries with their respective phonological representation through an automatic process comparable to Biadsy et al. (2009). The definite article assimilation is handled through rewrite rules because it involves an interaction between a stem and a prefix.

### 4.6 Tokenization Schemes

Tokenization is important for NLP tasks such as machine translation because it reduces word sparsity (Habash and Sadat, 2006; Zalmout and Habash, 2017b). Many tokenization schemes with different granularities and normalization rules exist, and the selection of tokenization scheme depends on the task on hand.

In MADAMIRA, tokenization happens after analysis and disambiguation through an expensive regeneration process. Our contribution is the insight that since a particular tokenization is completely dependent on the analysis, we can specify the tokenization details in the database entry. This is a tradeoff of a bigger database (space) with a faster tokenization (time). We specifically add four tokenization schemes D1, D2, D3 and ATB (Habash, 2010), in both normalized and unnormalized forms. We refer to the normalized schemes as tokenization, and to the unnormalized schemes as segmentation. A normalized ATB tokenization for the word كتبوها *ktbwhA* 'they wrote it' is كتبوا+ها *ktbwA+hA* 'they_wrote +it', whereas an unnormalized ATB tokenization (segmentation) for the same word would be كتبو+ها *ktbw+hA*. In the lex-

icon, the entry for the suffix in this analysis has a different feature for each of these schemes.

We extended our database with the tokenization features in a semi-automated process. For each scheme, we manually determined the list of affixes that would be detached. For each of these affixes, we generated the tokenized form. Stems do not have any parts to detach, but some stems have to be normalized for some tokenization schemes. We used our CALIMA$_{Star}$ generator to automatically get the normalized forms of these stems. The resulting tokenizations of a word are the concatenation of the tokenizations of the prefix, stem, and suffix of the word's analysis.

### 4.7 Multiple POS Tag Sets

There are many Arabic POS tag sets used by different researchers and in different tools, e.g., Buckwalter (Buckwalter, 2002), MADA (Pasha et al., 2014), Columbia Arabic Treebank (CATiB) (Habash and Roth, 2009), CATiBex (Marton et al., 2013), Universal Dependencies (UD) (Nivre et al., 2016), and Kulick (Kulick et al., 2006). It is desirable to link these POS tag sets to each other. CALIMA$_{Star}$ currently supports four POS tag sets: the Buckwalter POS tag set, and the MADA POS tag set, both of which are part of the AL-MOR database, as well as the CATiB and UD POS tag sets. We chose to start our extension with the CATiB and UD POS tag sets for their importance to the work on Arabic dependency parsing. This goal steered us to output the CATiB and UD POS tags following the ATB tokenization, which is the commonly used tokenization format in treebanking and parsing. This extension was an automatic mapping from both the Buckwalter and MADA POS tag sets. We plan to add more POS tag sets to our database in the future.

### 4.8 Lemma and POS Probability

Inspired by Khalifa et al. (2016) who used lemma and POS tag probabilities for out-of-context disambiguation, we added three different probability scores for lemma, POS (MADA POS) and joint lemma-POS, for each stem entry in the database. The scores were generated from the *train* set (Diab et al., 2013) of the PATB. We used the SRILM toolkit (Stolcke, 2002) to generate the scores with no smoothing. In Section 6, we show that these scores can be used to select the correct POS tag and lemma out of context with a high accuracy.

---

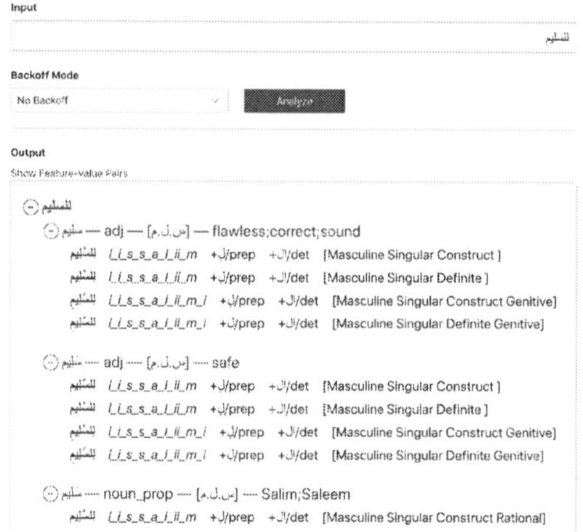

(a) The analysis output of the word للسلم *llslym* grouped by lemma and POS.

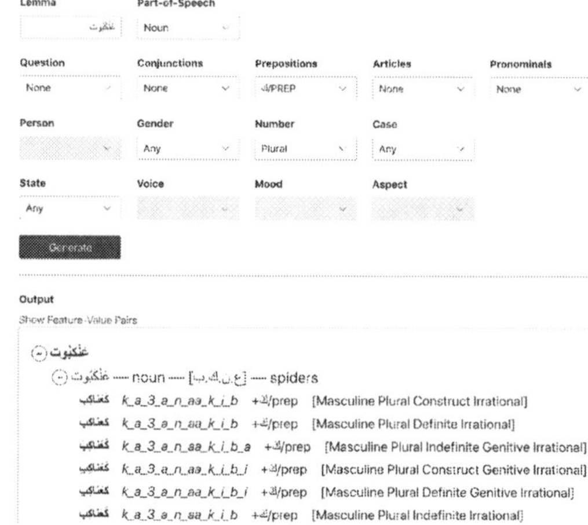

(b) The generation output for the nominal lemma عَنكَبوت *ςanokabuwt* 'spider' as plural with the preposition كَ *ka* 'as'.

Figure 1: A screen capture of the CALIMA$_{Star}$ analyzer and generator interfaces.

## 5   CALIMA$_{Star}$ Engine

The CALIMA$_{Star}$ engine is a new implementation of the analysis and generation algorithms described in Section 3 with some extensions. It uses the database described in Section 4.

**CALIMA$_{Star}$ API**   The CALIMA$_{Star}$ engine is implemented in Python. We provide a command-line tool interface as well as an API. CALIMA$_{Star}$ is a part of a collection of Arabic NLP tools we plan to release.

**Analysis and Generation Extensions**   All of the algorithmic extensions in the CALIMA$_{Star}$ engine are minor, and intended to accommodate the additional features in the database. Examples include the special handling of functional gender and number as discussed in Section 4.1, the concatenation of prefix, stem and suffix features for added POS tags and tokenization schemes. The concatenation of the CAPHI string and the pattern requires rewrite rules because of prefix-stem interactions.

**Reinflection**   Inspired by the SIGMORPHON 2016 Shared Task on morphological reinflection (Cotterell et al., 2016), we provide a reinflection functionality in the CALIMA$_{Star}$ API, which makes use of the existing analysis and generation components. The input to the CALIMA$_{Star}$ reinflector is an already inflected word and a desired set of feature-value changes. The system analyzes the word, adjusts its features given the input

feature-value pairs, and generates the reinflected form(s). The reinflector is also used as a backoff mode for the generator when the input lemma is not recognized.

**Web Interface**   We created a web interface for the CALIMA$_{Star}$ analyzer and generator – see Figures 1 (a) and (b), respectively. The analyzer interface expects an input word and a selected backoff mode. Options for backoff include no backoff, proper-noun backoff, or any POS backoff. The generator interface minimally expects a lemma and POS for input; feature values can be specified as needed. The generator interface changes which features are allowed to select values for depending on the input POS. For example, in Figure 1 (b), the verbal features, person, voice, mood and aspect, are disabled because the input POS is a noun. There are two output modes for both analyzer and generator interfaces. The first output mode is a user-friendly display of words grouped by lemma, POS tag, root and English gloss. For each inflected word, the interface shows its diacritization, phonology, clitics, and inflectional features, in a human-readable form. This output mode is what Figures 1 (a) and (b) show. The second mode presents the output in a feature-value pair format more suitable for debugging and programming interfaces.

The engine and web interface are linked from `http://resources.camel-lab.com/`.

## 6 Evaluation

In this section we validate our system and evaluate it against other systems in terms of speed and coverage.

### 6.1 Internal Validation

We ran a number of tests to validate our database extensions. All these tests were run on the PATB *dev* set (Diab et al., 2013) from PATB parts 1, 2 and 3, except where indicated.

**Analysis** This test aimed to validate that we are producing all the analyses that are produced by ALMOR. We ran the tokens in the dataset through ALMOR and CALIMA$_{Star}$, and verified that every analysis produced by ALMOR is also produced by CALIMA$_{Star}$. CALIMA$_{Star}$ produced more analyses on average than ALMOR. And naturally, the CALIMA$_{Star}$ analyses were richer than the ALMOR analyses.

**Generation** Since we do not have a manually annotated version of this data set with all of our extensions, we relied on automatic matching of CALIMA$_{Star}$ analyses against the ALMOR analyses used to train and evaluate MADAMIRA (Pasha et al., 2014).[7] This matching allowed us to extend the ALMOR analyses with functional gender and number features. We used the lemma and extended features as input to the CALIMA$_{Star}$ generation component. CALIMA$_{Star}$ produced the full diacritized word in all cases.

**Reinflection** Validating the reinflection component required us to have a source inflected word, and a target inflected word. We grouped the extended ALMOR analyses from the Generation test above by lemma and POS tag, and generated all possible pairs of words that share a lemma and POS tag. For each pair, we used the features of the first word to reinflect the second word, and vice versa. Our system produced the correct diacritized word in all cases.

**Functional Gender and Number Analysis** This test aimed to validate that the database extension for functional gender and number was consistent with the manual annotation. For this test, we analyzed every word that was manually annotated for functional gender and number, and con-

firmed that the analyzer is producing an analysis with the expected functional feature values. Our system produced the expected values in all cases.

**Tokenization** We tested our D3 tokenization extensions, as it is the most complex tokenization scheme in our database. We ran our test set in MADAMIRA to produce the D3 tokenization. We then compared the tokenization produced by MADAMIRA to the tokenization produced by CALIMA$_{Star}$ for the analysis that is equivalent to MADAMIRA's top analysis (modulo our extensions). We matched MADAMIRA's diacritized tokenization in 99.5% of the cases, and we matched the undiacritized tokenization in 99.9% of the cases. The only undiacritized mismatches are the result of MADAMIRA tokenization errors in words such as بِحَيْثُ *bHyθ* 'with/by + where; whereby', which MADAMIRA tokenizes as بِ +حَيْثُ *b+ bHyθ* instead of بِ+ حيث *b+ Hyθ*. This validation test also brought to light some minor cases which we intend to fix in future releases of the database.

**Lemma and POS Probability** We carried out preliminary experiments on the use of the different probability scores (Section 4.8) for out-of-context POS and lemma selection. We found that the top-one choice among the CALIMA$_{Star}$ analyses ranked using the joint lemma-POS score preformed the highest with 92%, 90% and 88% accuracy in terms of POS, lemma, and POS+lemma, respectively. The results are comparable to the maximum likelihood disambiguation baseline reported by Zalmout and Habash (2017a), which supports the use of morphological analyzers as a backbone for the different NLP task.

### 6.2 Comparison with other Systems

We compare CALIMA$_{Star}$ to four other morphological analyzers: AraMorph,[8] SAMA 3.1 (Graff et al., 2009), ALMOR and MADAMIRA,[9] in terms of coverage (out-of-vocabulary (OOV) rate and analyses per word) and speed performance (words, analyses, and features per second). We ran the experiments on one million words from the Arabic Gigaword corpus (Parker et al., 2011). The results of the comparison are in Table 2.

---

[7]The ALMOR analyses were themselves automatically matched against the gold PATB annotations in a similar manner to Habash and Rambow (2005).

[8]We used the AraMorph 1.2.1 version, and implementation of BAMA 1.2 that was optimized by Jon Dehdari from SourceForge https://sourceforge.net/projects/aramorph/files/aramorph/1.2.1/.

[9]We ran MADAMIRA in 'analyze only' mode.

| System | | | Coverage | | Speed | | |
|---|---|---|---|---|---|---|---|
| **Engine** | **Database** | **Features #** | **OOV %** | $\frac{Analysis}{Word}$ | $\frac{Word}{Second}$ | $\frac{Analysis}{Second}$ | $\frac{Feature}{Second}$ |
| **AraMorph** | AraMorph | 4 | 1.7 | 2.1 | 43.5K | 93K | 372K |
| **SAMA** | SAMA | 4 | 1.4 | 10.2 | 2.3K | 24K | 96K |
| **ALMOR** | ALMOR | 22 | 1.4 | 10.7 | 1.1K | 12K | 269K |
| **MADAMIRA** | ALMOR | 22 | 1.6 | 10.7 | 6.8K | 73K | 1,742K |
| **CALIMA**$_{Star}$ | ALMOR | 22 | 1.3 | 10.7 | 8.2K | 88K | 1,938K |
| **CALIMA**$_{Star}$ | CALIMA$_{Star}$ | 40 | 1.3 | 18.9 | 5.4K | 102K | 4,094K |

Table 2: A comparison of five systems, AraMorph, SAMA, ALMOR, MADAMIRA and CALIMA$_{Star}$, in terms of coverage (OOV and analyses per word) and speed (word, analyses, features per second).

The first three columns of Table 2 specify the systems, the databases, and the number of features in the databases. AraMorph was run on the AraMorph database, and SAMA was run on the SAMA database. Both of these contain four features: the diacritization, Buckwalter POS tag, lemma, and English gloss. ALMOR and MADAMIRA both use the ALMOR database, which produces 22 features: the same four features of AraMorph/SAMA in addition to the MADA POS tag, four proclitic features, person, aspect, voice, mood, gender, number, state, case, enclitic, rationality, source, stem, and stem category. CALIMA$_{Star}$ was run on the CALIMA$_{Star}$ database described in Section 4, which has 40 features: the 22 ALMOR features in addition to functional gender and number, CAPHI, root, pattern, tokenization and segmentation in four schemes (D1, D2, D3, and ATB), CATiB and UD POS tags, and POS, lemma, and joint lemma-POS probability scores. We also ran the CALIMA$_{Star}$ engine with the ALMOR database as a comparison point.

**Coverage** The OOV rates of the different analyzers are generally close to each other. The differences stem from two sources. First, AraMorph's database is an older version of SAMA/ALMOR/CALIMA$_{Star}$ with less lemmas (~38K vs ~40K lemmas). And secondly, different engines handle numbers, foreign words, and digits in different ways, with the CALIMA$_{Star}$ engine outperforming all others.

The number of analyses per word is strongly connected to the database being used. AraMorph has less coverage, in terms of affixes and stems, and that is why it produces a smaller number of analyses per word. ALMOR and MADAMIRA both use the same database, thus producing the same number of analyses per word. CALIMA$_{Star}$ extends the suffix lexicon to fully cover the state and case analyses resulting in the largest number of analyses per word.

**Speed** The last three columns of Table 2 compare the speed of the systems, in terms of words per second, analyses per second, and features per second. In terms of words per second, AraMorph is the fastest system. Comparing the ALMOR, MADAMIRA and CALIMA$_{Star}$ engines using the same database (ALMOR), CALIMA$_{Star}$ is the fastest of the three. However, using the larger CALIMA$_{Star}$ database slows the CALIMA$_{Star}$ engine down to second place in this three-way comparison. That said, CALIMA$_{Star}$ produces more analyses per seconds and features per second than all the other systems.

## 7 Conclusion and Future Work

CALIMA$_{Star}$ is an Arabic analyzer and generator that supports a large number of morphological features. It has as an API and a web interface, and will be released publicly. Compared with four commonly used Arabic analyzers, CALIMA$_{Star}$ has better coverage and is very competitive speed-wise.

In the future, we will extend our database in terms of lexical entries, features, and dialects. We will also integrate our system into existing disambiguators and parsers (Pasha et al., 2014; Shahrour et al., 2016; Zalmout and Habash, 2017a). Finally, we plan on conducting task-based evaluations where we can assess the added value of some of the new features.

**Acknowledgments** We thank the annotators who helped with gender, number and rationality features: Linda Alamir-Salloum and Sara Hassan.

**References**

Ahmed Abdelali, Kareem Darwish, Nadir Durrani, and Hamdy Mubarak. 2016. Farasa: A fast and furious segmenter for Arabic. In *Proceedings of the 2016 Conference of the North American Chapter of the Association for Computational Linguistics: Demonstrations*, pages 11–16, San Diego, California.

Imad A. Al-Sughaiyer and Ibrahim A. Al-Kharashi. 2004. Arabic morphological analysis techniques: A comprehensive survey. *Journal of the American Society for Information Science and Technology*, 55(3):189–213.

Sarah Alkuhlani and Nizar Habash. 2011. A Corpus for Modeling Morpho-Syntactic Agreement in Arabic: Gender, Number and Rationality. In *Proceedings of the 49th Annual Meeting of the Association for Computational Linguistics (ACL'11)*, Portland, Oregon, USA.

Mohamed Altantawy, Nizar Habash, and Owen Rambow. 2011. Fast Yet Rich Morphological Analysis. In *Proceedings of the 9th International Workshop on Finite-State Methods and Natural Language Processing (FSMNLP 2011)*, Blois, France.

Mohamed Altantawy, Nizar Habash, Owen Rambow, and Ibrahim Saleh. 2010. Morphological Analysis and Generation of Arabic Nouns: A Morphemic Functional Approach. In *Proceedings of the seventh International Conference on Language Resources and Evaluation (LREC)*, Valletta, Malta.

Kenneth Beesley, Tim Buckwalter, and Stuart Newton. 1989. Two-Level Finite-State Analysis of Arabic Morphology. In *Proceedings of the Seminar on Bilingual Computing in Arabic and English*.

Kenneth R. Beesley. 1996. Arabic finite-state morphological analysis and generation. In *Proceedings of COLING-96, the 16th International Conference on Computational Linguistics*, Copenhagen.

Fadi Biadsy, Nizar Habash, and Julia Hirschberg. 2009. Improving the Arabic Pronunciation Dictionary for Phone and Word Recognition with Linguistically-Based Pronunciation Rules. In *Proceedings of Human Language Technologies: The 2009 Annual Conference of the North American Chapter of the Association for Computational Linguistics*, pages 397–405, Boulder, Colorado.

Mohamed Boudchiche, Azzeddine Mazroui, Mohamed Ould Abdallahi Ould Bebah, Abdelhak Lakhouaja, and Abderrahim Boudlal. 2017. AlKhalil Morpho Sys 2: A robust Arabic morpho-syntactic analyzer. *Journal of King Saud University-Computer and Information Sciences*, 29(2):141–146.

Abderrahim Boudlal, Abdelhak Lakhouaja, Azzeddine Mazroui, Abdelouafi Meziane, MOAO Bebah, and M Shoul. 2010. Alkhalil Morpho Sys1: A morphosyntactic analysis system for Arabic texts. In *International Arab conference on information technology*, pages 1–6. Benghazi Libya.

Tim Buckwalter. 2002. Buckwalter Arabic Morphological Analyzer Version 1.0. Linguistic Data Consortium, University of Pennsylvania, 2002. LDC Catalog No.: LDC2002L49.

Ryan Cotterell, Christo Kirov, John Sylak-Glassman, David Yarowsky, Jason Eisner, and Mans Hulden. 2016. The SIGMORPHON 2016 shared task on morphological reinflection. In *Proceedings of the 14th SIGMORPHON Workshop on Computational Research in Phonetics, Phonology, and Morphology*, pages 10–22.

Mona Diab, Nizar Habash, Owen Rambow, and Ryan Roth. 2013. LDC Arabic treebanks and associated corpora: Data divisions manual. *arXiv preprint arXiv:1309.5652*.

Mona Diab, Kadri Hacioglu, and Daniel Jurafsky. 2004. Automatic Tagging of Arabic Text: From Raw Text to Base Phrase Chunks. In *Proceedings of the 5th Meeting of the North American Chapter of the Association for Computational Linguistics/Human Language Technologies Conference (HLT-NAACL04)*, pages 149–152, Boston, MA.

David Graff, Mohamed Maamouri, Basma Bouziri, Sondos Krouna, Seth Kulick, and Tim Buckwalter. 2009. Standard Arabic Morphological Analyzer (SAMA) Version 3.1. Linguistic Data Consortium LDC2009E73.

Nizar Habash. 2007. Arabic Morphological Representations for Machine Translation. In A. van den Bosch and A. Soudi, editors, *Arabic Computational Morphology: Knowledge-based and Empirical Methods*. Springer.

Nizar Habash. 2010. *Introduction to Arabic Natural Language Processing*. Morgan & Claypool Publishers.

Nizar Habash, Fadhl Eryani, Salam Khalifa, Owen Rambow, Dana Abdulrahim, Alexander Erdmann, Reem Faraj, Wajdi Zaghouani, Houda Bouamor, Nasser Zalmout, et al. 2018. Unified guidelines and resources for Arabic dialect orthography. In *Proceedings of the International Conference on Language Resources and Evaluation (LREC)*.

Nizar Habash, Ramy Eskander, and Adbelati Hawwari. 2012. A Morphological Analyzer for Egyptian Arabic. In *NAACL-HLT 2012 Workshop on Computational Morphology and Phonology (SIGMORPHON2012)*, pages 1–9.

Nizar Habash and Owen Rambow. 2005. Arabic tokenization, part-of-speech tagging and morphological disambiguation in one fell swoop. In *Proceedings of the 43rd Annual Meeting of the Association for Computational Linguistics (ACL'05)*, pages 573–580, Ann Arbor, Michigan. Association for Computational Linguistics.

Nizar Habash and Owen Rambow. 2006. MAGEAD: A Morphological Analyzer and Generator for the Arabic Dialects. In *Proceedings of ACL*, pages 681–688, Sydney, Australia. Association for Computational Linguistics.

Nizar Habash, Owen Rambow, and Ryan Roth. 2009. MADA+TOKAN: A toolkit for Arabic tokenization, diacritization, morphological disambiguation, POS tagging, stemming and lemmatization. In *Proceedings of the Second International Conference on Arabic Language Resources and Tools*. The MEDAR Consortium.

Nizar Habash and Ryan M Roth. 2009. CATiB: The Columbia Arabic Treebank. In *Proceedings of the ACL-IJCNLP 2009 Conference Short Papers*, pages 221–224.

Nizar Habash and Fatiha Sadat. 2006. Arabic Preprocessing Schemes for Statistical Machine Translation. In *Proceedings of the Human Language Technology Conference of the NAACL, Companion Volume: Short Papers*, pages 49–52, New York City, USA.

Nizar Habash, Abdelhadi Soudi, and Tim Buckwalter. 2007. On Arabic Transliteration. In A. van den Bosch and A. Soudi, editors, *Arabic Computational Morphology: Knowledge-based and Empirical Methods*. Springer.

Salam Khalifa, Sara Hassan, and Nizar Habash. 2017. A morphological analyzer for Gulf Arabic verbs. In *Proceedings of the Workshop for Arabic Natural Language Processing 2017 (co-located with EACL 2017)*, Valencia, Spain.

Salam Khalifa, Nasser Zalmout, and Nizar Habash. 2016. YAMAMA: Yet Another Multi-Dialect Arabic Morphological Analyzer. In *Proceedings of the International Conference on Computational Linguistics (COLING): System Demonstrations*, pages 223–227.

Seth Kulick, Ryan Gabbard, and Mitch Marcus. 2006. Parsing the Arabic Treebank: Analysis and Improvements. In *Proceedings of the 5th Conference on Treebanks and Linguistics Theories*, pages 31–32.

Mohamed Maamouri, Ann Bies, Tim Buckwalter, and Wigdan Mekki. 2004. The Penn Arabic Treebank: Building a Large-Scale Annotated Arabic Corpus. In *NEMLAR Conference on Arabic Language Resources and Tools*, pages 102–109, Cairo, Egypt.

Yuval Marton, Nizar Habash, and Owen Rambow. 2013. Dependency parsing of Modern Standard Arabic with lexical and inflectional features. *Computational Linguistics*, 39(1):161–194.

Joakim Nivre, Marie-Catherine de Marneffe, Filip Ginter, Yoav Goldberg, Jan Hajic, Christopher D. Manning, Ryan McDonald, Slav Petrov, Sampo Pyysalo, Natalia Silveira, Reut Tsarfaty, and Daniel Zeman. 2016. Universal dependencies v1: A multilingual treebank collection. In *Proceedings of the Tenth International Conference on Language Resources and Evaluation (LREC 2016)*, Portorož, Slovenia.

Robert Parker, David Graff, Ke Chen, Junbo Kong, and Kazuaki Maeda. 2011. Arabic Gigaword Fifth Edition. LDC catalog number No. LDC2011T11, ISBN 1-58563-595-2.

Arfath Pasha, Mohamed Al-Badrashiny, Mona Diab, Ahmed El Kholy, Ramy Eskander, Nizar Habash, Manoj Pooleery, Owen Rambow, and Ryan M Roth. 2014. MADAMIRA: A Fast, Comprehensive Tool for Morphological Analysis and Disambiguation of Arabic. In *Proceedings of the Language Resources and Evaluation Conference (LREC), Reykjavik, Iceland*.

Anas Shahrour, Salam Khalifa, Dima Taji, and Nizar Habash. 2016. CamelParser: A system for Arabic syntactic analysis and morphological disambiguation. In *Proceedings of COLING 2016, the 26th International Conference on Computational Linguistics: System Demonstrations*, pages 228–232.

June E Shoup. 1980. Phonological aspects of speech recognition. *Trends in speech recognition*, pages 125–138.

Otakar Smrž. 2007. ElixirFM — Implementation of Functional Arabic Morphology. In *Proceedings of the 2007 Workshop on Computational Approaches to Semitic Languages: Common Issues and Resources*, pages 1–8, Prague, Czech Republic.

Andreas Stolcke. 2002. SRILM an Extensible Language Modeling Toolkit. In *Proceedings of the International Conference on Spoken Language Processing*.

Michelle Vanni and Rémi Zajac. 1996. The Temple Translator's Workstation Project. In *Proceedings of a workshop on held at Vienna, Virginia: May 6-8, 1996*, pages 101–106.

Nasser Zalmout and Nizar Habash. 2017a. Don't throw those morphological analyzers away just yet: Neural morphological disambiguation for Arabic. In *Proceedings of the 2017 Conference on Empirical Methods in Natural Language Processing*, pages 704–713, Copenhagen, Denmark.

Nasser Zalmout and Nizar Habash. 2017b. Optimizing tokenization choice for machine translation across multiple target languages. *The Prague Bulletin of Mathematical Linguistics*, 108(1):257–269.

# Sanskrit n-Retroflexion is Input-Output Tier-Based Strictly Local


**Thomas Graf**
Department of Linguistics
Stony Brook University
Stony Brook, NY 11794, USA
mail@thomasgraf.net

**Connor Mayer**
Department of Linguistics
University of California, Los Angeles
Los Angeles, CA 90046, USA
connormayer@ucla.edu



## Abstract

Sanskrit /n/-retroflexion is one of the most complex segmental processes in phonology. While it is still star-free, it does not fit in any of the subregular classes that are commonly entertained in the literature. We show that when construed as a phonotactic dependency, the process fits into a class we call *input-output tier-based strictly local* (IO-TSL), a natural extension of the familiar class TSL. IO-TSL increases the power of TSL's tier projection function by making it an input-output strictly local transduction. Assuming that /n/-retroflexion represents the upper bound on the complexity of segmental phonology, this shows that all of segmental phonology can be captured by combining the intuitive notion of tiers with the independently motivated machinery of strictly local mappings.


## 1 Introduction

Subregular phonology seeks to identify proper subclasses of the finite-state languages and transductions that are sufficiently powerful for natural language phenomena (see Heinz 2018 and references therein). In addition to establishing tighter bounds on cross-linguistic variation, many of these subclasses are also efficiently learnable in the limit from positive text (Heinz et al., 2012; Jardine and McMullin, 2017).

Sanskrit /n/-retroflexion, also called *nati*, is noteworthy because it has been known for a long time to be subregular but to occupy a very high position in the subregular hierarchy when construed as a phonotactic dependency (Graf, 2010; Jardine, 2016). Its singularly high complexity stems from the combination of a locally specified target (/n/ immediately before a sonorant) with both a non-local trigger (a preceding retroflex) and three independent blocking effects, one of which is itself subject to blocking. Established classes such as *strictly local* (SL) and its extension *tier-based strictly local* (TSL; Heinz et al., 2011) cover a wide range of phonological phenomena, yet they provably cannot enforce the phonotactic conditions of *nati*.

However, as we show in this paper, *nati* can be handled by a natural extension of TSL. In TSL, a tier projection function masks out all segments that do not belong to some specified subset of the alphabet. This allows for simple non-local dependencies to be regulated in a local fashion. More involved patterns can be accommodated by increasing the complexity of the tier projection. In order to capture *nati*, the projection function has to consider two factors when choosing whether or not to project a symbol: I) the local context in the string, and II) which symbols are already on the tier. This makes it a special case of input-output strictly local maps, which is why we call this extended version of TSL *input-output TSL* (IO-TSL).

IO-TSL is a natural extension of TSL — it subsumes it as a special case and expands on recent proposals to make tier projection structure-sensitive. De Santo and Graf (2017) propose input strictly local maps to handle certain cases noted as problematic for TSL in McMullin (2016), and similar proposals are made in Baek (2017) and Yang (2018) for phonology and Vu et al. (2018) for syntax. Mayer and Major (2018), on the other hand, suggest based on Graf (p.c.) that backness harmony in Uyghur is TSL with output strictly local tier projection; Graf and Shafiei (2018) apply the same idea to syntax. Input-output strictly local projection merely combines these two extensions.

The paper is laid out as follows. We first introduce TSL (§2.1) and subsequently generalize it to IO-TSL (§2.2), some properties of which are discussed in §2.3. The empirical facts of *nati* are presented in §3 based primarily on Ryan (2017), followed by our IO-TSL analysis in §4.




*Proceedings of the 15th SIGMORPHON Workshop on Computational Research in Phonetics, Phonology, and Morphology*, pages 151–160
Brussels, Belgium, October 31, 2018. ©2018 The Special Interest Group on Computational Morphology and Phonology
https://doi.org/10.18653/v1/P17

## 2 Defining IO-TSL

### 2.1 TSL

Throughout the paper, we use $\varepsilon$ to denote the empty string, $S^*$ for the Kleene closure of $S$, and $S^+$ for $S^*$ without the empty string. We use $S^k$ to denote the proper subset of $S^*$ that only contains strings of length $k$, and we write $s^k$ as a shorthand for $\{s\}^k$.

Let $\Sigma$ be some fixed alphabet and $s \in \Sigma^*$. The set $f_k(s)$ of $k$-*factors* of $s$ consists of all the length-$k$ substrings of $\rtimes^{k-1} s \ltimes^{k-1}$, where $\rtimes, \ltimes \notin \Sigma$ and $k \geq 1$.

**Definition 1.** A stringset $L \subseteq \Sigma^*$ is *strictly k-local* (SL-$k$) iff there is some $G \subseteq (\Sigma \cup \{\rtimes, \ltimes\})^k$ such that $L = \{s \in \Sigma^* \mid f_k(s) \cap G = \emptyset\}$.

Intuitively, $G$ defines a *grammar* of forbidden substrings that no well-formed string may contain. The class SL of strictly local stringsets is $\bigcup_{k \geq 1}$ SL-$k$.

**Example 1.** The string language $(ab)^+$ is generated by the grammar $G := \{\rtimes\ltimes, \rtimes b, aa, bb, a\ltimes\}$ and thus is SL-2. For instance, $aba$ is illicit because $f_2(aba) \cap G = \{a\ltimes\} \neq \emptyset$, whereas $f_2(abab) \cap G = \emptyset$.

For every $T \subseteq \Sigma - \{\varepsilon\}$, a *simple tier projection* $\pi_T$ is a transduction that deletes all symbols not in $T$:

$$\pi_T(\sigma u) := \begin{cases} \varepsilon & \text{if } \sigma u = \varepsilon \\ \sigma \pi_T(u) & \text{if } \sigma \in T \\ \pi_T(u) & \text{otherwise} \end{cases}$$

**Definition 2.** A stringset $L \subseteq \Sigma^*$ is *tier-based strictly k-local* (TSL-$k$) iff there exists a $T \subseteq \Sigma - \{\varepsilon\}$ and an SL-$k$ language $K \subseteq T^*$ such that $L := \{s \in \Sigma^* \mid \pi_T(s) \in K\}$. It is TSL iff it is TSL-$k$ for some $k$.

TSL languages are string languages that are SL once one masks out all irrelevant symbols.

**Example 2.** Consider all strings over $\{a, b, c\}$ that contain exactly one $b$ and exactly one $c$. This language is TSL-3: let $T := \{b, c\}$, and $K := \{bc, cb\}$, which is an SL-3 language (the reader is invited to write down the grammar for $K$). The licit string $aabac$, for instance, is first projected to $bc$, which is a member of $K$. The illicit $aaba$, on the other hand, is projected to $b \notin K$.

### 2.2 IO-TSL

The power of TSL can be increased by changing the nature of the tier projection $\pi$. In particular,

it can be generalized to strictly local maps (Chandlee, 2014). Due to space constraints, we immediately define input-output strictly local projections without discussing the earlier work on subregular mappings on which our idea builds. The interested reader should consult Chandlee (2014, 2017) and Chandlee and Heinz (2018).

An $(i, j)$-*context* $c$ is a 4-tuple $\langle \sigma, b, a, t \rangle$ with $\sigma \in \Sigma$, $t$ a string over $\Sigma \cup \{\ltimes\}$ of length $j - 1$, and $a$ and $b$ strings over $\Sigma \cup \{\rtimes, \ltimes\}$ of combined length $i - 1$. The context specifies that $\sigma$ should be projected whenever both of the following hold: it occurs between the substrings $b$ (look-back) and $a$ (look-ahead), and the tier constructed so far ends in $t$. The value of $i$ determines the size of the input window, which includes the look-ahead and look-back spans, as well as the symbol itself. The value of $j$ indicates how far back along the tier we can look, including the current symbol. Given a set of contexts $c_1, c_2, \ldots, c_n$, we call it an $(i, j)$-*context set* $C(i, j)$ iff for every $c_m$ $(1 \leq m \leq n)$ there are $i_m \leq i$ and $j_m \leq j$ such that $c_m$ is an $(i_m, j_m)$-context.

Note that in a context set $C(i, j)$, $i$ and $j$ refer to the *maximum* input and output window sizes considered by any $(i, j)$-context. The individual $(i, j)$-contexts may vary in size within these bounds. This is merely a matter of notational convenience and does not affect generative capacity.

**Definition 3.** Let $C$ be an $(i, j)$-context set. Then the *input-output strictly $(i, j)$-local* (IOSL-$(i, j)$) tier projection $\pi_C$ maps every $s \in \Sigma^*$ to $\pi'_C(\rtimes^i \star s\ltimes^i, \rtimes^j)$, where $\pi'_C(ub \star \sigma av, wt)$ is

$$\begin{array}{ll} \varepsilon & \text{if } \sigma av = \varepsilon, \\ \sigma \pi'_C(ub\sigma \star av, wt\sigma) & \text{if } \langle \sigma, b, a, t \rangle \in C, \\ \pi'_C(ub\sigma \star av, wt) & \text{otherwise.} \end{array}$$

for $\sigma \in \Sigma$ and $a, b, t, u, v, w \in (\Sigma \cup \{\rtimes, \ltimes\})^*$.

The first argument to $\pi'_C$ is the input string, with $\star$ as a diacritic to mark the position up to which the string has been processed. The second argument contains the symbols that have already been projected. A schematic diagram of the projection function $\pi_C$ that arises from $\pi'_C$ is shown in Fig. 1.

**Example 3.** Let $\Sigma := \{a, b, c\}$ and consider the tier projection that always projects the first and last symbol of the string, always projects $a$, never projects $c$, and projects $b$ only if the previous symbol on the tier is $a$. This projection is IOSL-(2,2). The context set contains all the contexts below, and only those:

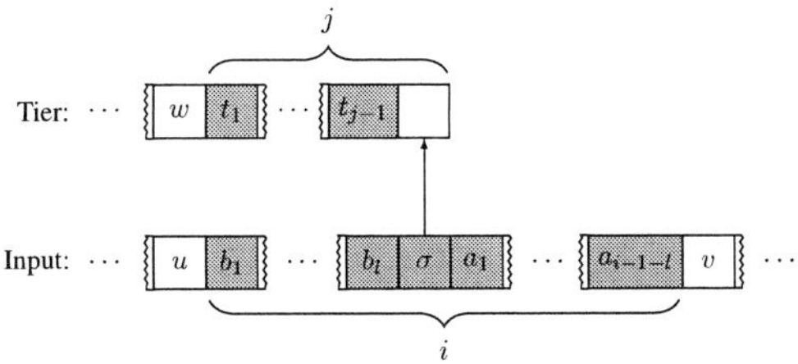

Figure 1: The projection function $\pi_C$. Grey cells indicate symbols in the input and tier strings that are considered when deciding whether to project $\sigma$.

- $\langle \sigma, \rtimes, \varepsilon, \varepsilon \rangle$ for all $\sigma \in \Sigma$,

- $\langle \sigma, \varepsilon, \ltimes, \varepsilon \rangle$ for all $\sigma \in \Sigma$,

- $\langle a, \varepsilon, \varepsilon, \varepsilon \rangle$,

- $\langle b, \varepsilon, \varepsilon, a \rangle$.

The first two of these contexts ensure that any segment is projected if it occurs at the beginning of the string or the end of the string. The third context ensures that $a$ is always projected as all occurrences of $a$ will be trivially preceded and followed by $\varepsilon$ in the input and preceded on the tier by $\varepsilon$. The final context ensures that $b$ is projected regardless of what precedes or follows in the input, but only if the previous symbol on the tier is $a$. Given the previous constraints, this is equivalent to saying that $b$ is only projected if it is the first $b$ encountered after seeing an $a$ earlier in the string.

**Definition 4.** A stringset $L \subseteq \Sigma^*$ is *input-output tier-based strictly $(i, j, k)$-local* (IO-TSL-$(i, j, k)$) iff there exists an IOSL-$(i, j)$ tier projection $\pi_C$ and an SL-$k$ language $K$ such that $L := \{s \in \Sigma^* \mid \pi_C(s) \in K\}$. It is IO-TSL iff it is IO-TSL-$(i, j, k)$ for some $i$, $j$, and $k$.

Note that TSL-$k$ is identical to IO-TSL-$(1, 1, k)$, which shows that IO-TSL is indeed a generalization of TSL.

### 2.3 Some properties of IO-TSL

It is fairly easy to show that IO-TSL languages are definable in first-order logic with precedence and hence star-free. We conjecture that IO-TSL is in fact a proper subclass of the star-free languages.

**Conjecture 1.** *IO-TSL $\subsetneq$ Star-Free.*

Consider the star-free string language $L := aL'a \cup bL'b$ where $L'$ is $(d^+cd^+ed^+)^+$. In order to ensure the long-distance alternation of $c$ and $e$, one has to project every $c$ and every $e$, and in order to

ensure the matching of the first and last segment those have to be projected too. But then the set of well-formed tiers is $a(ce)^+a \cup b(ce)^+b$, which is not in SL because it violates suffix substitution closure (cf. Heinz, 2018). Hence $L$ is not IO-TSL (although it is in the intersection closure of TSL). A fully worked out proof would have to show that all other IOSL tier projections fail as well.

Like most subregular language classes, IO-TSL is not closed under relabeling. This follows from the familiar insight that $(aa)^+$, which isn't even star-free, is a relabeling of the SL-2 language $(ab)^+$. We state a few additional conjectures without further elaboration.

**Conjecture 2.** *IO-TSL is not closed under intersection, union, relative complement, or concatenation.*

**Conjecture 3.** *IO-TSL is incomparable to the following classes:*

- *locally threshold testable languages (LTT),*

- *locally testable (LT),*

- *piecewise testable (PT),*

- *interval-based strictly piecewise (IBSP; Graf, 2017, 2018)*

- *strictly piecewise (SP; Rogers et al., 2010)*

If correct, these properties of IO-TSL would mirror exactly those of TSL, further corroborating our claim that IO-TSL is a very natural generalization of TSL.

That said, IO-TSL is a fair amount more complex than TSL. In the next section, we discuss the empirical facts of Sanskrit /n/-retroflexion that motivate the introduction of this additional complexity.

## 3 Sanskrit n-retroflexion

Sanskrit /n/-retroflexion, also called *nati*, has been studied extensively throughout the history of linguistics, and has received particularly close scrutiny within generative grammar. The notorious complexity of the phenomenon is the product of the interaction of multiple (individually simple) conditions: long-distance assimilation (§3.1), blocking by preceding coronals (§3.2), mandatory adjacency to sonorants (§3.3), blocking by preceding plosives (§3.4), and blocking by following retroflexes (§3.5).

Even a cursory look at the previous literature is beyond the scope of this paper, so we refer the reader to Ryan (2017) for a detailed literature review and analysis of the phenomenon. We draw data from Müller (1886), Hansson (2001), and Ryan (2017) and use the transcription conventions from Ryan (2017). Page numbers for the sources are indicated in the table captions of the data.

## 3.1 Base pattern

The central aspect of *nati* is simple: underlyingly anterior /n/ becomes retroflex [ɳ] when it is preceded in the word by a non-lateral retroflex continuant (one of /ɻ/, /ɻ̊/, /ɽ̊/, or /ʂ/). The retroflex trigger can occur arbitrarily far to the left of the nasal target. Tables 1 and 2 respectively show the alternations in the instrumental singular suffix /-eːna/ when attached to roots without and with a trigger. Triggers, blockers, and targets are bolded in all tables.

| Form | Gloss |
|---|---|
| káːm-e**ː**na | 'by desire' |
| baːɳ-e**ː**na | 'by arrow' |
| muːɖ^ɦ-e**ː**na | 'by the stupid (one)' |
| joːg-e**ː**na | 'by means' |

Table 1: Forms with no *nati* (Ryan, 2017, p. 305)

| Form | Gloss |
|---|---|
| na**ɻ**-e**ː**ɳa | 'by man' |
| manuʂj-e**ː**ɳa | 'by human' |
| **ɻ**aːg^ɦaʋ-e**ː**ɳa | 'by the Rāghava' |
| puʂpaug^ɦ-e**ː**ɳa | 'by the heap of flowers' |
| b**ɻ**afimaɳja | 'kind to Brahmans' |
| niʂaɳɳa | 'rested' |
| akʂaɳʋat | 'having eyes' |

Table 2: Basic *nati* examples (Ryan, 2017, p. 305 and Müller, 1886, p. 44)

Viewing *nati* as a phonotactic phenomenon rather than a mapping from underlying representations to surface forms, we can formalize it as the constraint that no [n] may appear in the context $R \cdots \_$, where $R$ is a non-lateral retroflex continuant. This does not constitute an analysis, but it clarifies the formal character of the process. As we will see in the remainder of this section, though, the context is in fact much more complicated than just $R \cdots \_$.

## 3.2 Unconditional blocking by intervening coronals

If a coronal segment (including retroflexes) occurs between the trigger and the target, then *nati* is blocked. The only exception to this is the palatal glide /j/ (cf. Table 2) — this is an important point that we will return to in §4.3. Crucially, [ɳ] itself is a coronal blocker, meaning the assimilation process only affects the first in a series of eligible targets. An exception to this is geminate /nn/ sequences, where both instances of /n/ undergo *nati* (cf. Table 2; this complication will also be discussed in §4.3). Examples of *nati* blocked by an intervening coronal are shown in Table 3. Leaving aside geminates for the moment, the illicit context for [n] now becomes $R\overline{C}^*\_$, where $\overline{C}$ matches [j] and all segments that are not coronals.

| Form | Gloss |
|---|---|
| **ɻ**át^h-e**ː**na | 'by chariot' |
| ga**ɻ**uɖ-e**ː**na | 'by Garuḍa' |
| p**ɻ**a-**ɳ**inaːja | 'lead forth' |
| ʋa**ɻɳ**-anaːnam | *no gloss* |

Table 3: Intervening coronal blocking (Hansson, 2001, p. 227 and Ryan, 2017, p. 305)

## 3.3 Mandatory adjacency to sonorant

Next, the /n/ must be immediately followed by a non-liquid sonorant to undergo *nati*. More precisely, the following symbol must be a vowel, a glide, /m/, or /n/ itself (Whitney, 1889). No other nasals can occur following /n/ due to independent phonotactic constraints in the language (Emeneau, 1946). Like the special status of /j/ and geminates, this will become important in §4.3 but can be ignored for now.

Examples of cases where *nati* is blocked by the following sound, or lack thereof, are shown in Table 4. Again updating the illicit context for [n], we get $R\overline{C}^*\_S$, where $S$ is a vowel, glide, /m/, or /n/.

| Form | Gloss |
|---|---|
| b**ɻ**afiman | 'brahman' |
| t**ɻ**=**n**-t-te | 'split (3Pl middle)' |
| ca**ɻ**-a-**n**-ti | 'wander (3Pl)' |

Table 4: Blocking when no non-liquid sonorant follows (Hansson, 2001, p. 229 and Ryan, 2017, p. 318)

154

### 3.4 Conditional blocking by preceding velar and labial plosives

In addition to coronals blocking when they intervene between the trigger and the target, velar and labial plosives can also block *nati*, but only when two conditions are met at the same time: I) the plosive occurs immediately before the target, and II) a left root boundary $\sqrt{}$ intervenes between the target and trigger. Left root boundaries are generally omitted for clarity when they occur at the left edge of a word. Table 5 shows that left root boundaries alone are not sufficient to block *nati*. Table 6 shows cases where a labial or velar plosive blocks *nati* across a left root boundary, and Table 7 shows cases where such a plosive does not block because no left root boundary intervenes.

| Form | Gloss |
| --- | --- |
| pɹa-$\sqrt{}$ɳaɕ-ja-ti | 'vanishes (3s)' |
| vʏtɹa-$\sqrt{}$ɦáɳa | 'Vr̥tra-killing' |
| pɹa-$\sqrt{}$miːɳ-aː-ti | 'frustrates (3s)' |

Table 5: *Nati* occurring across left root boundaries (Ryan, 2017, pp. 320, 321, 324)

| Form | Gloss |
| --- | --- |
| pɻ-$\sqrt{}$aːp-noː-ti | 'attains (3s)' |
| pɻ-$\sqrt{}$aːp-nu-aːh | 'should attain (2s opt.)' |
| pɹa-$\sqrt{}$bʰag-na | 'broken' |

Table 6: Labial/velar blocking with intervening root boundary (Ryan, 2017, pp. 318, 321)

| Form | Gloss |
| --- | --- |
| $\sqrt{}$ɹug-ɳá | 'break (pass. part.)' |
| $\sqrt{}$tʏp-ɳV- | 'be satisfied (pres. stem)' |
| $\sqrt{}$ɹéːkɳas | 'inheritance' |

Table 7: No labial/velar blocking (Ryan, 2017, p. 319)

To accommodate these new facts, we change the context to $R\alpha\_S$. Here $\alpha$ is any string that does not contain a coronal and does not match $\cdots\sqrt{}\cdots P$, where $P$ is a velar plosive or a labial plosive.

### 3.5 Conditional blocking by following retroflex

There is one final complication: *nati* is blocked when a retroflex occurs somewhere to the right of the target /n/. Like with blocking by plosives, though, two conditions must be met: I) as above, a

left root boundary separates the trigger and the target of *nati*, and II) no coronal intervenes between /n/ and the blocking retroflex (so coronals "block" retroflex blocking). Keep in mind that, as in §3.2, /n/ itself is coronal and thus can act as a blocker, a point that will be important in §4.

Table 8 shows cases where a following retroflex blocks in the presence of a left root boundary intervening between trigger and target, and Table 9 shows cases where it does not block because a coronal intervenes between the target and the blocker, or no intervening boundary is present. Note in the final example of Table 9 that an intervening left root boundary between the trigger and the blocker has no effect — the boundary must occur before the targeted /n/.

Ryan (2017) notes that it is unclear from the data whether the retroflex blocking is truly unbounded, or if the blocker must occur within a certain distance of the target. We assume the pattern is unbounded here, but it does not significantly alter the analysis if this is not the case.

| Form | Gloss |
| --- | --- |
| pɹa-$\sqrt{}$naʂ-ʈum | 'to vanish (inf.)' |
| pɹa-$\sqrt{}$nʏt- | 'dance forth' |
| pɹa-$\sqrt{}$nakʂ- | 'approach' |

Table 8: Following retroflex blocking (Ryan, 2017, p. 325)

| Form | Gloss |
| --- | --- |
| pɹa-$\sqrt{}$ɲeː-tʏ | 'leader' |
| $\sqrt{}$bɹaːɦimaɳ-éː-ʂu | 'Brahmins (loc. pl.)' |
| $\sqrt{}$pɻ-ɳa-k-ʂi | 'unite (2s)' |
| $\sqrt{}$puɹaːɳa-$\sqrt{}$ʏʂi | 'ancient rishi' |

Table 9: No following retroflex blocking (Ryan, 2017, p. 325, 326)

With this last piece of data in place, we can finally give a full description of *nati* as a phonotactic constraint on the distribution of [n] in surface forms.

**Definition 5** (nati). No [n] may occur in a context $R\alpha\_S\beta$ such that the following hold:

- $R$ is a non-lateral retroflex continuant, and

- $S$ is a vowel, glide, /m/, or /n/ and

- none of the following blocking conditions are met:

- $\alpha$ contains a coronal $C$, or

- $\alpha$ matches $\cdots \sqrt{}\cdots P$, where $P$ is a velar plosive or labial plosive, or

- $\alpha$ contains $\sqrt{}$, and $\beta$ contains a retroflex that is not preceded by a coronal in $\beta$.

This description can be translated into a first-order formula with precedence to show that *nati* is star-free. In the next section, we show that it is also IO-TSL.

## 4  Formal analysis

The IO-TSL analysis of *nati* is a bit convoluted, but more straightforward than one might expect. All the heavy lifting is done by the tier projection mechanism (§4.1). In any case where the projection considers the context at all, it uses a look-ahead of 1 or 2, a look-back of 1 in the string, a look-back of 1 on the tier, or a mixture of these options. In particular, $P$ and $C$ have complex tier projection conditions. Our projection function creates tiers of a very limited shape that are easily shown to be SL-3 (§4.2). While our analysis uses abstract symbols such as $R$, $P$, and $C$, the complexity of *nati* remains the same even if one talks directly about the relevant segments instead (§4.3).

### 4.1  Tier projection

As contexts make for a verbose description, we opt for a more informal specification of the IOSL tier projection. The projection rules for each symbol are sufficiently simple that this does not introduce any inaccuracies.

An IOSL-$(3, 2)$ tier projection for *nati* is shown below. For each condition we list its individual complexity. Note that the rules below merely specify how tiers are constructed, not which tiers are well-formed. This is left for §4.2.

- Always project $R$.   *IOSL-(1,1)*

- Project $S$ if it is immediately preceded by [n] in the input.   *IOSL-(2,1)*

- Project $\sqrt{}$ if the previous tier symbol is $R$.   *IOSL-(1,2)*

- Project $P$ if the previous tier symbol is $\sqrt{}$ and the next two input symbols are [n] and $S$.   *IOSL-(3,2)*

- Project $C$ if the previous tier symbol is $R$, $\sqrt{}$, or $S$, unless $C$ is [n] and the next input symbol is $S$.   *IOSL-(2,2)*

- Project every retroflex (not just those matching $R$) if the previous tier symbol is $S$.   *IOSL-(1,2)*

- Don't project anything else.   *IOSL-(1,1)*

Table 10 shows variations of the previous data points with the tiers projected according to the rules above.

Let us briefly comment on the intuition behind these projection rules. We always want to project $R$ since this is the only potential trigger for *nati*. For [n], we do not want to project all instances as this may end up restricting the distribution of an [n] that is not a suitable target anyways. In addition, we do not want to project [n] itself as this would make it impossible to distinguish an [n] that was projected as a potential *nati*-target from one that was projected as an instance of $C$. So instead, we project the sonorant after [n]. As a sonorant has no other reason to appear on the tier, it can act as an indirect representative of an [n] that may be targeted by *nati*.

The left root boundary $\sqrt{}$ matters only if it occurs between $R$ and [n]. Since we build tiers from left-to-right, we cannot anticipate the presence of [n] on the tier, and in the input string there is no upper bound on how far [n] might be from $\sqrt{}$. Hence we have to project $\sqrt{}$ after every $R$, even if $R$ does not end up triggering *nati*. A redundant instance of $\sqrt{}$ on the tier is no problem.

As for $P$, its presence matters only when it occurs before a potential *nati* target, so we project it only in these configurations. We also impose the requirement that the previous tier symbol is $\sqrt{}$ as $P$ needs a left root boundary between $R$ and [n] to become a blocker. This kind of mixing of input and output conditions is not necessary for $P$, but it is essential for $C$.

The coronal $C$ is the strongest blocker. In contrast to $\sqrt{}$, it does not depend on other material in the string, so it should be projected not only immediately after $R$ but also if the previous tier symbol is $\sqrt{}$ (from which we can infer that the tier symbol before that is $R$). A $C$ between [n] and a retroflex inhibits the latter's ability to block *nati*, so we also need to project $C$ if the previous tier symbol is $S$ (our tier stand-in for [n]). As arbitrary retroflex segments are projected only if the previous tier symbol is $S$, projecting $C$ after $S$ effectively blocks projection of retroflexes. Note that we do not project $C$ when it is an [n] before

$S$ as this is a potential *nati*-target and hence $S$ is projected anyways.

## 4.2  SL grammar

Once the IOSL tier projection is in place, specifying the forbidden substrings is a simple task. Consider a segment [n] that is followed by $S$ and hence a potential target for *nati*. If there are any $R$ that can trigger *nati*, it suffices to consider the closest one. Given such a configuration $R \cdots [\text{n}]S$, any tier will have the shape below:

$$\cdots R \, (C \mid \surd (C \mid P)) \, S \, (C \mid S \mid \text{retroflex}) \cdots$$

Here $(X \mid Y)$ means "$X$ or $Y$ or nothing".

Based on this abstract template, the following substrings are illicit because they indicate an [n] in a configuration where *nati* should apply:

- $R \, S$, and

- $R \, \surd \, S \, X$ (where $X$ is $\ltimes$, $C$, or $S$).

That these are the only four substrings that need to be forbidden is illustrated in Table 10. But note that $\surd$ is always immediately preceded by $R$ on the tier, so the illicit substrings for the second case can be shortened to $\surd \, S \, \ltimes$, $\surd \, S \, C$, and $\surd \, S \, S$. Therefore the longest forbidden substring has at most 3 segments and the dependencies over the tier are SL-3. As a result, *nati* is IO-TSL-(3,2,3); these surprisingly low thresholds suggest that *nati* is still fairly simple from a formal perspective.

### 4.3  Removing abstract symbols

There are still a few minor points that merit addressing. As noted in §2.2, IO-TSL is not closed under relabeling, so the fact that the abstract patterns used in the previous sections are IO-TSL does not imply that *nati* itself is. This is the case only if one can compile out the abstract symbols $R$, $S$, $C$, $P$, and retroflex into specific segments like [n], [j], and [ɭ]. No problems arise in cases where no segment corresponds to more than one abstract symbol. For example, [j] only matches $S$. If [j] were also a coronal blocker, then it would also match $C$ and the account in the previous section would no longer work since it would not be clear if a [j] on a tier represents a blocker $C$ or a sonorant $S$. In such a case, the use of abstract symbols would simplify the pattern in an illicit way. There are two instances of overlap in our analysis: $R$ versus arbitrary retroflexes, and [n] belonging to both $C$ and $S$.

Regarding the split between $R$ and arbitrary retroflexes, it is actually unclear from the data whether the two are distinct classes. The available data includes only instances of segments matching $R$ acting as blockers, though Ryan (2017) suggests based on his analysis that all retroflexes should be able to block. But even if the two are distinct, that is unproblematic for our account. The projection of $R$ is less restricted than that of arbitrary retroflexes as the latter are only projected if the previous tier symbol is $S$. This discrepancy matters only in cases where a $C$-segment occurs after [n]. In this case, arbitrary reflexives do not project whereas $R$ still does. Projecting an $R$-segment after a $C$ has no consequences, though. If the preceding substring matches $\surd \, SC$, then projecting $R$ won't salvage it. If it does not match this pattern, projecting $R$ won't make the tier ill-formed. Hence the minimal difference between $R$ and arbitrary retroflexes — if it exists — is immaterial for our account.

That [n] belongs to both $C$ and $S$ is not much of an issue, either. Since $S$ is projected only after [n], an [n] on the tier could be an instance of $S$ only if there are [nn] clusters targeted by *nati*. In such cases, the entire cluster undergoes *nati*. For example, we see [niṣaṇṇa], not *[niṣaṇna] (cf. Table 2). There are two solutions to this. One option is to treat these not as [nn] clusters, but rather as a single segment [nː]. As long as the projection of $S$ is generalized to be sensitive to both [n] and [nː], this data is handled correctly by our analysis. Alternatively, we could rely on the fact that [nn] clusters in our data are always followed by $S$. Hence we can limit $S$ to vowels, glides, and [m] and still end up with a sonorant on the tier after each potential *nati*-target. Either way there are again safe ways to deal with the apparent overlap between the abstract symbols.

We find it interesting in connection to this that [j] is both sonorant and coronal but does not act as a coronal blocker. If it did, it would belong to both $C$ and $S$, without an easy fix to rescue our analysis. Although Ryan (2017) accounts for the special status of [j] on the basis of its articulatory properties, the fact that its behavior is also predictable from a computational perspective is intriguing. Be that as it may, the important point is that the account in §4.1 and §4.2 captures *nati* even if the abstract symbols are compiled out to the actual segments.

| Example | Tier | Forbidden substring | Example | Tier | Forbidden substring |
|---|---|---|---|---|---|
| naɻeːɳa | aɻɳ⋉ | – | √ɻugɳá | ɻɳ⋉ | – |
| *naɻeːna | aɻa⋉ | ɻa | *√ɻugná | ɻá⋉ | ɻá |
| pɻaɳinaːja | ɻɳa⋉ | – | pɻa√neːtɻ | ɻ√ɳɻ⋉ | – |
| caɻanti | ɻt⋉ | – | *pɻa√neːtɻ | ɻ√eːtɻ⋉ | √eːt |
| ʋɻtɻa√ɦáɳa | ɻtɻ√ɳ⋉ | – | √bɻaːɦmaɳéːʂu | ɻɳʂ⋉ | – |
| *ʋɻtɻa√ɦána | ɻtɻ√a⋉ | √a⋉ | *√bɻaːɦmanéːʂu | ɻéːʂ⋉ | ɻéː |
| pɻ√aːpnoːti | ɻ√poːt⋉ | – | pɻa√nakʂ | ɻ√aʂ⋉ | – |

Table 10: Selected data points and ungrammatical variants from Tables 2 to 9 with their tiers and forbidden subsequences (if any); ⋉ is added to each tier for the sake of exposition.

## 4.4 Relevance and interpretation

Our analysis establishes IO-TSL as a tighter upper bound on the complexity of *nati* when construed as a single phonotactic constraint over strings. This does not mean, though, that this is the only viable view of *nati*, as it could have been analyzed as a collection of individually simple constraints (cf. Ryan, 2017), a condition on graph structures in the sense of Jardine (2017), or a mapping from underlying representations to surface forms. These are all insightful perspectives, but they are orthogonal to our goal of bounding the overall complexity of *nati*. Our finding that *nati* (and probably segmental phonology as a whole) is IO-TSL is analogous to claims that syntax yields mildly context-sensitive string languages (Joshi, 1985) even though the actual representations are trees with a tree-to-string mapping. The IO-TSL nature of *nati* provides a rough complexity baseline on which more nuanced and linguistically insightful notions of complexity can be built.

We do find it interesting that IO-TSL as a natural generalization of TSL is sufficient to capture *nati*. But IO-TSL is still too liberal an upper bound. Just like the TSL-extensions used in Baek (2017), De Santo and Graf (2017), and Yang (2018), IO-TSL allows for unattested phenomena such as first-last harmony (Lai, 2015). Future work may identify subclasses of IO-TSL that allow for *nati* but not first-last harmony. IO-TSL in its current form is nonetheless a fairly restrictive upper bound on *nati*.

One final point of contention is our treatment of *nati* as a long distance process, rather than local retroflex spreading as suggested by Ryan (2017). Unfortunately, there is no clear evidence that the posited local spreading is visible in the output string. Spreading of unpronounced material would be an instance of *feature coding*, which destroys subregular complexity because every regular language can be made SL-2 this way (see e.g. Rogers 1997). Ryan's analysis may still be more appropriate from a linguistic perspective, but for our purposes it may incorrectly nullify the complexity of *nati*.

## 5 Conclusion

We have shown that even a highly complex process like *nati* can be regarded as a local dependency over tiers given a slightly more sophisticated tier projection mechanism that considers both the local context in the input and the preceding symbol(s) on the tier. This extension is natural in the sense that it co-opts mechanisms that have been independently proposed in the subregular literature as a more restricted model of rewrite rules. Moreover, the complexity is fairly low as *nati* fits into IO-TSL-$(3, 2, 3)$. A careful reanalysis of the data may be able to lower these thresholds even more by incorporating independent restrictions on the distribution of some segments. Allowing the tier projection to proceed from right to left might also affect complexity.

The effect of the increased power on learnability is still unknown. IO-TSL-$(i, j, k)$ is a finite class given upper bounds on $i$, $j$, and $k$, which immediately entails that the class is learnable in the limit from positive text (Gold, 1967). This leaves open whether the class is efficiently learnable, as is the case for TSL (Jardine and McMullin, 2017) and the strictly local maps IO-TSL builds on (Chandlee et al., 2014, 2015). But IO-TSL adds two serious complications: the learner does not have access to the output of the tier projection function in the training data, and inferring correct contexts presupposes correctly built tiers.

## Acknowledgments

We would like to thank David Goldstein and Canaan Breiss for helping us better understand *nati*.

## References


Hyunah Baek. 2017. Computational representation of unbounded stress: Tiers with structural features. Ms., Stony Brook University; to appear in *Proceedings of CLS 53*.

Jane Chandlee. 2014. *Strictly Local Phonological Processes*. Ph.D. thesis, University of Delaware.

Jane Chandlee. 2017. Computational locality in morphological maps. *Morphology*, pages 599–641.

Jane Chandlee, Rémi Eyraud, and Jeffrey Heinz. 2014. Learning strictly local subsequential functions. *Transactions of the Association for Computational Linguistics*, 2:491–503.

Jane Chandlee, Rémi Eyraud, and Jeffrey Heinz. 2015. Output strictly local functions. *Mathematics of Language*.

Jane Chandlee and Jeffrey Heinz. 2018. Strict locality and phonological maps. *Linguistic Inquiry*, 49:23–60.

Aniello De Santo and Thomas Graf. 2017. Structure sensitive tier projection: Applications and formal properties. Ms., Stony Brook University.

M.B. Emeneau. 1946. The nasal phonemes of Sanskrit. *Language*, 22(2):86–93.

E. Mark Gold. 1967. Language identification in the limit. *Information and Control*, 10:447–474.

Thomas Graf. 2010. Comparing incomparable frameworks: A model theoretic approach to phonology. *University of Pennsylvania Working Papers in Linguistics*, 16(2):Article 10.

Thomas Graf. 2017. The power of locality domains in phonology. *Phonology*, 34:385–405.

Thomas Graf. 2018. Locality domains and phonological c-command over strings. To appear in *Proceedings of NELS 2017*.

Thomas Graf and Nazila Shafiei. 2018. C-command dependencies as TSL string constraints. Ms., Stony Brook University.

Gunnar Ólafur Hansson. 2001. *Theoretical and Typological Issues in Consonant Harmony*. Ph.D. thesis, University of California, Berkeley.

Jeffrey Heinz. 2018. The computational nature of phonological generalizations. In Larry Hyman and Frank Plank, editors, *Phonological Typology*, Phonetics and Phonology, chapter 5, pages 126–195. Mouton De Gruyter.

Jeffrey Heinz, Anna Kasprzik, and Timo Kötzing. 2012. Learning in the limit with lattice-structured hypothesis spaces. *Theoretical Computer Science*, 457:111–127.

Jeffrey Heinz, Chetan Rawal, and Herbert G. Tanner. 2011. Tier-based strictly local constraints in phonology. In *Proceedings of the 49th Annual Meeting of the Association for Computational Linguistics*, pages 58–64.

Adam Jardine. 2016. Computationally, tone is different. *Phonology*, 33:247–283.

Adam Jardine. 2017. The local nature of tone-association patterns. *Phonology*, 34:385–405.

Adam Jardine and Kevin McMullin. 2017. Efficient learning of tier-based strictly $k$-local languages. In *Proceedings of Language and Automata Theory and Applications*, Lecture Notes in Computer Science, pages 64–76, Berlin. Springer.

Aravind Joshi. 1985. Tree-adjoining grammars: How much context sensitivity is required to provide reasonable structural descriptions? In David Dowty, Lauri Karttunen, and Arnold Zwicky, editors, *Natural Language Parsing*, pages 206–250. Cambridge University Press, Cambridge.

Regine Lai. 2015. Learnable vs unlearnable harmony patterns. *Linguistic Inquiry*, 46:425–451.

Connor Mayer and Travis Major. 2018. A challenge for tier-based strict locality from Uyghur backness harmony. In *Formal Grammar 2018. Lecture Notes in Computer Science, vol. 10950*, pages 62–83. Springer, Berlin, Heidelberg.

Kevin McMullin. 2016. *Tier-Based Locality in Long-Distance Phonotactics: Learnability and Typology*. Ph.D. thesis, University of British Columbia.

Friedrich Max Müller. 1886. *A Sanskrit Grammar for Beginners: In Devanagari and Roman Letters*. Longmans, Green, and Co., London.

James Rogers. 1997. Strict $LT_2$ : Regular :: Local : Recognizable. In *Logical Aspects of Computational Linguistics: First International Conference, LACL '96 (Selected Papers)*, volume 1328 of *Lectures Notes in Computer Science/Lectures Notes in Artificial Intelligence*, pages 366–385. Springer.

James Rogers, Jeffrey Heinz, Gil Bailey, Matt Edlefsen, Molly Vischer, David Wellcome, and Sean Wibel. 2010. On languages piecewise testable in the strict sense. In Christan Ebert, Gerhard Jäger, and Jens Michaelis, editors, *The Mathematics of Language*, volume 6149 of *Lecture Notes in Artificial Intelligence*, pages 255–265. Springer, Heidelberg.

Kevin Ryan. 2017. Attenuated spreading in Sanskrit retroflex harmony. *Linguistic Inquiry*, 48(2):299–340.

Mai Ha Vu, Nazila Shafiei, and Thomas Graf. 2018. Case assignment in TSL syntax: A case study. Ms., Stony Brook University and University of Delaware.

William Dwight Whitney. 1889. *Sanskrit Grammar*. Oxford University Press, London.

Su Ji Yang. 2018. Subregular complexity in Korean phonotactics. Undergraduate honors thesis, Stony Brook University.

# Phonological Features for Morphological Inflection

**Adam Wiemerslage**[☼] and **Miikka Silfverberg**[☼🏵] and **Mans Hulden**[☼]
Department of Linguistics
University of Colorado[☼]
University of Helsinki[🏵]
`first.last@colorado.edu`

## Abstract

Modeling morphological inflection is an important task in Natural Language Processing. In contrast to earlier work that has largely used orthographic representations, we experiment with this task in a phonetic character space, representing inputs as either IPA segments or bundles of phonological distinctive features. We show that both of these inputs, somewhat counterintuitively, achieve similar accuracies on morphological inflection, slightly lower than orthographic models. We conclude that providing detailed phonological representations is largely redundant when compared to IPA segments, and that articulatory distinctions relevant for word inflection are already latently present in the distributional properties of many graphemic writing systems.

## 1 Introduction

Models of morphology are important to many tasks in Natural Language Processing, but also present new challenges of their own. Morphologically complex languages require analysis that is often only captured at the morpheme level, but is essential for syntactic or semantic representations. This requires effective morphological analysis, which often receives less attention than other subfields of Natural Language Processing. One relevant task in morphology is that of morphological inflection: automatically generating the inflected form of a lemma according to a given morphological specification. An example of this in English is $"walk" + 3 + \text{SG} + \text{PRES} \rightarrow "walks"$. There has been recent success in adopting the encoder-decoder architecture (Kann and Schütze, 2016), which has been effective in machine translation (Cho et al., 2014), to this task.

In this work, we explore representing the inputs to such an encoder-decoder model for morphological inflection in two additional ways: IPA segments and bundles of phonological distinctive features. Representing the inputs to an inflection model in phonetic space can unify the character inventory between languages with separate orthographies. The shared character inventory could also enable transfer learning in some instances where it otherwise would be impossible. There are also confusing idiosyncrasies in some orthographies that are not necessarily present in an IPA representation. For example, there are many instances of gemination in English that do not occur in the phonetic realizations of such words, as in ⟨control⟩ → ⟨controlled⟩. English also exhibits several examples of the same sound expressed by completely different orthographic realizations as in ⟨fly⟩ → ⟨flies⟩, or conversely ⟨arch⟩ (/tʃ/) ∼ ⟨monarch⟩ (/k/). Furthermore, a phonetic representation serves as an interface to an even richer representation of characters: phonological distinctive features.

We explore this by representing each IPA segment in a sequence as the combination of its distinctive features. This is potentially useful because (1) a model can learn representations for a fixed set of distinctive features, rather than for each unique IPA segment, and (2) the differences between similar phonemes should be more readily apparent in the distinctive feature representations than the IPA representations. When tasked with generating the past tense of the English verb "stop", transcribed as /stɑp/, a model may need to distinguish between both /t/ and /d/ as past tense suffixes, having seen such examples as "kick": /kɪk/ → /kɪkt/, or "rig": /ɹɪg/ → /ɹɪgd/. Rather than the model needing to learn good representations for both /p/ and /k/ as unrelated segments that precede a /t/ in the past tense, a phonological distinctive feature representation would explicitly capture that they share the feature [−voice]. This encourages a model to more quickly find the parameters that correctly gener-



*Proceedings of the 15th SIGMORPHON Workshop on Computational Research in Phonetics, Phonology, and Morphology*, pages 161–166
Brussels, Belgium, October 31, 2018. ©2018 The Special Interest Group on Computational Morphology and Phonology
https://doi.org/10.18653/v1/P17

ate this voicing assimilation, and produce the form /stɑpt/. That is, the model that learns from phonological features should quickly be able to generalize that this English past tense is realized as /t/ before voiceless segments. Similarly, in the example of "rob": /ɹɑb/ → /ɹɑbd/, the generated /d/ can be conditioned on [+voice] rather than the individual segment /b/.

An alternative hypothesis is that the proposed distinctive feature representation may, however, not have such a profound effect on the inflection model. This is because distributional representations of IPA segments or phonemic graphemes have been shown to capture good approximations of the distinctive feature space (Silfverberg et al., 2018). In order to test these two hypotheses, we experiment on a subset of data provided by task 1 of the CoNLL-SIGMORPHON 2017 Shared Task on Universal Morphological Reinflection (Cotterell et al., 2017), which introduced 42 more languages than the year before (Cotterell et al., 2016) for a total of 52 languages. We use an existing tool to perform G2P on the data, and, as a second step, to produce distinctive feature vectors from the resulting IPA segments. We evaluate the resulting models on their ability to generate IPA segments.

**Related Work**  Phonetic distributional vectors have been explored for their effectiveness in several NLP applications; especially for informing scenarios that utilize borrowing or transfer learning (Tsvetkov et al., 2016). Phonological distinctive features have also been successfully used to inform NER (Bharadwaj et al., 2016). However, to our knowledge, there does not seem to be work in learning distributional properties of phonological features that compares them directly to vectors of IPA segments.

## 2   Encoder-Decoder Architecture

Our model is implemented as an RNN Encoder-Decoder with attention, built to imitate the model introduced by Kann and Schütze (2016), variations of which found much success in the 2017 CoNLL-SIGMORPHON shared task. The system, pictured in Figure 1, works by learning an encoder RNN over a sequence of embeddings for the input characters or morphological tags. In practice, the encoder is bidirectional. The decoder RNN is initialized with a sequence boundary token, and each state of the decoder is predicted based on the state of the previous timestep, the previous

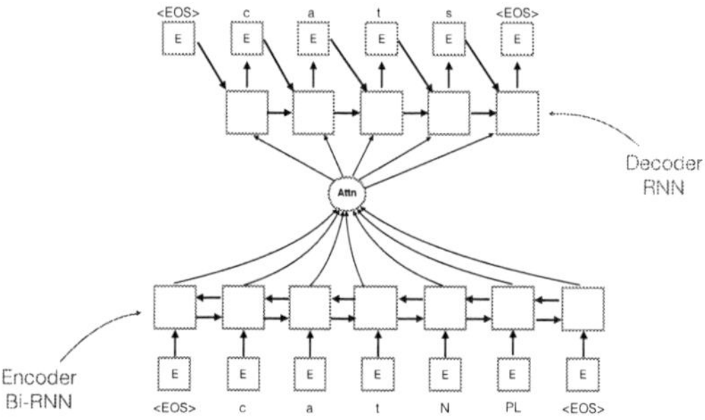

Figure 1: The encoder-decoder with an attention mechanism used for morphological inflection

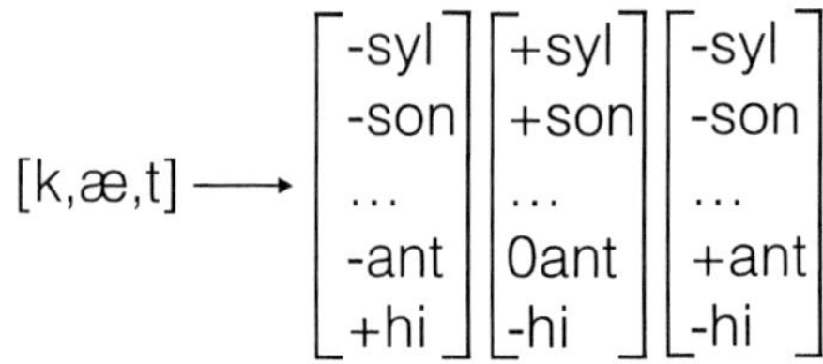

Figure 2: PanPhon transforms a sequence of IPA segments into a matrix of features

output embedding, and all of the encoder states $e_i \in Encoder$. We then use an attention mechanism (Bahdanau et al., 2014) to 'attend' over the encoder states, assigning a score to each $e_i$ given the previous decoder state $d_{j-1}$. The scoring function (Luong et al., 2015) is calculated as

$$score(e_i; d_{j-1}) = tanh([d_{j-1}; e_i] \times W) \quad (1)$$

where $W$ is a parameter matrix that is learned during training, and $[x; y]$ indicates the concatenation of $x$ and $y$. These scores are then normalized by applying a softmax over all encoder states in $Encoder$ to compute each $\epsilon_{i,j-1}$.

Finally, the attention vector is computed as the weighted mean of all encoder states according to their normalized score: $A(d_{j-1}, E) = \sum_{i=0}^{n} \epsilon_{i,j-1} e_i$, which is concatenated to the previously decoded embedding before being passed through the decoder. We implement this model in PyTorch (Paszke et al., 2017), using Gated Recurrent Units (GRU) (Cho et al., 2014) for the encoder and decoder, and optimize with stochastic gradient descent.

## 3   Embedding Inputs

The inputs to this model are sequences of character and tag embeddings. To this end, each Unicode character codepoint or tag is a one-hot vector $c$, and an embedding matrix $E \in \mathbb{R}^{|\Sigma| \times n}$ is

|  | **Medium** | | | | **High** | | | |
|---|---|---|---|---|---|---|---|---|
|  | Shared task | Text | IPA | Features | Shared task | Text | IPA | Features |
| English | 94.70 | 89.70 | 72.50 | 72.70 | 97.20 | 96.60 | 77.00 | 76.10 |
| German | 80.00 | 71.80 | 60.80 | 59.90 | 93.00 | 89.50 | 82.30 | 83.20 |
| Hindi | 97.40 | 84.80 | 89.80 | 86.50 | 100.00 | 99.80 | 99.60 | 99.90 |
| Hungarian | 75.10 | 67.10 | 65.50 | 63.90 | 86.80 | 83.70 | 82.80 | 82.60 |
| Persian | 91.90 | 84.10 | 85.00 | 82.30 | 99.90 | 99.10 | 99.20 | 98.70 |
| Polish | 79.90 | 67.10 | 63.40 | 64.30 | 92.80 | 88.20 | 88.20 | 88.90 |
| Russian | 84.10 | 66.90 | 66.80 | 67.60 | 92.80 | 89.20 | 86.50 | 88.90 |
| Spanish | 91.70 | 76.50 | 82.10 | 81.30 | 97.50 | 95.20 | 96.40 | 96.60 |
| **AVG** | **86.85** | **76.21** | **72.61** | **72.73** | **95.0** | **92.66** | **89.00** | **89.36** |

Table 1: Overall accuracy for each model (orthographic, IPA-based, and distinctive feature-based), and comparison with the CoNLL-SIGMORPHON 2017 shared task top performing system for each language.

computed to store the parameters that map the $|\Sigma|$-dimensional one-hot vectors to n-dimensional dense vectors, where $\Sigma$ is the character and tag vocabulary. Similarly we use a matrix $I \in \mathbb{R}^{|\Sigma_{IPA}| \times n}$ for embedding IPA segments, where $\Sigma_{IPA}$ is the IPA segment and tag vocabulary. To produce the IPA sequence, we use the Python library Epitran, which performs rule-based G2P on language specific mappings (Mortensen et al., 2018).

We then use the Python library PanPhon (Mortensen et al., 2016), which maps IPA segments to features as in Figure 2, to obtain vectors of phonological distinctive features. The features are represented numerically whereby each index of the vector corresponds to a specific feature such as $[\pm coronal]$ and stores a value from the set $\{1, 0, -1\}$. These values correspond to 'exhibits feature', 'unspecified for given class of sounds', and 'does not exhibit feature', respectively. In practice we map -1 to 0 to obtain strictly binary feature vectors. Now, each IPA segment can be represented as a vector $v$ which has a 1 for each feature that it exhibits, and a 0 otherwise. The embedding matrix $F \in \mathbb{R}^{|p| \times n}$, where $p$ is all features, tags, and symbols is no longer just a lookup for IPA segments. Tags are still one-hot vectors, and symbols are one-hot vectors for any character that has no phonological features (e.g. a space, or apostrophe). But the vector for an IPA segment now has a one for each feature that it exhibits, in contrast to the one-hot vectors.

The operation $vF$ is equivalent to summing each $F_i$ for which $v_i = 1$. In this way, an IPA segment is the sum of all of its distinctive feature embeddings. In practice, we can take the matrix-matrix product of the entire sequence of feature vectors and $F$ to calculate the matrix that represents a sequence of embeddings. The overall workflow involves passing from orthographic input sequences, through Epitran, and then PanPhon, and finally to phonological distinctive feature embeddings.

## 4 Experiments and Results

We evaluate these models on 8 languages that are at the intersection of CoNLL-SIGMORPHON data, Epitran, and PanPhon supported languages, selected to exhibit typological diversity. The languages, split into 2 training settings per the shared task data: Medium (~1,000 training examples), and High (~10,000 training examples), and their accuracies are given in Table 1. In the high data setting using orthographic inputs, our implementation performed comparably to the best shared task systems for each language. The slight degradation in performance can be attributed to the fact that we did not use ensemble voting, as the top performing systems in the shared task did (Cotterell et al., 2017), and that this is a comparison to the maximum score of 25 systems per language, which increases the likelihood that the optimal initialization will have been found. In the medium setting, the difference in accuracy is much more apparent. This is due to the fact that all of the top performing systems in the shared task also used either some type of data augmentation method (Zhou and Neubig (2017), Silfverberg et al. (2017), Sudhakar and Kumar (2017), Kann and Schütze (2017), Bergmanis et al. (2017)) a hard alignment method (Makarov et al., 2017), or both (Nicolai et al., 2017). These results illustrate the common observation that neural systems require a large amount of data to be very accurate,

| | ENSEMBLE ORACLE RESULTS | | | |
| --- | --- | --- | --- | --- |
| | Medium | | High | |
| | All inputs | Text | All inputs | Text |
| English | 94.20 | 94.20 | 97.90 | 97.50 |
| German | 79.50 | 81.20 | 93.10 | 94.30 |
| Hindi | 94.50 | 90.30 | 100.00 | 100.00 |
| Hungarian | 78.60 | 77.40 | 90.10 | 90.10 |
| Persian | 91.40 | 90.40 | 99.70 | 99.60 |
| Polish | 79.40 | 78.70 | 93.70 | 92.6 |
| Russian | 78.30 | 76.80 | 94.10 | 92.50 |
| Spanish | 89.2 | 86.90 | 98.5 | 97.0 |
| AVG | **85.64** | **84.49** | **95.89** | **95.45** |

Table 2: Ensemble Oracles for each language. If the correct word form is predicted by any of the 3 models, then it is classified as correct. This is compared against 3 text models.

which can be partially addressed by artificially expanding the training data, or enforcing some copy bias into the system.

For both phonetic representation experiments, the decoded outputs are in the inventory of IPA segments, the gold standard of which comes from the deterministic mappings implemented in Epitran. This means that they differ only in terms of the input representation in the encoder. Models trained on both IPA and feature inputs perform comparably to the text model on both the medium and the high setting. There are two main points of interest in the results. (1) The lower performance on average of the IPA and feature models when compared to the text model is almost exclusively due to differences in accuracy for German and English. We attribute this on the one hand to the fact that the orthography of English is often dissimilar to pronunciations and that their orthographies reflect etymological information which is useful in determining a word's inflectional behavior (Scragg, 1974). An example of the discrepancy between spelling and pronunciation is that the English vowel space has about 13 phonetic vowels (Ladefoged and Johnson, 2014), whereas in the orthographic alphabet, there are only 5. Furthermore, the unstressed vowel, schwa (ə), can essentially replace any vowel in an unstressed context. We observe that the majority of inaccuracies in the English predictions are related to vowels, and most commonly to a schwa. This indicates that converting the character space to IPA can introduce some new complications. Regarding German, there is no obvious explanation for the lower accuracy, and we believe that a more detailed analysis of the G2P performance is needed in order to explore this. Experiments on orthographically and morphophonemically similar languages may also be revealing.

An Ensemble Oracle of all three models is given in Table 2 in order to check if the systems vary in what they learn to predict. The results show that this ensemble outperforms each individual system for any given language. However, when compared to an Ensemble Oracle of three text models, the results are rather similar. The increase in accuracy may simply be due to varying parameters from different random initializations, yielding an effect that is similar to the boosted scores that can be observed in many of the shared task results.

More interesting is the fact that (2) both the IPA and feature representation seem to yield extremely similar accuracies with a paired permutation test p-value of 0.43 over all languages. Even when the training data is rather sparse as in the medium setting, the accuracies remain extremely similar. This suggests that the distributional properties of IPA segments capture the information expressed by distinctive features. Any benefit that representing a segment in terms of its features might have is *already available in the IPA embeddings*. To further compare these representations, we experiment with models that combine the IPA and feature representations. We attempt to simply add a 'feature' to the distinctive feature vectors for each IPA segment. That is, the feature vector for /ə/ would have a 1 for all of its distinctive features, and an additional 1 for that specific segment. We also experiment with concatenation of the embedding found from the feature vector combination and the IPA embedding. The input to the model is a vector of double the embedding size to account for concatenation. The results, given in Table 3, show that neither experiment seems to have much effect, and the accuracies reflect the initial results.

## 5 Conclusion and Future Work

We have experimented with morphological inflection on 8 different languages and compared results between an input space of IPA segments, and one represented as bundles of phonological distinctive features. The results show that both types of inputs behave similarly. This indicates that the distributional properties of IPA segments align with those found by phonological distinctive features, at least to the extent that articulatory information is relevant to inflection. Furthermore, when compared to a baseline of a purely orthographic space, it is ev-

| | INPUT COMBINATION RESULTS | | | |
|---|---|---|---|---|
| | Medium | | High | |
| | Addition | Concat | Addition | Concat |
| English | 71.10 | 68.70 | 77.40 | 77.70 |
| German | 56.60 | 56.40 | 84.40 | 84.50 |
| Hindi | 93.00 | 90.80 | 99.70 | 99.70 |
| Hungarian | 62.90 | 63.70 | 83.50 | 83.40 |
| Persian | 84.20 | 84.10 | 99.20 | 99.60 |
| Polish | 60.80 | 66.60 | 88.90 | 89.20 |
| Russian | 65.90 | 64.80 | 90.50 | 90.00 |
| Spanish | 80.80 | 84.40 | 97.80 | 97.50 |
| AVG | **71.91** | **72.44** | **90.18** | **90.20** |

Table 3: Results for the combination of feature and IPA embeddings. Addition refers to the inclusion of a specific phoneme 'feature'. Concat refers to concatenating the embedding of both input types.

ident that for many languages the results are still mostly redundant, and if there is a large discrepancy in accuracy it is in favor of the orthographic inputs.

There is still work to be done to explore if there are scenarios where bundles of distinctive features provide an advantage. That is, in the case of transfer learning where the phonology of a language is known, it becomes possible to approximate vector representations for unseen segments. Similarly, distinctive features may be better at representing segments that rarely appear in a training set for a given language.

## Acknowledgements

The second author was supported by The Society of Swedish Literature in Finland (SLS). NVIDIA Corp. donated the Titan Xp GPU used for this research.

## References

Dzmitry Bahdanau, Kyunghyun Cho, and Yoshua Bengio. 2014. Neural machine translation by jointly learning to align and translate. In *ICLR 2015*.

Toms Bergmanis, Katharina Kann, Hinrich Schütze, and Sharon Goldwater. 2017. Training data augmentation for low-resource morphological inflection. In *Proceedings of the CoNLL SIGMORPHON 2017 Shared Task: Universal Morphological Reinflection*, pages 31–39, Berlin, Germany. Association for Computational Linguistics.

Akash Bharadwaj, David R. Mortensen, Chris Dyer, and Jaime G. Carbonell. 2016. Phonologically aware neural model for named entity recognition in low resource transfer settings. In *Proceedings of the 2016 Conference on Empirical Methods in Natural Language Processing, EMNLP 2016, Austin, Texas, USA, November 1-4, 2016*, pages 1462–1472.

Kyunghyun Cho, Bart Van Merriënboer, Caglar Gulcehre, Dzmitry Bahdanau, Fethi Bougares, Holger Schwenk, and Yoshua Bengio. 2014. Learning phrase representations using RNN encoder-decoder for statistical machine translation. *arXiv preprint arXiv:1406.1078*.

Ryan Cotterell, Christo Kirov, John Sylak-Glassman, Géraldine Walther, Ekaterina Vylomova, Patrick Xia, Manaal Faruqui, Sandra Kübler, David Yarowsky, Jason Eisner, and Mans Hulden. 2017. The CoNLL-SIGMORPHON 2017 shared task: Universal morphological reinflection in 52 languages. In *Proceedings of the CoNLL-SIGMORPHON 2017 Shared Task: Universal Morphological Reinflection*, Vancouver, Canada. Association for Computational Linguistics.

Ryan Cotterell, Christo Kirov, John Sylak-Glassman, David Yarowsky, Jason Eisner, and Mans Hulden. 2016. The SIGMORPHON 2016 shared task: Morphological reinflection. In *Proceedings of the 14th SIGMORPHON Workshop on Computational Research in Phonetics, Phonology, and Morphology*, Berlin, Germany. Association for Computational Linguistics.

Katharina Kann and Hinrich Schütze. 2016. MED: The LMU system for the SIGMORPHON 2016 shared task on morphological reinflection. In *Proceedings of the 14th SIGMORPHON Workshop on Computational Research in Phonetics, Phonology, and Morphology*, Berlin, Germany. Association for Computational Linguistics.

Katharina Kann and Hinrich Schütze. 2017. The LMU system for the CoNLL-SIGMORPHON shared task on universal morphological reinflection. In *Proceedings of the CoNLL SIGMORPHON 2017 Shared Task: Universal Morphological Reinflection*, pages 40–48, Berlin, Germany. Association for Computational Linguistics.

Peter Ladefoged and Keith Johnson. 2014. *A Course in Phonetics*. Nelson Education.

Minh-Thang Luong, Hieu Pham, and Christopher D. Manning. 2015. Effective approaches to attention-based neural machine translation. *CoRR*, abs/1508.04025.

Peter Makarov, Tatiana Ruzsics, and Simon Clematide. 2017. Align and copy: UZH at SIGMORPHON 2017 shared task for morphological reinflection. In *Proceedings of the CoNLL SIGMORPHON 2017 Shared Task: Universal Morphological Reinflection*, pages 49–57, Berlin, Germany. Association for Computational Linguistics.

David R. Mortensen, Siddharth Dalmia, and Patrick Littell. 2018. Epitran: Precision G2P for many languages. In *Proceedings of the Eleventh Interna-

*tional Conference on Language Resources and Evaluation (LREC 2018)*, Paris, France. European Language Resources Association (ELRA).

David R. Mortensen, Patrick Littell, Akash Bharadwaj, Kartik Goyal, Chris Dyer, and Lori Levin. 2016. PanPhon: A resource for mapping IPA segments to articulatory feature vectors. In *The 26th International Conference on Computational Linguistics: Technical Papers*, page 34753484.

Garrett Nicolai, Bradley Hauer, Mohammad Motallebi, Saeed Najafi, and Grzegorz Kondrak. 2017. If you can't beat them, join them: the University of Alberta system description. In *Proceedings of the CoNLL SIGMORPHON 2017 Shared Task: Universal Morphological Reinflection*, pages 79–84, Berlin, Germany. Association for Computational Linguistics.

Adam Paszke, Sam Gross, Soumith Chintala, Gregory Chanan, Edward Yang, Zachary DeVito, Zeming Lin, Alban Desmaison, Luca Antiga, and Adam Lerer. 2017. Automatic differentiation in PyTorch. In *NIPS-W*.

Donald George Scragg. 1974. *A history of English spelling*, volume 3. Manchester University Press.

Miikka Silfverberg, Lingshuang Jack Mao, and Mans Hulden. 2018. Sound analogies with phoneme embeddings. In *Proceedings of the Society for Computation in Linguistics (SCiL)*, volume 1, pages 136–144.

Miikka Silfverberg, Adam Wiemerslage, Ling Liu, and Lingshuang Jack Mao. 2017. Data augmentation for morphological reinflection. In *Proceedings of the CoNLL SIGMORPHON 2017 Shared Task: Universal Morphological Reinflection*, pages 90–99, Berlin, Germany. Association for Computational Linguistics.

Akhilesh Sudhakar and Anil Singh Kumar. 2017. Experiments on morphological reinflection: CoNLL-2017 shared task. In *Proceedings of the CoNLL SIGMORPHON 2017 Shared Task: Universal Morphological Reinflection*, pages 71–78, Berlin, Germany. Association for Computational Linguistics.

Yulia Tsvetkov, Sunayana Sitaram, Manaal Faruqui, Guillaume Lample, Patrick Littell, David R. Mortensen, Alan W. Black, Lori S. Levin, and Chris Dyer. 2016. Polyglot Neural Language Models: A Case Study in Cross-Lingual Phonetic Representation Learning. In *NAACL HLT 2016, The 2016 Conference of the North American Chapter of the Association for Computational Linguistics: Human Language Technologies, San Diego California, USA, June 12-17, 2016*, pages 1357–1366.

Chunting Zhou and Graham Neubig. 2017. Morphological inflection generation with multi-space variational encoder-decoders. In *Proceedings of the CoNLL SIGMORPHON 2017 Shared Task: Universal Morphological Reinflection*, pages 58–65, Berlin, Germany. Association for Computational Linguistics.

# Extracting morphophonology from small corpora

**Marina Ermolaeva**
University of Chicago / Chicago, IL, USA
`mermolaeva@uchicago.edu`



## Abstract

Probabilistic approaches have proven themselves well in learning phonological structure. In contrast, theoretical linguistics usually works with deterministic generalizations. The goal of this paper is to explore possible interactions between information-theoretic methods and deterministic linguistic knowledge and to examine some ways in which both can be used in tandem to extract phonological and morphophonological patterns from a small annotated dataset. Local and nonlocal processes in Mishar Tatar (Turkic/Kipchak) are examined as a case study.


## 1 Introduction

Morphophonology, or the interface between morphology and phonology, encompasses a wide range of phenomena. While this paper primarily focuses on learning phonological rules from a dataset, it is difficult to draw generalizations based only on surface strings, since the rules may be morphologically specific. The challenge goes beyond learning which phonotactic sequences are allowed, also incorporating surface realizations of morphemes and rules governing their distribution.

Large unannotated corpora are used by a large portion of the existing work on learning phonological patterns e.g. approaches to learning vowel harmony (Goldsmith and Riggle 2012; Szabó and Çöltekin 2013; Flinn 2014). However, in the case of rare languages, a large corpus may be unavailable. On the other hand, *small* hand-annotated examples or texts are a natural output of linguistic fieldwork and readily available even for under-resourced and under-studied languages.

*Interlinear glossed text* is a format traditionally utilized in linguistic papers for presenting language data. It annotates each morpheme with a label, or *gloss tag*. When the amount of data is insufficient, the role of such linguistic knowledge in

making generalizations becomes more prominent; see (Wax 2014; Zamaraeva 2016) for approaches to extraction of morphological rules that take this path.

When it comes to morphophonology, agglutinative languages are of special interest. They tend to exhibit a variety of interacting processes which give rise to multiple surface realizations of most morphemes.[1] A small dataset is very likely to contain only a subset of possible allomorphs – an additional challenge for the learning algorithm. As a case study, this paper focuses on Mishar dialect of Tatar language (Turkic/Kipchak). The data sample used here is a hand-glossed collection of texts elicited from native speakers in the course of fieldwork (MSU linguistic expedition 1999–2012) (3090 word tokens; 1740 types).

## 2 (Morpho)phonological processes

One common type of alternations stems from *local* processes, where the context is immediately adjacent to the segment undergoing the change. The same surface segment may arise from different processes. For example, the ablative suffix (1) has different realizations after voiceless consonants, nasals, and elsewhere. The locative morpheme (2) demonstrates only a two-way distinction after voiceless consonants and elsewhere. The plural suffix (3) is also sensitive to a two-way distinction, drawing a line between nasal consonants and other segments.

(1)  a.  kibet-**tän**       c.  urɣn-**nan**
         shop-ABL              place-ABL

     b.  kɣz-**dan**
         girl-ABL

---

[1] For example, the idea of correlation between agglutination and vowel harmony goes back to (Baudouin de Courtenay 1876, 322–323), and its history and development are documented in (Plank 1998).




*Proceedings of the 15th SIGMORPHON Workshop on Computational Research in Phonetics, Phonology, and Morphology*, pages 167–175
Brussels, Belgium, October 31, 2018. ©2018 The Special Interest Group on Computational Morphology and Phonology
https://doi.org/10.18653/v1/P17

(2) a. jɤrt-**ta**  
    yard-LOC

   c. ten-**dä**  
    night-LOC

  b. kɤz-**da**  
    girl-LOC

(3) a. at-**lar**  
    horse-PL

   c. ujɤn-**nar**  
    game-PL

  b. kɤz-**lar**  
    girl-PL

While this data does hint at certain general phonotactic patterns (e.g. a voiceless stop is never followed by an affix beginning with a voiced obstruent), the contexts cannot be inferred exclusively from surface strings; each morpheme has to be considered separately. Moreover, even the same set of alternants may be found in multiple processes. Consider the following voicing alternation:

(4) a. matur-**lɤg**-ɤ  
    pretty-NOMIN-P3

  b. jaxšɤ-**lɤk**-ka  
    good-NOMIN-DAT

(5) a. kal-**gan**  
    stay-PFCT

  b. čɤk-**kan**  
    exit-PFCT

The difference between (4) and (5) lies in the *directionality* of the {g, k} alternation: the obstruent in the former is located at the left edge of the affix and assimilated to the preceding segment; in the latter it is sensitive to the voicing of the following segment.

Another prominent source of allomorphy is vowel harmony. This process is *nonlocal* in the sense that it only affects a subset of segments (in this case, the set of vowels); all other segments are transparent and do not interact with the rule in any way. Vowel harmony can be analyzed of in terms of *underspecification* (Archangeli 1988): vowels in affixes lack some feature specifications, and their surface realization is dependent on the closest fully specified vowel.

In Mishar Tatar, vowels are subject to fronting harmony controlled by the root; most affixes have front and back allomorphs.

| | [−BK, −RND] | [−BK, +RND] | [+BK, −RND] | [+BK, +RND] |
|---|---|---|---|---|
| [+HI, −LO] | i | ü | ɤj | u |
| [−HI, −LO] | e | (ö) | ɤ | (o) |
| [−HI, +LO] | ä | | a | |

Table 1: Mishar Tatar vowels

(6) a. bala-lar-ɤbɤz-ga  
    child-PL-P1PL-DAT

  b. täräz-lär-ebez-gä  
    window-PL-P1PL-DAT

These phenomena are not completely free of exceptions and problematic cases. Two instances of non-canonical vowel harmony in suffixes attached to borrowed roots are presented in (7). Similarly, (8a) shows the expected voiced variant of PFCT arising after a vowel while (8b) demonstrates the exceptional unvoiced variant in an identical phonological context. Another issue is true allomorphy triggered by morphosyntactic features as opposed to phonological context; and determining which is the case is in itself a nontrivial task. For example, in (9) 2PL is realized differently depending on the TAM (tense/aspect/mood) marker on the verb.

(7) a. tarix-ɤ  
    history-P3

   b. činovnig-ɤ  
    official-P3

(8) a. i-**kän**  
    AUX-PFCT

   b. di-**gän**  
    speak-PFCT

(9) a. bar-a-**sɤz**  
    go-ST.IPFV-2PL

   b. bar-dɤ-**gɤz**  
    go-PST-2PL

## 3 Finding alternations

### 3.1 Alternations as sets

Consider the following rule encoding Mishar Tatar vowel harmony:

(10) $\begin{bmatrix} +\text{SYL} \\ 0\,\text{BK} \end{bmatrix} \rightarrow [\alpha\text{BK}] \;/\; \begin{bmatrix} +\text{SYL} \\ \alpha\text{BK} \end{bmatrix} ([-\text{SYL}])^{*}$ __

(11) $\{e, ɤ\} \rightarrow e \;/\; (e\,|\,i\,|\,ä\,|\,ö\,|\,ü)\,(b\,|\,d\,|\,g\,|\ldots)^{*}$ __  
$\{e, ɤ\} \rightarrow ɤ \;/\; (ɤ\,|\,ɤj\,|\,a\,|\,o\,|\,u)\,(b\,|\,d\,|\,g\,|\ldots)^{*}$ __

This rule can be represented succinctly using feature bundle notation (10): any vowel not specified for $[\pm\text{BK}]$ receives these values from the closest vowel to the left. However, underspecified vowels can be equivalently thought of as sets of fully specified segments, and the rule as the condition determining which member of the set appears on the surface, e.g. (11). An *alternation* can then be defined as the set of all surface outcomes of a process, each associated with a set of contexts that trigger it.

At this proof-of-concept stage we adopt the following *simplifying assumption*: alternations occur between segments (i.e. one-segment substrings), or between a segment and zero, and the context of each alternant is a segment, not necessarily adjacent to the alternant. Further implications of this assumption for contexts will be examined in section 4.1.

## 3.2 String differences

The learning algorithm proposed here is based on the notion of string differences introduced by (Goldsmith 2011). This approach required defining an alphabet of symbols $A$ and a binary concatenation operator $\bullet$ (also represented by simple juxtaposition). The alphabet is augmented by adding a null element for concatenation (indicated $\emptyset$) as well as inverse for each letter in $A$. The inverse of $a \in A$ is $a^{-1}$, and $aa^{-1} = a^{-1}a = \emptyset$. Moreover, $(ab)^{-1} = b^{-1}a^{-1}$. These definitions establish *group structure* over the set of all strings in the extended alphabet.

The *right difference* of strings $s$ and $t$ is defined as $\frac{s}{t}R = t^{-1} \bullet s$. Similarly, the *left difference* of $s$ and $t$ is $\frac{s}{t}L = s \bullet t^{-1}$. The following examples clarify this notation:

(12)    $\frac{jumps}{jumped}R = (jumped)^{-1}jumps =$
$(ed)^{-1}(jump)^{-1}jumps = (ed)^{-1}s = \frac{s}{ed}$

(13)    $\frac{undo}{redo}L = undo(redo)^{-1} =$
$undo(do)^{-1}(re)^{-1} = un(re)^{-1} = \frac{un}{re}$

For our purposes, it is sufficient to interpret string differences as ordered pairs of strings.[2] In its turn, *left/right commonality* can be defined as the longest common prefix/suffix of two strings. The left commonality of *jumps* and *jumped* is *jump*, and the right commonality of *undo* and *redo* is *do*.

Given a *paradigm* (set of strings) $P$ with $n$ elements, its left/right *self-difference array* is the $n \times n$ array $D$ such that $D[i][j]$ is the left/right difference of $P[i]$ and $P[j]$. The array of commonalities is defined similarly. A paradigm is *regular* if each row in its self-difference array has a single common nominator and all elements in its commonality array are identical (ignoring the main diagonal).

|         | jump            | jumps           | jumped          | jumping          |
| ------- | --------------- | --------------- | --------------- | ---------------- |
| jump    |                 | $\frac{\emptyset}{s}$ | $\frac{\emptyset}{ed}$ | $\frac{\emptyset}{ing}$ |
| jumps   | $\frac{s}{\emptyset}$ |                 | $\frac{s}{ed}$  | $\frac{s}{ing}$  |
| jumped  | $\frac{ed}{\emptyset}$ | $\frac{ed}{s}$  |                 | $\frac{ed}{ing}$ |
| jumping | $\frac{ing}{\emptyset}$ | $\frac{ing}{s}$ | $\frac{ing}{ed}$ |                  |

Figure 1: Regular paradigm: right self-differences of $\{jump, jumps, jumped, jumping\}$

|         | try             | tries           | tried           | trying           |
| ------- | --------------- | --------------- | --------------- | ---------------- |
| try     |                 | $\frac{y}{ies}$ | $\frac{y}{ied}$ | $\frac{\emptyset}{ing}$ |
| tries   | $\frac{ies}{y}$ |                 | $\frac{s}{d}$   | $\frac{ies}{ying}$ |
| tried   | $\frac{ied}{y}$ | $\frac{d}{s}$   |                 | $\frac{ied}{ying}$ |
| trying  | $\frac{ing}{\emptyset}$ | $\frac{ying}{ies}$ | $\frac{ying}{ied}$ |                  |

Figure 2: Non-regular paradigm: right self-differences of $\{try, tries, tried, trying\}$

This notion of self-difference is still limited to prefixes and suffixes. Let $P = \{w_1, ..., w_n\}$ be a paradigm whose left and right self-difference arrays are regular, with $l$ and $r$ denoting its (unique) left and right commonality respectively. Omitting some details for the sake of space, we define the set of *internal difference substrings* of $P$ as $\{l^{-1}w_1r^{-1}, ..., l^{-1}w_nr^{-1}\}$.

Under the assumptions outlined previously, the task of identifying alternations reduces to finding segment-sized (or smaller) differences between realizations of the same morpheme. The following recursive definition captures this idea:

(14)    An *alternation* is the set of internal difference substrings of a paradigm that is regular if any previously determined alternations are ignored and, moreover, satisfies two conditions:

     (i)    the paradigm's left or right commonality is a non-empty string;

     (ii)    none of the difference substrings are longer than one character.

## 3.3 A two-step algorithm

In the input, morphs are arranged into sets by gloss tag, each morph forming its own *group*. A fragment of the input is shown below.

(15)    Q: $\{[mɤ], [me]\}$
PST: $\{[dɤ], [de], [tɤ], [te]\}$
P1PL: $\{[bez], [ebez], [ɤbɤz]\}$

The definition introduced in (14) lends itself naturally to a two-step iterative algorithm that calculates self-differences for each set of morphs, identifying alternations as it proceeds. The *extraction step* employs the definitions introduced above to find all possible alternations between groups within each set. The *reduction step* collapses all groups in each set that are identical up to known alternations, essentially factoring out some of the

<hr>

[2] As Goldsmith (2011) points out, one can also think of the right difference of $s$ and $t$ as a *function* that maps $t$ to $s$.

169

differences and making more alternations accessible to subsequent passes. The algorithm alternates between extraction and reduction until the number of groups stops decreasing.

Consider the toy example in (15). The first iteration starts out with no known alternations; the only morph set conforming to (14) is Q. The extraction step discovers one alternation: {e, γ}. The reduction step then collapses all morph groups that are identical up to this alternation:

(16)  Q: $\left\{\left[\begin{smallmatrix} m\,γ, \\ m\,e \end{smallmatrix}\right]\right\}$

  PST: $\left\{\left[\begin{smallmatrix} d\,γ, \\ d\,e \end{smallmatrix}\right], \left[\begin{smallmatrix} t\,γ, \\ t\,e \end{smallmatrix}\right]\right\}$

  P1PL: $\left\{\left[b\,e\,z\right], \left[\begin{smallmatrix} e\,b\,e\,z, \\ γ\,b\,γ\,z \end{smallmatrix}\right]\right\}$

At the second iteration (17), members of the {e, γ} set are now treated as the same segment, and PST and P1PL satisfy the conditions of (14). They yield two new alternations, {d, t} and {∅, e, γ}, allowing the reduction step to collapse both PST and P1PL:

(17)  Q: $\left\{\left[\begin{smallmatrix} m\,γ, \\ m\,e \end{smallmatrix}\right]\right\}$

  PST: $\left\{\left[\begin{smallmatrix} d\,γ, \\ d\,e, \\ t\,γ, \\ t\,e \end{smallmatrix}\right]\right\}$

  P1PL: $\left\{\left[\begin{smallmatrix} ∅\,b\,e\,z, \\ e\,b\,e\,z, \\ γ\,b\,γ\,z \end{smallmatrix}\right]\right\}$

At this point no further reduction is possible, and the algorithm halts.

## 3.4 Intermediate results

The Mishar Tatar sample contained 55 different gloss tags and 160 surface realizations. The algorithm converged after three iterations, collapsing the morphs into 85 groups.

| | |
|---|---|
| Correct | {d, n, t}, {d, t}, {∅, k, g}, {l, n}, {k, g}, {∅, e, γ}, {a, ä}, {e, γ} |
| Incomplete | {∅, γ}, {∅, ä} |
| Incorrect | {g, s}, {n, ŋ} |

Table 2: Extracted alternations

The following output snippets illustrate the work of the reduction step. Multiple processes affecting the same morpheme can be learned (18); this also holds for alternations with zero (19). Not every set of morphs is reduced to a single group; the algorithm has successfully learned that the

ATTR gloss corresponds to three different attributivizer suffixes, each of which has multiple realizations (20).

```
(18)  ---- PL          (20)  ---- ATTR
      ---- Group 0           ---- Group 0
      [['n' 'ä' 'r']         [['s' 'γ' 'z']
       ['n' 'a' 'r']          ['s' 'e' 'z']]
       ['l' 'ä' 'r']         ---- Group 1
       ['l' 'a' 'r']]        [['l' 'e']
(19)  ---- ORD                ['l' 'γ']]
      ---- Group 0           ---- Group 2
      [['e' 'n' 'č' 'e']     [['g' 'e']
       [' ' 'n' 'č' 'e']      ['g' 'γ']
       ['γ' 'n' 'č' 'γ']]     ['k' 'e']]
```

One interesting observation is related to the learner's ability to retain group boundaries if the groups appear to represent distinct morphemes. This has a practical potential for detecting inconsistencies in labelling – such as the COMP gloss tag being used for the complementizer *dip* and the comparative suffix *-r{aä}k* (21), when CMPR is expected for the latter (22).

```
(21)  ---- COMP       (22)  ---- CMPR
      ---- Group 0           ---- Group 0
      [['d' 'i' 'p']]        [['r' 'a' 'k']]
      ---- Group 1
      [['r' 'ä' 'k']
       ['r' 'a' 'k']]
```

## 4 Learning contexts

### 4.1 Rules and locality

Above, we have introduced a method of detecting likely phonological processes and collecting them as sets of alternating segments. This section makes the next logical step and focuses on patterns governing the distribution of alternants.

A straightforward way to formalize this task and define its boundaries is grounded in formal language theory. Two classes of subregular languages are particularly relevant to the discussion of phonology. One of them is Strictly Local languages (McNaughton and Papert 1971; Rogers and Pullum 2011). Given an alphabet $\Sigma$, a Strictly $k$-Local (SL) grammar can be expressed as a set of strings in $\Sigma$ of length at most $k$. The corresponding language is the set of all strings in $\Sigma$ that do not contain any of the strings in the grammar. Tier-based Strictly Local grammars (TSL) (Heinz et al. 2011) are a generalization of SL grammars. A $k$-TSL grammar can also be defined as a set of illicit strings; however, they only apply to a certain subset, or *tier*, of elements in $\Sigma$, ignoring any intervening elements that do not belong to the subset.

How can this model be used to produce a practical representation of a phonological process? One way is to link each alternant occurring in a surface form to a set of *trigger segments*, indicating whether they occur to the left or right. Each alternation should also be associated with a set of transparent segments – non-tier elements in TSL terms. This is essentially a *bigram model*, encoding dependencies between pairs of elements, and has a clear counterpart in 2-TSL grammars. Given an alternation with $n$ variants, the process of learning the rule boils down to determining the directionality and partitioning the set of segments into $n + 1$ subsets of triggers (for each alternant) and transparent segments.

## 4.2 Mutual information

*Mutual information* (MI) is a measure of dependence between two random variables, or the reduction of uncertainty in one random variable through the other (Cover and Thomas 2012).

(23) $MI(X;Y) =$
$$\sum_{x \in X} \sum_{y \in Y} p(x, y) \log_2 \frac{p(x,y)}{p(x)p(y)}$$

For the task at hand, it is convenient to think of MI as the expected value of *pointwise mutual information* (PMI). In its turn, PMI is an indication of how much the probability of a particular pair of events differs from what it is expected to be assuming independence (Bouma 2009). Intuitively, PMI measures correlation (positive or negative) between events.

(24) $PMI(x; y) = \log_2 \frac{p(x,y)}{p(x)p(y)}$

The PMI metric is naturally applicable to learning of vowel harmony. In our case, the algorithm is expected to learn the triggers and transparent segments for each process, which translates into calculating PMI values with respect to each specific alternation. Instead of the full set of bigrams in the corpus, the input for this procedure is the set of bigrams containing an alternant (member of the alternation in question) and a context segment.

A character bigram can be defined either locally, as a *substring* in a word, or nonlocally, as a *subsequence* (potentially non-contiguous pair), using left or right contexts of the alternant. These two parameters – *locality* and *directionality* – yield four different modes of collecting bigrams; see Table 3 for a concrete example.

|  | Left | Right |
|---|---|---|
| Local | šɤ | ɤŋ |
| Nonlocal | #ɤ, bɤ, aɤ, šɤ | ɤŋ, ɤ# |

Table 3: Bigrams for {e, ɤ} in the word *bašɤŋ*

Consider the voicing alternation {d, t} and the harmonic pair {e, ɤ}. Both have triggers to the left of the target; the former is a local process, while the latter is nonlocal. Both alternations are present in the past tense suffix:

(25)    a.   ker-**de**        c.   ɤrɤš-**tɤ**
           enter-PST         scold-PST

      b.   kɤčkɤr-**dɤ**    d.   teš-**te**
           shout-PST         fall-PST

Presented in Figure 3 and Figure 4 are heat maps showing PMI values calculated for the alternations in question. High positive values in cells indicate attraction, whereas negative values correspond to elements repelling each other. Cells without values indicate unattested bigrams.

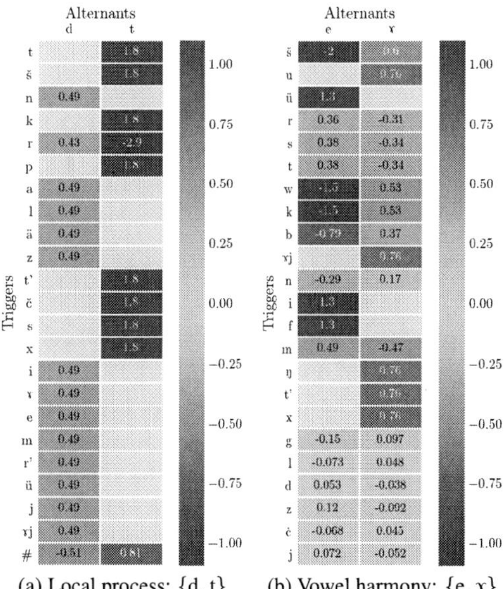

(a) Local process: {d, t}     (b) Vowel harmony: {e, ɤ}

Figure 3: PMI heat maps for local left bigrams; higher values indicate stronger attraction between segments

Local bigrams yield a very clear picture for the voicing alternation {d, t}. In Figure 3a, unexpected pairs – voiced trigger and unvoiced alternant, or vice versa – are either absent or have very low PMI values. However, local bigrams do not perform well on the vowel harmony pair $\{e, \gamma\}$. Figure 3b does indicate correct preference for some vowels, but the absolute values are comparably high for a number of consonants as well. With nonlocal bigrams the results are almost reversed. For $\{d, t\}$ (Figure 4a), the pattern is obscured. However, nonlocal processes such as vowel harmony yield some correct information: for $\{e, \gamma\}$ (Figure 4b) more vowels and fewer consonants exhibit strong positive or negative correlation tendencies.

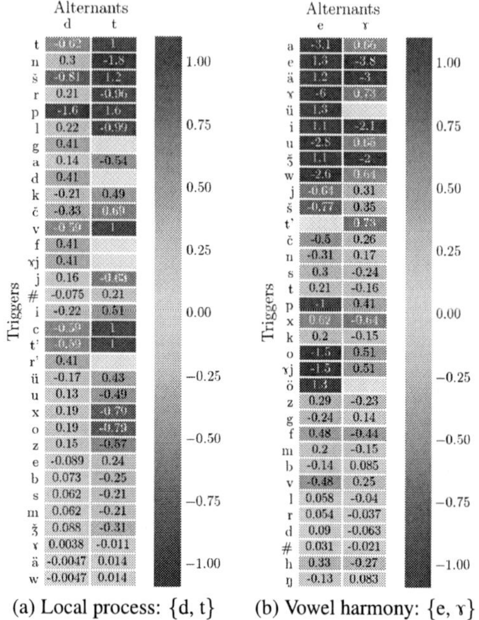

(a) Local process: $\{d, t\}$     (b) Vowel harmony: $\{e, \gamma\}$

Figure 4: PMI heat maps for nonlocal left bigrams

The heat maps demonstrate that PMI values can be successfully used to match triggers to alternants. What is needed at this point is a procedure that would assign correct sets of transparent segments to each process – namely, the empty set for local processes and the set of consonants for vowel harmony.

Augmenting local bigrams with the notion of transparent segments produces a generalization applicable to both local and nonlocal processes. A left (right) local bigram consists of an alternant and the closest non-transparent segment to its left (right). One option, then, is to compare context segments directly in terms of how likely they are to be transparent for a given alternation. A non-transparent segment is expected to have high absolute PMI values – positive with the alternant it

triggers and negative with all other alternants. The definition of MI (23) can be rewritten as follows:

$$(26) \quad MI = \sum_{x \in X} p(x) \sum_{y \in Y} p(y|x) PMI(x; y)$$

Fixing $x$ and normalizing the value by its probability to avoid unnecessarily high scores for rarely attested segments, we obtain the following metric:

$$(27) \quad MI(x) = \sum_{y \in Y} p(x, y) PMI(x; y)$$

This allows to *rank* context segments by their MI value. The bigrams have to be calculated in the nonlocal mode to capture information about long-distance dependencies. Intuitively, the higher a segment is ranked, the more likely it is to be transparent with respect to the alternation in question. For each segment, the ranking also shows the alternant that corresponds to the highest PMI value. The ranking for $\{e, \gamma\}$ (left contexts) is shown in (28).

```
(28)    ---- Alternation: {'e', 'ɣ'}:
        ŋ:      ɣ      0.00001362
        h:      e      0.00001943
        #:      e      0.00003585
        d:      e      0.00004618
        r:      e      0.00004704
        . . .
        z:      e      0.00034681
        ö:      e      0.00042929
        o:      ɣ      0.00051578
        ɣj:     ɣ      0.00051578
        k:      e      0.00053448
        . . .
        u:      ɣ      0.01335405
        i:      e      0.01762960
        ü:      e      0.01845926
        ɣ:      ɣ      0.03614305
        ä:      e      0.03741840
        e:      e      0.04574272
        a:      ɣ      0.04901854
```

As expected, most vowels have high values, whereas consonants tend to score low. Some vowels still end up in the middle – in particular, *o* and *ö*, which are uncharacteristic for this dialect and generally found in borrowed roots. Provided that the alternation set itself has been identified correctly, for every trigger segment the highest PMI value unerringly points at the correct alternant unless the segment is transparent.

### 4.3 Phonological viability and rule evaluation

Due to the limited data, the learner cannot be expected to have access to all possible contexts. Moreover, as shown in (28) above, the rankings of segments produced by calculating PMI tend to contain some degree of noise. It is at this point that phonological features come into play. Adopting the standard textbook definition, a *natural class* is a set of segments that share a particular value for some feature or a set of features (Odden 2013). A rule is considered *phonologically viable* just in case the sets of triggers of all alternants correspond to disjoint natural classes.[34]

Phonological viability introduces a straightforward way of producing generalizations. Combined with PMI rankings, it can be used to generate phonologically meaningful rules for known alternations. First, each trigger set is extended with segments in its natural class that have not occurred in the context of the given alternation. Second, any transparent segments that were accidentally added to the transparent list is removed from it if they are also found in one of the expanded trigger sets. These modifications produce *generalized rules*.

We use two metrics to evaluate and compare these rules. The primary objective is to explain as many instances of the given alternation as possible. This intuition is easy to formalize: an example is *explained* if it contains a correct trigger which is either adjacent to the alternant or separated only by transparent segments. Another option is to calculate the average PMI over all (segment, alternant) pairs, following the standard definition of mutual information shown in (24).

### 4.4  Assembling the pieces

In order to determine the best cutoff point in the ranking, each alternation $A$ is processed as follows. At initialization, MI values are calculated once with nonlocal bigrams in order to rank the segments; all subsequent calculations are performed with local bigrams. The set of transparent segments, $Transp_A$, starts out empty. The algorithm traverses the ranking, starting with the lowest MI value. At each step, the selected segment is added to $Transp_A$, and both metrics (mutual information and explained examples) are recalculated. Thus, $Transp_A$ is expanded incrementally until it

contains all segments in the ranking; every step produces a new rule with triggers assigned according to the current PMI values. If the rule is phonologically viable, it is converted into a generalized rule, and the metrics are recalculated once more. The procedure is performed twice for each alternation, on left and right contexts separately. Once it halts, the best generalized rule is selected – which means that only phonologically viable configurations are eligible candidates.

The results are summarized in Table 4. For each alternation, MI and explained examples ratio (EE) are shown for the best rule based on left and right contexts. Colored rows indicate that the learner has both partitioned the set of attested context segments and determined whether the trigger is to the left or to the right correctly with respect to the ground truth.

| Alternation | MI (left) | EE (left) | MI (right) | EE (right) |
|---|---|---|---|---|
| {d, n, t} | 1.4277 | **1.0000** | 0.0000 | 0.0000 |
| {d, t} | 0.8079 | **0.9864** | 0.0421 | 0.3143 |
| {∅, k, g} | 0.4951 | **0.4909** | 0.0000 | 0.0000 |
| {l, n} | 0.5547 | **0.9738** | 0.0514 | 0.1154 |
| {k, g} | 0.0814 | **0.1653** | 0.0000 | 0.0000 |
| {∅, ɣ, e} | 0.8431 | **0.6220** | 0.6205 | 0.5357 |
| {a, ä} | 0.8319 | **0.9733** | 0.8331 | 0.8387 |
| {e, ɣ} | 0.8825 | **0.9857** | 0.7148 | 0.7912 |
| {∅, ɣ} | 0.8113 | 1.0000 | 1.0000 | 1.0000 |
| {∅, ä} | 0.1651 | 0.4688 | 0.5586 | **1.0000** |

Table 4: Rule evaluation for correct and incomplete alternations

As mentioned in section 2, some alternations are involved in multiple processes. For instance, {k, g} conflates two assimilation processes with different directionality, while {∅, ɣ, e} corresponds to a combination of a local and nonlocal processes. As expected, they have lower scores.

The algorithm yields promising results for both local and nonlocal processes, provided that the alternation set itself is non-problematic. The vowel harmony case is further illustrated by the final heat map showing all non-transparent segments in the best generalized rule for {e, ɣ} in Figure 5. In particular, compare Figure 5 to Figures 3b and 4b and the ranking in (28).

---

[3]This is a simplification, as one of the trigger sets may form an unnatural class that corresponds to the general case – a fact captured by the Elsewhere Condition (Kiparsky 1973). The definition of phonological viability implements the Elsewhere Condition to some degree, as no natural class requirement is imposed on the set of transparent segments.

[4]Under this definition, classes of segments specified by disjunction are generally unnatural. While languages have a tendency to favor natural classes (definable by feature conjunction) in their rules (Halle and Clements 1983), exploring more relaxed definitions for the purposes of determining acceptable rules is an interesting avenue of future work.

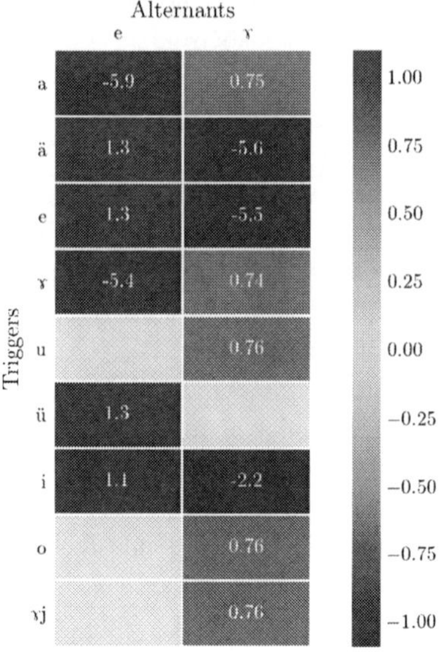

Figure 5: Final PMI heat map for vowel harmony: {e, ɣ}, left contexts

One way to gain insight into the procedure of context learning is to plot the step-by-step change of metric values depending on the set of transparent segments.

Figures 6–7 show graphs for left and right contexts with respect to the {t, d} and {e, ɣ} alternations. Each graph has context segments, ordered according to the MI ranking, along its x-axis. Each point corresponds to a step performed by the algorithm – or, equivalently, to a rule whose set of transparent segments contains all items on the x-axis up to and including that point. In addition, circle markers are present at every phonologically viable step and indicate values obtained by generalized rules.

Graphs for local and nonlocal processes display strikingly different behaviour. The typical picture for a local process is a monotonic sequence: both metrics start out high but decline steadily as more segments are declared transparent. For left-triggered processes, right contexts show noticeably lower values throughout the procedure – especially so if only phonologically viable steps are considered.

For vowel harmony (Figure 7) the plots start low and show a distinct peak once a sufficient number of segments are moved to the transparent set. The peak corresponds to the last consonant in the ranking.

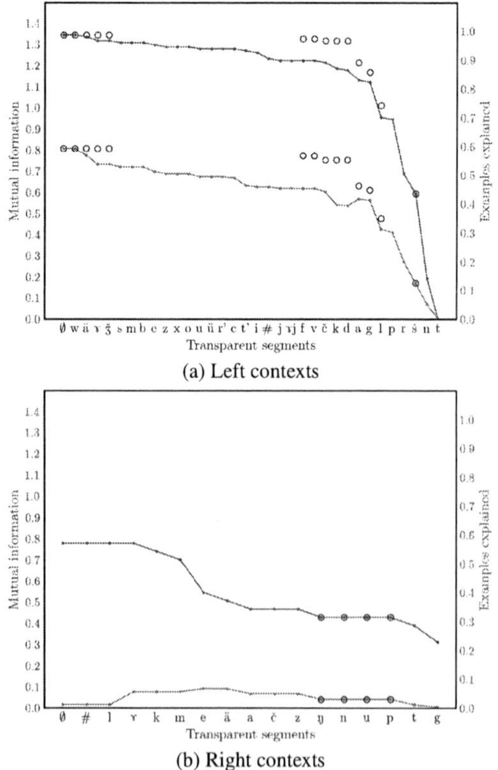

(a) Left contexts

(b) Right contexts

Figure 6: MI and explained examples for {t, d}

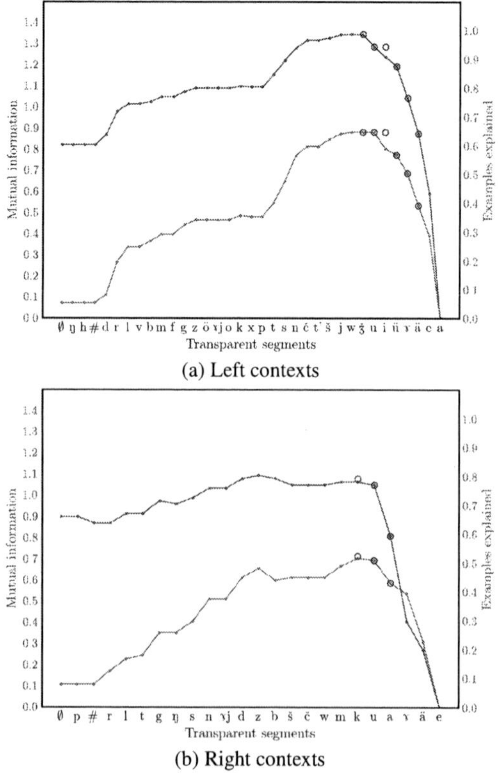

(a) Left contexts

(b) Right contexts

Figure 7: MI and explained examples for {e, ɣ}

While the values for left contexts are still higher, the difference is not as great. This is an expected result: since vowels serve as both triggers and targets of harmony, most vowels in non-final syllables would have a harmonizing vowel both to the left and to the right.

## 5 Discussion

This paper presents an approach to learning (morpho)phonological phenomena from small annotated datasets that combines information-theoretic methods with linguistic information. The proposal includes an algorithm that discovers phonological alternations (represented as sets of segments) shared by multiple morphological paradigms. The notion of mutual information is used to assign a set of contexts to each alternant. Possible rules are then restricted to phonologically plausible configurations via a procedure reminiscent of regularization in machine learning. This approach is applicable to both local and nonlocal processes.

All these should be taken as interim results. One option for future work is to explore interaction between alternation sets. For example, it may be possible to decompose the complex $\{\emptyset, e, \gamma\}$ alternation by first factoring out the known vowel harmony pattern $\{e, \gamma\}$, leaving a simple local process. Other steps that follow directly from the results described here include predicting and reconstructing morphs that are absent from the dataset and, as a more practically oriented goal, identifying inaccuracies and instances of mislabelling in the data.


## References

Diana Archangeli. 1988. Aspects of underspecification theory. *Phonology*, 5(2):183–207.

Gerlof Bouma. 2009. Normalized (pointwise) mutual information in collocation extraction. *Proceedings of GSCL*, pages 31–40.

Jan Baudouin de Courtenay. 1876. Rez'ja i rez'jane. *Slavjanskij sbornik*, 3:223–371.

Thomas Cover and Joy Thomas. 2012. *Elements of information theory*. John Wiley & Sons.

Gallagher Flinn. 2014. Modeling neutrality in Mongolian vowel harmony. Manuscript.

John Goldsmith. 2011. A group structure for strings: Towards a learning algorithm for morphophonology. Technical report, Technical Report TR-2011-06, Department of Computer Science, University of Chicago.

John Goldsmith and Jason Riggle. 2012. Information theoretic approaches to phonological structure: the case of finnish vowel harmony. *Natural Language & Linguistic Theory*, 30(3):859–896.

Morris Halle and George N. Clements. 1983. *Problem book in phonology: a workbook for introductory courses in linguistics and in modern phonology*. MIT Press.

Jeffrey Heinz, Chetan Rawal, and Herbert G. Tanner. 2011. Tier-based strictly local constraints for phonology. In *Proceedings of the 49th Annual Meeting of the Association for Computational Linguistics*, pages 58–64, Portland, Oregon, USA. Association for Computational Linguistics.

Paul Kiparsky. 1973. "Elsewhere" in phonology. In Paul. Kiparsky and Stephen R. Anderson, editors, *A festschrift for Morris Halle*, pages 93–106. New York: Holt, Rinehart & Winston.

Robert McNaughton and Seymour Papert. 1971. *Counter-Free Automata*. MIT Press.

MSU linguistic expedition. 1999–2012. Fieldwork materials. Lomonosov Moscow State University.

David Odden. 2013. *Introducing Phonology*. Cambridge University Press.

Frans Plank. 1998. The co-variation of phonology with morphology and syntax: A hopeful history. *Linguistic Typology*, 2:195–230.

James Rogers and Geoffrey Pullum. 2011. Aural pattern recognition experiments and the subregular hierarchy. *Journal of Logic, Language and Information*, 20:329–342.

Lili Szabó and Çagrı Çöltekin. 2013. A linear model for exploring types of vowel harmony. *Computational Linguistics in the Netherlands Journal*, 3:174–192.

David Allen Wax. 2014. *Automated grammar engineering for verbal morphology*. Ph.D. thesis, University of Washington.

Olga Zamaraeva. 2016. Inferring morphotactics from interlinear glossed text: combining clustering and precision grammars. In *Proceedings of the 14th SIGMORPHON Workshop on Computational Research in Phonetics, Phonology, and Morphology*, pages 141–150.

# Author Index


Çöltekin, Çağrı, 111

Adda, Gilles, 32
Adda-Decker, Martine, 32
Awashima, Hideki, 84

Besacier, Laurent, 32

Cardenas, Ronald, 131

Dolatian, Hossep, 66

Elsner, Micha, 11
Erdmann, Alexander, 54
Ermolaeva, Marina, 167
Eryani, Fadhl, 140
Eskander, Ramy, 78

Godard, Pierre, 32
Graf, Thomas, 151
Granell, Ramon, 125

Habash, Nizar, 54, 140
Heinz, Jeffrey, 66
Hulden, Mans, 161
Hussain, Syed-Amad, 11

Khalifa, Salam, 140
Kirkedal, Andreas Søeborg, 21
Kondrak, Grzegorz, 43

Magri, Giorgio, 1
Mayer, Connor, 151
Maynard, Hélène, 32
Miller, Amanda, 11
Muresan, Smaranda, 78

Najafi, Saeed, 43
Nicolai, Garrett, 43

Obeid, Ossama, 140
Oiwa, Hidekazu, 84

Pater, Joe, 93
Pierrehumbert, Janet, 125
Prickett, Brandon, 93

Rambow, Owen, 78

Rialland, Annie, 32

Silfverberg, Miikka, 161
Sofroniev, Pavel, 111

Taji, Dima, 140
Tikhonov, Aleksey, 117
Traylor, Aaron, 93

Wiemerslage, Adam, 161

Yamashita, Michiharu, 84
Yamshchikov, Ivan, 117
Yvon, François, 32

Zeldes, Amir, 101
Zeman, Daniel, 131

**Association for Computational Linguistics**
209 N. Eighth Street
Stroudsburg, Pennsylvania 18360



ISBN 978-1-5108-7426-8